CW00950977

THE INTERNATIONAL TAXATION SYSTEM

THE INTERNATIONAL TAXATION SYSTEM

edited by

Andrew Lymer
University of Birmingham
United Kingdom

and

John Hasseldine
University of Nottingham
United Kingdom

KLUWER ACADEMIC PUBLISHERS
Boston / Dordrecht / London

Distributors for North, Central and South America:
Kluwer Academic Publishers
101 Philip Drive
Assinippi Park
Norwell, Massachusetts 02061 USA
Telephone (781) 871-6600
Fax (781) 681-9045
E-Mail < kluwer@wkap.com>
Distributors for all other countries:
Kluwer Academic Publishers Group
Distribution Centre
Post Office Box 17
3300 AH Dordrecht, THE NETHERLANDS
Tel.: + 31 (0) 78 657 60 00
Fax: + 31 (0) 78 657 62 54

E-Mail < services@wkap.nl>

 Electronic Services < http://www.wkap.nl>

The international taxation system / edited by Andrew Lymer and John Hasseldine.
    p.cm.
  Includes bibliographical references and index.
  ISBN 1-4020-7157-4 (alk.paper)
    1. Taxation--Law and legislation. 2.Double taxation. 3.Income tax--Foreign income.
  I. Lymer, Andrew. II. Hasseldine, John.

K4475 .I58 2002
341.4'844--dc21   2002075243

Copyright © 2002 by Kluwer Academic Publishers

All rights reserved. No part of this work may be reproduced, stored in a retrieval system, or transmitted in any form or by any means, electronic, mechanical, photocopying, microfilming, recording, or otherwise, without the written permission from the Publisher, with the exception of any material supplied specifically for the purpose of being entered and executed on a computer system, for exclusive use by the purchaser of the work.

Permission for books published in Europe: permissions@wkap.nl
Permissions for books published in the United States of America: permissions@wkap.com
Printed on acid-free paper.
Printed in the United States of America

The Publisher offers discounts on this book for course use and bulk purchases.
For further information, send email to <david.cella@wkap.com> .

Contents

Contributors   vii

Preface   xi

1. Introduction to Taxation in an International Context   1
    ANDREW LYMER AND JOHN HASSELDINE

Part 1: The Global Tax Environment

2. History of Taxation   21
    WILLIAM D. SAMSON

3. History of International Business Taxation   43
    PAUL HEWITT, ANDREW LYMER AND LYNNE OATS

4. Internet Challenge to Tax System Design   61
    NEIL WARREN

5. Anti-Avoidance and Harmful Tax Competition: From Unilateral to
    Multilateral Strategies?   83
    MARIKA TOUMI

6. The Future International Tax Environment   105
    SIMON JAMES

vi

Part 2: Aspects of International Taxation

7. The Role of Tax Treaties in International Taxation   123
    WALTER O'CONNOR

8. Foreign Tax Credits   135
    ROBERT RICKETTS

9. International Transfer Pricing   157
    JAMIE ELLIOTT AND CLIVE EMMANUEL

10. International Tax Aspects of Income Derived from the Supply of
    Intellectual Property: Royalties vs. Business Profits   181
    KEVIN HOLMES

11. Taxing Non-Residents: A U.S. Perspective   207
    PEGGY HITE

12. Taxes and Compensation   229
    AMIN MAWANI

Part 3: Comparative Analyses

13. Taxing Companies and Their Shareholders: Design Issues   249
    LYNNE OATS

14. Administrative and Compliance Costs of International Taxation 273
    JEFF POPE

15. Binding Rulings: A Comparative Perspective   291
    ADRIAN SAWYER

Index   317

Contributors

Jamie Elliott is Senior Manager in the International Tax Group at Deloitte & Touche. Prior to his appointment, he held academic positions at the University of Southampton and the London Business School. He has researched extensively on many aspects of International Transfer Pricing. He is co-author of *"Financial Accounting and Reporting"* (Elliott and Elliott). He completed his Ph.D degree ("Managing International Transfer Pricing Policies") at the University of Glasgow in 1999.

Clive Emmanuel is Director of the Centre for International Finance and Accounting and Ernst and Young professor at the University of Glasgow. His research on international transfer pricing with Jamie Elliott has attracted CIMA Foundation support and he currently supervises three doctoral candidates working in the area.

John Hasseldine is the Co-Chair of Tax Management Research-Net and Director of the International Centre for Taxation Management Research at the Nottingham University Business School. He has held prior academic positions in the U.S. and in New Zealand. He researches and consults in the areas of tax compliance and tax administration. Currently, he is leading a four-year cross-national ESRC research project on improving voluntary tax compliance in the U.K. He completed his Ph.D degree in Accounting at the Kelley School of Business, Indiana University in 1997. He is on the editorial board of *Advances in Taxation* and is a U.K. correspondent for the *Bulletin for International Fiscal Documentation*.

Paul Hewitt is a Researcher in Taxation at the University of Birmingham in the UK. He is currently working on a research project addressing the impact of electronic commerce and electronic business practices on international taxation.

Peggy Hite is a Professor of Accounting at the Indiana University Kelley School of Business where she is the Chair of the Honors Program. Professor Hite received her Ph.D in 1986 from the University of Colorado. She has published in numerous journals including *The Accounting Review, The Journal of the American Taxation Association, The National Tax Journal, Public Opinion Quarterly, Public Finance, Journal of Economic Psychology and Advances in Taxation.* Professor Hite's research interests include taxpayer compliance, taxpayer-client relationships, and progressivity preferences. Professor Hite has won several teaching awards at the department, school, and university level.

Kevin Holmes is Principal Research Associate at the International Bureau of Fiscal Documentation (IBFD), Amsterdam, The Netherlands and Visiting Professor of Taxation at Eötvös Loránd University in Budapest, Hungary. He is co-editor of the *International Guide to the Taxation of Transfers of Technology* and a member of the editorial board of the *Bulletin for International Fiscal Documentation.* He was formerly Head of the IBFD's Government Consultancy Department and a tax partner of an international accountancy firm. He has a Ph.D degree from Victoria University of Wellington, New Zealand.

Simon James is Reader in Economics, School of Business and Economics, University of Exeter, Visiting Fellow, School of Finance, Australian National University, a Chartered Tax Adviser and Fellow of the Chartered Institute of Taxation. His 40 published research papers are mainly concerned with taxation and his 15 books include *The Economics of Taxation: Principles Policy and Practice.* He has also edited a four-volume collection of tax papers entitled *Taxation: Critical Perspectives on the World Economy,* which will be published by Routledge in 2002.

Andy Lymer is a Senior Lecturer at the University of Birmingham in the U.K. where he teaches the unusual combination of courses in U.K. taxation, international taxation and information systems. He has held visiting positions in Australia (at ATAX, University of New South Wales, the University of Sydney and Curtin Institute of Technology) and in the U.S. (at Texas Tech University). His research interests in tax include information technology impacts in tax practice and administration, transfer pricing developments and the impact of electronic commerce on taxation systems. He is the joint author of an annually produced guide to U.K. taxation entitled *"Taxation: Policy and Practice"*, produced by Thomson, and now in its ninth edition. He is the Managing Editor of the AccountingEducation.com web community.

Amin Mawani is an Associate Professor of Taxation at the Schulich School of Business at York University in Toronto, Canada. His research and teaching interests are in the area of taxation of employee stock options. Amin Mawani earned his Ph.D in Taxation from the University of Waterloo, his MA in Public Economics from the University of Toronto, and his Bachelor of Commerce in Finance from the University of Alberta. Amin is also a Certified Management Accountant (CMA) and a Certified Financial Planner (CFP).

Lynne Oats is a Lecturer in Taxation at Warwick Business School. She was previously a Senior Lecturer in Taxation at Sheffield Hallam University and at Curtin University of Technology, Western Australia. She completed her Ph.D at the University of Western Australia in 2000 and is currently researching in the areas of corporation tax, tax policy and U.K. tax history.

Walter O'Connor is Professor of Taxation and Accounting at Fordham University in New York where he is the Director of the Masters in Taxation Program and Area Chair of Accounting and Taxation. He was a Fulbright scholar in Macroeconomics and completed his Ph.D at City University of New York / Baruch. He now serves as Editor-in-Chief of *The International Tax Journal* and is retired Vice Chairman International of KPMG. He has published four books and numerous articles in academic and professional journals.

Jeff Pope is an Associate Professor in Economics at Curtin University of Technology, Perth, Australia. He pioneered the estimation of tax compliance costs in Australia in the late 1980s and early 1990s, with five (co-authored) books being published by the Australian Tax Research Foundation. His research has focused on tax compliance costs in the Asia-Pacific region, including the (co-authored) book *Taxation and Compliance Costs in Asia Pacific Economies*. Jeff has undertaken research for the Australian Business Coalition for Tax Reform and served on Government and business tax review committees. He is widely published in tax compliance costs and taxation policy in Australia and internationally.

Robert Ricketts is Frank M. Burke Chair in Taxation at Jerry S. Rawls College of Business Administration at Texas Tech University, in Lubbock, Texas. He teaches in the areas of corporate taxation, partnership taxation and international taxation, and conducts research on tax policy and the effects of tax rules on investor and taxpayer behaviour. He is co-editor of *Fundamental Concepts of Taxation*, a textbook on the U.S. income tax system. He received his Ph.D degree in Accounting from the University of North Texas in 1988.

William D. Samson is the Roddy-Garner Professor of Accounting at the University of Alabama. He is the 2002 President of the Academy of Accounting Historians, and served the organisation in a variety of offices including four years as co-editor of its journal: *The Accounting Historians Journal*. He recently completed a tax history project examining tax rates over time. In 1997, Bill has received national recognition for his teaching activities he specialises in teaching income taxation of individuals and tax planning courses. Bill received his Ph.D in 1981 from the University of North Carolina, has taught for 25 years and is a North Carolina CPA.

Adrian Sawyer, M Com (Hons), LLB, is a senior lecturer in taxation and business law at the University of Canterbury, Christchurch, NZ. He specialises in tax compliance and administration research, as well as insolvency law. He is both a chartered accountant and barrister and solicitor of the High Court. He has been a consultant for the NZ Inland Revenue Department on several occasions, including issues involving self-assessment, tax compliance and most recently binding rulings. He is a tax commentary writer for Brookers and Butterworths in New Zealand, is widely published, and is a co-editor of the *NZ Journal of Taxation Law & Policy*.

Marika Toumi, Maitrise de Droit, LLM, is a researcher at Nottingham University Business School where she works on an ESRC-funded project on the role of tax agencies in increasing voluntary tax compliance. She has worked in Coopers & Lybrand's International Tax Department and taught at Warwick University. She is now researching for her Ph.D thesis, a socio-legal and comparative study of tax avoidance and legal control.

Neil Warren is an Associate Professor of Economics in the Australian Taxation Studies Program (ATAX) at the Faculty of Law, University of New South Wales and since 1994, has been Research Director of the Australian Tax Research Foundation. He has consulted widely to both Commonwealth and state governments on taxation issues and advised on taxation policy and tax administration issues in a number of international development projects in the Asia-Pacific. In addition, he has advised numerous private sector organisations on taxation issues and written extensively on most economic aspects of tax policy design and development.

Preface

Although we have entitled this book 'The International Taxation System', the term 'international tax' is in fact a misnomer. When we speak of international tax what we are really referring to is the international aspects of domestic tax laws. There is no overriding global law of taxation, no single international tax authority ensuring compliance and tax payment. Tax laws are creations of national states that, from time to time, interact with one another where they describe the taxation of cross-border activity.

To understand the taxes that will be imposed on any individual taxpayer, business taxpayer or personal, you need to understand the national tax laws of the countries in which some potentially taxable activity is occurring. This book focuses on the trends in taxation that have received wide (i.e. multiple country) acceptance – and which therefore are collectively termed international tax - and the underpinning, but differing, national views on the interpretation of these trends - which is termed comparative taxation.

Teaching materials currently available in the area of international taxation appear in a wide range of technical and discursive styles. They also are founded in multiple disciplines because of the nature and importance of taxation – including at least accounting, legal, economic and political science disciplines. Why is another book needed in this area? As teachers of taxation we were concerned that much of this material focused heavily on the USA and the range of resources that were in fact appropriate for support of teaching of international taxation outside of the USA were very limited. The remit we accepted therefore was to create materials, at appropriate depth and with suitable breadth, to support the teaching of international taxation right across the world, with necessary support for comparative analysis. We have attempted to build on the material available in the USA, but also to integrate a wider international viewpoint on the subject into the resources we have created.

This book is mainly targeted at taught university-level study of international taxation. For most universities, this is undertaken at a post-graduate, Masters, level. The authors of the chapters of this book have therefore mainly been asked to assume that basic taxation knowledge is available to readers from a first, nationally focused, course in taxation that most will have been gained from prior study. To cover the possibility that some users may not have such a background, however, we have included some introductory support (see 'Introduction to International Business Taxation' particularly) that introduces appropriate foundation principles of taxation needed for the study of international taxation. However, this text is not an introduction to taxation theory, or to any particular national tax system.

The rest of the remit given to each of our authors was also common. Each chapter introduces the reader to the topic being examined, leads you through the key issues related to the topic, and provides details on further reading and discussion issues in each case. Each chapter provides enough material for a two-hour lecture on the topic at hand, with pre- and post- reading suggested as appropriate.

The range of resources we, as educators, would like to have available in this area, and the different perspectives that could usefully be taken on most of this topics from different disciplinary focuses, lead to a long wish list of different chapters for the book. Of course, some limitation on this range had to be imposed because of the physical constraints of the publication process. We therefore choose to opt for a publication deal with a publishing partner who was willing to think imaginatively about how best to provide a wide range of resources for this topic – not just what would appear in the printed part. Kluwer Academic were willing supporters of this idea. For this reason the book is therefore just one part of a range of materials, managed by us as editors, available to support the study of international and comparative taxation. Readers are encouraged to visit the website that provides a companion to this printed text. It contains materials that directly link to the chapters chosen to form a part of this book. It also, however, provides other chapters on different topics, other teaching and study support, and other useful links and content to provide a complete framework for the study of this topic. These materials as a set provide a wide variety of perspectives, content and focus. This allows the educator a wide choice of approaches to this increasingly important topic of study and provides a range of viewpoints for the student seeking to understand this topic area.

Website address: http://www.taxstudent.com/international

As editors, we would like to acknowledge the support of the various people who have played key roles in the production of this text. These particularly include Marika Toumi, of Nottingham University in the UK, who played an essential role in the management of the production of the text. We also acknowledge the support from the publishers, especially from our Publishing Editor at Kluwer Academic, David Cella. Other support was offered from various members of the Tax Research Network (TRN – http://www.trn.org.uk) that we gratefully acknowledge.

We would welcome feedback on the materials in this text, and on the website, including suggestions for additional materials. Please address these comments to int_tax@taxstudent.com. (Please note however, we will not be able to answer questions on international taxation via this address)

Please note, whilst every attempt has been made to be accurate in the production of the content of this text, the information should not be used, or relied upon, for tax planning purposes in any way. Neither the authors, editors nor publishers will accept any liability for actions taken on the basis of information contained in this text, or on the website.

Andrew Lymer and John Hasseldine
May 2002

Chapter 1

Introduction to Taxation in an International Context

ANDREW LYMER and JOHN HASSELDINE
University of Birmingham, U.K. and University of Nottingham, U.K.

Key words: international tax; double taxation; tax treaties; jurisdiction

Abstract: This chapter provides an outline to taxation in an international context. It discusses the importance of taxation as both an individual and business planning activity, outlines what a tax is, why Governments charge them and how they can be arranged. It then discusses how these domestic structures for tax are changed to be applied to cross border transactions where more than one country is involved. It discusses the key problem of international taxation, that of double tax, and how this arises from jurisdictional conflicts in the rights to tax. The chapter also discusses how double tax can be relieved in practice. It concludes with a brief introduction to other key issues in international taxation; neutrality, tax avoidance/evasion and transfer pricing.

1. INTRODUCTION

This chapter introduces the reader to the subject of International Taxation. This is a key topic in the development of effective business planning for a business that wishes to trade internationally and also a fundamental consideration for an individual when thinking of working overseas, or earning income from a non-domestic source of some kind (e.g. buying an investment in an overseas country).

Whenever anyone, a business or otherwise, considers trading or investing beyond the borders of the country in which they are based one of the key plans they must make is how taxation will affect their economic decisions. Whilst tax will probably not be the only concern (e.g. other important issues are economic and political stability, banking regulation quality, and so on), tax can be a very significant cost in performing international trading transactions and ignoring its impact on cost structures, and hence profitability, could be courting with disaster. Taxes on business transactions exceed 30% in many countries around the world – ignoring this fact would have a major impact on investment appraisal calculations. International Taxation is the consideration of rules for determining how an entity trading in more than one country ('cross-border') will pay tax. It explains when taxes are paid, to whom and how much will be paid. Understanding the international tax system enables a taxpayer to examine the impacts of entering into international transactions between two, or more countries.

This chapter provides an overview of the international taxation system as currently operated around the world. It sets this discussion into an overview of the role tax plays in the global economy. Many of the issues it touches upon are further developed elsewhere in this book, and in the other resources available via the website. However, this chapter should be your starting point for these other resources, as it will provide you with the general foundation needed to understand them fully.

2.   FUNDAMENTAL ISSUES

2.1   What is Tax?

Before considering the basic principles of International Taxation, we need to make sure we know what *a tax* is. James (1998), in his Dictionary of Taxation, provides a commonly used definition:

> 'A compulsory levy made by public authorities for which nothing is received directly in return'.

This definition suggests that the nature of a tax is that it is a payment made, (a cost incurred) without the usual associated receipt, normal to other transactions, of any consideration in return. The word 'directly' used in the definition is of course important. A government will charge its citizens, and businesses trading within its borders, tax in order to raise revenue to fund the provision of the public sector. Most taxes paid however, are not directly associated with a public sector provision the taxpayer will receive in return but are more loosely linked to the idea of benefits they gain from their link with that country. For example, their taxes will help support economic stability, the availability of a skilled workforce, the physical infrastructure, and so on.

The IBFD International Tax Glossary (IBFD, 1996) helpfully lists inclusions and some exclusions in their definition to aid our understanding. They suggest a tax would not include charges (e.g. user charges - as these are normally made in return for something direct) or penalties, but includes social security contributions (because of their compulsory nature and indirect consideration returns).

2.2   Why and How do Governments Tax?

Governments, whether elected by popular vote or otherwise, take on the role of governing a country. In order to carry out this governing function, a government will need to spend money in its economy. This may be direct expenditure, such as employing civil (public) servants to carry out direct governing functions, but will also include much wider expense than this where governments will spend money to support particular areas of the economy (e.g. paying subsidies or offering grants), provide a support system for their citizens (e.g. provision of a social security or health system) and other functions to occur such as development of economic stability, regulation and so on.

To do all of these functions a government must therefore raise finances to enable this money to be spent. By far the largest source of this revenue in most countries is levies (i.e. taxes) charged by the government, and paid by its citizens (individual and corporate).

In most countries citizens of other countries that are investing or trading in the country are also drawn into this group of taxpayers as they too receive at least some of the benefit from their presence in the private sector. Taxes are therefore an inevitable factor of a society in which a public sector is present.

A subsequent question is how does a Government decide what to tax to raise this revenue? These decisions are partly politically motivated but also follow basic economic principles of fiscal policy making. They must also be responsive to changing economic situations within a country, and between countries.

This complex combination of factors will lead to the dynamic collections of taxes (or 'tax systems') we see around the world. No two tax systems are identical in any two countries, nor in fact will they remain constant even within a country as a government responds to changes in its economy, or in the wide global context in which it is found.

The basic economic principles on which a 'good' tax system design have been well understood for many years. They were presented, for example, in a key economic text, produced by an economist called Adam Smith in the 18th century, called 'The Wealth of Nations'. In this book[1] Adam Smith outlined the following four principles of sound tax system design:

---

[1]   Book V, Chapter II Part II, 'of Taxes'.

a) Equity – fair in its impact on taxpayers
b) Certainty – taxpayers should be able to determine the tax impact of their
   economic decisions at the point at which they make their decisions
c) Convenience – easy to pay for the taxpayer
d) Efficiency – it should not have an effect on the allocation of resources i.e.
   people will not change their economic decisions as a result of tax (in ways
   not so designed for the tax) or be inefficient in administration (i.e. cost as
   little to administer as possible)
   Of course, other factors should also be considered in the development and
reform of tax systems. For example, flexibility, the tax system must be
designed to continue to function appropriately in a changing environment
(e.g. as the economic situation in the country changes).
   Governments therefore have a difficult task to determine the basis on
which their tax system should be formed, but this is a necessary function of
the Government to enable it to have any effect within its jurisdiction.

2.3   Bases of Taxation

Having established why a government taxes, the next question to discuss is
how these principles can be put into practice. Rules related to taxation can be
classified into three categories – referred to as the 'bases of taxation'. These
bases are helpful in determining how various activities are to be taxed:
Income – how income flows from wealth are taxed; Capital – how stores of
wealth are taxed; and Expenditure – how expenditure of wealth is taxed.
   All taxes will fall into one or other of these categories and most tax
systems will include at least one tax from each category. Taxes on income and
on capital are normally created so as to make the taxpayer directly responsible
for payment of the tax due. These taxes are therefore typically referred to as
direct taxes. Taxes on expenditure are typically paid via the recipients of the
expenditure (e.g. the retailer) who act as tax collectors on behalf of the
government. Therefore these taxes are paid indirectly to the government by
the taxpayer and are thus referred to as indirect taxes.

2.4   Impact of International Trade on Domestic Monetary Flows

The discussion so far in this chapter really applies to establishing a tax
system within a single country (a single 'jurisdiction'). If a country did no
business with other countries, i.e. no products, services or financing were
imported or exported, then the tax system could be developed in a way that

best suits the local economy, its Government's objectives and its taxpayers' attitudes. This is an unrealistic scenario however, for any country operating in the modern environment. In reality, large sums of money transfer across borders, in various forms, on a daily basis as part of the normal business activities of many businesses. Therefore the tax system of any one country must be able to cope with firstly, inflows of 'wealth' from other countries (i.e. belonging to people or businesses from other countries and to whom any returns on that wealth will belong) and outflows of wealth from individuals and business entities within its own jurisdiction to other countries.

Many Governments will argue that anyone gaining a benefit, even if indirectly, from its expenditures should contribute towards the cost of that expenditure in some form – usually as a tax of some sort. This leads most governments to develop their tax system to enable them to collect tax revenue from as many sources as gain benefit from their public sector expenditures. The form, and extent, of this taxation will vary depending on the principles applied by the government. Some will favour direct taxation forms, others indirect taxation as their focus. In most cases a mixture of taxes are applied. For example, in the largest 14 industrialised countries, direct taxation (from domestic and international sources) accounted for 63.4% of government revenues in 1999 compared with only 29.0% in developing countries (Sandford, 2000, p. 8). This is contrasted with indirect taxes making up between 40% and 70% of government revenues in 61% of non-oil producing developing countries compared to all less than 40% of government revenues in the largest 14 industrialised countries. The more industrialised a country becomes, the more it relies on direct taxation sources to collect taxation from its citizens and others choosing to invest in its country.

3. THE CENTRAL PRINCIPLE OF TAXATION

3.1 Jurisdictional Rights

An important concern in building an effective tax system for the real world is what right any particular government has to tax any particular individual's, or individual company's, wealth (in whatever form or however it flows). This 'jurisdictional right to tax' is a central principle of international taxation. Its resolution (i.e. when in fact does a government have the right to tax and when not) is central to most international tax issues.

How this right is enacted is entirely a decision for an individual country. No international authority exists that can force a country to collect, or not collect, a particular tax or apply a particular set of tax rules on a tax base.[2] In practice, however, most countries are keen to use the tax system to raise revenues where they can and will therefore follow international patterns of tax system design in the main. However, it can often also be a useful tool for a Government not to raise taxes on a particular activity to influence economic behaviour in certain circumstances. This can happen, for example, when a country, keen to have money invested with them that may otherwise be placed elsewhere, offers tax 'breaks' (incentives – such as reductions in future taxes to be paid) to wealthy individuals or businesses in return for their investments.

3.2   Source vs. Residency Principles of Taxation Rights

At the heart of a jurisdictional right to tax is the principle of residence. If a taxpayer, individual or corporate, fulfils a country's rules for residency then they will be subject to that jurisdiction's tax rules. This is true for all countries. The reach of this taxable status may also go beyond physical residence to citizenship (domicile) if someone is not actually resident or operating from that country now, but had so in the past, or intends to do so in the future. The U.S. and the UK (amongst others) operate tax jurisdiction policies that may mean residents and non-resident citizens may have to pay tax to them.

Residency rules can be determined by fairly straightforward principles such as where was the taxpayer's country of birth/incorporation (e.g. as applies in the U.S.) or by more complex rules such as incorporation *or* place of effective management (e.g. as applies in the UK and Australia). The more complex the residency rules the more costly a tax system may be to operate for the Government, however, this is compensated for by widening the tax revenues that are generated as it is harder for individuals or companies to move activities out of the residency catchment (called 'going offshore').

Whilst these residency rules may appear straightforward, the jurisdictional right to tax does not usually stop at taxation of residents. Most countries also claim the right to tax non-residents/non-citizens, if they are earning income, investing wealth, or spending wealth in their jurisdiction. For example, if an American resident spends money in the UK whilst on holiday there they can expect to pay UK expenditure taxation (a VAT) on their purchases just as a UK resident would in the UK – no distinction on the basis of residency will be given between them. This is termed the source principle – the country of source of an activity producing a taxable event has a claim to tax the wealth

---

[2]   See Hamilton *et al* (1999), p1-16 to 1-19 for more on this topic.

flows involved, or stores created, when generated or held within their jurisdiction.

4. DOUBLE TAXATION

4.1 Source vs. Residence Clash

The application of both the residency and source principles of taxation together, as is usually the case in most international transactions, may lead to the taxation of the tax base more than once. This is referred to as double taxation. For example, if a U.S. resident places money on deposit in a bank in Australia then the return on that investment (the interest the bank will pay out) will be sourced in Australia, and therefore subject to Australian taxation rules for the reasons given in the section above. However, the U.S. will claim that the interest received forms part of the income of one of its residents and therefore the residency rule would entitle it to also tax this interest when received. This conflict, if not resolved somehow, would result in double taxation of the interest received – in Australia and again in the U.S.

A jurisdictional conflict can arise not only when there is a source v residence clash as in the case above, but also where residency rules between countries are inconsistent resulting in a taxpayer being considered a resident of more than one country for the same tax period ('dual residence clash'- Hamilton, *et al* 1999). This could perhaps occur if someone moves residence during a tax year, for example, and both countries then claim the taxpayer was resident in their jurisdiction for that tax year. It ca also occur where source rules clash, i.e. where two, or more, countries claim source taxing rights to a tax base, usually income (a 'dual source clash'). In each case double taxation will result if not resolved in some way.

Double taxation, a phrase used for however many times taxation is charged on the same tax source even if it is more than twice, is something that taxpayers feel 'uncomfortable' with. It is rare that people feel pleased to pay tax once of course, but paying it twice on the same source will not be liked at all. Double taxation therefore can be considered to be 'the central problem of international taxation' (Doernberg, 1997) and its handling (e.g. its relief) causes much of the complexity of international taxation and is the primary concern of taxpayers in dealing with their international tax affairs.

The chapters throughout this book show that some element of double taxation is often unavoidable when engaging in international activities – it is a cost that must be born when doing business internationally. However, minimising this double taxation is a key tax-planning goal in almost all circumstances. The desire to minimise taxes paid, and avoid double taxation if at all possible, has lead to the development of a large international tax-planning community as the number and volume of international transactions has grown.

Managing acceptable ways of avoiding double taxation also concerns tax authorities as they seek to protect their rights to tax and ensure taxpayers make fair tax contributions to their countries of residence as well as countries of source.

4.2   The OECD, the UN and the Tax Treaty Network

Double taxation between states (or provinces) in federal countries like the U.S. and Germany had been an issue for some time before international trade had grown very large and lessons were learned from the resolution of these inter-state activities in determining how international rules could be made to operate successfully. However, as international trade developed, before, between and particularly after the two world wars, the impact of double taxation reached a point where the attempts to handle conflicting rights to taxation between countries became inefficient to handle on a case by case, even country by country, basis.

Super-national organisations, such the League of Nations, its post-second world war successor the Organisation of Economic Co-operation and Development (OECD) and the United Nations (UN), became involved in representing national interests at an international level looking to find acceptable international solutions to the management of these conflicting rights. Despite not being tax raising bodies themselves they acted as aggregators of best practice and therefore much of the discussion on international taxation issues were handled through them.

A system of tax agreements (called treaties) became the way countries agreed to handle sharing the taxation rights for international activity. These treaties were largely bilateral (between two countries). On behalf of its international membership, the OECD worked to create a model for these treaties in the form of a standard 'outline' to help support efficient agreement resolution. The OECD Model Tax Treaty on Income and on Capital was first released in draft form in 1963 with a first full version being made available in 1977. It has undergone a number of amendments since then (1992, 1994, 1995, 1997 and some changes in 2000 – with further amendments planned for mid-2002). This model now forms the basis for the majority of treaties in existence between industrialised nations. The UN also produced a model tax treaty (first issued in 1980) that aimed to address tax issues between industrialised and developing nations, although was largely the same as the

OECD versions in many key respects. The UN model favours the source countries right to tax revenues a little more than the OECD model, as would be expected given its different bias. The U.S. also has its own model income tax convention. The latest version of this model was issued in September 1996 (Meldman and Schadewald, 2000).[3]

4.3   Role of Permanent Establishment Rules

A key feature of double taxation management is the agreement to share the rights to tax when more than one jurisdiction has a legitimate right to tax a transaction, or store of wealth.

Where both a source country and residence country share a right to tax the resident country will normally give up their right to the source country to become the principle taxing country. This right is not always completely relinquished, as discussed in the next section, as the residence country normally holds the rights to tax income in addition to the source country if it so wishes – i.e. the power rests with the residence country in this arrangement. The giving up of this right is normally only done however, in the case of business transactions where adequate taxable 'presence' exists in the source country. This is normally measured by the 'permanent establishment' rules.

Article 5 of the OECD Model Tax Treaty (1995) defines when a permanent establishment is normally considered to exist. It requires 'a fixed place of business through which a business of an enterprise is wholly or partly carried on'. This may be taken to include a place of management plus branches, offices, a factory, workshop, mine or quarry and building projects (in the latter case, only if lasting for more than twelve months). Some explicit exclusions also exist in the OECD definition where certain functions carried out will not normally lead to a permanent establishment. These include storage, displays or delivery of goods, their maintenance, or where only preparatory or auxiliary functions to the normal business functions are engaged in.

Where a permanent establishment exists in a country, then wealth generated in that country can primarily be taxed by that country (i.e. the source country dominates the right to tax). Conversely, where no permanent establishment can be said to exist when trading in a country then that country

---

[3]   Further details on the history and current use of Model Tax Treaties/Conventions can be found in Ogley (1992) and Picciotto (1992). The standard contents of the model tax treaties form the core subject of interest for anyone studying international taxation. They will be studied in depth in a later chapter of this book.

will have no rights as the principle country to tax that activity even though it was sourced within that country. The principle taxing rights revert instead to the country of residence.

The role of the permanent establishment rules is therefore of great importance in international taxation of business transactions. Where a permanent establishment does not exist, the source country may still extract some tax on the wealth flow when that wealth leaves the country to be stored elsewhere (such as when repatriated to its owner in another country). This tax will usually take the form of a withholding tax – usually a percentage of the value of the wealth flow – and often at a much lower rate than would have been charged on the generation of that wealth had a permanent establishment existed.

4.4   The Relief of Double Taxation

As double taxation is the central problem of international taxation, its relief is a key issue for international tax systems. Double tax will arise when the resident country claims a right to tax something a source country has already taxed, so double tax relief is dealt with by the resident country not in the source country.

There are four different ways in which the resident country can handle double taxation. The method chosen for any particular transaction will depend on the countries between which the wealth is flowing, the nature of any tax treaty in force between these countries and the nature of the transaction involved.

The four methods that may be chosen from by the resident country are exemption, deduction, credit or no action (i.e. where double taxation will apply). The difference between these options are best illustrated with a simple example, as below:

In a simple group of two companies, the foreign company of the group (with a permanent establishment in its source country) earns a profit of $100,000 and remits all its profits (after source country tax) to its parent. The parent then may have to pay further taxes to its resident country before the income of the group can be determined. Assuming the foreign source country taxation for this profit is 30% and the resident taxes are 35%, the four options shown in Table 1 below apply for relief of double taxation.

In case one, neither country is acting to relieve double taxation and so the group pays tax in both countries – a total of 65% in all. This is the worst case for the taxpayer in this scenario but is not uncommon in practice as it can occur whenever no double tax treaty exists between two countries and no unilateral tax credit provision exists.

In case two, the resident country relieves double taxation by allowing the resident company to pay residence taxes only on the remittance it receives after foreign taxes have been paid. This is referred to as the deduction method. In this case, this method would result in a total tax rate to the group of 54%.

Table 1. Options for Relief of Double Taxation

	1. Double tax	2. Deduction	3. Credit	4. Exemption
Foreign sourced income	100,000	100,000	100,000	100,000
Foreign taxes (@30%)	30,000	30,000	30,000	30,000
Net FSI	70,000	70,000	70,000	70,000
Domestic Taxes:				
@ 35% on $100,000	35,000			
@ 35% on $70,000		24,500		
@35% on $100,000 –			5,000	
foreign taxes paid				
FSI exemption				0
Total Group Income	35,000	45,500	65,000	70,000
Effective group tax rate	65%	54.5%	35%	30%

In case three, a credit is allowed for foreign taxes already paid against the residence country's tax bill. This means the resident country tax is calculated on the full group income, but then the group is allowed to credit foreign taxes already paid. This produces, in this scenario, a group tax bill of 35% (note – this is equivalent to the resident country tax rate, being the higher of the two rates applicable on this income).

Case four involves exemption of foreign sourced income from resident country tax (the exemption method). In this case, no resident country tax would be due as all the group's income was foreign sourced. This method is most commonly found in resident countries that import more capital than they export – termed capital importing countries. It is also often a feature of the tax systems of tax havens, or other tax motivated offshore financial centres (OFCs), as it can often produce the lowest total tax bill for the group (as in this scenario) and therefore attract residents to that country.

The most common tax relief method for capital exporting countries (typically the industrialised nations) is the tax credit method. This gives a lower rate of tax for their resident companies than may be the case with other methods (excluding the exemption method), as illustrated in this scenario – although this may not always be the case. The credit limit available to a resident company is often restricted, however, to prevent excessive tax loss to resident countries. For example, most countries that operate a tax credit system for double tax relief (e.g. the U.S., the UK, Australia etc) only allow foreign source income tax credits against the residence company's tax bills up to the limit of tax that would have been paid on that income had that same income been domestically earned (sourced) rather than foreign sourced. This means that tax credits will only be available to relieve all of the double taxation where a source country has a lower rate of tax than the resident country. Where the source country has a higher rate of tax then the maximum credit allowable will only be up to the resident country's tax bill and no excess credits will be available to relieve the other tax that has been paid. This will result in a higher amount of tax being paid overall by the group than would have been the case if they had sourced their income in a lower tax jurisdiction.[4]

5.   OTHER FEATURES

5.1   Types of Returns and Income

In planning an effective international tax system a country must consider a range of income flows and wealth stores to ensure an individual or company cannot bypass its tax system in ways that the country is not intending to allow. For example, individuals may invest in shares in a foreign company and receive returns on that investment in the form of dividends – so foreign source dividend income must be planned for in the tax system design. Individuals may however, 'roll-up' these returns into capital gains released when they sell their shares rather than taking dividends from the investment. Capital gains from foreign asset transactions must therefore be considered in the design of the international tax system.

The individual could also loan money to a foreign company instead of taking an equity stake. Returns to this investment would then come in the form of interest payments. This flow too must therefore be encompassed in the tax system design.

An individual may also receive returns from a fee or license for the use of an asset (e.g. from an intangible asset they own) lent to, or leased to, a foreign company or individual. These license fees usually are referred to as royalties and will also need including in the international tax system design.

---

[4]   Other restrictions on foreign source tax credit exist in practice in some countries as will be
      seen later in this book. A useful list of which countries apply which system of double tax
      relief in general can be found in the appendices to Ogley (1992).

A further way of extracting profits from a foreign investment may come by way of payments for services or administration costs. For example, parent company could charge a foreign subsidiary a fee to cover the costs of the centralised services it provides. As this may be used in some cases as a way of moving profit from the subsidiary to the parent then appropriate taxation of this flow must also be considered in the tax system design to limit this kind of abuse.

In general, dividend payments between companies and their investors are taxed using the source/residency rules as explained in the previous sections. These make up a large proportion of the international flows of taxable incomes. Double taxation will then be relieved using whichever method the resident country determines appropriate.

Other cross border relationships may not result in the creation of a permanent establishment in the source country and therefore will often be taxed by the source country using withholding taxes instead. These are also usually subject to double tax relief where a tax treaty exists, or are set at a very low rate by the source country (usually because of the conditions of a treaty) making the impact of any double taxation very small.

5.2   Neutrality in International Trade

One of the key features of an effective tax system design is efficiency (as was discussed in section three). This principle implies a tax system should aim to have a neutral impact on the economic decisions of its taxpayers (at least to limiting their effects on wider decisions than those that the tax system was designed to specifically influence). This means the tax system should be designed to operate 'in the background' (Doernberg, 1997).

This principle applies for international taxation as much as for the domestic tax system. In the international case neutrality can be considered in three ways; capital export neutrality, capital import neutrality and national neutrality (Doernberg, 1997).

Capital export neutrality is achieved where a taxpayer's choice of investment at home or overseas is not affected by taxation. This would imply the taxes paid, in total, on the investment would be the same wherever that investment is made. If this was achieved, it would result in resource allocation being determined entirely on non-tax decisions (i.e. would be tax neutral).

Capital import neutrality suggests all firms trading in a market are taxed at the same rates irrespective of the residence of the trader. Achieving this standard of neutrality would imply preventing overseas investors from being disadvantaged by being taxed in the country of source at the same rate as local investors and, in addition, by their country of residence, thus reducing their returns compared to source country investors who are only taxed by the source country.

The third neutrality standard is that of national neutrality. Under this standard residence country returns are shared between the taxpayer and the tax authority in the same way whether earned in the country of residence, or in a foreign country. This implies the impact of foreign taxes should match the impact of taxing the same income had it been generated within the resident country instead.

International tax systems will typically have elements of all three of these standards in their design. However, it is probably impossible in practice to operate all three fully, at the same point in time, for the same tax base such as income, where sovereign rights to tax must be maintained over a range of countries.

5.3   Tax Avoidance, Tax Evasion and Role of Tax Havens

Paying tax to a tax authority is not something most people wish to do more than they have to. The avoidance of tax is therefore a common activity amongst taxpayers. At a national level, this can contribute to a large 'gap' between expected, or potential, tax revenue for a government and that which it actually achieves.

No government can claim the right to more tax revenue that its tax law allows them to collect however, and therefore tax planning to avoid paying more tax than necessary (called tax avoidance) is a legitimate activity. Where you engage in breaking the law to reduce your tax bill (termed tax evasion), this will, however, result in criminal proceedings when discovered. A concern therefore arises as to at which point does legitimate tax avoidance become illegal tax evasion; the grey area between these often being referred to as tax 'avoision'.

This issue is addressed in some countries with specific anti-avoidance legislation (e.g. in Canada, New Zealand, and Australia). In other countries, such as the UK, other rules exist to address this problem such as preventing taxpayers using otherwise artificial means to reduce their tax bills.

Anti-avoidance legislation also exists at an international level where the opportunities to use the international tax system to reduce global tax bills are many. This legislation includes preventing simple movement of business activities offshore where these entities are just for tax minimisation purposes (e.g. as in the case of Subpart F regulations in the U.S. or Controlled Foreign Corporation legislation in Australia and the UK). They also cover the misuse of the various treaties that exist between countries to move taxable wealth around the world in tax efficient, but artificial, ways. This so called 'treaty shopping' activity is prevented in many tax treaties by limiting the tax benefits available under a treaty to those genuinely resident in one or other of the countries of the tax treaty (i.e. the ultimate beneficiary is in the resident country not a third country). The U.S. is the key global exponent of these restricted treaty rules[5] although other countries are now revising their treaties with other countries to also mirror these restrictions.

A further dimension to international tax planning activity is the role of tax havens.[6] Tax haven status is explicitly reserved for countries that actively pursue the low tax characteristics of a tax haven, many countries engage in activity that may reduce tax bills for at least some of its taxpayers. This may be offered in the form of 'tax breaks' or incentives to domestic investors (to encourage them to invest 'at home' rather than overseas), or to overseas investors (to place their investment in their country rather than elsewhere). The influence of 'tax competition' of this kind on tax avoidance activity is widespread and not just limited to tax havens countries.

The global influence of tax havens has been limited over the period of the development of the international tax system but has been growing steadily year on year. Recently the impact of tax havens, and more general offshore financial centres where tax breaks may be offered as investment inducements, became the subject of extensive OECD review as member countries agreed to act together against what they termed 'harmful tax competition or practices'.[7] This could mark the end of the widening of the impact of tax havens on tax avoidance – although they are unlikely to disappear altogether.

The offering of tax inducements or incentives, as outlined above, is also becoming less effective as some countries (again led by the U.S.) are acting to limit their impact on resource allocation (and therefore their tax revenues) via changes to their tax treaties. Where the residence country maintains the ultimate right to manage the amount of total tax that is paid by an international group, then it is straightforward for residence countries to deny the support of these tax breaks by limiting the lowering of their tax bills to match the source countries deductions. The honouring in the resident country of a source country's tax break is referred to as 'tax sparing'.

Despite these concerns, some countries do support specific tax incentive regimes by having have agreements explicitly listed in their tax treaties, often as a way of indirectly assisting developing countries. For example, the Australia tax treaties with Malaysia, Sri Lanka, Thailand, Vietnam and Fiji all

---

[5]   For an example, see Article 16 of the Australian/U.S. Double Tax Agreement
[6]   A tax haven is a country where tax rates are substantially lower than taxpayers would otherwise pay in another country
[7]   A later chapter in this book reviews these recent discussions in detail as this is an important current international taxation topic.

have clauses to offer a variety of tax sparing arrangements (Hamilton *et al*, 1999). However, these will disappear over time as the 1997 Australian budget proposed no further agreements of this kind would be made in the foreseeable future when these treaties come up for review.

6.   CONCLUSION

This chapter has introduced the reader to the topic of international taxation. The principles we have outlined are relatively new (many little more than 40 years old in practice) although founded upon economic fiscal theory that has served domestic tax systems for many hundreds of years. This novelty does mean however, that we are not at the point of a stable equilibrium for international tax systems and new developments are continually influencing the systems in place. For example, current influences include international tax competition, electronic business activity impacts, globalisation of equity markets, tax system harmonisation plans, altered balances between the use of indirect versus direct taxation, growth of the impact of intangible assets, and so on. These issues are each addressed in later chapters of the book, and elsewhere in the resources available via our website.

It is unlikely we will ever reach a stable equilibrium for international tax systems, however, as we continue to operate in an unstable business and regulatory environment that together exert changing pressures on the international tax system.

The reader is encouraged however, to contribute to the debate as to how international tax systems should be developed by getting to grips with the issues made available to you in this book, and via the website.

STUDY QUESTIONS

1. What is the difference between a tax and a user charge?
2. To what extent are Adam Smith's principles of taxation still relevant in the modern tax environment?
3. What is the 'central problem of international taxation' and what are the options of handling it?
4. What is a source vs. residence clash and why is the notion of a permanent establishment so important?
5. What is the difference between tax evasion and tax avoidance – in a) legal terms, and b) economic effect?

REFERENCES AND FURTHER READING

Doernberg, R. (1997), *International Taxation in a Nutshell*, St. Paul, MN: U.S. West
    Publishing Co.
Hamilton, R. Deutsch, R. and Raneri, J. (1999), *Guidebook to Australian International
    Taxation* (6th Student Edition). Prospect Publications: St. Leonards, NSW, Australia.
IBFD (1996), *International Tax Glossary* (3rd Edition), Ed S. Lyons. Amsterdam: International
    Bureau of Fiscal Documentation.
James, S. (1998), *A Dictionary of Taxation*, Cheltenham: Edward Elgar: Cheltenham .
Meldman, R. and Schadewald, M. (2000), *A Practical Guide to U.S. Taxation of International
    Transactions* (3rd Edition), Dordrecht: Kluwer Law International/CCH.
Picciotto, S (1992), *International Business Taxation*, London: Weidenfeld and Nicolson
    (Academic).
Ogley, A. (1992), *Principles of International Taxation*. London: Interfisc Publications.
Sandford, C. (2000), *Why Tax Systems Differ: A comparative study of the political economy of
    taxation*, Bath: Fiscal Publications.

For further information on Model Tax Treaties see the OECD website at http://www.oecd.org

Other details can be found on our website at http://www.taxstudent.com

PART ONE:

THE GLOBAL TAX ENVIRONMENT

Chapter 2

History of Taxation

WILLIAM D. SAMSON
University of Alabama, U.S.A.

Key words: tax history; income tax; estate tax; consumption tax

Abstract: Taxation is a mark of civilisation. Tax evolved and developed independently in
the great ancient empires. The concepts that evolved were transported to other
empires and cultures where tax ideas took root. This pattern continues through
to today as nations are influenced by developments in tax from other countries.
In this chapter, the evolution of property taxes, inheritance, estate and gift taxes,
consumption taxes such as excise taxes and sales taxes, and the income tax are
examined. These taxes are traced from their roots on through mutations. The
transportation of these taxes is also described.

'There is no art which one government sooner learns of another than that
of draining money from the pocket of people' – Adam Smith.

1.   INTRODUCTION

Tax emerges from the blurry past as being part of ancient empires. The
exact point in time when a tax was first instituted is unknown not only
because of poor historical records but also because of cultural and societal
structure of ancient empires. Empires such as the Egyptian, Mesopotamian,
Chinese, and Inca were theocratic: the religion and the government were
mixed – the king/emperor was viewed as a god. Paying tribute to this leader
was both a religious contribution and a governmental extraction. Hence,
'tithing', referred to in the Bible as contributions to the temple, was both a tax
and a contribution. Second, in early ancient empires, the people were often
considered the property of the king/emperor who owned everything. Often
civic projects and governmental actions were carried out by the subjects
performing services, i.e., building pyramids, serving as warriors in military

campaigns, constructing levees. These actions were imposed on the people as their duty to the emperor. Like the payments of tax, rendering services to the government was a form of taxation.

Tax payment by subjects to the central authority did emerge in these civilisations, perhaps when specialisation developed to the point that demanding everyone, for example, to work on the pyramid was inefficient and impractical. Instead, it became more efficient for the government to hire some citizens to perform the needed services, while the rest of the population engage in other activities, but pay for the government's expenditures.

The sections that follow explore taxation in ancient empires; property taxation; inheritance, estate, and gift taxes; consumption-based taxes; and income taxation. In these, sections emerge some recurring themes. Ideas about taxes, developed in a particular time and place, were transported to and adopted in other times and in other places. In the ancient civilisations, taxation arose independently such that taxes, like writing, characterised civilised society. Yet, it is the uncivilised acts of war that often seems to be the impetus for developing or adopting a new form of tax.

2.   TAXATION IN ANCIENT EMPIRES

Taxation occurred as ancient empires developed. One notes that taxation was implemented by different empires in different places and times; perhaps like temple and monument construction, taxation is a common phenomenon of human society.

Taxes have been traced by archaeologists as far back as King Scorpion the First's empire in southern Egypt between 3300 and 3200 BC. The archaeological record of taxation has been found in clay tablets the size of postage stamps and on jars and vases unearthed in King Scorpion I's tomb. The exciting part of the discovery is not only that taxation occurred so early, but that the tablets, jars and vases have the oldest use of writing with symbols representing constants and forming syllables-hieroglyphics. Previous discoveries found earlier records had used pictures. The writings from King Scorpion's tomb for the most part were tax records. These documents indicate the receipt of linen and oil as tithes-taxes-to King Scorpion I. Beside the record of amounts are a list of names of subordinates and institutions making the payment. As the archaeologist, Gunter Dreyer, who discovered the Scorpion I tomb observed, writing emerged as an innovation because of economic necessity rather than from creative expressions of humankind. Scorpion I had expanded his area of domination to the point that records of tax being paid were necessary. Thus, it seems that tax collection was a major impetus to the development of writing. Could taxation also have influenced the development of numbers and mathematics?

Taxation existed not only in Egypt but also Mesopotamia. Cuneiform tables dating back to as far as 2500 BC indicate tax payments made by the citizens of Babylonia. Though there is no record of the type of tax, the payment was made to and recorded by the temple, which was not only a religious organisation, but also a governmental institution in the theocracy (Garbutt, 1984). Given the needs of Mesopotamian society to build and maintain irrigation canals from the Tigris and Euphrates Rivers, taxes were necessary.

Taxation existed in other cultures. Half a world and 3000 years away from the Babylonia, knotted string records (called 'quipu') of the Incas revealed that tax payment was a major object being recorded. Interestingly, the distinction between taxation and tribute is blurred in the Incan Empire. The Incas conquered many tribes in building the Empire; each conquest required tribute to be paid by the conquered people to the central Inca government. The tribute/tax varied according to the prosperity of the conquered tribes, the size of the tribe, and the type of products that the tribe produced and used as tax payment. The taxation was instituted after the conquest and continued regularly. In turn, the Inca government produced a strong, stable, centralised authority, with administrators to rule the defeated people. Road building activities linked the empire together and such public effort required the tax payment. In addition, government maintained warehouses stored food to protect the various parts of the Empire from famine if crops in the region failed. 'Quipucamayocs' were the civil servants who recorded the payments of taxes in the knotted strings. The Incan empire and the Quipucamayocs died with the Spanish Conquistadors (Yeakel, 1983).

3. PROPERTY TAXATION

The general property tax has been traced to the tax on land to Athens in the time of Solon about 596 BC. As wealth increased in Greece at this time, this tax on land became extended to the wealth held in other forms. By 378 BC, Athenians were taxed on not only their houses and land, but also on slaves, cattle, furniture and money.

The early Roman Empire also employed the property tax; this tax was initially applied to land only at a time when the Roman Empire was primarily an agricultural state. As trade developed and wealth was held in other forms, the taxation of land alone evolved into a tax on personal property as well. Specific items such as ships, carriages, money, clothes, and jewellery became objects of taxation. In Roman provinces, the property tax remained a tax on land ownership only.

In the feudal system of the Middle Ages, land was the only form of real wealth. Teutonic and Saxon societies taxed land starting with taxes on the quantity of land and evolving into taxes based on gross then net production from the land. With the rise of towns and commerce by the 12th century, a tax on personality was instituted and became an important addition to the tax on land such that wealth irrespective of the form was being taxed. Thus, throughout Europe in the Middle Ages, the tax on land evolved into a general property tax on wealth.

In England during the 14th century, a property tax known as 'the fifteenth and the tenth' developed from an earlier form of tax in which the clergy and the nobles were taxed at a rate of two-thirds the tax on other citizens. This tenth and fifteenth tax was imposed on real estate: a tenth of the value of urban realty and a fifteenth of the value of all other realty. This basis was modified such that the fifteenth-tax rate was applied to land itself or land rents and the tenth rate was applied to 'movables' (personal property). This differential in rates of tax reflects the political strength of landed gentry who dominated Parliament over the tradesmen and craftsmen of the towns and villages. The rate differential also reflects the problem of tax collectors – that 'movables' often be hidden from the tax collector's view while real estate remained very visible, hence charged a lower tax.

By the end of the 12th century, the property tax had become well established in Europe as Italian states and Dutch states were using the general property tax for local taxation. The property tax would be used in European countries from the end of the Middle Ages through the Renaissance to the 21st century.

4.   INHERITANCE, ESTATE AND GIFT TAXES

These taxes are similar in the sense that they have evolved into taxes on the value of transfer property. The inheritance tax is on the property that an heir receives while the estate tax is on the total value of a decedent's net property that may be subdivided, perhaps among many heirs. Thus, either way these taxes are borne by heirs, one is paid by heirs directly, the other by the executor of the estate thus reducing the remainder to be distributed to heirs. The gift tax is paid by the donor on the value of property transferred to loved-ones while alive (as opposed to a gift-at-death).

The histories of inheritance and estate taxes are intertwined and distinctions between them are blurred. Several points should be noted from the outset. These taxes often were adopted from other countries. Thus, Adam Smith's point about the transferability of a tax development across borders can be readily seen in the inheritance-estate taxes. Second, war often caused these taxes to be imposed or increased. Third, these taxes evolved from a flat amount to a percentage amount of the property to a graduated rate structure. However, this evolution was uneven and often changes reverted to a previous form. Interestingly is the perseverance of certain tax features such as the exemption of tax on property left to surviving spouse, lower tax on 'direct' heirs, graduated tax rates and the 'gift in contemplation of death' being taxable to the estate.

Egypt, around 700 BC, is believed to have originated the first gift and inheritance tax. Here, a tax of 10% of the value was imposed on transfers of land. Cleverly, the Egyptian tax collectors recognised the need to keep a land register to enforce these taxes. The tax could be easily collected when the title to land was changed because of death. By 117 BC, both personal and real property became subject to inheritance tax. Unlike other cultures, no exemption, even to close lineal descendants, was provided. Tax evasion was achieved via phony sales of property to children. Greek states adopted the Egyptian inheritance tax during the later Hellenistic period. Though it seemed to have been often evaded, the inheritance tax was used by four Greek states and then adopted later by the Byzantine Empire. Thus, the practice of taxing the value of inherited property spread throughout the Mediterranean and the Middle East.

During the period of the Caesars, Rome adopted the inheritance tax directly from Egypt as it conquered the Nile. Under Triumvirate in 40 BC, Roman law required that all wills include a 5% bequest to the government. In 6 AD, Augustus kept his legions happy with personal contribution of much of his wealth to fund army pensions. Augustus then forced the Roman Senate to fund the rest of the pension requirement. After Augustus rejected several Senate proposals, he accepted the passage of a 5% inheritance tax. This tax avoided the Senate's imposing a tax on land. The new inheritance tax was known as 'vicesima hereditatium.' It exempted the legacies left to direct heirs (children, grandchildren) as well as the legacies of provincial citizens. Also exempted from tax were relatively small legacies. Funeral expenses were deducted in computing the property left as a legacy. Interestingly, property left in trust to yield an income for the life of the heir was taxed by a capitalisation of the income expected to be received during remaining life based on a 60-year life expectancy.

The Roman *vicesima hereditatium* produced significant revenues and was long lasting —more than two hundred years without major change except to extend the tax to provincial citizens. Hence, the Romans carried the inheritance tax to Great Britain during this period.

With the fall of Rome to Germanic people, the inheritance tax disappeared. The concept of property rights and inheritance had to be re-established in law first as the semi-nomadic people settled on the land. Life estates of vassals occupying land, but not owning the land, was the next barrier to the inheritance tax re-emerging. Finally, in the Middle Ages, the absolute ownership of all land by the king had to be dissolved. Eventually, three developments, the king's relief or *rachet*, the servile death due paid to noble, and the 'voluntary' bequest to Church, led to the re-establishment of inheritance and estate taxes in Europe.

The king's land ownership right and the vassals' ability to occupy the land for life then pass the life-time-right to the land to a direct descendant, arose during the Dark Ages. Further, the king, needing funds, often sold the title to land to heirs upon the death of a noble. This sale to heirs, called the 'relief' or 'rachet', became a form of inheritance tax. This practice spread throughout Europe, a noble's heirs paid the relief to the king upon the noble's death. This payment apparently occurred with each succession to the land, so that it took on the substance of an inheritance tax. William the Conqueror brought the relief from France when he became William the First of England.

In Germany and France, the relative power of the nobles and weaknesses of the emperor/king prevented the relief law from being instituted. With William's Norman Conquest of England, the Norman kings were powerful, while the nobility was weak. The relief in England eventually increased to a point, which caused nobles to rebel. In both the Charter of Henry I and in the Magna Carta, there are specific limits set on the relief amounts. The Magna Carta specified that an earldom or barony would cost 100 pounds, a knight's title would be 100 shillings and no other relief payments could be required.

During this time, there arose in England and, with the English invasion, in France, the practice of a noble being able to seize the most valuable possession of a vassal upon the vassal's death. This practice started with knights being outfitted with armour by nobles – the armour being returned at the death of the knight. The noble's seizing of the vassal's property at death, called the 'heriot,' evolved into a form of taxation. The 'heriot' practice lasted long after the Middle Ages: the practice ended in France with the French Revolution, in Germany after the Napoleonic Wars and in Eastern Europe after World War I.

After the fall of the Roman Empire, the Church began exhorting a bequest of the decedent's property, otherwise condemning the decedent's soul to the eternal fire. From this evolved a practice of the Church claiming the decedent's best animal (or second best if the best had been taken by the noble). Eventually the Church claimed the decedent's money, clothes, and tools as well. Pope Innocent IV encouraged the imposition of a death levy to be paid to the Church of one-third the decedent's property, justifying this large a take because the decedent had probably not fulfilled his annual tithing obligation several years during his lifetime so the death seizure was considered the catch-up opportunity.[1]

While most of Europe did not follow Innocent's proclamation to the full extent, in England the Church did try to fully impose the Church's death duty. This led to resentment and protests. Finally, in 1529, the English Parliament acted to limit the Church's claim on the estate to (a) 10 shillings if the estate was valued at more than 40 pounds, and (b) 3 shillings, 4 pence if the estate was worth less than 40 pounds.

In the early Renaissance period, Italian city-states began to tax legacies. The rate structure was a flat rate and varied from city to city between 2% and 5% of the value of inherited property. While the rules differed among the city-states, it was common to exempt legacies of direct descendants, small bequests, as well as charitable contributions.

The Dutch states adopted the inheritance tax during various dates between 1591 and the early 1600s as a way of paying for the ongoing war against Spain. The rates of tax varied from state to state and ranged between 2-½% and 6 ⅔% of the value of inherited property.

German states followed the Dutch example and imposed a 5% tax on inheritances as a way to pay for the war to stop the Turkish insurgence into Europe. The emergency of having the Ottoman empire threaten Germany made it easy to justify the tax as one-twentieth being paid to protect the other nineteen parts of the estate. The tax was seen as not being an imposition because it came from the property of the dead. Interestingly, the German states' inheritance taxes continued long after the Turkish threat to Central Europe subsided.

Other European countries instituted inheritance taxes during the Age of Discovery. In the explorer nations of France, Spain, and Portugal, this tax was instituted as a registration fee for recording title to property. Heirs, wanting the title to property changed to themselves, had to pay this registration fee to transfer the property's recorded ownership. France began this type of tax in 1539 while Spain and Portugal adopted the tax a hundred years later. The inheritance tax, if measured by length of time utilised, was successful in all three nations as it continued until the age of Napoleon. From Spain, the inheritance tax was carried to its colonies in the Western Hemisphere.

---

[1] Interestingly, the untaxed gains on appreciated property are a modern justification for the estate tax.

During the end of the 1600s, the inheritance tax – the relief – changed to the stamp tax on wills probated by the Ecclesiastical Court. This form of inheritance-estate tax was instituted in Great Britain by the 1694 Stamp Act. It, like the British monarchs, William and Mary, came to England from Holland. Like the Dutch tax of the time, the tax was instituted to pay for the war with Spain. The initial rate was 5 shillings, subsequently increased to 10 shillings on wills probated by the court, thus requiring the official stamp of the court. As with the French, Spanish and Portuguese registration tax, the English Stamp Tax lasted for a hundred years. It too was carried to the New World and became deeply resented by the Americans as the stamp tax expanded and increased with the British revenue needs.

While the American Revolution was being fought, the British ended the stamp tax. Its repeal came about with the publication of Adam Smith's *Wealth of Nations* in which Smith argued for a tax upon the value of inherited property as opposed to the flat fee stamp tax. Parliament instituted a new inheritance tax in 1779 and imposed graduated tax amounts upon larger inheritances. The tax was 10 shillings on inheritance from £20 to £100, 30 shillings on inheritances from £100 to £300, and 50 shillings on inheritances greater than £300.

Perhaps the wealth-dominated Parliament was loath to make such changes. However, in a series of subsequent acts, the tax eventually evolved into a percentage of value of the inheritance. Forcing Parliament's actions was the need for revenues in fighting war with not only its American colonies, but also with France.

The ongoing war with France caused England to adopt the legacy duty in 1796. This tax was based on the total value of property-real and personal-received from the decedent. The tax exempted spouses and direct descendants (children, grandchildren) and legacies under £100. A flat rate of tax – depending on the relationship between heir and decedent – was applied to all other legacies. The initial rates were 2% for siblings, 3% for aunts, uncles, nephews, nieces and cousins, 4% for great aunts, great uncles or second cousins, and 6% by all others. These rates did not stay at this level for very long. Napoleon's successes increased the British revenue needs, so rates rose in 1804, in 1805 and again in 1815. Legacies of direct descendants were taxed at 1% while the rates of the other classes of heirs were raised to 3%, 5%, 6%, and 10%. This tax structure remained virtually unchanged for one hundred years.

The French Revolution and the impact of Napoleon's conquests in Europe made significant changes to the inheritance tax throughout the Continent. In France, in 1789, there were separate taxes imposed on inheritances of 'movables' and 'immovables'. Initially movables were taxed at a lower rate than immovables but this distinction between the two taxes soon was abolished and one set of rates applied to both. The rates of these taxes depended upon the relationship of the heir to the decedent. This tax continued from the Revolutionary period throughout the nineteenth century.

Significantly, the tax rates on inheritances increased during the century to as high as 11¼% for legacies to unrelated heirs. This tax, plus the tax registration of wills as well as stamp taxes on judicial proceedings involving the settlement of estates, meant, in practice, that the French government's take could be as high as 15% to 20% of the estate's value from the combination of taxes. Forced sales of family property often followed a death, as these taxes proved onerous. Reform did finally occur at the beginning of the twentieth century.

French occupation of Spain changed the Spanish inheritance tax to one similar to the French tax. A tax on movables and a separate tax on immovable property left to heirs were instituted in the 1820s. Like the French tax, the rate depended on the heir's relationship to the deceased with rates as high as 12% if property was left to non-relatives. As in France, it would take a new century to institute major change.

French occupation of the Low Countries brought unification of Dutch provinces to form the nation of Holland. Provincial inheritance taxes were replaced by a general one in 1805. The rate of tax depended upon the heir's relationship to the deceased. The rates ranged from 5% to 10%. In 1809, the rate was increased to as high as 13% due to the need for revenues. After the French defeat at Waterloo, the rates were reduced to the 1805 level.

Throughout Europe during the 1800s, the inheritance tax system remained largely unchanged from the Napoleonic era. However, in the late 19th century, new thoughts and ideas began to sweep the Continent. With political upheavals of average citizens and workers trying to overthrow inequities of king-nobility-landlord legacies of the Medieval period, progressive rate structure began to be adopted to solve social and political ills.

In England in 1894, a progressive estate tax plus a 1% tax on the value of property at settlement and replaced the previous legacy and succession duties. The new tax, based on the total value of the estate, had 13 rate brackets and peaked at 8% on estates larger than £1,000,000. As the typical pattern, these rates were increased. By 1910, the top estate tax rate was 10%. World War I would cause further increases in the British estate tax to be as high as 20% on estates in excess of £1,000,000 in 1914, with an exemption if an estate tax had been imposed on the property within the previous five years.

British Dominions also used progressive rates and imposed an estate tax rather than an inheritance tax. Australian states used progressive rates two decades earlier than Great Britain and all but one Australian state imposed the estate rather than the inheritance tax by 1914. New Zealand also used a progressive rate structure (top rate 10%) with its estate tax from 1881. By World War I, the top tax rate had been increased to 15%.

The South African states followed the English changing their inheritance taxes to estate taxes with progressive rates during the 1905 to 1910 era.

Canadian provinces first used the inheritance tax in 1892 and like older European taxes made the rate on the legacy a flat percentage rate based on the heir's relationship to the deceased. The progressive rate estate tax replaced the inheritance tax in several provinces before 1914.

On the Continent, France stayed with the inheritance tax, but in 1901 made the tax very progressive – to be as high as 18½% on large legacies received by non-relatives. This progressive rate – based on relationship and amounts received - became even more progressive in 1910 when the to rate was increased to 29%. These taxes were driven by the socialists' rising political strength and the need for tax revenue to pay for the military build-up prior to World War I.

Spain, like France, clung to the inheritance tax, but followed the French in making the rates progressive based on the amount of legacy received for each of eleven categories of heirs (based on relationship of heir and decedent).

The Scandinavian countries adopted progressive rates for their estate and inheritance taxes during the period prior to World War I. Norway utilised progressive rates starting in 1905 for its inheritance tax. The rate depended on the amount received as an inheritance as well as the heir's relationship to the deceased. Denmark adopted a similar tax in 1908 and Sweden did so in 1914.

Japan adopted a progressive-rate inheritance tax in 1905 to pay for the war it had fought with Russia. Reflecting the Spanish legacies, South American countries, for the most part, had adopted inheritance taxes prior to the start of the 20th century.

The United States has a long varied history of taxing inheritances and estates. During the Colonial Period, Virginia imposed a 'probate duty' paid to the royal governor on probate estate documents that needed a public seal. After the Revolution in 1797, Congress instituted a stamp duty on inheritances. The charge depended upon the size of the legacy with inheritances under $50 exempt from tax as were amounts received by surviving spouses and lineal descendants. Inheritances valued at between $50 and $100 paid 25¢, $100 to $500 paid 50¢, $500 to $5,000 paid $1.00, and $5,000 to $10,000 paid $2.00. Legacies in excess of $10,000 were charged an additional $1 for each $5,000 increment in excess of $10,000. Congress repealed this federal tax in 1802.

Among the states, there were several experiments with inheritance and estate taxes. In 1825, Pennsylvania imposed a 2½% tax on the value of inherited property in excess of the $250 of exemption. The rate was doubled to 5% in 1846. Louisiana adopted a 10% inheritance tax on legacies left to foreign heirs. Virginia adopted a fee for probates of estates in 1843. This fee structure continued through the Civil War when the fee was raised to $2.50 and changed to a proportional percentage of the estate in 1869. During the Civil War, the federal government instituted a national inheritance tax (1861). This tax exempted legacies of less than $1,000 and had a differential rate structure depending on the heir's relationship with the deceased. The rate structure was increased in 1864 to be as high as 6% on legacies left to non-relatives. The tax was repealed in 1874. From the Civil War to the 1900s, the majority of states instituted some form of inheritance or estate tax.

The Income Tax Act passed by Congress in 1894 contained a federal inheritance tax, along with the individual income tax. The federal inheritance tax would have taxed legacies at a rate of 2% after exempting $4,000 of value. However, this tax was never imposed because the U.S. Supreme Court declared the 1894 Income Tax Act unconstitutional.

The federal inheritance tax came back unchallenged in 1898 as a means to pay for the war with Spain. This U.S. tax was progressive with the rate being a function of both the size of the legacy and the relationship between heir and recipient. The top rate was 15% for legacies of more than one million dollars left to non-relatives. The federal inheritance tax was repealed in 1902.

With World War I raging in Europe, the United States adopted the estate tax in 1916. Unlike the inheritance tax, this was on the entire value of the estate, rather than on the pieces given to heirs. The 1916 federal estate tax was progressive: starting at 1% or the first $50,000 of value of estate property and increasing in rate by 1% increments on large estate values reaching the 10% rate on estate values in excess of $5,000,000.

The ink was barely dry on the 1916 Tax Act when the 1917 Tax Act doubled the rates and added two higher rate brackets: 22% on estate values between $8,000,000 and $10,000,000 and 25% of estate values in excess of $10,000,000. The U.S. war effort drove the need for greater tax revenue. However, the estate tax was quickly reduced in 1919 with the end of World War I.

In 1924, the United States experimented with the tax on the values of gifts, since these gifts potentially reduced the size of estates subject to the estate tax. The gift tax was repealed, then was reinstated in the late 1920s. Revenue needs during the 1930s caused Congress to increase the estate rates in a steeply progressive fashion to 70% on estates in excess of $50,000,000.

From the 1920s to the 1970s, the federal gift tax was separately computed from the federal estate tax with a lower rate of tax imposed upon gifts. Since 1976, the estate tax has been unified with the gift tax such that the tax is on the wealth transferred either at death or during the life of the property owner. The progressivity of rates has been maintained with the top tax rate on such transfers set at 55% for the last two decades of the twentieth century.

The American adoption of the estate tax during World War I followed British tax leadership. In Britain, the tax rate on estates was increased several times as the war dragged on until the top rate reached 40%. Estates of those killed in war-related deaths were exempted from the estate tax. To prevent the American problem of transferring property by gifts prior to death, the British estate tax imposed the tax on gifts made within three years of death by including such transfers as part of the final estate value.

Also following the British lead, Australia began taxing estates in 1914 and added the tax on gifts made with contemplation of death (estate tax avoidance in mind) in 1924. The Australian tax was a national tax in addition to the state inheritance and estate taxes.

New Zealand's estate tax reached a top tax rate of 50% in 1920, while South Africa instituted a top tax rate of 17% during this period. The South African estate tax is noteworthy for experimenting with a 'vanishing exemption' in which estates of under £1,000 were exempt, and this exemption amount was reduced £1 for each £1 of estate value over £1,000. Hence, the full value of estates over £2,000 was taxed.

In France during World War I, the inheritance tax rates were increased to as high as 36% for heirs unrelated to the decedent. The rate structure was sharply progressive based on not only the size of the legacy but also the relationship of the heir and deceased and also a granting of a large deduction based on family responsibilities. This inheritance tax was adopted along with a special estate duty and a gift tax with graduated rates. The combination of the estate duty and the inheritance tax could impose a tax rate as high as 59% on legacies left to unrelated parties. Unlike the American estate tax experience, there was no immediate reduction in estate tax rates after World War I. Only by 1924 was there a reduction when France acted to limit the estate tax to no more than 80% of the value of the estate and allowed instalment payments to make the tax convenient to executors who were faced with business and other illiquid assets in the estate.

Germany, like the other combatants in World War I, used the death tax to pay for the war. In 1919, its inheritance rate was set as high as 70% on large legacies left to unrelated heirs.

5. CONSUMPTION-BASED TAXES

Taxes on exchanges of goods have been widely used since ancient times. The tax on consumption was utilised in ancient Egypt. In Rome, the tax on sale of slaves at auction was imposed for a time. Customs and duties – taxes on the value of goods imported or exported – probably had the start as ancient traders such as the Phoenicians paid maritime chiefs for protection or these traders plied their ships across areas controlled by these rulers. These tolls were also used by the Romans, as merchants and traders paid directly for protection. Fees for government services evolved into taxes on the exchange or transportation of goods. As these taxes developed, so too did smuggling, as it became economically worthwhile to evade such taxes.

In England during the Dark Ages, customs and tariffs fell into disuse as little trade with the Continent was taking place. However, the rise of cross Channel commerce in the 13th century, along with the rise of royal power and the need to finance the Crusades, led to the evolution of these taxes. In particular, John I began collecting 'a fifteenth' from merchants shipping goods into or out of the country. This became the 'custom': that a fifteenth belonged to the king. The proceeds of the custom were used to finance a navy, which protected the shipping goods on the high seas. In 1266, the custom was increased from a fifteenth (6 ⅔%) to a tenth (10%).

In England during the next centuries, customs and duties became a major source of revenue for the king. Other trading countries such as Holland, also used this form of taxation.

In Colonial America, the British used customs and duties as a way of insuring trade directly with England by taxing goods from other countries imported to the American Colonies at very high rates – making British goods more attractive to the American consumer. This practice of taxing imports to control trade was later used in the U.S. in the 19th and early 20th centuries via the 'protective' tariff which was designed more to discourage imports and encourage consumption of domestic goods rather than collection of revenues.

Excise taxes are taxes on specific goods. Often luxuries and 'bads' are subject to these taxes. What is a luxury today may be a necessity tomorrow – such as the telephone, the automobile, electricity – all of which are still taxed (tax on phone bills, tax on tires, batteries, gasoline, tax on electric bills). Other excise taxes are imposed on forms of entertainment such as movie tickets and tickets to sporting events. Excise taxes are also imposed in a rigorous way on alcohol (beer, wine and whisky), on gambling, on guns and ammunition, and on tobacco products as a way to make the products more expensive and thus reduce the demand for them. Such taxes on the consumption of specific goods can be traced back to the eighteenth century. The infamous British 'tea tax' that sparked the American Revolution is an example. Ironically, the newly formed United States' first national tax was the Whisky Tax that also sparked a rebellion – the Western Pennsylvania frontier farmers rose up against the new American government in 1791.

By contrast to the excise tax, the general sales tax is a relatively modern tax. Unlike the excise, which is levied on specific goods, the general sales tax is levied on all purchases of goods. The heavy debt burden of Germany and France after World War I caused these two counties to impose a 'turnover tax' on the sale of goods. These taxes quickly were passed on to the purchaser by the seller, with the consumers ultimately paying these taxes in the form of higher prices. Canada, in 1920, adopted a manufacturer's sales tax, purportedly levied on the manufacturer when goods were sold to wholesalers or retailers. Again, it seems likely that some of the tax was ultimately borne by the consumer via higher prices.

The general retail sales tax became widely used when 30 countries adopted it during the 1930s. Among these countries were Australia, Austria, Belgium, Canada, France, Germany, Hungary, Italy, and the USSR (Blakey and Blakey, 1940, p. 64). This also was the time that state governments began using the sales tax within the United States. The fall in revenue caused by the worldwide depression was the main reason, as other tax sources seemed to dry up, for the adoption by countries and states of the general retail sales tax. By 1937, 31 out of 48 states had adopted it.

The value-added tax is an even more recent form of tax, though its roots have been traced back several centuries (Crum, 1982). The value-added tax was first adopted by France in 1954 and Denmark in 1967. It quickly spread to most other European countries and to Canada as well. In the United State, only Michigan and Louisiana have taxes based on the value added by the producer of goods. Michigan's tax adoption (1953) predates the French adoption. The major distinction is that the Michigan version of the value added tax is on the net value (revenue minus cost of production) that each producer adds in a chain of production. By contrast, the European tax is based on the sales amounts and is charged to the buyer. The tax is thus 'pushed forward' to the consumer.

6.   INCOME TAXATION

While various societies had tried to use progressive taxes in the past,[2] the most influential attempts were during the tumultuous late eighteenth century.

---

[2]   See Seligman (1909).

In the 1790s, the British were faced with paying for its continuous warfare with the French. Struggles with the financing of these emergencies led to taxation innovations in both countries. Among the most noteworthy was the British adoption of a tax on the rental value of houses, a forerunner of a more comprehensive income tax. This British tax had a graduated rate structure. At the same time, French revolutionaries also imposed a tax on houses; however, it was much more progressive than that of the British. This French tax was, in essence, class warfare and was intended to drive (and succeeded in driving) wealthy citizens from their homes. Large French estates were broken up when nobles were forced into bankruptcy by the tax.

In Great Britain, William Pitt fathered the income tax as part of his 'Triple Assessment' in 1798. This tax was expanded to a general income tax in 1799. Not by accident, Parliament chose income as the tax base instead of increasing the tax on property. The political makeup of the Houses of Lords and Commons, which were dominated by land interests, led Parliament to look for signs of ability to pay other than wealth. The rising class of merchants and professionals owned little real estate and earned income from sources other than rents. This class became the target of the British income tax, which was essentially a flat rate tax. This tax ended with the Napoleonic Wars in 1816. Despite its class roots, the income tax was justified by the argument that the merchant class benefited greatly from the British war economy. Thus, to a degree, the tax was an attempt to tax 'excess profits' created by the war. This, in turn, enabled the government to use the proceeds of the tax to pay for the war. The class tax and the war profits aspects of the income tax would be repeated later when the tax was adopted in the United States.

The British re-instituted the income tax in 1842, with a rate that was essentially proportional. It remained a flat rate tax for the next 65 years, during which the debate over the concept of rate progressivity raged on in Great Britain. In 1880, under Gladstone's leadership, the British modified the income tax to include an exemption amount and 'abatements' (reduced rate on wages) for lower income taxpayers. The debaters were divided, not surprisingly, along class lines, with the wealthy being the most opposed to any notion of progressivity. The British adopted a progressive rate structure for their income tax at the turn of the century, when the 'super tax' rates on income beyond a relatively large threshold were introduced. Other European countries instituted the income tax in the latter half of the nineteenth century and embraced progressive rate structures.

In the U.S., the states were first to adopt the income tax rather than the federal level of government. In the southern states, the income tax evolved from a license (occupation) tax during the 1840s. Because of economic booms primarily owing to westward expansion during the 1830s, states had undertaken large road and canal building projects. Initially, several states had chartered private companies. In return for construction, the companies would operate the projects and charge tolls. However, private resources were quickly exhausted and the states stepped in to finish these undertakings. Like the private developers, the states continued to underestimate the completion costs and overestimate the revenues; thus, states also faced bankruptcy from the project debts that were coming due. The solution was to raise taxes to pay off the heavy state debt burden.

The southern states in particular were influenced by British developments and caused them to experiment with the income tax as a means to pay for the internal public work projects. Like the British Parliament, southern state legislatures were dominated by large landowners who objected to taxing real estate or other property (slaves). Instead, in Virginia, North Carolina and Alabama, the legislatures enacted business taxes that were flat fees initially, the modern equivalent to a license or occupation tax. This tax was changed to a proportional tax on revenue and finally evolved to a proportional tax on income. The targets of this tax were the merchants and professionals who were the backbone of growing towns. Soon the use of the income tax spread to most of the Southern states. By the time of the War Between the States, Virginia had begun to use a progressive rate structure.

The emergency of the Civil War caused the income tax to be adopted on a national basis. Both the South and the North imposed an income tax. The Confederate income tax ended with the surrender at Appomatox in 1865. The Union's income tax continued until 1872, when most debts from the Civil War had been paid. It is interesting to note that the income tax of the Civil War was the first time that a major national tax had been imposed on U.S. citizens since 1818. Prior to the war, the federal government had relied on revenues from the sale of land from *external* tariff revenue. The income tax was the nation's first major *internal* revenue and the income tax was selected over other tax bases.

Also noteworthy is the fact that the tax rate adopted for the federal income tax was initially a flat tax rate of 3% applied to all income in excess of $800. The revenue need of the Union to pay for the war forced this 1861 tax to be increased even before the original act had become effective. In 1862, the income tax was quickly modified to tax all income in excess of a $600 exemption. The tax rates were 3% on income in excess of $600 and 5% on income in excess of $10,000. Thus, with almost no debate, (1) the federal government adopted an income tax and (2) while initially a flat rate, the income tax was quickly changed to a progressive rate system. The emergency of war along with Lee's threat to invade Washington D.C. forced national attention to more important matters than tax policy arguments. As would often be repeated, economic considerations, particularly revenue needs of the government, dictated the rate structure of the tax, rather than tax policy and equity considerations. The linkage of the income tax with progressive tax rates was abandoned after the end of the Civil War, when the tax reverted to a flat rate of 5% on income in excess of $5,000.

In the U.S., the next attempt to establish an income tax was led by the populist and progressive parties which held political strength in the 1880s and the 1890s among farm and working classes (especially in the South, the Midwest and the far West). These groups felt that the tariffs were too high and protected Northeastern industry to the detriment of the rest of the country which bore the cost of higher-priced goods. The income tax was seen as a replacement for reduced tariff revenues. However, it was clear that the incidence of the income tax would be quite different from that of the tariff. Indeed, the proponents of the income tax saw it as a weapon against wealthy monopolists and the Eastern industrialists who benefited most from the tariff. The income tax movement culminated in 1894 with the passage of a federal income tax. However, this success was short-lived because the Supreme Court, in *Pollack v. Farmers' Loan & Trust Co.*, 157 U.S. 429 (1895), struck down the tax statute for being unconstitutional. Particularly noteworthy is that the 1894 tax contained a flat rate structure: a relatively innocuous 2% rate applied to income in excess of a relatively large exemption of $4,000.

In 1909, Congress did succeed in passing the *Corporate Excise Tax* on the 'privilege of doing business as a corporation'. This tax was 1% of profits. Upon review, the Supreme Court upheld the tax as constitutional. Perhaps, the Court was more impressed with the form, rather than the substance, of the tax.

Also in 1909, proponents of the income tax began a drive for an amendment to override the constitutional limitations on direct taxes. By early 1913, thirty-six states had ratified the amendment, which reads simply, 'The Congress shall have the power to lay and collect taxes on income, from whatever sources derived, without apportionment among the several states, and without regard to any census or enumeration'.

Upon ratification of the U.S. Constitution amendment in 1913, the U.S. Congress passed an income tax law which imposed a tax rate of 1% on income in excess of an exemption of $4,000 for married taxpayers and $3,000 for single taxpayers. The 1913 income tax also contained a *surtax* (the U.S. equivalent of the British *super tax*) exempting all income under $20,000. The surtax rates went from 1% to 6%, with the 6% rate imposed on income in excess of $500,000. When combined with the normal tax, the 1913 income tax ranged to a maximum of 7%. Because of the generous exemption level, only a small percentage of citizens were subject to any income tax, and a much smaller percentage was taxed at rates higher than 1%. This very large exemption was perhaps instituted for the purpose of administrative simplicity, since the Bureau of Internal Revenue was very limited and not prepared to deal with the complexity of the new income tax. This administrative simplicity theory for the large exemption is contrary to another possibility: that Congress was carrying out the will of the masses by installing a tax that would burden the rich. In any event, the belief persists that the 1913 income tax was a *class* tax aimed at extracting and confiscating wealth, or alternatively, rectifying the abuses of regressive tariffs by reducing the concentration of wealth, particularly of the Northern industrialists (who seem to have been direct beneficiaries of the high tax on imports that burdened the rest of the U.S. citizens).

The new income tax, with its low rates and large exemption, represented a fresh source of revenue needed once America started preparing for World War I. In a rapid succession of tax acts, the *normal* tax was raised from 1% to 2% in 1916, to 4% in 1917, and to 6% in 1918. In addition, the exemption amount was reduced in 1917 to $1,000 for single and $2,000 for married taxpayers. The *surtax* rates were increased rapidly by these World War I tax acts. Within a span of five years after the passage of the Sixteenth Amendment, the top income tax rate would climb to as high as 82%.

Many of the same economic, political, social and cultural forces that influenced the U.S. federal income tax also helped shape the Dominion Income Tax of Canada. Therefore, it is not surprising that the Canadian experience with income tax progressivity has been similar to that of America. The Canadian income tax was instituted in 1917 to help finance the World War I effort. The 'normal' tax rate was set at 4% on income above $1,500 (single taxpayers) or $3,000 (married taxpayers). A 'super tax' with graduated tax rates was also imposed. The combined rates meant that income over $100,000 was taxed at 29%.

As with the U.S. experience during World War I, the Canadian income tax increased annually. In 1918, the exempt level of income was cut to $1,000 for single and to $2,000 for married taxpayers. The super tax also was increased and reached 50% on income in excess of $1 million. In addition, a 35% surtax (a tax on the tax amount) was imposed, thus extending the tax rate to 72% on income over $1 million. These amounts were remarkably similar to those used in the U.S. at the same time.

While the income tax was being lowered slightly in 1919 in the U.S., the Canadian income tax rates increased in 1919 and 1920. However, in the early 1920s, both the Canadian and American tax rates were reduced, although the former's tax rates remained somewhat above the latter's rates.

As in the U.S., the Canadian income tax was increased during the 1930s, with the first boost in 1932 from 2% to 3% for the lowest bracket and 61% on income above $500,000. Again, the Canadian and American income tax rates, brackets and exempt levels of income seem very close in amounts during the Depression Era.

During World War II, the Canadian withholding system was instituted, as in the U.S., to collect income tax from the wages of workers. Similar to the U.S., the income tax was relied on to finance the war effort and tax rates became very high. After the war, the Canadian income tax rates remained high, as were the rates in the United States. For example, the 1963 income tax in Canada had 17 brackets, a top tax rate of 80% on income of $175,000, an initial bracket of 11%, and $3,200 of income exempt from tax for a family of four. By comparison, the 1963 U.S. federal income tax had 24 brackets with the top tax rate of 91% on income over $400,000 and the lowest bracket rate of 20% on income in excess of $3,400 (exempt amount for a family of four). Most interestingly, the U.S. income tax was reduced in 1964 to a top rate of 77% and the lowest bracket rate to 16%, certainly making the federal income tax even more Canadian-like.

The similarities of trends in Canadian and U.S. income taxes have continued. In the early 1970s, the Canadian income tax top rate was 47% with a relatively low $60,000 income threshold, reached in a thirteen-step rate bracket from 17%. While this rate structure differed from that of the U.S. at the time, it seems that Canada was ahead: it was not until Reaganomics of a decade later that the U.S. adopted a thirteen-step, 50% top tax rate structure. By this time, the Canadian income tax had been reduced to a top tax rate of 34%, with ten-rate bracket steps from a 6% initial rate. When the U.S. used a two-rate bracket structure of 15% and 28% in the late 1980s, Canada was using a three-rate structure from 17% to 29%. Again, Canada may have been slightly ahead of U.S developments, because it was not until 1991 when the U.S. began using a three rate structure of 15%, 28% and 31%.

7.   CONCLUSION

This chapter explored developments of taxation across form, across time and across geography. While the subject of world-wide history of taxation is too immense to be covered in a mere few pages, this chapter has tried to focus on the evolution of various forms of tax and the transference of the developments from country to country. By no means is the history here complete.

Themes that seem to be recurring are that taxation arose independently across isolated empires. Yet, tax developments were transported to other societies and nations. Wars were a major stimulus for tax developments as governments' revenue needs in war caused changes and innovations. Likewise, war often allowed tax changes to be made as citizens accepted a new tax in light of national emergencies. Once adopted, a tax typically was modified and increased over time. When the tax burden became extreme, rebellions occurred. Thus, taxation has had a lively history throughout the ages as societies search for revenue, which can only be obtained with either voluntary support or coercion of taxed citizens.

STUDY QUESTIONS

1. Why do civilised societies tax? Why isn't taxation a part of primitive societies? Where can you reside today and not be subject to taxation? What are the negatives in choosing places to live where there are no taxes?
2. In less developed societies, what types of taxes are likely to be imposed? Why? In highly developed societies, what forms of taxation are likely? Explain why.
3. Is compulsory service for the state a form of taxation? Under what situations is compulsory service most likely? When has it most recently been tried?
4. Trade has been taxed from ancient times. Why do governments tax cross-border trading activities? How can the taxation of such trade be justified on a policy basis? What is the behavioural reaction to such a tax? What are the economic consequences of taxing international trade?
5. What is the reason that certain taxes have evolved from a flat fee to one-rate to a progressive rate structure? Give an example of tax with this pattern of development?

REFERENCES

Afosa, K. (1985), 'Financial Administration of Ancient Ashanti Empire', *The Accounting Historians Journal*, Vol. 12(2), pp. 109-115.

Blakey R. G. and Blakey, G. S. (1940), *The Federal Income Tax*, New York, Longman Green and Company.

Crum, R. P. (1982), 'Value-Added Taxation: The Roots Run Deep into Colonial and Early America', *The Accounting Historians Journal*, Vol. 9(2), pp. 25-41.

Garbutt, D. (1984), 'The Significance of Ancient Mesopotamia in Accounting History', *The Accounting Historians Journal*, Vol. 11(11), pp. 83-101.

Jose, M.L. and Moore, C.K. (1998), 'The Development of Taxation in the Bible: Improvements in Counting, Measurement and Computation in the Ancient Middle East', *The Accounting Historians Journal,* Vol. 25(2), pp. 63-80.

Kozub, R.M. (1983), 'Antecedents of the Income Tax in Colonial America', *The Accounting Historians Journal*, Vol. 10(2), pp. 99-116.

Mann, H. (1984), ' Thus Spake The Rabbis—The First Income Tax?', *The Accounting Historians Journal*, Vol. 11(1), pp. 125-133.

Paul, R.E. (1954), *Taxation in the United States*, Boston: Little Brown and Company.

Samson, W.D. (1985), 'The Nineteenth Century Income Tax in the South', *The Accounting Historians Journal*, Vol. 12(1), pp. 37-52.

Samson, W.D. (1996), 'The Evolution of the U.S. Income Tax: The History of Progressivity and Influences from Other Countries,' in A. Richardson (Ed), *Disorder and Harmony: 20th Century Perspective on Accounting History*, The Seventh World Congress of Accounting Historians (CGA Canada Research Foundation Research Monograph No. 23), pp. 205-227.

Seligman, E.R.A. (1909), *Progressive Taxation*, New York: MacMillan Company, 2nd edition.

Seligman, E. R.A. (1911), *The Income Tax*, New York: MacMillan Company.

Seligman, E.R.A. (1931), *Essays In Taxation*, New York: MacMillan Company.

Shultz, W.J. (1926), *The Taxation of Inheritance*, Boston: Houghton Mifflin Company.

Smith, A. (1976), *An Inquiry into the Nature and Causes of the Wealth of Nations*, Oxford: Clarendon Press.

Solas, C. and Otar, I. (1994), 'The Accounting System Practiced in the Near East During the Period 1220-1350 Based on the Book *Risale-I Felekiyye*', *The Accounting Historians Journal*, Vol. 21(1), pp. 117-135.

Wells, S.C. and Flesher, T. K. (1994), 'Lessons for Policymakers from the History of Consumption Taxes', *The Accounting Historians Journal*, Vol. 21(1), pp. 103-126.

Yeakel, J.A. (1983), 'The Accountant-Historians of the Incas', *The Accounting Historians Journal*, Vol. 10(2), pp. 39-51.

i

Chapter 3

History of International Business Taxation

PAUL HEWITT, ANDREW LYMER and LYNNE OATS
University of Birmingham, U.K. and University of Warwick, U.K.

Key words: history, international business taxation, multinational enterprise, OECD

Abstract: The current systems of international, cross border, taxation are complex. This complexity is partly due to the incremental development of the systems now in place to deal with cross border trade activity. This chapter reviews first the key developments of international business and the development of the multinational enterprise and then discusses some of the developments related to the systems for international taxation that arose to address this cross border trading growth. Knowledge of tax history is an important foundation for understanding current tax practice and examining the possibilities for future tax reform. This chapter seeks to provide at least the core elements of this foundation for the reader.

1.   INTRODUCTION

This chapter introduces the reader to the history of international taxation of business activity.[1] As with any history, it is difficult to decide what to include, and what to leave out, where to start, and where to stop. However, as tax systems are largely developed on an incremental basis, only with a grasp of the past can a student of tax expect to understand the current system and the future prospects for tax reform. This will include some knowledge of what has been tried before, how these methods worked and why they were discarded when they were, what order historical developments occurred in

---

[1]   This chapter only focuses at the history of cross border business activity. The developments in international personal taxation mirror many of the business taxation developments but are a study in their own right that are not covered here. See Samson's History of Taxation chapter for more details on this topic.

and why, why various tax relationships exist now are as they do and so on. Whilst one short chapter can not expect to fully address all these issues, it does provide the reader with the foundations necessary to understand other parts of this book, and to provide a basis for their own further, perhaps country or subject specific, study as they may require.

2.   HISTORY OF INTERNATIONAL BUSINESS

Before we address the relatively recent history of international taxation of business activity, it is useful to review the developments of international business itself. This can be traced back over two thousand years before Christ was born. Traders from Mesopotamia, Greece and Phoenicia made themselves very rich by engaging in Mediterranean trade (Liu, 1998, p.xiii). As time passed, the Greeks took full advantage of both their military and intellectual leadership by asserting their authority over trade in this area. Indeed, by the year 500BC, trade was so much more advanced in Greece compared to anywhere else that this nation had already mastered mass production (Taggart and McDermott, 1993, p. 1).

Just as the Greeks had managed to utilise their armies to become the international business superpower of their time, so the Romans achieved the same regional dominance a few hundred years later. However, although it can be claimed that the sheer military might of Rome led to the foundation of her Empire, it can be argued that the promotion of international business itself played a vital role. The Pax Romana, or Roman peace, ensured that merchants would receive protection from Roman soldiers and a safe passage along the roads to Rome where they would eventually conduct business (Czinkota *et al.*, 1989, p. 5).

One of the effects of this international business was that it created a very high standard of living. States and tribes outside of the Empire envied this so much that, although some had to be persuaded by force, many were keen to willingly ally themselves with Rome hoping to share in the prosperity. These allies were of course required to pay tribute and taxes to Rome in return for their protect, governance and the rights to trade within the Empire (Czinkota *et al.*, 1989, p. 5).

When the Roman Empire entered decline, Constantinople became the successor to Rome as the generally accepted centre of international trade and remained so for approximately one hundred and fifty years until 650AD. Almost the entire continent of Europe during this time was ruled by men who disagreed with the notion of cross-border trade (Taggart and McDermott, 1993, p. 2). International trade did not recommence until some centuries later when the Italian cities of Venice and Genoa began to exploit their location to maximise its business potential. They shipped goods on a regular basis to the Crusaders who had by now established themselves on the east coast of the Mediterranean. Nautical erudition and hence international trade supremacy had passed to the Spanish by the late sixteenth century, after which time it was considered that the only way for a nation to become wealthy was by acquiring colonies around the World. Countries such as England, France, Holland, Spain and Portugal began to build empires, action that faltered only with the inception of the Industrial Revolution (Taggart and McDermott, 1993, p. 2).

In more recent times, international trade has developed into a much more genuinely global activity. Before World War I, many countries still had colonies around the globe in which they would invest directly. For example, in 1914 Britain was easily the largest foreign capital stakeholder due largely to the size and nature of her Empire. Indeed, by this time she had invested almost the same amount of funds overseas as all the other developed countries put together (see Table 1 below) (Casson, 1983, p. 86). Even at such an early stage of international trading there were distinct geographical patterns that varied depending upon the home country of the investor. Language, cultural, political and trading ties as well as geographical distance were all much more important factors than they are today, which explains why seventy two per cent of U.S. investment was in other areas of the American continent and also why British investment was so distributed (Casson, 1983, p. 90).

Table 1. Estimated stock of accumulated foreign direct investment by country of origin - 1914 (*Source: adapted from Casson, 1983* p. 87)

	$m	%
	14,302	100.0
USA	2,652	18.5
Canada	150	1.0
Britain	6,500	45.5
Germany	1,500	10.5
France	1,750	12.2
Belgium, Italy, Netherlands, Sweden and Switzerland	1,250	8.7
Others	500	3.5
Total	14,302	100.0

3.   THE DEVELOPMENT OF THE MULTINATIONAL ENTERPRISE

Most of the foreign direct investment that occurred in the years preceding the outbreak of World War I did not involve internationally integrated activities but simply overseas investment in foreign enterprises. However, by the middle of the nineteenth century two American companies, namely Colt Industries Incorporated and the Singer Company, and J & P Coats, a Scottish company, were already conducting business in a way not dissimilar to the way in which multinational corporations operate today in that their activities relied on mutual contributions from their different geographic elements. Shortly after the turn of the century the list had grown to include, amongst others, Ingersoll Rand, General Electric, International Harvester, HJ Heinz and Bayer (Taggart and McDermott, 1993, p. 2) and the birth of the multinational enterprise (MNE) had occurred.

The Great War and the Russian Revolution put a temporary stop to international trade and multinational enterprise growth. The cost of fighting such a long war took its toll and several European investors had no alternative but to sell some of their pre-war investments. The associated political upheaval of these events reduced corporate activity still further (Casson, 1983, p. 91). The United States, however, did not suffer as much economic damage as other countries and directed international investments towards new manufacturing industries in the post war period. However, the crash of 1929 soon put an end to cross border dealings and also had ramifications for the eventual resumption of global trade. The Depression instigated great caution amongst investors and World War II limited the movement of international capital until after 1945 (Picciotto, 1992, p. 3).

International activity picked up again quickly after the end of the Second World War. Multinational enterprises then developed considerably in the 1960's and 1970's. This unprecedented expansion of their activities was greatly assisted by technological advances such as the development of jet aircraft and more efficient international communication devices. Geographically dispersed operations could be conducted with much more ease than had previously been possible. This development was however fairly focused on a relatively few businesses. The 1957 census conducted by the U.S. Department of Commerce showed that less than 6% of the 2,800 U.S. enterprises with foreign affiliates or operations controlled over 80% of total U.S. overseas assets and sales. This situation is not restricted to American firms. In 1962, 46 enterprises, or less than 8% of the total number of British enterprises with foreign operations, accounted for over 71% of total British manufacturing investments overseas (Dassbach, 1989, p. 1).

The comparative slowing of the rate of growth of American multinationals at the end of the 1960's paralleled a rapid expansion of European and Japanese organisations (Channon, 1979, p. 4). The rebuilding process that had had to take place after World War II had enabled a number of large companies to establish themselves in these two geographic regions. Soon, however, despite rapid growth made possible by the Common Market and hence very low duties, the new European companies needed to venture further afield and eventually moved into the U.S. and Canada. Great success was achieved between 1966 and 1980, for the ratio of European investments in the U.S. to that of American investments in Europe evened out from 37% to 49% (Ghertman and Allen, 1984, p. 12).

The oil crisis, that had ended the domination of the Seven Sisters[2] and largely levelled out the power of American and European organisations, sparked a recession in the mid-1970's. The incredible growth of the global economy that was witnessed throughout the 1960's and early 1970's was brought to a sudden halt as oil prices rocketed. Then, just as economies were recovering in the late 1970's, a second wave of increased oil prices caused further global recession that lasted until 1982 (Ghertman and Allen, 1984, p. 62).

After 1982, cross border investment flows improved again quickly. In 1982, global outward investment stood at $24 billion. From 1984 throughout the remainder of the 1980s, this figure increased annually by 30% and in 1988 and 1989, totals equalled $154 billion and $174 billion respectively. Japan, the United Kingdom and the U.S. have been the driving forces behind this huge increase (OECD, 1991, p. 9).

The era of the multinational enterprise was well established by the end of the 1980s but a further boost to cross border trading volumes was given by the development of the Internet and ubiquitous global communications in the mid to late 1990s. These developments significantly widened the range of businesses that became multinationals by lowering the cost barriers to entry to international trade. Almost any business, with the desire to, can now become a multinational with remarkably little effort and cost.

---

[2] The 'Seven Sisters' was a term given to the seven largest oil companies: Exxon, Standard Oil, Gulf Oil, Texaco, Mobil, BP and Royal Dutch/Shell.

4.   FINANCIAL ISSUES RAISED BY THE GROWTH OF MULTINATIONAL ENTERPRISES

When the decision is taken to conduct business on an international or multinational level, new financial issues arise because the regulations to which a company must adhere often differ markedly from country to country. Usually, organisations comply with the new sets of rules they become exposed to by trading internationally and bear the extra cost associated with this requirement in their business profitability. However, it is widely accepted that some enterprises take advantage of the loopholes in regulatory systems that can develop from trading on an international scale. One very notable characteristic of multinational corporations is that more than one set of taxation rules may need to be abided by. One particular policy problem associated chiefly with such enterprises is the taxation attributes of transfer pricing (Safarian, 1983, p. 78)[3], but even simple source vs. residency conflicts can significantly increase the costs of complying with tax regulations imposed on companies by the countries in which they are trading.

The structures of many international businesses were becoming increasingly complex by the start of the 1930's. By positioning subsidiaries around the globe, they were able to limit the amount of tax that the enterprise as a whole would have to pay. Mitchell B. Carroll raised the question of the grounds for the 'transfer price'. In reports to the League of Nations in 1932 and 1933, he recognised that *'profits can be shifted from place to place, the purpose frequently being to transfer them to the country with a low rate of tax or no income- tax at all'* by fixing *'the transfer price from the factory to the selling establishment at so high figure as to show little or no profit in the books of the sales branch'* (The League of Nations, 1932; 1933).

The financial issues for international trade are now well recognised by both tax authorities and also by companies themselves. In both cases there is a need however, for careful planning and appropriate communication to ensure that such issues do not hinder the free development of business in ways that would be detrimental to global business advancement.

---

[3]   See the chapter in this volume by Elliott and Emmanuel who discuss the influence of transfer pricing on multinational behaviour and tax costs.

5. EFFORTS TO ALLEVIATE FINANCIAL BARRIERS TO INTERNATIONAL BUSINESS: THE TAX TREATY

Historically, international trade had been taxed via indirect means – often in the form of customs duties on importation. At the beginning of the twentieth century, a general move away from indirect tax sources occurred in national taxation systems with a corresponding increase in focus on direct sources.[4] This change of focus was also visible in the way international activity became taxed. Whilst duties remained in place, whole new systems of taxation were developed around the taxing of business profits. The issues of jurisdictional right to tax arose from this new focus where genuine conflicts occurred as to where cost and revenue were generated and could be expensed.[5] Where foreign investments were made they became taxed on the export of the associated returns or profits either in the form of withholding taxes, or direct taxes where permanent establishment was to be found in the country of the source of the profits.

A further key development in the national approach to international taxation occurred in the U.S. Revenue Act of 1918 (ss 222 and 238) that introduced the notion of foreign tax credits into U.S. national tax systems for the first time. The availability of tax credits greatly reduced the total tax burden of foreign investments and helped promote U.S. companies around the world.[6] Although these credits were restricted (firstly in the 1921 Revenue Act and significantly in the 1986 Tax Reform Act) they have played an important role in enabling overseas investment and cross border trade.

One of the other features of the increasingly liberalised international system which generated the growth of international investment after World War II were international tax agreements, the basic principles of which quickly spread once they had been initially laid out by supra-national bodies. 'The key legal mechanism for the co- ordination of states' jurisdiction to tax international business has been the bilateral tax treaty' (Picciotto, 1992, p. 38). These arrangements resolve jurisdictional rights to taxation between countries over the various income flows that multinationals create. Whilst a useful practical tool, they require continual renegotiation and development as

---

[4] This was clearly visible for example in the impact of the U.S. Revenue Act of 1917 which created the tax rules associated with the 16th Amendment ratified in 1913 and introduced the federal individual and corporate income tax system.

[5] For more information on jurisdictional conflicts in respect of taxation see Lymer and Hasseldine's chapter introducing international taxation in this volume.

[6] The important role of foreign tax credits, in the USA and elsewhere, is discussed in the Ricketts chapter in this volume.

states, eager to attract new foreign investment, offer financial inducements to companies in order to tempt them to trade within their borders (Picciotto, 1992, p. 38). The bilateral tax treaties provide a network of relationships between trading countries and a degree of stability for corporate tax planning, but do not provide a truly international resolution of cross-border taxation, leaving a number of key problems unresolved or at best uncertainly or inconsistently applied.

5.1   Brief Historical Example – The Zollverein

One of the first examples of a tariff treaty was the Zollverein undertaken by Prussia during the early stages of the nineteenth century.[7] The country exported raw products on the whole, her mines were unworked and manufacturers were still using handlooms and spinning wheels. Trade was restricted due to the fact that tariffs in the thirteen 'enclaves' that made up Prussia ranged from oppressive to virtually non-existent and in no two provinces were duties uniform. In total, there were 67 different tariffs involving 3,800 different types of goods. Without uniformity, the collection of these tariffs was very difficult indeed as the external borders of Prussia were 8,000 kilometres in length and touched twenty-eight different states (Marriott and Robertson, 1946, p. 290).

Karl Georg Maassen recognised this and he can take much of the credit for the first move towards standardisation that was enacted in the law in May 1818 (Marriott and Robertson, 1946, p. 290). Amongst the immediate requirements of this Tariff Reform Act was the removal of barriers to trade, all raw materials were to be imported free of charge and other categories of products would be subject to an average duty. For example, manufactured goods had a duty of ten per cent. Internal customs duties were no longer applied (Marriott and Robertson, 1946, p. 291).

In 1819 the Prussian Finance Minister, Motz, concluded the first tariff treaty with one of the enclaves, namely Schwarzburg-Sondershausen and three years later Weimar, Gotha, Mecklenburg-Schwerin, Schaumburg-Lippe, Rudolstadt, and Bamberg woke up to the advantages of the policy instigated by Prussia (Marriott and Robertson, 1946, p. 291). The southern states of Germany had also been negotiating between themselves and in 1828 arrived at a customs union of their own. One year later, north met south in a treaty that approximated, although did not amalgamate, the two systems. This eventually happened in 1833 and a true Zollverein came into existence for the

---

[7]   See Marriott and Robertson (1946, p. 290+) for a full discussion of the development and importance of this tariff treaty.

major part of Germany. It catered for seventeen states and 26,000,000 million people between whom free trade could then be conducted (Marriott and Robertson, 1946, p. 293).

But the Union did not stop there. States and free cities continued to join the Zollverein and furthermore, negotiations had taken place with foreign powers. In 1831, states incorporated in the Zollverein were relieved of paying tolls imposed by the Netherlands upon products passing down the Rhine. Treaties were entered into with Great Britain and Belgium too in 1841 and 1844 respectively (Marriott and Robertson, 1946, p. 294). The importance of the Zollverein cannot be overstated. It played a more than substantial role in increasing imports and exports by 100 per cent between 1834 and 1842.

5.2   Foundations of a Multinational Agreement

The foundations of a truly internationally co-ordinated tax treaty were set in the inter-war period through the work of the League of Nations which commissioned four economists, namely Professors Bruins, Einaudi, Seligman, and Sir Joshua Stamp, to produce a report into how different national approaches to taxation could be reconciled (Picciotto, 1992, p. 19). Firms were becoming involved in international trade and investment like never before and global co-operation was needed to resolve the problem of double taxation that was arising from unresolved jurisdictional taxation right conflicts (Ogley, 1993, p. 36). Their report in 1923 revealed that no simple general principle could be possible in order to achieve an acceptable allocation of jurisdiction to tax across the world. However, it did propose four options for reconciling national differences (Picciotto, 1992, p. 19):

1. The use of a foreign tax credit system, as by then in operation in the USA (which whilst giving priority to the source country did leave residual taxing powers, and hence the determination of the actual rate of tax to be paid with the resident country)
2. The full relieving of non-residents by the source country.
3. An agreement, at an international level, to determine the basis of allocating profits between source and residence countries (some form of what is now referred to as global formulae apportionment)
4. Different types of tax could be assigned based on 'the primary economic allegiance of the income in question'. This would imply the source country has first claim to tax profits of the business however, returns on investment would be taxed in the country of residence.

Whilst work on these proposals was being undertaken, the Financial Committee of the League of Nations created a board of Technical Experts consisting of government tax officials from Belgium, Czechoslovakia, France,

Britain, Italy, the Netherlands and Switzerland because it was becoming increasingly concerned by the lack of any internationally agreed principles (United Nations, 1980, p. 6). It was thought that companies were finding ways of evading their tax burdens by moving capital around and so the International Economic Conference that took place in Genoa in 1922 passed a resolution insisting that the problem of tax evasion be dealt alongside that of international double taxation. In Geneva in October 1928 at a General Meeting of Government Experts on Double Taxation and Tax Evasion four model conventions were discussed after the technical experts had recommended that such action be taken in their first report in 1925. All had been sent to a number of governments, prior to the meeting, regardless of whether or not they were members or non-members of the League (such as the USA which was not a member - United Nations, 1980, p. 7). Two of these four conventions concerned mutual assistance, one the assessment and the other in collection of taxes. The propositions were comprised of the work done by the economists and the government officials and again favour was expressed for the principle of taxation of income by the country of residence (i.e. the source country exempting non-residents). However, it was also recognised that capital-importing countries would be unlikely to relinquish their right to tax foreign investors so a method would have to be found to placate both the country of source and of residence (Picciotto, 1992, p. 23).

Initially, interest was shown in the American idea of a foreign tax credit. Despite this method giving priority to the country of source and maintaining residual taxation rights for the country of residence, its unilateral simplicity was misleading, as income from subsidiaries abroad would be taxed at the higher of the source or residence rates. This would inevitably then lead to the country in which the overseas branch was located to simply increase its tax rates. For these reasons, the Technical experts favoured the idea of splitting up (allocating) the income flows between countries (Picciotto, 1992, p. 22).

Of the four conventions that the conference in Geneva in 1928 produced, Convention One became the most important. This dealt with direct taxes and had three sections. Together, they established the fundamental basic principles dominating international tax systems today, particularly that the country of source could only tax the business profits of a foreign business if there was a Permanent Establishment within its borders through which the income had been generated and that the home country could retain the rights to tax its residents on their global income, perhaps subject to a credit or exemption for foreign taxes paid on business profits at source (Picciotto, 1992, p. 24). The initial definition of the term 'permanent establishment' given in this Convention did not include within it affiliated companies or subsidiaries.

They were to be treated as separate entities and taxed as such (Picciotto, 1992, p. 23).

Although the permanent establishment requirement was the key to international compromise over which authority had jurisdictional right to levy tax on the profits of a business, several hindrances prevailed. For example, the British government saw no reason why it should give up its right to tax British residents on their worldwide income. Sir Richard Hopkins drew up a list of the arguments that supported this view for the Chancellor of the Exchequer in 1933 (Picciotto, 1992, p. 25). The 1928 conference also left unresolved whether the source country could impose taxes on investment returns (i.e. non-business profits) such as in the form of withholding taxes, or on how allocation of business profits should be undertaken when a business entity has residence in more than one country. Both problems were later to need resolving.

Mitchell B. Carroll addressed the open question of business profit allocation in work produced for the League of Nations in the early 1930s (becoming known as the Carroll Report – League of Nations 1932; 1933). His detailed work on trying to understand what rules were then in existence around the world for such allocations led to the League's 1935 Allocation Convention. This addressed one of the two open questions from the 1928 conference. It produced what has now become the 'arm's length' principle rule for determining prices and cost allocations for tax purposes by establishing separate accounts for calculation of business profits in related entities.

The work done by the League of Nations was however significant despite these limitations. In the period between the wars, approximately sixty general treaties that dealt with the problem of double taxation of income and property were finalised and there were a great deal more agreements made concerning specific tax matters (Picciotto, 1992, p. 25).

The tense economic and political atmosphere of the late 1930's meant that it was not until 1943 and 1946 at meetings in Mexico and London respectively that model conventions in mutual assistance were finally drawn up based on the 1928 and 1935 meeting outputs (Picciotto, 1992, p. 49). The Fiscal Committee had been able to continue its work during World War II from Princeton University in the United States and had arranged western hemisphere Regional Tax Conferences in Mexico City in 1940 and 1943 which were attended by representatives from Argentina, Bolivia, Canada, Chile, Colombia, Ecuador, Mexico, Peru, the United States, Uruguay and Venezuela (United Nations, 1980, p. 7). The latter of the two meetings saw the adoption of Model Bilateral Conventions for the Prevention of the Double Taxation of Income, the Prevention of Double Taxation of successions and for the Establishment of Reciprocal Administrative Assistance for the Assessment and Collection of Direct Taxes (United Nations, 1980, p. 8).

5.3   Post-War Proposals

Three years later in England, a new document was produced which built on the contents of the Mexico draft of 1943, particularly in the area of property and wealth taxation. The two papers were published alongside each other rather than the latter replacing the former. Together they were responsible for the post-war development of international taxation cohesion, whilst at the same time being unable to disguise their differing basic principles, most notably the ongoing source versus residence controversy (Picciotto, 1992, p. 49). The League of Nation's Fiscal Committee recognised that the two documents differed and put it down to the fact that the membership of the London meeting was different to the one held in Mexico City three years earlier (United Nations, 1980, p. 8). Although both drafts stated that the income produced by a Permanent Establishment should be subject to source-based taxation, the Mexico draft went further and addressed the remaining key question from the 1928 meeting. It declared that payments of interest, dividends and royalties should also be subject to source-based tax. The London draft however, addressed this issue differently and made interest taxable in the country of the beneficiary; it made dividends exempt from tax if they were being paid to a parent company from a subsidiary – otherwise they were subject to tax in the country of the payer; tax on royalties was only levied in the country of utilisation if they were paid to a related company (Picciotto, 1992, p. 50).

5.4   OECD Undertakings

After the dismembering of the League of Nations in 1946, the Economic and Social Council of the United Nations set up a Fiscal Commission to 'study and advise the Council in the field of public finance, particularly in its legal, administrative and technical aspects' (United Nations, 1980). This Commission and its Committee on International Tax Relations had a life of eight years before passing on the focus of action in the area of international taxation to the OEEC[8] (United Nations, 1980, p. 8). The OEEC created its own Fiscal Committee in 1956 and in 1958 commissioned it to produce a new convention that would alleviate double taxation and hence stimulate international investment. The Committee used as its base the London model

---

[8]   Organisation for European Economic Cooperation

treaty of 1946 and other treaties that had been entered into since that date (Picciotto, 1992, p. 53). The opinion of the Fiscal Committee at that time was that 'since the work of the League of Nations, the value of a Model Convention has been universally recognised not only by the national authorities, but also by the taxpayers themselves' (OECD, 1963, p. 25, para.49).

In 1961, the OEEC became the OECD[9]. In 1963 it published its first Double Taxation Convention on Income and Capital (United Nations, 1980, p. 9). Alongside the draft, the organisation had prepared commentaries that were designed to help interpret the various sections of the document. The idea behind their inclusion was that any disputes that should arise concerning the meaning of the articles of the Convention could be resolved using definitive explanations of intention and meaning (Picciotto, 1992, p. 53).

Although this new draft, like the others, was based on work done by the League of Nations, it incorporated within it new issues that were emerging due to the rapid growth of foreign direct investment. From the 1960's, MNEs started to become much more genuinely global and were able to manipulate international tax systems by making use of offshore financial centres and tax havens in order to pay as little tax as possible. These actions undermined the fairness of national fiscal policies and unilateral action was undertaken by some home countries of multinational enterprises in an attempt to tax the income of 'their' companies (Picciotto, 1992, p. 54). Steps taken by a country in isolation resulted only in partial success however, due to political and jurisdictional difficulties that had long been visible, and had led to the need for tax treaties and related conventions in the first place (OECD, 1981, p. 4). However, the collaboration of countries to reduce double taxation, and guard against tax evasion, had previously involved at least some mutual assistance, particularly in the field of the recovery of taxes, and substantial progress had been made through bilateral tax conventions during the 1960's.

In 1967, the Fiscal Committee of the OECD began to revise the 1963 Double Taxation Convention. As international movement of resources grew easier, so it continued to facilitate taxpayers' non-compliance and create further complications in tax allocation that could lead to unwanted double taxation. The revision led to the publication of the 1977 Model Double Taxation Convention on Income and Capital (United Nations, 1980, p. 9). This proved to be an extremely influential document because it provided a framework for negotiation that had already acquired the broad agreement of most developed countries (Ogley, 1993, p. 36).

---

[9] Organisation for Economic Co-operation and Development

One of the most important features of the OECD Model Convention is Article 9, entitled Associated Enterprises. This deals with transfer pricing and allows taxation authorities to enforce the arm's length principle, i.e. the right to adjust the price at which goods and services are bought and sold within a group of companies (Ogley, 1993, p. 37).

Agreement to employ the arm's length principle was a very large step taken by the OECD countries to make their presence in foreign countries more attractive to source governments. By 1976, the year in which the OECD 'Guidelines for Multinational Enterprises' had been adopted, these companies were playing an important part in numerous economies around the World (OECD, 1994, p. 11). The capability of MNEs to organise their finances in such a way as to manipulate the national frameworks of countries in which affiliates had been set up had led to concerns about financial and legal conflicts between companies and authorities (OECD, 1994, p. 12).

The Guidelines for Multinational Enterprises that have been proposed by the OECD are designed to help ensure that large global organisations can work in harmony with the governments of the countries in which they have chosen to invest. They have been the subjects of reviews in 1979, 1982, 1984, and 1991, but amendments have been scarce because their effectiveness depends a great deal upon their stability (OECD, 1994, p. 7). OECD Member countries support these voluntary guidelines and believe that their extension to other countries around the world would greatly assist international co-operation (OECD, 1994, p. 7). The Guidelines have helped the growth of international direct investment. Today, there is greater acceptance of multinationals as countries compete against each other to attract larger shares of the limited amount of investment capital. This not only includes the most developed countries with the largest economies in the World, but also those from Eastern Europe, Asia, Africa and Latin America, where older opinions concerning the role foreign investment can play in national economic development are gradually being replaced (OECD, 1994, p. 8).

Further revisions to the OECD Model Double Tax Convention have occurred at regular intervals throughout the 1980s and 1990s. A further reform is proposed for mid-2002. By the mid 1990s more than 200 treaties had been agreed between OECD members based on the various model treaties (Ault, 1993). This had risen to nearly 350 by 2002, and now more than 1,500 such agreements are in place around the world between other countries.[10]

A version of the Double Taxation Convention has also been issued by the United Nations. Whilst this document differs very little from the OECD version, the OECD focus is on principles for treaties between developed

---

[10] Source: OECD website April 2002.

countries and therefore is not always suitable for use between developing countries or between developed and developing countries – at least not in ways that may be considered acceptable to the developing nation. The UN version of the Convention addresses some of the concerns that have been raised by developing countries, which are usually source countries, over the inequity of the OECD model.

6.   MULTILATERAL AGREEMENTS

The network of bilateral double tax agreements has grown exponentially in recent times and is viewed by many as being inadequate in dealing with modern commerce, in particular electronic commerce, and also with developments in tax policy. One possible solution would be the wider use of multilateral agreements.

An early multilateral agreement was executed in 1922 between Italy, Austria, Hungary, Poland, Romania and Yugoslavia (Harris, 1996 p288-292). Multilateral agreements are difficult to negotiate, however, as the Nordic experience demonstrates. Hamaekers (1986) notes 'preparation and negotiation of a multilateral convention is extremely difficult'. This convention took 11 years from commencement to negotiations to the signing of the treaty. This negotiation difficulty was a primary reason for the avoidance of the formulae apportionment systems being passed over in favour of separate accounting conventions and arms length principles from the 1928 League of Nations conference onwards.

The limited success to date in forming multilateral agreements demonstrates that a multilateral solution to current problems in international taxation will not emerge from the existing bilateral framework (Oats and Fernandez, 1999). The failure of multilateral agreements to so emerge could be said to stem from a number of factors. These now include the 'lock in' effect of existing arrangements, to add to the longstanding concerns of huge global, cultural and political diversity. There are significant difficulties, in particular, in relation to developing countries. In the context of multilateral information exchange, Bird (1988, p. 298) notes 'with the best will in the world, no one can endow most developing countries with the considerable expertise needed to make use of any information they might receive from other countries'.

The possible need for multilateral agreements in at least some aspects of international tax has however, recently been discussed again in the context of re-examination of international tax systems and electronic business where

greater need for mutual agreement now exists to effectively manage tax
relationships than previously had been the case.[11]

7.   CONCLUSION

The participation of international organisations since the First World War
in the attempt to co-ordinate international tax systems has not rapidly led to
the resolution of all the tax issues created by the growth of international
business activity. However, companies and governments alike appear to be
resolved to working together to alleviate potential problems where both
parties will otherwise suffer. The widespread use of the OECD 'Guidelines',
and the acceptance of the Model Tax Convention as the basis for most
national tax treaties is evidence of this fact. Attitudes to the role of the
multinational in international, and therefore national, business environments
have changed a great deal since the 1970s when they came to prominence.
Large corporations are no longer looked upon solely with suspicion, but are
indeed now an integral, and probably vital part of the international economy.
Although this does not mean all is smooth in the relationships between
Multinational Enterprises and their host countries, particularly where either
party tries to misuse its power to influence the other, companies that follow
the suggestions of the OECD can be fairly confident that they will receive a
warm welcome from governments and will be able to take advantage of new
markets on the basis of mutual respect and confidence with national
authorities (OECD, 1994, p. 12). We have come a long way towards creating
an acceptable, if not perfect, international tax system that has freed business
to develop according to market need. How the system will develop in the
future remains uncertain, although some clues are provided by James' chapter
in this book.

STUDY QUESTIONS

1. In what way does foreign direct investment differ from truly multinational
   activity in respect of its taxation implications?
2. Could a business ever be truly multinational?
3. What would be the international tax implications of a business achieving
   full multinational status?

---

[11] See the chapter in this volume by Warren who explores the influence of electronic business
on International Taxation systems.

4. Could the world benefit from a single international tax entity? What conditions would be necessary to create and sustain such an entity? How might it determine, set, collect and allocate international taxes?
5. What have been the key contributions of the Model Taxation Convention? How would international taxation have differed had they not been created in the way they were?
6. What influence has the OECD's 'Guidelines for Multinational Enterprises' had on the global systems of taxation?
7. What would be the benefits, to both taxpayers and tax authorities, of wider use of multilateral tax agreements? Would their use result in any disadvantages?

REFERENCES

Adams, J. (1977), The International Taxation of Multinational Enterprises in Developed Countries, London: Associated Business Programmes Ltd.

Ault, H. (1993), 'The Role of the OECD Commentaries in the Interpretation of Tax Treaties', in Alpert, H. and van Raad, K. (Eds), *Essays on International Taxation*, Deventer, the Netherlands: Kluwer law and Taxation Publishers, pp. 61-68.

Bird, R. (1988), 'Shaping a New International Tax Order', *Bulletin for International Fiscal Documentation,* p. 298.

Casson, M. (1983), The Growth of International Business, London: Allen & Unwin.

Channon, D. and Jalland, M. (1979), Multinational Strategic Planning, London: Macmillan.

Czinkota, M., Kivoli, P. and Ronkainen, I. (1989), International Business, London: Dryden.

Dassbach, C.H.A. (1989), Global Enterprises and the World Economy, London: Garland.

Ghertman, M. and Allen, M. (1984), An Introduction to the Multinationals, London: Macmillan.

Hamaekers, H. (1986), 'Multilateral Instruments on the Avoidance of Double Taxation, *Bulletin for International Fiscal Documentation*, p. 99.

Harris, P. (1996), Corporate/Shareholder Income Taxation and Allocating Taxing Rights Between Countries, Amsterdam: IBFD.

League of Nations (1932), 'Taxation of Foreign and National Enterprises', Study of the tax systems and the methods of allocation of the profits of enterprises operating in more than one country, Vol. I (France, Germany, Spain, the UK and the USA), no.C.73.M.38, 1932 II A 3, Geneva.

League of Nations (1933), 'Taxation of Foreign and National Enterprises', Vols. II and III, and 'Methods of Allocating Taxable Income', Vol. IV; Allocation Accounting for the Taxation Income of Industrial Enterprises by Ralph C. Jones; Doc. No. C.425.M.217 1933 II A 18, Geneva.

Liu, L.G. (1998), Internet Resources and Services for International Business, Phoenix, Arizona: Oryx Press.

Marriott, J.A.R. and Robertson, C.G. (1946), The Evolution of Prussia: The Making of an Empire, Oxford: Oxford University Press.

Oats, L. and Fernandez, P. (1999), 'Creation of a Cyber Entity', *New Zealand Journal of Taxation Law and Policy,* Vol. 5(2), pp. 96-107.

OECD (1963), Draft Double Taxation Convention on Income and Capital: Report of the OECD Fiscal Committee, Paris: OECD publications.

OECD (1981), OECD Model Convention for Mutual Administrative Assistance in the recovery of tax claims - Report of the OECD Committee on Fiscal Affairs, Paris: OECD publications.

OECD (1991), The OECD Declaration and Decisions on International Investment and Multinational Enterprises, Paris: OECD publications.

OECD (1994), The OECD Guidelines for Multinational Enterprises, Paris: OECD publications.

Ogley, A. (1993), Principles of International Taxation, London: Interfisc Publishing.

Picciotto, S. (1992), International Business Taxation, London: Weidenfeld & Nicolson.

Rounds, T.A. (1992), 'Tax Harmonisation and Tax Competition - Contrasting Views and Policy Issues in 3 Federal Countries', *Publius - The Journal of Federalism* 22

Safarian, A.E. (1983), Governments and Multinationals: Policies in the Developed Countries, Washington D.C: British-North American Committee.

Taggart, J. H. and McDermott, M. C. (1993), The Essence of International Business, London: Prentice-Hall.

United Nations (1980), United Nations Model Double Taxation Convention Between Developed and Developing Countries, New York: United Nations publication.

Note: One of the best guides available to the history and foundations of the modern systems of international business taxation is Picciotto's book as listed above. This is particularly recommended for anyone interested in historical developments.

Chapter 4

Internet Challenge to Tax System Design

NEIL WARREN

ATAX, University of New South Wales, Australia

Key words: e-commerce; internet; source and residence rules; permanent establishment; transfer pricing; tax administration; harmful tax practices

Abstract: The growth of the internet poses a challenge to both tax system design and to tax administrations. Governments and international agencies are aware of this challenge but are uncertain as to its likely magnitude. However, there is no doubting that e-commerce and the anonymity of the internet offers real opportunities for those seeking to avoid and evade tax. This paper seeks to identify the key issues which need to be considered in any evaluation of the internet challenge to tax design. It notes that core tax concepts are under challenge and outlines the response of governments as well as agencies such as the OECD. While there is a view that current tax laws can be made to work in the new environment, if this is not the case and a tax-what-you-can system develops, equity and economic efficiency will be major casualties from the growth of the internet.

1.   BACKGROUND

The internet is being heralded as the next revolution to sweep the world. How can this be and why is something which is technically nothing more than a series of computer networks linked together by a series of telephone lines, constitute a revolution? The answer lies in the concept of technology convergence.

The internet offers a simple framework for bringing together all electronic media into one delivery platform. This means that all your electronic interactions with the rest of the world can be undertaken using just one media - the internet. Whether it is video, data retrieval, telephony, banking, shopping, reading, or just plain entertainment, the internet has the potential to deliver all these to your home and place of work through one connection to the outside world. This is possible because what you send over the internet is not important. If you are using email, then your email software digitises this information and sends it to other mail programs on a server connected to the internet. Equally, if the internet is being used for audio communication then audio is digitised and sent by telephony software and if video, then between video software to similar software on another computer connected to the internet. In fact, the internet has unlimited uses with the only constraint being that all communication must take place using the accepted communication protocols.

The purpose of this paper is to examine how the development of e-commerce using the internet will affect the design, operation, and administration of tax systems. With this knowledge, we will be better able to consider what tax challenges and tax policy responses are likely as a result of these developments.

2.   THE E-COMMERCE TAX CHALLENGE

2.1   Business Challenge

E-commerce poses both threats and opportunities to business[1]. The opportunities come from the scope producers have for reducing their need to use intermediaries in order to contact consumers - this has become known as the process of disintermediation. With the internet enabling direct business-to-consumer (B2C) and business-to-business (B2B) transactions seamlessly across domestic and international frontiers, large markets are now accessible by relatively small businesses. When the trade is in digitised goods and services, an additional benefit is that these businesses confront opportunities to manage their affairs in such a way as to minimise the tax burden on their trading activities.

For example, this could be achieved by locating a web server from which digitised goods can be downloaded in a jurisdiction which has low taxes and no information sharing with the country of residence of the ultimate owner of the web server. Alternatively, with sophisticated encryption of transactions a business could mask its activity from domestic tax authorities on a web server sited locally. With disintermediation also come less taxation points and therefore less information against which to check compliance with tax laws.

---

[1]   A useful private sector site reporting on breaking e-commerce tax issues can be found at www.ecommercetax.com

Clearly, the internet offers businesses considerable scope for the minimisation of both income and consumption taxes, an issue that is examined in Section 3.

2.2   Tax Administration Challenge

For taxation authorities, three facts must be accepted about the internet: firstly it is here to stay and will continue to grow; secondly, only band width and security limit its rate of growth and finally, nothing any one government can do will stop its growth.

Since the internet lacks order and discipline, tax authorities are confronted by a technology that is capable of being used to undermine the tax administration system. Since tax systems rely on voluntary compliance maintained by having a mix of help and enforcement, then the internet poses a real threat. If there is no domestic paper trail and transactions are encrypted, the activities of internet users will be all but invisible to the host nation so the task of the cyber tax police will be nearly impossible.

This would render concepts traditionally applied under tax systems useless in the face of the activities of taxpayers intent on tax evasion at a global level. This will especially be true if some countries present themselves as tax havens for locating websites. This implies that only multilateral actions by tax authorities can address the challenge posed by electronic commerce, an issue pursued in Section 4.

2.3   Sub-national Government Challenge

The internet has important implications not only for national government tax collectors but also for those in sub-national jurisdictions.

The tax systems of State and regional governments are clearly under challenge from the internet. The first wave of this challenge is coming from the growth of internet banking and gambling. Anyone can now open overseas bank accounts and make payments to and from it via the internet. For the Australian States, this meant that their Financial Institutions Duty (FID) on deposits in financial institutions was not sustainable in an electronic age. It was of no surprise that it was eventually abolished in July 2001 in return for equivalent funding from the Federal GST.

State gambling taxes are also vulnerable and it is this vulnerability which lies behind the recent UK change to cut taxes on gambling (announced in the 2001 budget[2]). A particular motivating factor in the UK was that UK based

---

[2]   See the following article on UK gambling tax changes brought about due to the growth of internet based gambling: www.nottingham.ac.uk/business/workabst.html#2001.3

gambling institutions were setting up gambling websites in offshore tax havens, which was undermining UK revenue from this source. For the gambler, the attraction of gambling in some offshore country with a reputable gambling institution is obvious - better chances of winning because of a lower tax take and lower overheads. It will be interesting to see if the proposed substantial cuts in gaming taxes on the UK resident gambling institutions is capable of meeting the internet challenge.

Quite clearly, the internet offers the challenge of increased tax competition for both State and national governments. Undoubtedly, this will impose considerable longer-term pressure on nations to harmonise both their tax base and tax rates.

There will also be considerable pressure to adopt a system of enforcing tax laws across jurisdictions, such as a move towards the introduction of global tax file numbers that are quoted on all internet transactions and much improved information sharing.

2.4   Conclusion

The growth of the internet poses a number of fundamental challenges to tax systems including[3]:
a) basic concepts underlying:
   - income taxes
   - capital taxes
   - consumption taxes
b) foundations for model tax treaties;
c) opportunities for tax evasion (by not reporting transactions) and tax avoidance (through the opportunities the internet offers for transfer pricing); and
d) tax administration and tax compliance.

Governments are acutely aware of the challenge posed by the internet. In the case of the OECD Committee on Fiscal Affairs, they developed a set of Taxation Framework Conditions, the key conclusion of which was that the taxation principles that guide governments in relation to conventional commerce should also guide them in relation to electronic commerce[4]. The

---

[3] See for example, the work program on electronic commerce and taxation by the OECD at www.oecd.org/subject/electronic_commerce/documents/taxation.htm

[4] This is also a view expressed by the Australian Tax Office (ATO) in its two reports on *Tax and the Internet* (see www.ato.gov.au.)

OECD also held the view that existing taxation principles can be made to implement these principles[5].

This has resulted in a work program focussed on[6]:

- whether a web site or a server can constitute a permanent establishment giving rise to tax jurisdiction in a country;
- how payments for digitised products should be characterised under tax treaties;
- for consumption tax, obtaining a consensus on defining the place of consumption and on internationally compatible definitions of services and intangible property;
- adopting conventional identification and internationally compatible information requirements.

Quite clearly, electronic commerce is hastening a major rethink of hereto-accepted principles underlying tax system design. It is to the nature of this challenge that we turn our attention in the remainder of this paper.

The all-important question is whether the current taxation rules and design need to be re-written or re-interpreted to suit the new market situation or whether the tax rules have to be completely re-thought and the tax system re-designed.[7]

3. JURISDICTIONAL ISSUES

International double taxation agreements (DTA's) provide domestic taxation authorities with rules which enable them to determine the tax liability of those carrying on a business or earning income in any country which is a signatory to the DTA. These rules cover important issues such as the residency of the taxpayer, sources of income, income of a permanent establishment (PE), and the allocation of income.

Generally, a country uses residency rules to tax residents on their worldwide income and source rules to tax non-residents on income derived

---

[5] See discussion in the reports released by the various Technical Advisory Groups (TAG) charged with reporting on how a range of tax issues are impacted upon by e-commerce. These reports can be accessed at www.oecd.org/daf/fa/e_com/public_release.htm More general information on OECD research into e-commerce issues is available at www.oecd.org/daf/fa/e_com/e_com.htm.
See additional links at www.oecd.org/subject/e_commerce/ec_links.htm

[6] *op cit*

[7] These and related issues are also examined in Section 7 of the ATO's first report on *Tax and the Internet*.

domestically. Since e-commerce ignores national frontiers, it therefore challenges these rules.

In this section, we shall examine how e-commerce has the potential to impact directly on the effectiveness of the concepts underlying a DTA.

3.1   Residency

Typically, domestic tax rules allow tax authorities to tax residents on their worldwide income but non-residents only on that income generated domestically.

3.1.1   Residency of a Person

For an individual, residency can be potentially defined in a number of ways including where they are domiciled; by a 183-day rule; where they have family business or social ties; or where they have their permanent residence. What status then does electronic residency in a country have even though there is no physical residency by this taxpayer? After all, by using the internet, a taxpayer can effectively reside and conduct business in any number of jurisdictions. For individuals, telecommuting using the internet is now simple, easy and cheap so what is the status of a physical residency concept for individuals based on a so-called 183-day rule?

What if this person is an e-resident who crosses international boundaries many times every day and effectively resides in multiple jurisdictions. With no clear records of a border crossing, they would be taxed in their country of physical domicile but is this appropriate?

After all, there is only a weak link between a person's physical location and the jurisdiction in which they are electronically resident - so who in this case has the greatest claim on this persons income? The trouble is that current tax rules are unsympathetic to the new sophisticated methods of working and deals with this situation in an arbitrary and inefficient way.

> How might the tax laws be made flexible enough to enable the concept of residency to accommodate work practices which are globally based and where physical location is less important than economic ties?

One possible solution is a 'facts-and-circumstances test' with a person taxed not on the basis of location but on the basis of the facts surrounding their situation.

How then are we to make operational a tax that is imposed in the country to which a person commutes rather than the country in which they are physically resident? This approach also brings into question the purpose of taxation. If it is to fund the benefits and infrastructure available to a person in their country of residence, then this approach is maybe inappropriate.

The 'facts-and-circumstances test' therefore has problems since it flies in the face of one of the primary purposes of taxation - the provision of benefits that accrue to those physically located in a region. Moreover, a 'facts-and-circumstances test' is likely to be extremely difficult to apply in practice whereas fact-based rules such as physical presence are operational even if not completely appropriate.

3.1.2   Residency of a Corporation

In the case of companies, residency has typically been determined as the place of incorporation or the place of central management and control (CMC). CMC has been variously determined as being where the business exists, or where the directors exercise their management and control. The location of directors has proven particularly important in determining a company's residency. However, if the directors all reside in different countries and communicate using internet based technology such as emails, chatrooms, and video and audio conferencing, then CMC related rules may not be effective.

Could a company have dual residency if it is electronically managed by directors in two countries?

What then is the status of an internet based business that is mirrored in several countries and where the directors are based in a number of countries?

3.2   Source

Source rules outline fundamental principles that underlie domestic tax systems. For non-residents this rule ensures they are generally only taxed on income from domestic sources while residents are taxed on income from all sources.

In the Australian case, these rules are based on legislation and common law precedent and the courts in determining source, have examined the essence of the business that derived the income and where that essence is located (ATO, 1999, para 5.2.9) as well as other factors such as: where any relevant contracts are negotiated or concluded; where they are performed; the governing law of such contracts; the currency in which the transaction is carried out; and the place where payment is made.

The problem for tax authorities is that an internet-based business is able to influence these factors and therefore be able to determine the source of income from different locations and therefore influence their aggregate tax liability.

For example, if an activity is deemed to be 'carried on' where an e-commerce web server is located then the location of the server can be manipulated for tax advantage. Also, if where a contract is signed determines the source of profits on sales, a website could be configured to ensure that businesses provide an 'offer to sell' to customers ensuring that the website is the place where the contract was concluded.

> What also happens if contracts are concluded offshore at offshore
> websites but the services are provided by domestic residents?

Clearly, traditional concepts of source are open to manipulation. The question then is, can the current domestic legislation and precedents from common law rules be capable of being applied to e-commerce transactions - or should more general principles of source be devised and applied. The latter would appear to be the preferable approach.

3.3   Permanent Establishment

A permanent establishment (PE) is a location where a business enterprise is wholly or partially carried on. With disintermediation made possible by the internet, global businesses can now operate through websites and without the physical presence of a branch office (PE) in countries around the world. For governments in technology-importing countries where this physical presence is removed, there is a potential loss of revenue from locally sourced income.

In Article 7 of the OECD Model Treaty, an enterprise of a contracting state is generally exempt from taxes on profits derived from business carried on in the *other* contracting state unless those profits are attributable to its PE located in that *other* contracting state. Article 5 in the OECD Model Treaty defines business premises that are PEs as[8]:

1. a place of management;
2. a branch;
3. an office;
4. a factory;
5. a workshop; and
6. a mine, an oil or gas well, a quarry or any other place of extraction of natural resources.

It would appear that some form of permanent physical presence characterises each of these cases. How should a website be treated? The fact

---

[8]   See www.oecd.org/daf/fa/treaties/treaty.htm downloadable at
www.oecd.org/daf/fa/treaties/MTCArticles.pdf

is that carrying on business via the internet challenges the whole concept of a PE and therefore how we should determine the business income of an enterprise.

If the website holds information (equivalent to a warehouse) for a business and then sells this information by executing orders and arranging for shipments then it has all the characteristics of a PE. However, if the website does not have a permanent physical presence because it can be moved, replicated and masked with considerable ease, what (if any) is its permanent location? After all, these websites are nothing more than software (or computer programs) running on hardware (the web server computer). Moreover, while a website might be akin to a PE for a fleeting moment, because it can be mobile in seconds or mirrored at many locations around the world, then it is not clear if it is a PE. It is this observation that led the U.S. Treasury (1996) to conclude that the concept of a PE should be abandoned and that we should move to rely exclusively on a residence-based tax system - but this is not a solution for most countries that are capital and technology importers.

The UN's Model Tax Treaty defines a PE more broadly than the OECD, including dependent agents who maintain a stock of goods from which they make deliveries on behalf of their principals[9]. In this case, a website, or an electronic establishment (EE), could be considered a dependent agent which automatically delivers goods and services to clients on behalf of the principal once an electronic contract is signed at the website.

Is this broader concept of a PE enforceable? What if a country becomes a website (tax) haven, refusing to share information with other countries on who are the owners of the websites operating within their borders? Tax agencies need an information trail and website havens would destroy the information flow. Tax evasion and avoidance would become a major concern.

DTAs will need to be capable of coping with PE and EE so that physical appearance becomes less important than the activities carried on. The OECD TAG on PEs released a draft on this issue in December 2000[10]. This draft

---

[9]   www.un.org

[10] Related discussion can be found in: *Clarification on the application of the Permanent Establishment definition in e-commerce: changes to the commentary on the model tax convention on article 5*, 22 December 2000, OECD Committee on Fiscal Affairs, downloadable from 2001 www.oecd.org/daf/fa/e_com/ec_1_PE_Eng.pdf; and *Attribution of profit to a Permanent Establishment involved in Electronic Commerce Transactions*, A discussion paper from the Technical Advisory Group on monitoring the application of existing treaty norms for the Taxation of Business Profits, February 2001, downloadable from 2001 www.oecd.org/daf/fa/e_com/ec_3_ATTRIBUTION_Eng.pdf *Tax Treaty Characterisation Issues arising from e-Commerce*, Report to Working Party No. 1 of the OECD Committee on Fiscal Affairs by the Technical Advisory Group on Treaty

distinguishes between the web server and the web software and data used on the web server. A web server hosting a website was seen as not a PE but once the web server was used to conduct business then it could be considered a PE. Whether it is a PE should be determined on a case by case basis according to what functions are performed by a business on the web server.

It is also important that the rules applied to determining a PE in relation to e-commerce should not be different from those for a conventional business for fear of encouraging traditional businesses to relocate their selling activities to a website offshore. For governments, disintermediation and the vagaries of what constitutes a PE have potentially significant revenue implications and it is not surprising that there is an air of urgency in the efforts to clarify just when and where a PE exists.

3.4   Income Characterisation

Typically, income received from different sources by non-resident businesses is subject to different withholding tax regimes. The characterisation of income by a business can significantly influence their withholding tax burden. The challenge from e-commerce is the scope it provides for income to be characterised in a form that incurs the lowest withholding tax rate. For example, if an Australian business purchased software over the internet, this supply of goods from the website (assuming it is not a PE) could be characterised by the operator of the website as either income from sales (hence adding to business profits and subject to residency taxation of the website owner) or as a royalty for the right to use or for use of the copyright. If this website was located in Australia and viewed as a royalty, it would be subject to an Australian withholding tax of 10% to 30% of the gross payment depending on the country to which it is paid. If viewed as sales, it would be taxed in the country where the website owner has its PE. Significant revenue risk arises for the government from the scope for business owners to manipulate the outcome to their tax advantage.[11]

Characterisation of Electronic Commerce Payments, 1 February 2001, downloadable at www.oecd.org/daf/fa/treaties/Treatychar_finalrep.pdf; and *OECD Discussion Draft on the Attribution of Profits to Permanent Establishments*, downloadable from www.oecd.org/daf/fa/tr_price/peprofit_english.pdf

[11] See *Treaty Characterisation Issues Arising from e-Commerce*, Report to Working Party No. 1 of the OECD Committee on Fiscal Affairs, Technical Advisory Group (TAG) on Treaty Characterisation of Electronic Commerce Payments, 1 February 2001 www.oecd.org/daf/fa/e_com/ec_2_TREATY_CHAR_Eng.pdf

Technical Advisory Group revised report: '*General Conclusions of Treaty Characterisation Issues and Analysis of Typical E-Commerce Transactions*, 1 Sept 2000, It is stated that the

For example, royalties are defined in Article 12 of the OECD Model Tax Convention[12]. Royalties:

...means payments of any kind received as a consideration for the use of, or the right to use, any copyright of literary, artistic or scientific work including cinema films, any patent, trade mark, design or model, plan, secret formula or process, or for information concerning industrial, commercial or scientific experience.

It is possible that payments that are akin to royalties such as software license fees could be characterised as tangible supplies. Likewise, tangible supplies could be characterised as royalties because they can be manipulated and modified. If payments for rights in an intangible such as the right to use a software program are not royalties[13] then a royalty must be defined as a right to do any of the acts comprised in the copyright such as modification and reproduction.[14] Some distance is yet to be travelled in addressing risks that arise from the characterisation of income for tax advantage.

3.5   Income Tax Base Allocation Issues

Shifting of the global income of a multinational through transfer pricing to a jurisdiction that has low tax rates has long been a concern for tax authorities. The growth of the internet and secure global company-based intranets make the task of preventing such reallocation considerably more difficult because this new technology enables more sophisticated and more widespread access to tax base shifting for not only companies but also individuals.

Intranets are private (company wide) secure networks that operate on the same protocols as the internet. Intranets are a threat to the tax systems because they provide global corporations with scope to rearrange their internal structure and cost sharing arrangements across international frontiers to minimise their global tax liability.

Using an intranet, firms could mask the extent of their transfer pricing activities by purchasing services from service companies (which could be just a website) in a low tax country or by purchasing labour services around the world in a way that a tax authority would find difficult to monitor or dispute. Without a secure and verifiable electronic trail for tax authorities to follow,

---

majority of characterisation comments were in relation to downloading of digital products. See also ATO Tax and the Internet, 2nd Report, Section 5.4.

[12]   See www.oecd.org/daf/fa/treaties/MTCArticles.pdf
[13]   Op cit ftn 11
[14]   ATO Taxation Ruling TR 93/12 and ATO Taxation Ruling IT 2660, accessible by searching law.ato.gov.au/atolaw/index.htm provides further insight into this issue.

global profits could be readily transferred to low tax jurisdictions. Electronic signatures attached to transactions for which the tax authority holds one of the two digital keys necessary to change this file once locked with one of the keys, is one solution for tax authorities in their attempts to maintain integrity in the tax system.

The OECD view[15] is that current domestic laws, double tax agreements and OECD rules and guidelines are basically adequate and effective in addressing any e-commerce challenge. The reality is however, as we noted above, that the internet will make the challenge much more complicated and difficult[16]. Issues that will be difficult for tax authorities to resolve are what are appropriate cost-sharing arrangements for a multinational when operating across international borders; who has ownership of intangibles; and how do we disentangle complex internet transactions. However, the key to answering these issues is remembering that the internet and intranets do not fundamentally change the nature of what a business is doing currently - it only makes it more difficult to ensure compliance with domestic laws.

It is this reasoning that led the United States Treasury (1996) to adopt residence based taxation as the preferred base for tax and for a move away from source based taxes. Obviously, such a move would benefit the U.S. Government but would do little for capital and technology importing countries and would, as has been the case, be fiercely argued against as an inevitable outcome of the growth of the internet[17].

3.6   Consumption Tax Base Allocation Issues

Cross-border shopping has always been a concern to governments, especially those at the sub-national level who impose retail sales taxes. The scope for consumers to use mail order houses to purchase goods has always been an issue. This has typically been addressed through state sales taxes being defined as sales and use taxes - with the good or service taxed where it is used, not necessarily where it is purchased. Enforcement is clearly an issue but is possible in the case of large bulky goods such as motor vehicles.

However, e-commerce opens new dimensions for consumers to avoid and evade national sales taxes, raising the spectre of this being more than just a sub-national government problem. National GSTs are already quite capable of

---

[15]   The OECD view is that to date, electronic commerce has presented neither fundamentally new nor categorically different problems for transfer pricing.' De Zilva(2000), p651, and OECD, *Transfer Pricing* Guidelines at www.oecd.org/daf/fa/tr_price/transfer.htm

[16]   See OECD conference proceedings at www.oecd.org/daf/fa/e_com/e_com.htm. Also Boyle, Peterson, Schottensin (1999, p. 378) and Chapman, Steiss, and Pantaleo (1997, p. 1402)

[17]   ATO (1999, para 7.7.11)

capturing internet based offshore purchases of physical goods (by taxing them at the point of importation). B2B supply of intangibles over the internet is also captured by the application of a reverse charge rule but B2C transactions involving intangibles is more problematic.

Obvious problem areas are computer software downloads over the internet, or the sales of downloadable music (as with MP3) or videos. If the supplier is not connected in any way with the jurisdiction in which the consumer resides, then the purchases could be purchased GST free. Even if the national government legislated that the consumer must apply a reverse charge rule and reimburse the national government for GST on offshore purchases, this would be unenforceable. What the national government could not do is legislate to require businesses offshore that sell to local residents to register for the local GST. How can they force domestic laws on non-residents?

A solution might be the imposition of an origins based VAT on international transactions and a CVAT (McLure, 2000[18]) on flows between sub-national jurisdictions each with a VAT. However, an origins based VAT would require a VAT clearing house and the EU attempts have been long and fruitless in the pursuit of this objective, despite the present lack of any national frontiers for trade purposes. In contrast, a CVAT system has been proposed for countries which operate sub-national VATs. In this situation, each state would levy it own VAT rate and impose a different rate - the CVAT rate - on interstates sales and a zero-rate on international sales. The CVAT rate might be set equal to the weighted average of the rates in the various states.

> Bird and Gendron (2001, p. 302) state that: 'Like the introduction of income tax withholding and indeed the VAT form of sales taxation itself, this new idea in fiscal technology may prove to be one of the key innovations in tax thought of the century'. Do you agree? What problems do you foresee with a CVAT system?

3.7   Tax Havens (and Harmful Tax Practices)

In recent years, the OECD[19] has taken an aggressive position on the growth of harmful tax practices, which are tax regimes designed to erode the tax base of other countries. These practices include tax policies designed to attract investment away from jurisdictions to which it would normally go or which enable residents of one jurisdiction to legally avoid tax due in their

---

[18] See also the options discussed in Bird and Gendron (2001).
[19] www.oecd.org/daf/fa/harm_tax/harmtax.htm

country of residence. In response, in 2000 the OECD released a report on *Towards Global Tax Co-operation*[20] which not only identified potentially harmful tax practices of member countries, but also some 35 non-member countries who were deemed to be tax havens and therefore operating harmful tax practices.

In response, the OECD released guidelines on harmful tax practices[21], which were designed to limit the growth of such practices both in member and non-member countries. The guidelines have two key elements: a standstill provision and a rollback provision. The standstill provision requires member countries to refrain from adopting harmful tax practices and from extending or strengthening existing harmful tax practices. The rollback provision requires members to eliminate harmful tax practices within five years. In relation to non-member countries operating tax havens, they have been presented with a *Framework for a Collective Memorandum of Understanding on Eliminating Harmful Tax Practices*[22]. By preparing such an MOU[23], these tax havens will escape potential OECD member country sanctions.

Of particular concern to the OECD is that globalisation and in particular the growth of the internet will potentially encourage the proliferation of harmful tax practices. This current action against tax havens can be seen as symbolic of the action they take against those countries that become e-commerce or website tax havens. The primary driving force here is that harmful tax competition will drive tax rates down in member countries which will in turn erode those countries tax base and directly impact on government expenditure programs.

> Will these activities by the OECD eliminate harmful tax practices? Can the tax havens deliver on their *Commitment Letters* and *Schedule of Commitments* to the OECD?

4.   COMPLIANCE CHALLENGE

The challenge posed by the internet to tax systems is clearly fundamental. Most vulnerable are income taxes and taxes on private consumption of intangibles. The reality is that tax systems survive on a combination of enforcement through penalties and voluntary compliance. What happens if

---

[20] www.oecd.org/daf/fa/harm_tax/Report_En.pdf
[21] www.oecd.org/media/MOUrev20novR1.pdf
[22] www.oecd.org/media/release/nw00-123a.htm
[23] Several of these tax havens have already provided undertakings to the OECD. See www.oecd.org/daf/fa/harm_tax/advcom.htm

individuals and companies see in the internet technology an opportunity to avoid or at worst, evade their tax liability without detection by masking both their identity and their activity?

4.1 Identification

The problem for all governments is that their investigative and enforcement powers are typically restricted to national boundaries - unless other nations also co-operate. The internet challenge comes from the use of this technology to make it difficult to identify the parties to a particular transaction, the timing of that transaction and its value. Without this information, tax authorities cannot ensure the tax laws are being enforced at the key taxing points. This is not a problem with traditional commerce but it is potentially with e-commerce.

In Recommendation 17 of the first *Tax and the Internet* report (ATO, 1997), the Australian Tax Office recognised the potential limitations of their *Financial Transactions Reports Act* which could mean certain internet based transactions are not reported to AUSTRAC[24], particularly under the 'cash dealer' definition. The most significant problems arise when individuals and businesses move away from local financial institutions to those in another country which does not have the reporting requirements, financial system regulations,[25] or consumer protection laws. This might mean no verifiable paper trail (with no receipts and no periodic statements) for the ATO. This problem might also occur domestically if businesses and consumers move over to a greater use of stored value cards (SVC) which would operate independently of the banking system.

The move by the OECD on the harmful tax practices of tax havens is part of a recognition by all governments that the integrity of their tax systems will only be maintained if there is global information sharing. Without this sharing of information, domestic enforcement (and hence sanctions through penalties) will be rendered ineffective as businesses recognise that 'playing-by-the-rules' is optional. While having a few tax evaders is probably tolerable and inevitable in any system, systematic evasion (and avoidance) is intolerable

---

[24] AUSTRAC is the Australian agency that collates information on financial transactions from those required to under the *Act*.

[25] In recent testimony before a US Senate Committee, Manhattan District Attorney Robert M. Morgenthau said there is now $800 billion on deposit in Grand Cayman. This is twice as much as is on deposit in all of the banks in New York City, and is the equivalent of 20% of all dollar deposits in the United States. See the following link for more information www.ecommercetax.com/doc/072901.htm

and it is this threat that cheap and easy access to the internet provides businesses and individuals around the world.

4.2   Information Trail

Tax systems only work when accurate and verifiable information is available on a taxpayer's activities. Business carried on at a website poses a number of challenges, especially identifying who is the taxpayer for income tax and GST purposes. The problem is that tracing the ownership of websites and the activity on them could prove problematic if the jurisdiction in which they are located is uncooperative. A similar problem could occur within a multinational's intranet - with the identity of the buyer and the nature of the transaction proving difficult to determine.

The ATO (1999, p. 132) recently noted that 'while most business websites adequately identify the business owner, recent ATO audit experience reveals that for approximately 15% of domain named websites it was not possible to identify from the website, or the domain name registration databases, the entities conducting the business'. The lack of transparency at websites as to their owners is a real issue for tax authorities. However, requiring websites to be officially registered and for that registration to include information on the owner(s), contact details, country of location, and trading name(s) could be difficult because the great majority of websites are not intended for undertaking commercial activity.

However, even if this information was available, the fact that there is only an electronic trail to follow and not a paper trail poses a number of fundamental problems for the tax authority. Firstly, is the electronic data being provided by the website owner verifiable (and therefore reliable), especially if the data is being encrypted? While encryption is clearly necessary for security reasons, it also enables the website owner to deny or restrict access to this information by the tax authority (although fines might subsequently be imposed) but more importantly, it would enable undetectable alteration of the information collected by the website on business activity. If the website of a local business owner is located offshore, then the latter outcome is a very real possibility. Even information sharing with this offshore jurisdiction would not address this problem since the business owner could hide his activities from both governments - which brings us again to the issue of tax havens.

4.3 Tax Havens

The biggest threat to the information paper trail comes from the growth of e-commerce tax havens[26]. Exchange of Information (EOI) protocols in DTAs is a start but only applies to treaty partners and would not apply to tax havens. It requires little imagination to appreciate that the harmful tax practices actions of the OECD has as one of its key objectives greater information sharing with jurisdictions which do not have DTAs with OECD members.

It is not surprising therefore that the OECD requires tax havens identified as having harmful tax practices to sign an MOU which states that by 31 December 2002, they will make available beneficial ownership information and the financial books and records of businesses; that by 31 December 2003, they will enable the effective exchange of information (criminal tax matters) and access to bank information; and that by 31 December 2005, they will provide the effective exchange of information on all tax matters[27].

Note that this exchange of information relates not only to the business owners and to their accounts' information, it also relates to bank information. In fact, the key to an effective tax system in the world of e-commerce is a compliant (regulated) banking sector. The ultimate method of identifying a business's activities is to access related banking information.

By encouraging these countries to agree to exchange information with OECD countries, a pre-emptive strike has been made against the growth of e-commerce tax havens. What this action does acknowledge is the current real limits to the territoriality of a nation when it seeks to enforce its laws when there is no DTA with the tax haven country. However, the OECD action backed with sanctions against tax havens is a very powerful move against the current and potential future actions of tax havens in the area of harmful tax practices related to setting up e-commerce tax havens[28].

---

[26] See www.offshore-e-com.com/html/factfile.html#ecomtax especially the case studies at www.offshore-e-com.com/html/case.html

[27] See the MOU at www.oecd.org/media/release/nw00-123a.htm

[28] The OECD actions are only effective if supported by member countries. The US has indicated recently that it is relaxing its demands on tax havens. The new US approach would only require transparency and access to information on offshore accounts. See www.ecommercetax.com/doc/072901.htm

5.   SHOULD WE MOVE TO A TWYC SYSTEM?

If tax laws are not enforceable and taxpayers use the internet to play a *catch-us-if-you-can* game of tax avoidance and evasion, then the resulting tax system is neither efficient, nor equitable nor sustainable.

What then is the solution? Two extremes could be considered. The first could involve the introduction of a world tax office with responsibility for issuing global tax file numbers and co-ordinating the administration and revenue collection in tax systems around the world. In this case, the tax systems administered by a world tax office might not be too different from those currently is operation - the main difference being greater information sharing and the tagging of all transactions with the global tax file numbers of the sender and recipient. Clearly, this system would require a considerable level of international co-operation (and potential loss of autonomy), especially on how to share the revenue raised.

The other extreme is where there is no information sharing or international co-operation and the domestic tax system is adapted to operate in the new global e-commerce environment where evasion and avoidance is simple, easy and rife. In this case, the basic principle that should probably underlie the tax system would be the principle of *tax-what-you-can* (TWYC). The problem here is deciding what to chase and include in the base and what to overlook. This would be a very different way of thinking about tax design from the approach taken today. Such a system would require income, consumption, and wealth taxes to be rethought. What would such a TWYC system look like?

Undoubtedly, it would require consideration of the following proposals:
1. Residence based taxes administered through a series of withholding taxes such as schedular income taxes where different income sources are taxed at source under different rate schedules.
2. Imposition of taxes on the:
   - purchase of tangible consumption goods with a VAT (or GST)
   - use of tangible durable consumption goods with a *use* tax
   - stock of tangible assets with property taxes, annual wealth taxes, and succession and gift duties.

   Such a range of taxes would be designed in part to tax the accumulation of wealth from income tax evasion or from the adoption of a less than comprehensive income tax base.
3. Tax tangibles at higher rates than intangibles because electronic data flows are elusive whereas bulky goods and physical assets are readily identifiable. However, the effectiveness of such a rate regime depends on the elasticity of demand for tangibles as against intangibles and the scope for substituting out of the relatively highly taxed tangibles.

4. Tax internet service providers (ISP) on their turnover: Some U.S. States have sought to impose turnover taxes on ISPs. However, there is a poor correlation between ISP charges and the value of transactions undertaken by clients of the ISP and such taxes are likely to stifle rather than encourage the growth of the internet.

5. Tax Bit Flows: The European Commission put forward a proposal to tax bits flows[29] over the internet. The problem is that this approach lacks any discretion based on the nature of the flow and could hinder the development of the internet.

6. Foreign Exchange Regulation: Governments might consider forcing all FOREX related transactions through official banks. Combined with draconian penalties on banks (such as losing their licence) for non-compliance, this could limit the scope for tax evasion via the internet. However, this threatens the global moves towards deregulated markets and is a largely untenable solution. Moreover, with encrypted data flows, this may be pointless exercise.

7. Tobin Tax: This would be a tax that is levied on foreign exchange transactions. Such a tax has been the subject of considerable international debate since Nobel Laureate James Tobin proposed it over two decades ago. A primary goal of such a tax is to reduce speculative foreign exchange transactions. There are many criticisms of such a tax, probably the most significant being that all countries will need to adopt it if it is to be in any way effective.

6. WHAT TAX POLICY RESPONSE CAN WE EXPECT TO E-COMMERCE?

The reality is that a TWYC tax system is probably not tolerable from an equity or revenue perspective. Residence based taxes clearly favour selected countries and taxing tangibles will undoubtedly be regressive as will high consumption tax rates. Equally, low tax rates on mobile income sources such as capital income will favour higher income individuals.

How then should governments *constructively* respond to the e-commerce challenge? The earlier discussion highlighted the considerable effort being made by governments to determine what action is necessary to ensure the integrity of domestic tax systems in an e-commerce environment. The consensus would appear to be that countries will continue to work with their

---

[29] See europa.eu.int/index_en.htm Note that there are 8 bits in 1 byte, 1024 bytes in 1 kilobyte, 1024 kilobyte in 1 megabyte and 1024 megabytes in 1 gigabyte.

own tax legislation and tax systems but that they will be adapted marginally to accommodate the impact of the internet. Probably the greatest change required in the future will be considerably improved information sharing by tax authorities around the world accompanied by tighter financial regulation to ensure business data flows are verifiable against bank financial data. This will require multilateral agreements, which have proved difficult to achieve in the past. The problem is going to be that while tax administrators can perceive the risks to revenue, politicians see in e-commerce avenues to grow the economy and herein lies the dilemma - go for revenue or go for growth.

FURTHER READING

Australian Tax Office (1997), *Tax and the Internet, Volumes I and II*, Canberra: AGPS.

Australian Tax Office (1999), *Tax and the Internet Second Report*, Canberra: AGPS.

Becker, H. (1998), 'Taxation of Electronic Business in a Globalizing World - Ten Demands for an Adaptation', *INTERTAX*, Vol. 26(12), pp. 410-413.

Bird, R.M. and Gendron, P. (2001),'VATs in Federal Countries: International Experience And Emerging Possibilities', *Bulletin for International Fiscal Documentation Bulletin*, Vol. 55(7), pp. 293-309.

Bloom, A.S. and Giusti, R.S. (1997), 'International Tax Implications of Electronic Commerce on Outbound Transactions', *The International Tax Journal*, Vol. 23(4), pp. 45-61.

Boyle, M., Peterson, J. and Schottensin, T. (1999), 'The Emerging International Tax Environment for Electronic Commerce', *Tax Management International Journal*, p. 378.

Brown, C.A. (1994), 'The Canadian Income Tax Treatment of Computer Software Payments', *Canadian Tax Journal*, Vol. 42(3).

Burnstein, M.R. (1996), 'Conflicts on the Net: Choice of Law in Transnational Cyberspace', *Vanderbilt Journal of Transnational Law*.

Caccamise, W.C. (1988), 'U.S. Countermeasures Against Tax Haven Countries', *Columbia Journal Of Transnational Law Association*, Inc.

Capito, A. (1999), 'OECD permanent establishment in e-commerce context, Australian Tax Practice', *International Tax Bulletin*, Issue 2, pp. 4-5.

Chapman, L., Steiss C. and Pantaleo, N. (1997), 'Income_taxes.ca.com: International Tax Planning: The Internet, Electronic Commerce, and Taxes - Some Reflections Part 2', *Canadian Tax Journal*, Vol. 45(6), pp. 1378-1415.

Chapman, L., Steiss, C. and Pantaleo, N. (1997), 'International Tax Planning: The Internet, Electronic Commerce, and Taxes - Some Reflections: Part 2', Canadian Tax Foundation, *Canadian Tax Journal*, Vol. 45(6), p. 1402.

Cigler, J.D. and Stinnett, S.E. (1997), 'Treasury Seeks Cybertax Answers with Electronic Commerce - Discussion Paper', *Journal of International Taxation*, February, pp. 58-96.

De Zilva, A. (2000), 'E-Commerce: Make Hay While The Sun Shines', *Taxation in Australia*, Vol. 34(12), p. 651.

Glicklich, P.A., Levine, H.J., Goldberg, S.H. and Brody, E.S. (1997), 'Electronic Services: Suggesting a Man-Machine Distinction', *Journal of Taxation*, pp. 69-75.

Guttman, G. (1999), 'IRS Studying E-commerce Tax Problems', *Tax Notes*, p. 424.

Hamburger, A.S. (1997), 'The Corporate Income Taxation of Electronic Commerce', presented at the IBFD International Academy Seminar: *International Taxation of Electronic Commerce,* Amsterdam, 3 October 1997.

Hee Lee, C. (1999), 'Impact of E-Commerce on Allocation of Tax Revenue Between Developed and Developing Countries', *Tax Notes International,* pp. 2569-2580.

Hellerstein, W. (1997), 'Taxation of Electronic Commerce in the Unites States, National and Sub-national Issues' presented at the IBFD International Academy Seminar: *International Taxation of Electronic Commerce,* Amsterdam, 3 October 1997.

Hinnekens, L. (1998), 'The Challenges of Applying VAT and Income Tax Territoriality Concepts and Rules to International Electronic Commerce', *INTERTAX,* Vol. 26(2), pp. 52-70.

Horner, F.M. and Owens, J. (1996), 'Tax and the Web: New Technology, Old Problems', *Bulletin,* pp. 516-523.

Jenkins, P. (1999), 'E-commerce: Future State, The likely indirect tax treatment in the European Union', *The Tax Journal.*

Killius, J. (1999), 'Cross Border Business on The Internet: Income Tax Aspects' in IBFD International Academy, presented at the IBFD International Academy Seminar: *International Taxation of Electronic Commerce,* Amsterdam, 3 October 1997.

Kogels, H.A. (1999), 'VAT @ e-commerce', *EC Tax Review,* Issue 2, pp. 117-122.

Lejeune I., Canbien, J. and Joostens, M. (1999), 'E-commerce - The European Commission', *VAT Monitor,* Vol. 10(4), pp. 156-158.

Lejeune I.,Vanham, B., Verlinden, I. and Verbeken, A. (1998), 'Does Cyber-Commerce Necessitate a Revision of International Tax Concepts', *European Taxation,* pp. 50-58.

Marshall, B. and Knowles, D. (1998), 'Is Electronic Commerce Taxing?', *The Tax Journal,* pp. 12-14.

McLure, C.E. (2000), ' Implementing Sub-National VATs on Internal Trade: The Compensating VAT (CVAT), *International Tax and Public Finance,* Vol. 7, p. 723.

McNab, P. and Porter, D. (1998), 'Electronic Commerce: Determining Source', *The Tax Specialist,* Vol. 1(4), pp. 223-229.

McNab, P. (1998), 'International Reaction to Electronic Commerce: the Developments', *Australian Tax Review,* Vol. 27, pp. 219-233.

Merrick, F. (1999), 'Taxation of E-Commerce', Paper presented at *TIA International Tax Masterclass,* Sydney, 14 October 1999.

Morgan, J., Graham, D., Patel, Z. and Sanderson, C. (1997), 'Don't Be Afraid of the Internet', *International Tax Review,* pp. 19-22.

OECD (1997), *Electronic Commerce: Opportunities and Challenges for Governments,* Paris: OECD.

OECD (1998), *Electronic Commerce: A Discussion Paper on Taxation Issues,* Committee of Fiscal Affairs, Paris: OECD.

OECD (1999), 'A Borderless World: Realising the Potential of Global Electronic Commerce', OECD Conference, Ottawa, 7- 9 October 1998, SG/EC(99)1/FINAL.

OECD (1999), 'Business-to-Business Electronic Commerce: Status, Economic Impact and Policy Implications', DSTI/ICCP/IE(99)4/FINAL.

Owen, J. (1993), 'Globalisation: the implications for tax policies', *Fiscal Studies,* Vol. 14(3), pp. 21-44.

Owens J. (1997), 'The Tax Man Cometh to Cyberspace', *Tax Notes International,* pp. 1833-1852.

Pinto, D. (1999), 'Potential, Opportunity and Challenge for the ATO', Paper presented at the *ATO Tax Technical Conference,* Sydney.

Powers, J.P. (1997), 'United States of America' International Tax Issues in Cyberspace: Taxation of Cross-border Electronic Commerce, presented at the IBFD International Academy Seminar: *International Taxation of Electronic Commerce,* Amsterdam, 3 October 1997.

Roose, E.R. (1998), 'Global Taxation of Electronic Commerce', *Asia-Pacific Tax Bulletin,* pp. 248-259.

Sanderson, C., Merrill, P. and Dunahoo, C. (1998), 'Consumption Tax Treatment of Electronic Commerce: Issues and Policy Recommendations', *Tax Notes International,* pp. 1083-1087.

Schwarz, J. (1999), 'Transfer Pricing and Electronic Commerce', *Bulletin for International Fiscal Documentation,* pp. 286-290.

Sorensen, P.B. (1994), 'From the Global Income Tax to The Dual Income Tax: Recent Tax Reforms in the Nordic Countries', *International Tax and Public Finance,* Vol.1(1), pp. 57-79.

Spence, I. (1997), 'Globalization of Transnational Business: the Challenge for International Tax Policy', *INTERTAX,* Vol. 25(4), pp. 143-148.

Sprague, G. and Hersey, R. (1999), 'Letter to OECD re: Electronic Commerce', *INTERTAX,* Vol. 27(2), pp. 40-49.

Tillinghast, D.R. (1996), 'The Impact of the Internet on the Taxation of International Transactions', *Bulletin for International Fiscal Documentation,* pp. 524-526.

U.S.Dept. of Treasury (Office of Tax Policy), (1996), *Selected Tax Policy Implications of Global Electronic Commerce,* Washington DC: Dept of Treasury.

Warren, N. (1998), 'Taxation of Internet Trade', *Asia-Pacific Tax Bulletin,* pp. 412-419.

Yamanouchi, A. (1997), 'International Tax Issues Affecting Electronic Commerce and Banking', *Tax Notes International,* pp. 1619-1624.

Chapter 5

Anti-Avoidance and Harmful Tax Competition: From Unilateral to Multilateral Strategies?

MARIKA TOUMI
Nottingham University Business School

Key words: harmful tax competition, tax havens, anti-avoidance provisions, international taxation

Abstract: One of the consequences of globalisation is the increase in harmful tax competition. It result in governments introducing practices designed to encourage non-compliance with the tax laws of other countries. The chapter reviews some of the measures taken by countries to protect their tax base, such as CFC legislation and transfer pricing rules and the limitations of the unilateral approach to anti-avoidance. It then presents the content and context of the recent OECD multilateral initiative against harmful tax practices.

1.   INTRODUCTION

International tax avoidance and evasion through the use of tax havens has been one of the most important and long-standing concerns of the tax administrations of most OECD countries. With the expansion and acceleration of globalisation, the negative effects of avoidance and evasion have been tremendously amplified by tax competition. Countries concerned about the flight of capital and savings from their jurisdictions to low- or no-tax jurisdictions in turn engage in the cycle of tax competition to attract investment. This spiral involves enormous amounts of lost revenue for governments, as well as facilitating the laundering of proceeds from criminal activities. The phenomenon has reached such proportions as to be considered harmful and become a priority on the OECD Fiscal Committee's agenda.

However, against international avoidance, there has not been a co-ordinated international response. Anti-avoidance has so far consisted of an arsenal of unilateral and bilateral anti-avoidance measures taken by individual countries, essentially within the framework of the tax treaty network. This unilateral approach to taxation at international level has always been imperfect but it is now proving worryingly inadequate to tackle the scale of modern tax avoidance. This is why in 1998 the OECD launched an initiative of international co-ordinated action against harmful tax competition.

This chapter does not aim to offer an exhaustive list of anti-avoidance measures at international level. Rather, it sets to provide an overview of the issues of avoidance and harmful tax competition and to the reliance on unilateral and bilateral measures to tackle them. Controlled Foreign Company legislation and transfer-pricing measures will be examined as instances of such unilateral anti-avoidance provisions. The chapter will then be dedicated to the OECD attempt at co-ordinated action with its initiative against harmful tax competition.

2.   OVERVIEW OF INTERNATIONAL TAX AVOIDANCE AND HARMFUL TAX COMPETITION

2.1   The Origins of Offshore Finance[1]

The inter-dependence of countries' tax systems and economies is a new phenomenon that has appeared and grown with the internationalisation of trade and investment and the developments of technology. However, the issue of finding appropriate ways of taxing international trade is not new. From the end of the 19th century when income taxation became the major source of government revenue, both trade and investment represented a high percentage of GDP. The first tax treaties emerged in the 1930s as an answer to the question of the appropriate treatment of foreign income.

Tax havens are not a new phenomenon either. They were used since the 1920s-1930s, although mainly by wealthy individuals to shelter their private fortunes from their home tax authorities or from dictatorial regimes. For instance, the low-tax jurisdictions of the Channel Islands and the Isle of Man were used by the British; Panama and the Bahamas by the Americans; and Liechtenstein, Monaco, Switzerland and Luxembourg by the continental Europeans[2].

---

[1] This section draws heavily on the chapter on tax havens and international finance in Picciotto (1992).

[2] Ibid. p. 118.

The de-colonisation movement of the 1950s and 60s resulted in the birth of new tax shelter locations. Many newly independent small countries, without much prospect for economic development, saw financial business as an attractive option at a time when tourism was not offering signs of becoming the booming industry it now is. That period was also the golden era of post-war reconstruction and economic growth. Multinational companies emerged and contributed to the development of international finance.

Further, in the 1960s, balance of payment controls, aimed at limiting the outflow of investment capital, were introduced by the major capital lending countries. The emergence of these controls in the 'onshore' financial centres gave multinationals an additional incentive, other than tax avoidance, to turn towards less regulated parallel financial markets. Thus the discreet use of tax havens by a rich few gave way to the rise of the offshore financial centres, either for direct or portfolio investment.

The phenomenon has since grown so enormously to shift from being a tolerated side effect of international finance to being a threat to the equilibrium of the world economies. In 1968, international bank deposits in tax havens were estimated at $US10.6 billion, half held by banks, half by non-banks. Ten years later in 1978, the amount was estimated at $US385 billion (OECD, 1987). The present estimate puts the total size of offshore funds investment at around $US1 trillion[3], shared between more than one hundred locations world-wide that offer tax and other incentives to foreign firms and individuals.

2.2 The Tax Treaty Network

States' jurisdiction to tax international business is co-ordinated through the bilateral tax treaty. Hence, there is no multilateral convention but instead a network of hundreds of treaties separately negotiated at national level. This mechanism has been preferred to a global approach to the taxation of international business that would have required an international agreement between tax jurisdictions on the basis for fractional apportionment of the profits of transnational corporations. This was considered both politically and technically too difficult at the time and the international community opted for the bilateral treaty arrangement to allocate the jurisdiction to tax international trade. The OECD model provided the necessary minimum of co-ordination and uniformity and it was hoped that the network would develop into a global and comprehensive system.

---

[3] See Owens (2000).

The tax treaty mechanism has the main advantage of being flexible and adaptable to each pair of negotiating countries' circumstances. It also allows each State to retain sovereignty over their internal tax arrangements. However, it has important drawbacks that make it not only inappropriate to deal effectively with the challenges of international avoidance and evasion but have also contributed to their very existence and their increase, as Sol Picciotto points in his study of international business taxation[4]. The tax treaty system relies on negotiation between countries. This process of bargaining treaty provisions is slow, onerous, and not very co-ordinated in spite of the model treaty. The focus is on the trading of national benefits rather than on the establishment of an equitable and effective international regime. Because the treaty network protects national rather than international tax equity which was left undefined, it has encouraged and legitimised international tax planning and avoidance, which have been facilitated in turn by the combined phenomena of globalisation and tax competition.

2.3   Tax Competition

Tax competition arises when a particular jurisdiction, in its bid to attract some of the multi-billion offshore investments and savings opportunities, tailors its fiscal regimes and provides preferential tax treatment of offshore income to foreign investors. Such tax regimes target corporations in the banking, financing, insurance and leasing sectors as these are geographically mobile services, sensitive to tax differentials. The most significant activity in the 1990s is arguably offshore banking. The demand for international private banking (bank accounts, trust, and offshore companies) in particular has seen a surge with the increase in numbers of wealthy individuals worldwide. It is really its proportions, rather than its existence *per se*, that has made tax competition a harmful phenomenon. The huge amounts at stake, that countries can attract with tax incentives or detract if their regime is deemed unfavourable, constitute an unavoidable pressure on tax systems that are pushed into a race to the bottom to prevent capital flight.

Besides harmful tax competition, money laundering is another damaging effect linked to tax havens and offshore centres. Their secrecy and deregulated environment have provided facilities where the gains from criminal activities can easily be channelled and then recycled into transactions that are more legitimate. The activities that are served by this convenient screen include drug trafficking, arms and diamond trafficking, and public corruption.

---

[4]   Ibid. p. 29.

The criminal aspect of money laundering has facilitated the acceptance of co-ordinated international action, which was launched with the set up in 1989 by the G-7 of the Financial Action Task Force as an independent international body (based at the OECD) to combat money-laundering. The FATF established forty recommendations as an international standard against money laundering and, since the end of 1998, works on identifying key anti-money laundering weaknesses in jurisdictions inside and outside its membership. In February 2000, the FATF published an initial report and in June 2001, a follow-up review that contains a list of non-cooperative countries and territories[5]. This strategy has been reasonably successful in the sense that countries tend to bend to the stigma of the blacklist and take steps to comply with the FATF requirements.

The OECD initiative against harmful tax practices, which will be described in more details further in this chapter, has undertaken to follow the FATF model of the blacklist in its approach to tax avoidance and evasion. However, avoidance and evasion do not bear the same stigma of criminality than money laundering and the OECD has met more resistance to its own set of blacklists and measures than it expected.

The key features of tax havens and offshore financial centres are secrecy and deregulation. There are different degrees in which these features can be found in OFCs on which their respectability is dependent. Some of the OECD members themselves have allowed the growth of semi-regulated 'offshore' pockets within their conventional financial markets to attract funds from non-residents. The OECD initiative reflects the distinction between the preferential tax regimes (of which the Irish International Services Centres are one example), which aim to attract real economic activity, and the full-blown tax haven facilities that aim to facilitate either tax avoidance and/or tax evasion. The two separate but overlapping phenomena are targeted differently by the OECD initiative. However, This has made the stance of the OECD members against the endemic problem of tax competition seem ambiguous and attracted criticism from the blacklisted tax havens.

2.4   Urgency of the Problem

The acceleration of globalisation and the advances of computer and communication technologies have greatly contributed to worsening the effects of harmful tax competition. The removal of non-tax barriers to international commerce and investment and the resulting integration of national economies have increased the potential impact that domestic tax policies can have on

---

[5]   The reports are available from the following website: http://www.oecd.org/fatf

other economies. As multinationals develop more global business strategies, they also become more independent from any one country and thus less responsive to governmental action. In effect, roles have been reversed and governments are now subject to pressures by multinationals as they can threaten to, and easily do, shift their activities to more tax-friendly locations.

The member countries of the OECD have been concerned about the distortions in the pattern of trade and investment that harmful tax competition creates. The flight of capital towards tax havens or offshore financial centres can erode national tax bases of other countries. It may alter the structure of taxation by shifting part of the tax burden from mobile to less mobile factors (income from labour) and from income to consumption. It may also hamper the application of progressive tax rates and the achievements of redistributive goals. These circumstances pose a real and pressing threat to the equilibrium of the international tax system which unilateral and bilateral anti-haven measures alone will not be able to address.

3.   INSTANCES OF UNILATERAL ANTI-AVOIDANCE MEASURES

International tax planning and its abuse through avoidance and evasion emerged as an attempt to resolve some of the problems caused by the double taxation of profits generated by cross-border business. The tax treaty mechanism, which did not address the need for international principles of tax equity and in fact represented an alternative solution to compensate for their lacking, only imperfectly answered the issue of double taxation.

The treaty network set principles of international taxation which in broad terms are as follows: business profits are taxable by the State of residence of an enterprise (including a subsidiary) or if attributable to a permanent establishment. The returns on a capital investment (dividends, interest, fees, and royalties) are taxable in the country of residence of the recipient, and the source country's withholding taxes are then eliminated or severely reduced.

However, today, economic globalisation and the deregulation of monetary systems and financial flows, in combination with the fast development of electronic communication and trade make national borders less important. Production factors have also become more internationally mobile. Know-how and other intangibles count for an increasing part of product value. The reliance on fixed assets for production is being successively reduced, which means that manufacturing too has become more mobile. All these factors are putting an increasing strain on the traditional principles of international taxation.

Also left unresolved by the model tax treaties is the issue of taxation of export profits. This explains the protracted dispute that takes place at the World Trade Organisation between the EU and the U.S. over the American Foreign Sales Corporations for instance.

Again, there has not been a co-ordinated international response to address these issues and their increasingly uncontrollable by-products of avoidance and evasion. Until the recent OECD initiative, anti-avoidance was essentially left to individual countries' provisions. They have mainly focussed on the prohibition or control of movements of persons or funds, or the disallowing or disregarding of such movements for taxation purposes. National provisions include transfer-pricing rules to prevent TNCs from shifting profits between jurisdictions for avoidance purposes, and more recently CFC legislation that targets the use of tax havens. There are many more devices to try and counter avoidance and evasion achieved through hidden distributions, thin capitalisation, offshore investment funds, treaty shopping.... This section will not review all of these anti-avoidance measures but will focus on transfer pricing and CFC legislation as instances of unilateral action against tax avoidance.

3.1   CFC Legislation

The most significant type of tax legislation directly aiming at counteracting tax advantages due to the use of tax havens is what is called Controlled Foreign Company legislation (or subpart F-type legislation from its U.S. model). Broadly, what CFC rules do is tax the offshore subsidiary's income in the hands of its domestic shareholders to defeat avoidance of tax through abuse of the deferral or exemption systems. Countries that have a system of worldwide taxation allow a deferral of tax when a TNC based in its jurisdiction controls a foreign resident subsidiary that operates abroad. The deferral entails that the profits of the overseas subsidiary will be taxed in the jurisdiction of the parent company only when they are repatriated. This ensures an equal footing with local and multinational companies from jurisdictions that operate an exemption system, whereby dividends from overseas subsidiary and the profits of overseas branches are exempt from tax in the home country provided they derive from a real business activity.

However, the deferral system and the exemption system have been used for tax avoidance purposes to shelter income in a tax haven or, to convert passive income into exempt dividend income receivable from a low-tax country. CFC legislation first emerged in the U.S. in 1962 and has now been introduced by most industrialised countries as a unilateral anti-haven measure.

The provisions of the CFC legislation usually refer to essentially three factors that delimit its scope: (1) the participation held by the residents that defines control of the foreign company, (2) the nature of the income liable to tax, (3) the definition of low taxation.

1. Control: the basis of imposing a liability to tax on the undistributed income of a CFC is that it is 'controlled' by residents of the tax country. A broad definition of control is usually used to minimise potential loopholes, but most CFC laws specify that at least 50% of the shares in the CFC must be held by resident taxpayers in the taxing country.

2. Regarding the income liable to tax, national legislation adopts one of two approaches: the 'locational' approach or the 'transactional'. The majority of countries adopt the locational approach whereby the CFC provision targets low-tax jurisdictions and then narrows its scope further by targeting only certain types of income (income that is not derived from a genuine business activity). However, the U.S. and Canada adopt the transactional approach that targets 'tainted' income, regardless of where it arises. Income covered under this transactional approach is usually passive income and is defined in the country's CFC provision. Passive income comprises dividends, royalties, rents, capital gains and profits arising from administrative and management functions.

3. The low taxation is broadly defined in comparative terms as substantially less tax than would otherwise be paid in the company's country of residence. Countries define low taxation in a variety of ways in their domestic provisions.

More and more countries adopt CFC legislation. A 1996 OECD report on CFC legislation showed that 14 member countries had CFC rules compared with only 6 in 1987. This figure is now higher with Italy and New Zealand recently introducing CFC provisions in their tax law. However, CFC rules are not an anti-avoidance panacea. They are very complex to administer and do not deal adequately with financial services such as banking and insurance, which are generally considered to produce 'passive income'.

The OECD certainly does not wish to abandon unilateral anti-avoidance action altogether but rather proposes a combination of the traditional unilateral anti-avoidance measures such as CFC legislation with multilaterally co-ordinated action. In its 1998 Report on Harmful Tax Competition that will be examined in more detail in the second part of this chapter, one of the OECD recommendations was to reinforce the existing network of CFC legislation. Although the individual CFC rules are very similar with regards to their objectives and their structural features, there are substantial variations in technical details from country to country. In this push towards greater co-ordination, the OECD encouraged its members towards more congruence in their respective CFC regulation and even hinted that in further work, the Committee of Fiscal Affairs might elaborate minimum standards for the design of CFC regimes[6].

3.2 Transfer Pricing Legislation

As part of their anti-avoidance arsenal, most countries have transfer-pricing legislation to prevent TNCs from manipulating and shifting profits between jurisdictions in order to minimise or avoid taxation. Transfer pricing legislation gives the tax administration the authority to scrutinise international transactions between related companies and to determine whether they have been operated at arm's length. It requires companies or branches to draw up separate accounts that reflect these arm's length prices.

This is again an example of international taxation administered on a unilateral basis and of prevalence of national, rather than international equity. This mechanism has been preferred in the 1930s to the consolidation of the accounts of multinationals and an international formula apportionment to define the taxing rights of individual States. This would have involved agreeing at international level what factors to take into account in any formula apportionment and also the basis of accounting and was deemed too problematic. As mentioned earlier, it is on these principles of independent business and separate accounting that the network of double tax treaty has been based and developed. Again, this is not without shortcomings. Administrators use the arm's length profit criterion to determine the fair allocation of costs and profits between related companies. They compare the profitability of the group subsidiary with that of a comparable independent firm, which means that they ignore the fact suggested by economic theory that multinationals benefit from economies of scale profits from their integrated organisation.

The transfer-pricing issue is of great importance considering that more than 60% of cross-border transactions take place between affiliated companies[7]. Yet, the rules on transfer-pricing are inadequate, complex, and inconsistent in spite of recent OECD efforts to improve them. According to a new transfer-pricing survey including more than 1,000 large international enterprises, the transfer-pricing issues are their most or second most important tax problem[8]. The 1995 OECD Transfer-pricing Guidelines[9] have laid down

---

[6] OECD, *Harmful Tax Competition, An Emerging Global Issue*, Paris, OECD, 1998, p. 42.
[7] See Lodin (2001).
[8] See Ernst and Young International (2000).
[9] See OECD (1995).

some common principles to try and harmonise the diversity of national provisions but transfer-pricing remains a source of international tax uncertainty, not least because the actual principle of pricing intra-group transactions across borders in the age of electronic technology and intangibles is artificial and unsatisfactory.

Among the various transfer-pricing methods, the OECD recommends using the traditional transaction methods rather than the transactional profits. The latter should be used as a method of last resort when the traditional transaction methods cannot be reliably applied or cannot be applied at all. I will summarise in very brief terms the methods available, namely the traditional transaction method and the transactional profits method and point to some of the difficulties that they involve.

The traditional transaction method includes:

– The comparable uncontrolled Price (CUP). It is established by reference to the price of similar goods on the market. However, this is only appropriate when the goods are sufficiently common so that they can be compared to similar goods.
– The resale price method. A resale margin is deducted from the resale price to obtain the arm's length transfer price. This method is most appropriate where the seller adds little value to the goods. The greater the value added to the goods by the functions performed by the seller, the more difficult it is to determine an appropriate resale margin.
– The cost plus method. This is best for a product for which the costs are known. The arm's length resale price is found by adding a mark-up to these costs.

The transactional profit methods examine the profits that arise from particular controlled transactions. The OECD only recommends them as an alternative to the traditional methods mentioned above, as an approximation of transfer-pricing in a manner consistent with the arm's length principle. The OECD Guidelines accept the profit split method and the transactional net margin methods for that purpose. (For a detailed analysis of the transfer pricing issue, refer to the chapter by Jamie Elliott and Clive Emmanuel).

Apart from several issues with regards to the technological evolution in pricing of services and intangibles that have not been very well foreseen by the OECD Guidelines and finds them lacking only six years after their introduction, the implementation of the guidelines into domestic legislation has also been insufficient. They have not produced the expected convergence of the various national transfer-pricing rules[10]. Countries that introduced transfer-pricing rules after the publication of the OECD guidelines have not

---

[10] Supra, note 6.

followed them closely enough. Instead, they have considered them as a sort of minimum standard that could be improved upon and surpassed. Others have even gone against them. The pressures of tax competition mean that the rules have also been interpreted more or less aggressively. Thus the harmonising effect that was intended for the Guidelines has not been successful and highlights once again the limits of unilateral action in international taxation.

3.3   The Need for Multilateral Action

The international tax system has been tested to the limits by the dual tensions of avoidance and evasion from corporations or wealthy individuals, and of harmful tax competition in which governments offshore and onshore are increasingly engaging. The OECD in its 1998 report on harmful tax competition acknowledged the limitations of unilateral and bilateral actions and pointed more specifically to five points:

a) The jurisdictional limits to the powers of a country's tax authorities restrict the ability of these authorities to counter some forms of harmful tax competition;

b) A country may believe that taxing its residents in a way that neutralises the benefits of certain forms of harmful tax competition will put its taxpayers at a competitive disadvantage;

c) The necessity to monitor all forms of harmful tax competition and to enforce counter-measures effectively imposes significant administrative costs on countries adversely affected by such competition;

d) The uncoordinated unilateral measures may increase compliance costs on taxpayers;

e) The need for co-ordinated action at the international level is also apparent from the high degree of mobility of the activities that are the object of harmful tax practices. Considering this context and the absence of international co-operation, there is little incentive for a country that provides a harmful preferential tax regime to eliminate it since this would merely lead the activity to move to another country that continues to offer a preferential treatment.

The issues of demography and social welfare are also imperative factors that motivate the OECD member States' governments to consent to a more co-ordinated approach to the current problems of international taxation. The growing demands in public spending[11] and the unpopularity of tax increases with the electorates provide the political incentive for taking multilateral action to try to halt the shrinking of the industrialised countries' tax base. The

---

[11]   See Avi-Yonah (2000).

OECD initiative against harmful tax competition is an example of such multilateral attempt.

4. THE DEVELOPMENT OF A MULTILATERAL STRATEGY: THE OECD INITIATIVE AGAINST HARMFUL TAX COMPETITION

Before the stand taken in 1998, efforts to increase supervision of the Offshore Financial Centres had been hampered by several considerations. The deregulated services constitute the main source of revenue for the small states where they are located. Consequently, any action meant running the risk of seriously disrupting these economies without the guarantee of achieving any lasting result considering the possibility that if control is tightened too much in jurisdictions where regulatory authorities have power, the transactions and institutions would easily move to other locations harder to control.

It meant the usual unilateral or bilateral approaches to international taxation issues would be inadequate. Any efficient action had to be taken multilaterally in order to neutralise competitive edges. However, international co-operation requires political determination that the OECD did not gather until recently. Section three below argues that the change in EU tax policy that occurred in the mid-1990s was instrumental in providing the OECD with the necessary momentum to place the debate and actions on harmful tax competition in an international framework. The current section presents these OECD measures.

Discussions on the issue of tax competition started in May 1996 when ministers called upon the OECD to 'develop measures to counter the distorting effects of harmful tax competition on investment and financing decisions and the consequences for national tax bases, and report back in 1998'. The G-7 countries subsequently endorsed the request. The OECD Committee on Fiscal Affairs went on to create the 'Special Sessions on Tax Competition' under the auspices of which a report was prepared and adopted by the Committee on 20 January 1998.

4.1 The 1998 OECD Report

The OECD report entitled 'Harmful Tax Competition – An Emerging Global Issue' addresses harmful tax practices in the form of tax havens and harmful preferential tax regimes in OECD member countries and non-member countries and their dependencies. It focuses on geographically mobile activities such as financial and other service activities.

The OECD has adopted different approaches for tax havens and for preferential tax regimes on the grounds that in tax havens, the whole system is geared up to offering a low or no-tax environment to geographically mobile capital, while a harmful tax regime is merely a pocket of capital-attractive regulations within a 'normal' tax system. The OECD therefore justifies the difference in treatment by the difference in purpose of the tax systems considered as a whole. Whether the distinction is justified or not is arguable as both regimes contribute to the erosion of the tax base and undermine the fairness of tax structures. A more lenient attitude towards preferential tax regimes might convey the message that they are somewhat acceptable or not that harmful.

The Committee acknowledged that tackling harmful tax practices is a process that will require time and the co-operation of all involved (tax havens, OFCs and Member States). The report does not rely on goodwill alone however and sanctions are suggested in order to 'encourage' jurisdictions to co-operate. The report therefore set out a number of proposals, some involving measures to be applied immediately by the signatories, and others intended as steps in a longer-term perspective. The proposals are:

a) The establishment of Guidelines on harmful preferential tax regimes
b) The creation of a Forum on Harmful Tax Practices
c) The development of a list of havens to be completed within one year of the first meeting of the Forum
d) 19 recommendations for action at the level of domestic legislation (recommendations 1-7), in tax treaties (recommendations 8-14), and lastly those concerning intensification of international co-operation (recommendations 15-19)

4.1.1   The OECD Criteria to Identify Tax Havens

The report defines a set of four factors to be used in identifying *tax havens*:

1. No or only nominal effective tax rates
2. Lack of effective exchange of information
3. Lack of transparency
4. No substantial activities

A tax haven will be characterised by the combination of low or zero effective tax rates AND one or more of the other three factors.

To define *harmful tax practices* in otherwise high tax countries, the OECD report uses a slightly different set of four factors:

1. No or low effective tax rates
2. 'Ring-fencing' of regimes, whereby preferential tax regimes are partly or fully insulated from the domestic markets of the country providing the regime'
3. Lack of transparency, which makes it harder for the home countries of the investments to take defensive measures
4. Lack of effective exchange of information

Eight other factors are mentioned that help determine the existence of harmful preferential tax regimes: (i) an artificial definition of the tax base; (ii) a failure to adhere to international transfer-pricing principles; (iii) the exemption of foreign source income; (iv) a negotiable tax rate or tax base; (v) the existence of secrecy provisions; (vi) access to a wide network of tax treaties; (vii) the promotion of regimes as tax minimisation mechanism; (viii) the encouragement of purely tax driven arrangements.

4.1.2   The OECD Recommendations for Member State Actions

Concerning domestic legislation and practices, the OECD recommends member countries enforce, or adopt, a number of rules in a manner consistent with the aim of curbing harmful tax practices. Those rules regard: Controlled Foreign Corporations (CFC), foreign investment funds, transfer-pricing, and access to banking information. It also recommends restricting participation exemption and other systems of exempting foreign income to income that has not benefited from harmful tax practices; adopting rules on foreign information reporting; and making public the conditions for granting, denying or revoking advance rulings.

Regarding tax conventions, the 1998 Report recommends that treaties be modified to include restrictions to treaty benefit entitlement where entities and income have benefited from harmful tax practices. A clarification of anti-abuse rules and doctrines in treaties should also be included. The report recommends that a list should be drawn and maintained by the Committee of the provisions used by countries to exclude specific income or entities from treaty benefit. The list should serve as a reference for further tax convention negotiation and basis for discussion in the Forum. Moreover, the Report recommends as defensive measure that member countries terminate their tax treaties with tax havens. Finally, action is also prescribed for tax administrations: the intensification of exchange of information, co-ordinated enforcement regimes (joint audits, joint training activities), the assistance in recovery of tax claims.

The last set of guidelines regards international co-operation and mainly includes two types of provisions: a 'standstill' provision, which basically requires member States to freeze their harmful tax practices; a roll-back provision which requires member States to eliminate their harmful tax practices by 31 December 2001 at the latest.

Both Switzerland and Luxembourg refused to sign the report and to commit to the recommendations it contains. They expressed their disagreement with the non-comprehensive approach to tax competition taken by the OECD whose measures focus on geographically mobile activities and did not consider other factors such as economic, social and institutional circumstances in its assessment.

4.2   The 2000 OECD Report

In June 2000, the OECD issued its follow up report entitled '*Towards Global Tax Co-operation – Progress in Identifying and Eliminating Harmful Tax Practices*'. It outlines the results obtained up to date of the Forum's work and includes:

– Identification of potentially harmful preferential regimes in Member countries under the factors of the 1998 report;
– Identification of jurisdictions meeting the criteria for being tax havens under the factors of the 1998 report;
– Update on work with non-member economies and proposals for taking this work forward.

The 2000 report contains two lists. The first classifies 35 jurisdictions as tax havens judged by the criteria of the 1998 report. There were 47 jurisdictions initially identified as potential havens and reviewed by four working groups; of these, six were dropped from the list, and a further six made advanced commitments (Bermuda, Cayman Islands, Cyprus, Malta, Mauritius, San Marino), leaving the 35 listed in the table below.

Andorra*	Grenada	Niue
Anguilla	Guernsey/Sark/ Alderney	Panama
Antigua and Barbuda	Isle of Man	Samoa
Aruba	Jersey	Seychelles
Bahamas	Liberia*	St Lucia
Bahrain	Liechtenstein*	St Christopher and Nevis
Barbados	Maldives	St Vincent & the Grenadines
Belize	Marshall Islands*	Tonga
British Virgin Islands	Monaco*	Turks and Caicos Islands
Cook Islands	Montserrat	US Virgin Islands
Dominica	Nauru*	Vanuatu*
Gibraltar	Netherland Antilles	

* Countries that have not agreed to co-operate with the OECD as at April 2002.

Since the publication of the list, most of the listed havens have either been removed from it by the OECD (Barbados, Maldives, Tonga), or have agreed, more or less reluctantly, to commit to the OECD guidelines. As at April 2002, 7 jurisdictions still refuse to do so (Andorra, Liberia, Liechtenstein, Marshall Islands, Monaco, Nauru, Vanuatu).

The second list identifies 47 preferential tax regimes of OECD member countries as being potentially harmful. It is worth mentioning that holding company regimes were not part of that list of harmful practices but were merely mentioned as being under consideration. The two lists are under different timetables too. In the 1998 report, member countries have already committed themselves to eliminate the harmful features of their preferential tax regimes. They must eliminate those features by April 2003. The listed tax havens had not made such a commitment and had until the deadline of 28 February 2002, to decide whether they would co-operate with the OECD and commit to the aims of the Forum. They would then have until 31 July 2005 to eliminate harmful tax practices. Those who have not expressed their commitment by the February 2002 deadline have been named on a list of 'uncooperative tax havens' that the OECD drew after the deadline and may incur sanctions.

The principle of the Forum is that member countries will adopt a common approach to restraining harmful tax competition. It offers harmful tax havens and harmful preferential tax regimes the opportunity to 'clean up their act' and co-operate. If they refuse, the OECD prescribes a number of defensive measures that can be used against those jurisdictions that fail to co-operate. A certain degree of autonomy is left to member countries in the medium used to implement these measures (under their domestic legislation or under tax treaties).

A few of the defensive measures proposed by the OECD are:
- disallowing deductions, exemptions, credits or other allowances related to transactions with uncooperative havens or to transactions taking advantage of their harmful tax practices;
- requiring comprehensive information reporting rules for transactions that involve an uncooperative tax haven or that take advantage of their harmful tax practices, supported by substantial penalties for inaccurate reporting or non-reporting of such transactions;
- imposing 'transactional' charges or levies on certain transactions involving uncooperative tax havens

This is the OECD as it stood before the U.S. elections and the change in politics it brought with them. Since then, the Bush administration has somewhat slowed the OECD momentum and forced it to water down its objectives. The positions of the EU, the tax havens and the USA *vis-à-vis* the OECD initiative are examined in the next section.

5. MULTILATERAL ACTION REQUIRES POLITICAL MOMENTUM

5.1 The Concurrence of EU and OECD Policies Against Tax Competition

5.1.1 EU Tax Policy Focuses on Harmful Tax Competition

The stance taken by the OECD on harmful tax competition has coincided with the tax policy of the European Union shifting from the issue of tax harmonisation and tax neutrality to that of harmful tax competition. The new focus engineered by Mario Monti, EU commissioner for taxation from 1995 to 1999, achieved some success and gathered a consensus from the 15 Members resulting in the adoption of a number of measures, including a Code of Conduct against harmful tax practices.

Previously, EU tax policy strategy had been based on the grounds of tax neutrality. Co-ordination of taxes was promoted in a deliberately non-political manner as a technical, hence presumably consensual, means to achieving efficiency and neutrality[12]. It focused on removing from each domestic tax system the impediments to free trade and investment in the single market. This strategy however did not produce the expected unifying result. Instead, the debate became polarised into coalitions conflicting on EU politics. This policy generated two directives, but was eventually stalled.

When Monti took over the EU tax policy portfolio in 1995, he deliberately withdrew it from the counter-productive technical debate it had sunk into. He restored the political dimension of taxation and placed European tax policy within a broader political framework. The looming negative impact of uncontrolled tax competition on the welfare state and employment proved a powerful enough political motivation to unite EU members into the necessary consensus and taking action.

The new EU momentum has certainly been influential to the OECD initiatives and vice-versa. Under article 13 of the OECD Convention, the EU Commission takes part in the work of the OECD and both organisations share

---

[12] See Radaelli (1998).

a number of members. Further than the timing of their measures, their methods and substance are also consistent.

5.1.2   EU Measures Against Harmful Tax Competition

There are three major items in the EU 'tax package to tackle harmful tax competition'[13]. The first is an agreement reached on 1 December 1997 on a Code of Conduct with respect to business taxation. The second item concerns harmonising the taxation of savings. The last are measures to eliminate taxes on cross-border interest and royalty payments between companies.

The Code of Conduct for Business Taxation is a non-binding document by which Member States undertake to avoid measures that involve harmful tax competition. Similarly to the OECD 1998 Report, it identifies potentially harmful regimes in the field of business taxation and gives criteria for the assessment of harmful tax measures. It includes a commitment not to introduce new harmful tax regimes and to rollback existing regimes. The Code also includes a monitoring procedure.

The scope and operation of the EU Code and OECD Guidelines differ in the sense that the OECD guidelines are limited to financial and other service activities whereas the Code looks at business activities in general (although with emphasis on mobile activities). However, both sets of measures are compatible, particularly as regards the criteria used to identify harmful preferential regimes.

5.2   The Tax Havens' Reaction Against the OECD Initiative

The response from the tax havens to the OECD set of measures has been mixed. Six of them (Bermuda, Cayman Islands, Cyprus, Malta, Mauritius and San Marino) have accepted the OECD approach at least in principle and, in advance of the 2000 report, made a public political commitment to co-operate. They have thus not been named on the initial list. Most other havens have reacted differently. Although a good proportion of them has now agreed to commit to the OECD guidelines, they initially expressed outrage at the OECD methods that they condemned as neo-colonial bullying from the richest and most powerful nations[14]. They organised themselves into an 'Offshore Task Force' to counter the OECD and press it to consider them as negotiating partners rather than threaten them into submission. They also lobbied very

---

[13] See Commission of the European Communities (1997).
[14] See Ugur (2000).

vehemently the U.S. administration and legislature to get them to withdraw their support from the OECD initiative.

The criticism expressed by the offshore centres is understandable and it will be essential that member countries, as well as calling for co-operation from the tax havens, tackle their own harmful practices and persuade the recalcitrant Switzerland and Luxembourg to comply. If they fail to do so, they run the risk of being accused of double standards and of discrediting the OECD aims on harmful tax competition altogether. How could the OECD legitimately justify the imposition of sanctions on uncooperative havens on the one hand and tolerate the Swiss's non-participation on the other?

The havens' concerns were to some extent understood by the OECD which then established an alternative process that sets out in greater detail the terms of the commitment sought and a proposed timetable for implementation. This is presented in the OECD November 2001 progress report with the modifications to the OECD measures reflecting the improved dialogue with tax havens and the changes of the international political scene since 1998.

To date, 7 of the 35 blacklisted havens have still not been persuaded to commit to the OECD objectives (see table above).

5.3   The U.S. Position Towards the OECD Initiative

The arrival of the Bush administration at the White House also signalled a change of attitude towards the OECD initiative. In June 2001, Treasury Secretary O'Neill made it clear that he considered that some tax competition is good and that he wants action against preferential tax regimes soft-pedalled. He called for the OECD to refocus its initiative from harmful tax practices to the objective of exchange of information against tax evasion[15], however he supports maintaining the work against tax havens.

As a result, the OECD has seen its attempt at multilateral action lose some of its strength. The modifications to the proposals include:
a) An extension of the deadline for making commitments under the project to 28 February 2002;
b) Limiting commitment sought to 'transparency' and 'effective exchange of information';
c) The application of a potential framework of co-ordinated defensive measures (anti-tax avoidance measures) to apply to jurisdictions outside the OECD no earlier than it would apply to OECD member countries. This would be no earlier than 2003.

---

[15]   Paul O'Neill letter to the OECD, 7 June 2001.

Furthermore, the OECD's threat to apply widespread sanctions to jurisdictions that do not agree to its demands will probably have to be abandoned and replaced by leaving individual members or groups of them to take action individually. The organisation will probably also have to give up its efforts to end discriminatory tax practices, such as the 'International Business Companies' which offer privileged tax regimes to non-residents. That leaves essentially 'transparency' as a major goal of the initiative but even there, the U.S. only signed up to a very tight definition that includes the 'need for countries to be able to obtain *specific* information from other countries upon request in order to prevent the illegal evasion of their tax laws by a rich few'[16] but opposing *automatic* exchange of information.

6.   CONCLUSION

The political momentum for the co-ordinated OECD proposal is still strong in Europe. The rephrasing of its support by the U.S. leaves the OECD initiative essentially refocused on exchange of information issues, which would nevertheless constitute a major step forward, if the project is implemented. For this is were the real problem lies: can the OECD initiative be implemented considering the notable exception of Switzerland and Luxembourg, that are still persisting in their refusal to sign the 1998 protocol? All OECD member countries would need to be seen to comply before the initiative could be legitimately imposed on non-OECD countries.

It is significant indeed that many of the jurisdictions which have reluctantly agreed to co-operate with the OECD have made conditional commitments. The condition ties the havens' agreement to amend transparency and information exchange laws to all offshore jurisdictions and OECD members doing likewise. The future negotiations with Switzerland, Luxembourg and Liechtenstein will thus prove crucial to the success of the whole initiative.

STUDY QUESTIONS

1. Consider the impact of tax competition and increased capital mobility on foreign-source income, both from portfolio and from direct investment, and their consequences on tax rates and tax bases.

[16]   Paul O'Neill's statement to the G-7 meeting, May 2001.

2. Explain the objectives, functioning and conditions for application of Controlled Foreign Company legislation.
3. Compare the OECD initiative against harmful tax competition from the point of view of an OECD member country and from the point of view of a tax haven. List and analyse the differences between the OECD measures against preferential tax regimes and those against tax havens.
4. What are the limitations of unilateral and bilateral actions in international taxation?
5. 'Among the traditional differences between U.S. and Western Europe tax policy are: (a) the imposition of annual tax on net wealth as well as tax on bequest and gifts; (b) extremely high payroll tax rates; and (c) the use of value-added tax that has become harmonised. Because they are open economies, Western Europe, Canada and Japan are extremely sensitive to tax policies in other countries. On the one hand, they are reluctant to eliminate tax preferences for saving and domestic investment for fear that capital will flow abroad. On the other hand they are impressed with the success of tax reform in the United States, especially the large reduction of tax rates it provided.'
   Discuss this quote from Bruce Zagaris (1999) in the light of the OECD measures against harmful tax competition and the EU Code of Conduct.

REFERENCES

Avi-Yonah, R. (2000), 'Globalization, Tax Competition and the Fiscal Crisis of the Welfare State', *Harvard Law Review*, Vol. 113(7), pp. 1573-671.

Commission of the European Communities (1997), *A Package to Tackle Harmful Tax Competition in the European Union*, COM (97) 564 final, Brussels.

Ernst & Young International (1999), 'Transfer-pricing 1999 Global Survey: Practices, Perceptions and Trends for 2000 and Beyond', *Tax Notes International*, Vol. 19(20), p. 1907.

FATF (2000), *Review to Identify Non-Cooperative Countries or Territories - Increasing the Worldwide Effectiveness of Anti-Money Laundering Measures*, Paris: OECD.

FATF (2001), *Review to Identify Non-Cooperative Countries or Territories: Increasing the Worldwide Effectiveness of Anti-Money Laundering Measures*, Paris: OECD.

Hampton, M. (1995), *A Preliminary Analysis of the Offshore Interface Between Tax Havens, Tax Evasion, Corruption and Economic Development*, University of Portsmouth.

Hetherington-Gore, J. (2000), 'The EU and Offshore: A Review of the Year 2000', www.tax-news.com

Hetherington-Gore, J. (2001), 'The Future of Offshore as a Business Location Following the EU/OECD/FATF/FSF Initiatives', www.tax-news.com

Lodin, S. (2001), 'International Tax Issues in a Rapidly Changing World', *Bulletin for International Fiscal Documentation*, Vol. 55(1), pp. 2-7.

OECD (1987), *International Tax Avoidance and Evasion – Four Related Studies*, Fiscal Affairs Committee, Paris: OECD.

OECD (1995), *Transfer-pricing Guidelines for Multinational Enterprises and Tax Administration*, Fiscal Affairs Committee, Paris: OECD.

OECD (1998), *Harmful Tax Competition – An Emerging Global Issue*, Fiscal Affairs Committee, Paris: OECD.

OECD (2000), *Framework for a Collective Memorandum of Understanding on Eliminating Harmful Tax Practices*, Fiscal Affairs Committee, Paris: OECD.

OECD (2000), *Towards Global Tax Co-operation – Progress in Identifying and Eliminating Harmful Tax Practices*, Fiscal Affairs Committee, Paris: OECD.

OECD (2001), *The OECD's Project on Harmful Tax Practices – The 2001 Progress Report*, Fiscal Affairs Committee, Paris: OECD.

Ogley, A. (1993), *Principles of International Tax – A Multinational Perspective*, London: Interfisc Publishing.

Owens, J. (1998), 'Taxation Within a Context of Economic Globalisation', *Bulletin for International Fiscal Documentation*, Vol. 52(7), pp. 290-296.

Owens, J. (1999), 'Curbing Harmful Tax Practices', *OECD Observer*, Paris: OECD.

Owens, J. (2000), 'Towards World Tax Co-operation', *OECD Observer*, 21 November.

Owens, J. (2001), 'Promoting Fair Tax Competition', www.oecd.org

Picciotto, S. (1992), *International Business Taxation*, London: Weidenfeld and Nicolson.

Radaelli, C. (1998), 'Policy Narratives in the European Union: The Case of Harmful Tax Competition', Robert Shuman Centre Working Paper n.98/34, Florence: European University Institute.

Scholes, M.S., Wolfson, M.A., Erickson, M., Maydew, E.L., and Shevlin, T. (2002), *Taxes and Business Strategy: A Planning Approach*, 2nd edition, Upper Saddle River, NJ: Prentice-Hall.

Sorensen, P.B. (2000), 'The Case for International Tax Co-ordination Reconsidered', *Economic Policy*, Vol. 16(31), pp. 429-444.

Tanzi, V. (1998), 'The Impact of Economic Globalization on Taxation', *Bulletin for International Fiscal Documentation*, Vol. 52(8/9), pp. 338-343.

Zagaris, B. (1999), 'The Assault on Low-Tax Jurisdictions: a Call for Balance and Debate', *Tax Management International Journal*, Vol. 28(8), pp. 474-500.

USEFUL WEBSITES

For daily updated information on offshore jurisdictions: www.tax-news.com
The OECD website: www.oecd.org
The Financial Action Task Force website: www.oecd.org/fatf

Chapter 6

The Future International Tax Environment

SIMON JAMES
University of Exeter, U.K.

Key words: international tax systems; STEP analysis; management; tax competition

Abstract: This chapter examines trends that are likely to influence the shape of the future
international tax system. The basic strategic management technique of STEP
analysis is used to examine relevant changes to Social, Technological,
Economic and Political factors affecting taxation. Important future influences
include the increasing complexity of socio-economic systems and that trade will
become increasingly global and more competitive. Fundamental technological
developments, including the development of the internet and the world wide
web, have some important implications for tax systems including the continued
use of traditional tax concepts such as 'source', 'destination' and 'residence'.

1. INTRODUCTION

Taxation is one of the most important variables in economic decision-making, both nationally and internationally. As many commercial decisions have long-term implications they are likely to be affected by the way tax systems develop in the future. Perhaps surprisingly, textbooks on strategic management often devote very little space to tax considerations. For example, one of the best textbooks on business strategy is Johnson and Scholes (1999). However, the fifth edition published in 1999 and expanded to 972 pages does not even refer to taxation in the index. 'Taxation policy' is listed as a factor to be considered in conducting an analysis of environmental issues but there is no systematic analysis of taxation as a factor in management decisions.

The purpose of this chapter is therefore to examine the trends that are likely to influence the shape of the future international tax system. Although the management literature does not usually pay much attention to taxation issues, management techniques provide a useful framework for analysing such trends. This chapter uses the basic management technique of STEP analysis to explore the changes that are underway and presents some of the social, technological, economic and political factors involved. It soon becomes clear that important trends include the increasing complexity of socio-economic systems which is likely to increase the complexity of the tax systems that have to accommodate them. Nevertheless, the most dramatic changes will be associated with fundamental technological developments including the internet and the world wide web. The development of international electronic commerce presents a considerable challenge to existing tax systems and there are accounting implications. For example, certain economic events may no longer continue to have easily identifiable physical locations. Such changes will substantially increase the need for governments to co-operate and to co-ordinate their tax systems.

2.   GENERAL ISSUES

Taxation is an extremely important part of modern economies. Figures from the OECD (1999) indicate that for all OECD member countries tax revenue is substantial. If social security contributions are counted as taxation, as they should be on most definitions of taxation (James and Nobes, 2000, pp. 163-4), total tax revenue ranges between a third and a half of GDP at market prices for most OECD countries. Furthermore, there are some important developments, including the use of tax competition and tax harmonisation that have some important implications for national tax systems.

Predicting the future is, of course, very difficult and perhaps particularly so for taxation that is so embedded in economic systems and subject to constant change and modification. This chapter does not pretend to offer any precise picture of the future tax environment, but it attempts to examine some of the key factors that will influence it and to identify areas of potential difficulty. A limitation of many contemporary studies of taxation is that they are concerned with existing tax systems. Furthermore, comparative tax studies have tended to be confined to a limited number of issues or countries or both rather than taking a wider and more global view of the situation. These considerations are not just important for individual taxpayers. Governments also need to consider the likely future international tax environment. It is important for revenue authorities to anticipate the implications of future changes for tax systems before any significant undesirable consequences become apparent. As will be shown below, such developments may undermine the integrity of national tax systems and influence the ways in which governments can raise revenue in the future.

The development of an increasingly global economy adds a further important dimension topic but it has been suggested, by Yip (1997) for example, that most multinational companies appear to lack an adequate global strategy. It is fairly certain that many of them have not developed an adequate strategy that includes future tax issues either. To do this they will need to consider the way the international tax system is likely to develop and how it might affect their decisions regarding location, finance and operational issues.

Some work has been done and some trends identified. For example, Picciotto (1992, p. xiii) points out that the taxation of international income has been based formally on bilateral treaties but in practice its administration has relied on a 'community of specialists' consisting of business advisers and national officials. The growth of international corporations and their use of various devices such as transfer pricing and thin capitalisation to divert profits to countries with favourable tax regimes has put a great deal of pressure on other tax systems.

Nevertheless, the full implications of these and other factors, such as changes in technology, merit closer examination. The paper will begin with a simple model examining the process of tax change. It will then go on to summarise a STEP analysis and discuss particular factors such as technological developments and international tax competition.

3. THE DEVELOPMENT OF TAX SYSTEMS

There are several possible ways of modelling phenomena such as the development of tax systems and one helpful approach is the use of forcefield analysis developed from the work of Lewin (1951). Some individuals might view the development of tax systems as a process of rational reforms in changing circumstances. The drawback with that optimistic approach is that it is not reflected in the actual process of tax reform and does not take account of the complex array of different interests and factors involved in the way tax systems develop and the nature of the political process itself. It also overlooks the considerable innocence of many contributors to fiscal discussions with respect to the overall characteristics of an effective and equitable tax system (James and Nobes, 2000, pp. 20-103).

Forcefield analysis reflects the reality that at any time, there will be all sorts of different pressures for change developing, and there will also be a variety of forms of resistance to change. Inertia is also an important political factor as Rose and Karran (1987) demonstrate with particular reference to taxation. As they put it: '*if keeping out of trouble is a basic law of politics, then not making decisions about taxes is one way to avoid trouble - in the short run at least.'*

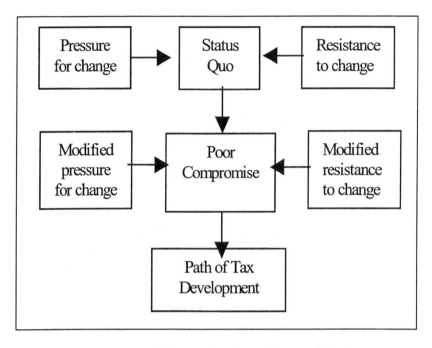

Figure 1. A Forcefield Approach to the Development of Taxation

A summary of this process is illustrated in Figure 1. Here the pressure for change meets the status quo with the latter supported by an array of forces resistant to change. The optimal outcome might be identified perhaps, as in this example, somewhere behind the resistance to change. Eventually the pressure for change might overcome the resisting forces, but the latter remain strong enough to deflect change from the optimal position and the result is an unsatisfactory compromise. This, of course, is only part of the continuous process of change so, as also indicated in Figure 1, the pressure and resistance to change is modified but continues and the optimal position is also changing. The development of tax systems can only be properly analysed when it is appreciated that it is a dynamic process.

There are many examples of such a scenario to choose from. One notable sequence of events arose from the pressure to reform local government finance in the UK. For many years there had been opposition to the main form of local authority taxation – rates. This finally led to the introduction of the poll tax which was such a fiscal disaster that it led to civil disobedience (Mair and Damania, 1992) and became a factor in the downfall of Prime Minister Margaret Thatcher (Gibson, 1990). The failure of the poll tax in turn led the introduction of the council tax, which is still far from the ideal form of local taxation.

There are many forces resistant to change but an important group of them relates to a lack of a clear view of the requirements of a good tax system, an appreciation of the need for change and how that change should be achieved. In an Australian context, the example given by Grbich (1997, p. 3) is that the 'bitter experience of the GST debacle and 20 years of faltering reform...have done nothing to clear up the confusion.' It would be worthwhile to outline the nature of optimal positions and the likely unsatisfactory compromises that might arise but this is beyond the scope of the present paper. What will be helpful in contributing to such an analysis, however, is to examine some of the main factors involved.

4.   METHODS OF ANALYSING DEVELOPMENTS IN TAXATION

If such a forcefield model captures something of the nature of the development of tax systems, the next stage is to examine more closely the pressures for change and the pressures resisting change, or to use other methods to predict the likely shape of the future international tax environment. There are several possible approaches but all must in some way or another incorporate likely developments in the international economic, social, technological and political environment in which individual businesses have to operate.

4.1   Economic Forecasting

One method is economic forecasting but used on its own this suffers from some severe limitations. Cairncross (1971, p. 123) wrote that:

> *To an economist it is a little shocking that forecasting should have been so long neglected as a subject of study...Anyone who jests at economic forecasting - as everybody does from time to time - is really expressing his scepticism of the scientific foundations of economics.*

Denis Healey as U.K. Chancellor of the Exchequer put it quite well when he said in his Budget speech of 12 November 1974 that:

The best forecast(s) that the Treasury can make of expenditure, imports and gross domestic product...give a spurious impression of certainty. But their origin lies in the extrapolation from a partially known past, through an unknown present, to an unknowable future according to theories about the causal relationships between certain economic variables which are hotly disputed by academic economists, and may well in fact change from country to country or from decade to decade. (quoted in James, 1984, p. 80).

Economic forecasting can contribute to our knowledge but its accuracy is questionable and it does not satisfactorily incorporate many of the factors relevant to the shape of future taxation.

4.2   Scenarios

Another possibility is to construct plausible scenarios of likely economic and social developments that can then be used to develop strategies (Schwartz, 1992; Johnson and Scholes, 1999, pp. 111-4). This is most appropriate for long term planning and Johnson and Scholes point out that for some sectors, such as the oil industry, there is a need to consider a long term view for planning for up to 20 years ahead.

Constructing scenarios also has some advantages and might be a worthwhile exercise elsewhere but it does not always analyse the relevant factors systematically.

4.3   STEP Analysis

A method that seems to offer a useful and systematic analysis in this context is known as STEP analysis in which the relevant Social, Technological, Economic and Political factors are examined in turn as laid out, for example, by Mercer (1992). There are alternative formulations of this approach such as the 'PEST' analysis by Johnson and Scholes (1999, pp. 104-7) which reorders the main categories into Political, Economic, Social and Technological. There are some other variants that incorporate additional dimensions but these will not be included here. In analysing the international tax environment using a STEP analysis, it is useful to look not only at the current position but also at likely future developments. The forcefield analysis approach suggests tax reform comes about when the pain of change finally outweighs the pain of continuing with the present system. Therefore, there might be considerable advantages in examining the powerful pressures likely to influence the development of international business taxation and how helpful tax reform might be anticipated.

5.   A STEP ANALYSIS OF THE DEVELOPMENT OF TAX SYSTEMS

STEP analyses have been undertaken in the private sector but very little has been done in this way for taxation. Some earlier work by James and Wallschutzky (1995) and by James (1995; 1997) examined such factors with respect to tax administration. It is not necessary to repeat that analysis in this chapter though one of the main conclusions was that tax systems will become increasingly complex in the future. There have also been studies of change with respect to particular taxes, for example by Chennells and Griffith (1997) who examined corporate income taxation. If the STEP procedure is followed with respect to international taxation, likely trends emerge fairly clearly as some of the key Social, Technological, Economic, and Political factors are dealt with in turn.

5.1   Social Aspects

Several important social trends will influence the development of tax systems. They include demographic changes, social mobility, and increasing levels of education and consumer awareness. In many countries, such factors are a major cause of the increasing complexity of tax systems. One of the main demographic factors is a steady increase in the average age in many populations. Older people in prosperous economies tend to have more complex financial affairs, with more of them accumulating or drawing on a range of investments and pensions. Families are becoming less stable in many countries and one result of a higher divorce rate is that the number and variety of sources of personal incomes are increasing. There is also an increase in social and geographical mobility. The level of education achieved by many people is rising which, together with increased incomes, may encourage and enable them to take a more effective and active interest in their tax affairs. These and similar sociological factors will increase the pressure on tax systems to become even more complex in order to take account of increasingly complicated and changing social circumstances.

5.2   Technological Aspects

Technological change is likely to cause the most drastic changes in the future tax environment. The most important phenomena are the development of the internet and the world wide web. The internet is a network of computer networks that enables computer users to share services and communicate with each other in ways that transcend national boundaries. The world wide web is the graphical hypertext part of the internet that incorporates images, video and audio elements as well as text. It can also contain embedded links to other web documents or information. As we know, the internet was originally designed to reduce the damage to communications by nuclear attack since there is no central computer that can be targeted. In the same way, the internet poses enforcement problems for revenue agencies as services and funds can flow in ways that are very difficult for revenue authorities to track.

Technological change is a major factor in the development of the global economy. Electronic commerce - the ability to undertake transactions involving the exchange of goods and services electronically - is a rapidly growing phenomenon (May and Wat, 1998). There are now both retail and wholesale catalogues of goods and services which are accessible on the world wide web. Many commercial items are suitable for trading over the internet, for example computer software and recorded entertainment. On-line information, including research databases, periodicals and some encyclopaedias are available, as are consulting and similar services and financial transactions and stock trading now take place electronically around the world.

Tax systems themselves, of course, have taken advantage of technological change, for example with the introduction of the facility to transmit tax returns electronically to the revenue authorities and also to pay taxes electronically (see for example James and Wallschutzky, 1993). The implications of the wider technological revolution have also begun to be examined in many countries. Work includes that done by the Australian Tax Office (1997) and Wallschutzky (1998) in Australia, Revenue Canada Taxation (1998), the Inland Revenue Department (1997) in New Zealand and by the Department of the Treasury (1996) in the USA. One issue is that in some ways physical national boundaries are less relevant than they once were and there is the possibility that different countries will try to assert inconsistent rules leading to conflict between different jurisdictions and uncertain and inconsistent taxation. It will be necessary to establish how existing tax systems are to be applied to international electronic commerce.

Tax systems have evolved in a world where commercial events take place in clearly identifiable physical locations. Tax can be levied on the 'source principle' whereby a country levies tax on income arising within its jurisdiction whether that income is for the benefit of residents or non-residents. Residence itself is also a basis of taxation. Usually taxpayers resident within a particular jurisdiction are taxed on a wider range of incomes than non-resident taxpayers. In terms of indirect taxation, tax can be based on the 'origin principle', that goods or services should be taxed according to where they originate or on a 'destination' basis when taxation is levied on the basis of where they are consumed. With electronic commerce transactions can take place on computer servers anywhere and in a sense occur in some form of intangible 'cyberspace'. It will not always be easy to see how such transactions fit into traditional concepts as 'source', 'residence', 'origin' and 'destination'.

One result in particular is that taxation based on the source of income is likely to prove more difficult to apply in the future. It may be that the emphasis will have to shift to taxation based on residence, though the concept of residence also encounters some difficulties when transactions are carried out in cyberspace. However, if residence did become more important for tax purposes this in turn may have implications for the migration of individuals and enterprises between countries and the effects of tax competition discussed below. Another area is the response to the difficulty of ensuring tax compliance in respect of electronic transactions that are difficult or impossible for revenue authorities to trace. Some forms of electronic money might pose similar problems to cash in terms of tax evasion. Other difficulties may also be involved in identifying who is party to various economic events and verifying records of electronic transactions. It would seem that there are important issues of this sort that will require considerable international co-operation in the future.

This could be difficult to achieve since, of course, not all countries have the same priorities. However, the benefits from the development of global electronic commerce in the form of increased wealth in all countries are very large. One aim therefore should be to avoid the creation of unnecessary barriers to its development, including taxation. To this end, a number of moves have been made. For example, the Organisation for Economic Co-operation and Development (OECD) held a conference on the subject in Turku, Finland in November 1997. As it made clear in a press release (of 26 November 1997), in the area of taxation, no single country can resolve the issues on its own. The OECD therefore suggested the creation of an internet forum where all parties could meet for discussions - in other words, there was the recognition that cyberspace solutions might be needed for cyberspace problems. The participants at the OECD conference indicated that they supported the well-established criteria of tax neutrality, fairness, certainty and the avoidance of excessive taxation. Such criteria remain a suitable guide for future progress. At the G7 conference on electronic commerce and business in the global marketplace, held in Bonn on 7-9 April 1997, one of the conclusions was the importance of creating certainty through a globally accepted legal and policy framework. Leading the way, the G7 Policy Group invited public discussion via the internet. A further OECD conference took place in Ottawa on 7-9 October 1998 on the theme of *A Borderless World: Realising the Potential of Global Electronic Commerce*. This was the first OECD ministerial level meeting that invited the active participation of international organisations, business, labour, consumer and public interest groups. Nearly one thousand people attended and it was hoped that the conference would 'help promote greater international policy comparability' concerning electronic commerce (OECD press release, Paris, 13 October 1998). Further discussion of taxation and electronic commerce appears in Hickey (2000), Mann *et al.* (2000) and the chapter by Neil Warren in this volume.

5.3   Economic Aspects

Powerful economic trends will also affect the development of the tax system. Although, of course, incomes can fall as well as rise, the general trend is for *per capita* income to rise. This is likely to contribute to the increasing variety and complexity of financial instruments and presents new challenges for regulation machinery (in a European context see for example McKenzie and Khalidi, 1996). Globalisation has been much discussed by commentators, such as Yip (1997) mentioned above, and seems to be accompanied by increasing mobility of capital and labour. Together with the sociological and technological factors already raised, it can be seen that one of the strongest trends is that taxation will continue to become more complex. Although there are movements towards tax simplification from time to time, they usually fall far short of becoming a consistent strategy for simplification and so the increase in complexity continues (James and Wallschutzky, 1997).

Another economic factor has been an increase in competitive pressure in many markets. In the past competition has often been restricted by physical distance between competing producers and because often only very limited information has been available to buyers and sellers. Many enterprises have survived because they have been located sufficiently far from effective competition or their customers have been not been fully aware of rival goods and services. With technological developments of the sort described above, physical distance becomes less important in many markets and consumers have access to a great deal more information than they had previously. All of this means that many enterprises are likely to face greater competition than they have done in the past. In the international setting, trade rivalry has led to a number of developments. These include tax competition between countries in order to attract or keep economic resources and increased pressure for greater tax harmonisation to overcome some of the perceived disadvantages of tax competition.

5.4 Political Aspects

Political factors present a range of pressures on the development of tax systems and some of these have already been considered by, for example, Radaelli (1997). They include the growth of the public sector and its consequent requirement for tax revenue, the environment, protective tariffs, tax competition and tax harmonisation.

One of the most dramatic economic changes in the twentieth century has been the growth of the public sector. OECD (1998b) figures suggest that member countries will have general government outlays ranging from about a quarter to over half nominal gross domestic product. A large proportion of this spending in industrialised countries is made up of different forms of welfare expenditure. The political environment is such that this major commitment is almost certain to continue at a high level (Boreham *et al.* 1996) and to influence the tax system, not only in its demand for revenue but also in the interaction between social welfare payments, economic incentives and tax liability.

There has also been an increasing concern for the environment. It has been recognised that some economic activities, such as those causing pollution, impose costs on the wider community and that it might be possible to improve the situation by assigning such costs to the consumers and producers by imposing a special tax. The result has been proposals for various forms of corrective taxes such as 'pollution charges', 'green taxes' and so on and these are examined by authors such as Cordes *et al.* (1990), Nicolaisen *et al.* (1991), Smith (1992), Symons *et al.* (1994) and Oates, (1995). As pollution and other environmental concerns are not limited to particular tax jurisdictions, a greater degree of international co-operation might be forthcoming.

Another concern is the use of tariff barriers to favour domestic production even though the resulting fall in international trade can make all countries worse off, including the one that originally imposed the tariffs (see, for instance Kindleberger and Lindert, 1978). The result may be global recession. The General Agreement on Tariffs and Trade (GATT) and its successor, the World Trade Organisation, have been a major force in reducing the average level of tariffs to only about 10 per cent of the level when GATT began its work in 1948 (*The Economist*, 16 May 1998). It is to be hoped that the mistakes of the past in this respect will not be repeated in the future but there are pressures to move in such a direction. What needs to be considered is international co-operation with respect to problems raised by technological advance, tax competition and tax harmonisation.

A different form of international rivalry takes the form of tax competition (for further discussion on harmful tax competition, see also the chapter by Marika Toumi in this volume). This may be defined as the 'competition between different tax jurisdictions to encourage businesses and individuals to locate in their areas' (James, 1998: 144) and the issue has stimulated tax policy debate in Europe (Radaelli, 1998). Clearly some countries may choose to have lower tax rates than others for all sorts of reasons. Defining 'harmful preferential tax regimes' precisely is therefore difficult but the OECD (1998a) suggested there are four key factors that might assist in identifying them, namely:

a) the regime imposes a low or zero effective tax rate on the relevant income;
b) the regime is "ring-fenced" (in other words, certain activities are isolated for tax purposes from other activities);
c) the operation of the regime is non-transparent; and
d) the jurisdiction operating the regime does not effectively exchange information with other countries.

Not all the effects of tax competition are negative. Tax competition is designed to provide an incentive for incoming investment and it might generate new as well as diverted investment. It has also been argued by those who wish to control public expenditure that tax competition might have a further beneficial effect in encouraging governments generally to keep tax rates down in order to avoid the loss of economic resources. However, there is a general presumption that artificial flows of economic resources encouraged only by the potential for tax avoidance are not likely to be in the interests of the global community as a whole. The world as a whole cannot make itself better off in this way. Instead it is likely to make itself significantly worse off if industries locate, not where it is economically most advantageous, but where the tax regime is most favourable. One concern of most revenue authorities is that it increases the scope for tax avoidance and possibly tax evasion as well. More immediately, it can cause difficulties for individual countries in maintaining the integrity of their tax systems.

The difficulty has been recognised by many commentators and some international organisations. For example, in May 1996 the Ministers of Member Countries of the OECD asked that organisation to 'develop measures to counter the distorting impact of harmful tax competition and financing decisions' and this resulted in the publication of the report already referred to above (OECD, 1998a). The Report pointed out that it is difficult for individual countries to combat such harmful tax practices without putting their taxpayers and economies at a competitive disadvantage. As well as a number of specific recommendations, the Report suggested there was a strong case to intensify international co-operation in formulating a response to the problem and one general dimension is the development of tax harmonisation.

A further development has been moves towards tax harmonisation and a prime example has been the European Union. Tax harmonisation has the advantage of reducing economic distortions caused by different tax systems in different countries. However there may be sound reasons why some countries have different tax arrangements and progress towards tax harmonisation has been slow and difficult (James, 2000).

6.   CONCLUSION

A basic analysis of the likely future international tax environment, such as that presented here, suggests that tax systems will become more complex in the future and trade will become increasingly global and more competitive. The most dramatic changes are those associated with technological developments, in particular the internet and the world wide web. Such technical advances have the potential to increase world prosperity on a large scale and unnecessary barriers to their adoption should be avoided. However, adapting existing tax systems to cope with economic transactions in cyberspace presents considerable challenges.

STUDY QUESTIONS

1. Why is it so difficult to achieve an optimal tax system?
2. What implications does an ageing population have for tax systems?
3. How might changes in technology affect taxation internationally?
4. What is tax competition and why is it important?
5. What are the advantages and disadvantages of tax harmonisation?

REFERENCES

Australian Tax Office (1997) *Tax and the Internet*, Vol. 1 and Vol. 2, Canberra: Australian Government Publishing Service.

Boreham, P., Hall, R. and Leet, M. (1996) 'Labour and citizenship: the development of welfare state regimes,' *Journal of Public Policy*, Vol. 16(2), pp. 203-227.

Cairncross, Sir Alec (1971) *Essays in Economic Management*, London: Allen and Unwin.

Chennells, C. and Griffith, R. (1997) *Taxing Profits in a Changing World*, London, Institute for Fiscal Studies.*

Commission of the European Community, (1992) *Report of the Committee of Independent Experts on Company Taxation* ("Ruding Report").

Cordes, J.J., Nicholson, E.M. and Sammartino, F.J. (1990) 'Raising revenue by taxing activities with social costs,' *National Tax Journal*, Vol. 43, pp. 343-356.

Department of the Treasury (1996) *Selected Tax Policy Implications of Global Electronic Commerce*, Washington DC: U.S. Department of the Treasury.*

Gibson, J. (1990) *The Politics and Economics of the Poll Tax: Mrs Thatcher's Downfall*, Cradley Heath: EMAS.

Grbich, Y. (1997) 'Tax Reform Prospects in Australia,' Keynote address at conference of the International Fiscal Association, New Zealand Branch, Mt. Ruapehu, Tongariro National Park, New Zealand, 7 March 1997.

Hickey, J. B. (2000) 'The Fiscal Challenge of e-commerce,' *British Tax Review*, pp. 91-105.*

Inland Revenue Department (1997) *Electronic Commerce*, Wellington, New Zealand, July.

James, S. (1984) *A Dictionary of Economic Quotations*, 2nd edition. London: Croom Helm.

James, S. (1995) *Self-Assessment and the UK Tax System*, London: Research Board of the Institute of Chartered Accountants in England and Wales.

James, S. (1997) 'Self-assessment and the UK Tax System,' *Australian Tax Forum*. Vol. 13, pp. 205-226.

James, S. (1998) *A Dictionary of Taxation*, Cheltenham: Edward Elgar.

James, S. and Nobes, C. (2000) *The Economics of Taxation: Principles, Policy and Practice*, 7th edition. Hemel Hempstead: Prentice Hall.

James. S. and Wallschutzky I. (1993) 'Returns to The Future: The Case For Electronically Submitted Tax Returns.' *British Tax Review*, Vol. 38, pp. 401-405.

James. S. and Wallschutzky I. (1995) 'The Shape of Future Tax Administration.' *Bulletin for International Fiscal Documentation*, Vol. 49, pp. 210-218.

James. S. and Wallschutzky I. (1997) 'Tax Law Improvement in Australia and the UK: the Need For a Strategy For Simplification.' *Fiscal Studies*, Vol. 18, pp. 445-460.

James, S. (2000) 'Can We Harmonise Our Views on European Tax Harmonisation?' *Bulletin for International Fiscal Documentation*, Vol. 54, pp. 263-269.

Johnson, G. and Scholes, K. (1999) *Exploring Corporate Strategy*, 5th edition. Hemel Hempstead: Prentice Hall.

Kindleberger, C. P. and Lindert, P. H. (1978) *International Economics*, 6th edition. Homewood, Illinois: Irwin.

Lewin, K. (1951) *Field Theory in Social Science*. London: Harper.

Mair, D. and Damania, R. (1992) 'Fiscal Crisis and UK Local Tax Reform.' *Local Government Studies*, Vol. 18, pp. 179-190.

Mann, J., Swinson, J. and Morrison, D. (2000) 'e-GST', *Revenue Law Journal*, Vol. 10, pp. 138-193.

May, J. and Wat, S. (1998) 'Tax and Electronic Commerce' *Asia-Pacific Journal of Taxation*, Vol. 2, pp. 37-44.

McKenzie, G. and Khalidi, M. (1996) 'The Globalization of Banking and Financial Markets: the Challenge for European Regulators', *Journal of European Public Policy*, Vol. 3(4), pp. 629-646.

Mercer, D. ed. (1992) *Managing the External Environment: A Strategic Perspective*. Sage Publications, London.

Nicolaisen, J., Dean, A. and Hoeller, P.B. (1991) 'Economics and the Environment: a Survey of Issues and Policy Options', *OECD Economic Studies*, No. 16, Spring.

Oates, W.E. (1995) 'Green Taxes, Can We Protect the Environment and Improve the Tax System at the Same Time?', *Southern Economic Journal*, Vol. 61, pp. 915-922.

OECD (1998a) *Harmful Tax Competition: An Emerging Global Issue*, Fiscal Affairs Committee, Paris: OECD.*

OECD (1998b) *Economic Outlook*, No. 65, June, Paris: OECD.

OECD (1999) *Revenue Statistics of OECD Member Countries*, Paris: OECD.

Picciotto, S. (1992) *International Business Taxation*, London: Weidenfeld and Nicolson.

Radaelli, C.M. (1997) *The Politics of Corporate Taxation in the European Union: Knowledge and International Policy Agendas,* London: Routledge.

Radaelli, C.M. (1998) *Policy Narratives in the European Union: the Case of Harmful Tax Competition*, San Domenico: European University Institute.

Revenue Canada Taxation (1998) *Electronic Commerce and Canada's Tax Administration: A Report to the Minister of National Revenue from the Minister's Advisory Committee on Electronic Commerce*, Ottawa, April.

Rose, R. and Karran, T. (1987) *Taxation by Political Inertia*, London: Allen & Unwin.*

Schwartz, P. (1992) *The Art of the Long View*, Century Business.

Smith, S. (1992) 'Taxation and the Environment: a Survey.' *Fiscal Studies*, Vol. 13, pp. 21-57.

Symons, E., Proops, J. and Gay, P. (1994) 'Carbon Taxes, Consumer Demand and Carbon Dioxide Emissions: a Simulation Analysis for the UK,' *Fiscal Studies*, Vol. 15, pp. 19-43.

Wallschutzky, I. (1998) 'The Implications of Electronic Commerce for the Australian Tax System.' Papers of the Third International Conference on Tax Administration, University of New South Wales, Sydney, 16-17 April.

Yip, G. S. (1997) *Total Global Strategy: Managing for World Wide Competitive Advantage*, Prentice Hall: Canada.

*   *Key readings are asterisked*

PART TWO

ASPECTS OF INTERNATIONAL TAXATION

Chapter 7

The Role of Tax Treaties in International Taxation

WALTER O'CONNOR
Fordham University, U.S.A.

Key words: tax treaty; model tax treaty; permanent establishment; residence

Abstract: Given the globalisation of the economies of the nations in the world, it became inevitable that the business rules of these nation states would interact. When taxpayers of one nation began to do business with taxpayers in other countries, conflicts and inconsistencies began to develop. Two or more nations started to tax the income and transactions of a single entity which created double taxation problems. Such problems could have deterred a business from operating globally. So some vehicle was needed that could not be provided by a single country acting on its own. Some agreement had to be entered into by two or more countries to prevent this deterrent from stifling worldwide business. Such agreements are the tax treaties in this paper.

1. INTRODUCTION

There are tax provisions in many treaties that countries sign with each other. While most attention of tax people is focused on tax treaties, there are tax elements in treaties of friendship and navigation and other treaties whose principal agenda is not taxation. The purpose of this chapter is to create an awareness of the purpose of tax treaties, how they interrelate to the internal tax law of a country, their major provisions from a substantive and administrative standpoint and how they can be utilised by individuals and business entities to operate globally with a lesser burden of taxation. The next section outlines some preliminary issues, and the third section outlines the main provisions of tax treaties.

2.   PRELIMINARY ISSUES

2.1   What is a Tax Treaty?

A tax treaty is an agreement between two countries that outlines a series of articles (provisions) which clarifies the tax rules between the countries on specific subjects. For example, a tax treaty will usually have an article dealing with dividends flowing from a corporation in one country to an investor in the other country. The tax laws of the United States state that dividends flowing out of the United States must bear a 30% withholding tax if paid to a person who is not a U.S. citizen or resident. However, if there is a tax treaty between the United States and the country of residence of the investor, then the 30% tax may be reduced to a low rate of tax.

2.2   Why Do We Need Tax Treaties

As a rule of global economics, tax rules should not impede or complicate business decisions. The words 'tax neutrality' are used to express this idea. This means that global consumers will get the best quality products at the lowest cost, if taxation does not get in the way.

Now this is an ideal. However, it is at least a goal to which we should strive. Assume a country required an 80% withholding tax on interest income because it wants to raise a significant amount of revenue from foreign investors. If you were the investor, would you place your money in this country? Probably not; but even if you did, you would want such a high return on your investment (ROI). The party receiving your funds would be hard pressed to make a profit.

Therefore, tax treaties try to facilitate international trade and commerce by easing the trade investments going across borders. The foregoing example of an 80% tax rate is unrealistic - but it makes the point. If a country believes it can obtain the funds it needs by burdening foreign businesses, it will soon find out its 80% rate will result in decreasing revenues. However, since it would be unlikely for that country to get the other to lower its national tax rate for everybody, the tax treaty approach is the appropriate vehicle.

Later in this chapter we will see how specific articles make it easier for people to engage in trade with, or invest money in, another country. At this point, suffice it to say, this trade and investment facilitation is a major objective of a tax treaty.

Another major objective of a tax treaty is the avoidance of double taxation. Assume one country has a 50% tax rate and another country also has a 50% tax rate. If a business from one country wants to engage in commerce in the other country, it will decide not to do so if it will be subjected to a total tax burden of 100%!

Many countries have unilateral provisions in their tax law to prevent double taxation. However, some do not. Again, it is unlikely that a country will change its entire tax law just because another country wants it to do so. Consequently, negotiating some type of double taxation relief in a tax treaty between the two countries is a practical way of solving this problem.

Finally, to facilitate trade and investment, tax treaties allow individuals to go to other countries without paying taxes if they are agents, directors, artists, athletes, students, pensioners, etc. In so doing, it makes it easier to keep taxation from complicating their lives.

2.3   Who Cares About Tax Treaties?

If a United Kingdom investor wants to invest in Japan, s/he will be interested in knowing what the overall tax burden will be on that investment. While Japan may not have jurisdiction over the person of the UK investor, it will have jurisdiction over the income from Japanese sources. Consequently, the withholding tax imposed by Japan and the UK tax imposed on the person of the investor, would be important to the investor.

Will the UK tax system give some relief to the investor for the Japanese withholding tax if there is no tax treaty? If there is a tax treaty between the UK and Japan, does it reduce the Japanese withholding tax burden? These questions are the reason tax treaties are important in the international tax world.

Assume a German business wants to trade with businesses in Brazil. Is the German business sufficiently involved in Brazil to require it to file tax returns in Brazil? That is, is the German business only doing business with Brazil or is doing business in Brazil? Most countries have tax rules that say, if you are engaged in business in our country, we want you to file tax returns and pay tax on the net income attributable to the business you are conducting in our country.

However, what degree of business penetration of a country results in a country determining whether a business needs to file a tax return? This varies with the tax laws of each country. So tax treaties are constructed so that a foreign business must have some establishment in the other country that is of a permanent nature. Unless there is such a permanent establishment, there would be no need to file tax returns in the host country.

Assume a French business is selling products to a subsidiary in Mexico. The French tax authorities contend the parent is selling at too low a price to its subsidiary. The Mexican tax authorities contend the Mexican subsidiary is buying at too high a price from its French parent. How is a disagreement like this resolved?

Without a tax treaty, the taxpayer is stuck between the two tax authorities – and possibly exposed to double taxation without relief.

Tax treaties have an article that deals with administrative relief in situations like these. The mutual agreement procedures in tax treaties create a competent authority mechanism so that the tax authorities can negotiate and try to work out a resolution of this double taxation problem.

There are many similar international tax problems like this e.g. transfer pricing. We still live in a world of national states (countries) that have to raise funds in order to build the roads, hospitals, armies, etc. to serve their citizens. Taxation is the way to do this. However, pressing too hard on foreigners can frighten them from investing in a country or doing business with the country.

Because of this dilemma for tax authorities, tax treaties are a mechanism for encouraging global trade and investing while still raising revenue but not scaring foreign businesses away.

2.4   What Countries Have the Largest Tax Treaty Network?

With these reasons for having tax treaties, which countries have them? More than 200 countries have tax treaties as of the beginning of the year 2000. All of the major economic powers of the world have a tax treaty network with the average country having entered about 90 tax treaties.

This gives some idea of the scope of the global tax treaty network. The fact that the United States does not have many tax treaties with less developed countries is of particular interest. Since a tax treaty is really a contract, this may not be too surprising, since each country in a tax treaty is bargaining to get something if it is going to give up something. This is a policy issue that each country must consider before it enters tax treaty negotiations.

For example, tax sparing is the policy of giving a tax credit for taxes forgiven by another country. The idea is that, if a less developed country wishes to forgive its taxes to encourage foreigners to invest in their country, the country of the investor should reduce its tax on the earnings received from the foreign country as if the less developed country actually imposed its tax.

Some developed countries, like Japan, have used tax sparing in its tax treaties with other Asian countries. The United States of America, on the other hand, has never agreed to tax sparing.

3.   MAIN PROVISIONS OF TAX TREATIES

With the foregoing introduction to the treaties, let us now look at some of the more important articles of the treaties. There are 29 articles in the model tax treaty of the United States of America. For our purposes, we will examine several of the most important articles. The reader is also encouraged to examine the articles in the OECD Model Tax Treaty as well as the treaties of the countries of greatest interest to you.

3.1   Scope of Treaty

In addition to income taxes, there are also tax treaties dealing with estate and gift taxation. For purposes of this book, we will concentrate on income taxation treaties, but those involved in inheritance tax matters should familiarise themselves with the estate and gift tax treaties.

In addition, as mentioned earlier, there are tax provisions in treaties entered into by many countries. While not tax treaties as such, you should be aware of these provisions for tax planning purposes.

Furthermore, there are countries around the world that have historically close ties with other countries, i.e. the British Commonwealth, the French Empire, the Netherlands influences in the Caribbean and Asia. Some countries extend their tax treaties to these former colonies (some of whom have the appellation 'tax haven').

3.2   Taxes Covered

This article of a tax treaty indicates the taxes in each signatory country that is covered by the treaty. It often indicates whether the taxes covered include those of subdivisions of the countries, such as provinces, cantons, launder, prefectures, states, etc. Given the importance of such subdivisions in many countries you should be alert to be certain that your tax reserves cover the all-important levies of the nation state and its subdivisions.

3.3   Residency of Taxpayers

On the individual tax side, many countries' tax people on their worldwide income if that individual is 'resident' in the country. But, how do the countries define resident? It varies from country to country. Assume two (or more) countries claim an individual is resident in their country. Result – double (or maybe triple) taxation.

In the past, this may not have been a practical problem, since some people could just cheat! Now with electronic technology improving the information tax authorities have and can get, detection is more sophisticated.

Nevertheless, the tax treaty articles on residency provides a series of rules having as a major objective making certain the countries will agree. The individual is resident in only one country. See these rules from a typical tax treaty:

2. *Where by reason of the provisions of paragraph 1, an individual is a resident of both Contracting States, then his status shall be determined as follows:*

   a) *he shall be deemed to be a resident of the State in which he has a permanent home available to him; if he has a permanent home available to him in both States, he shall be deemed to be a resident of the State with which his personal and economic relations are closer (centre of vital interests);*

   b) *if the State in which he has his centre of vital interests cannot be determined, or if he does not have a permanent home available to him in either State, he shall be deemed to be a resident of the State in which he has an habitual abode;*

   c) *if he has an habitual abode in both States or in neither of them, he shall be deemed to be a resident of the State of which he is a national;*

   d) *if he is a national of both States or of neither of them, the competent authorities of the Contracting States shall endeavour to settle the question by mutual agreement.*

3. *Where by reason of the provisions of paragraph 1 a company is a resident of both Contracting States, then if it is created under the laws of one of the Contracting States or a political subdivision thereof, it shall be deemed to be a resident of that State.*

4. *Where by reason of the provisions of paragraph 1 a person other than an individual or a company is a resident of both Contracting States, the competent authorities of the Contracting States shall endeavour to settle the question by mutual agreement and determine the mode of application of the Convention to such person.*

3.4   Withholding Taxes - Statutory versus treaty rates

Reduction (or elimination) of withholding taxes on such income is interest, dividends, royalties, rentals, income from personal services is covered in separate articles of the tax treaty dealing with each type of income. The U.S. withholding tax rates in its internal laws are reduced in the model tax treaty.

These reductions encourage the flow of resources to the United States from its trade and investment partners. Similar concessions are made by the other economic powers around the world in their tax treaties.

3.5   Permanent Establishments - Transfer Pricing Dilemma

Earlier in this chapter we discussed the issue of when a company has made such penetration of the economy of another country, so as to require the company to file a tax return or pay taxes based on its business profits in the host country. When a business reaches this point is very difficult to say, since it depends on the tax rules of the country in which the activity takes place.

To simplify this difficulty – and unclear exposure to taxation by companies engaging in international business – a tax treaty has an article which, in effect, says the business does not have to file a tax return unless it is doing business in the other county through a permanent establishment.

Some examples as to what constitutes a permanent establishment are the following:
a) a fixed place of business through which an enterprise is wholly or partially carried on
b) a place of management
c) a branch
d) an office
e) a factory
f) a workshop
g) a mine, an oil, or gas well, a quarry
h) a building site
i) a dependent agent

Yet to be resolved, is the issue of electronic commerce in this regard. If a company in Sweden used a satellite hovering over Chicago to sell its product to consumers throughout the United States, does it have a permanent establishment in the United States? Some countries are very wary of how businesses can economically perforate their borders via technology without the traditional means of bricks and mortar and human beings. Take this example, a U.S. company sells its products to a subsidiary in Korea. The Korean tax authorities state that 10 activities are being conducted in Korea and the subsidiary is paying too high a price for the goods purchased from the U.S. parent and assesses additional tax on an increased income. The Korean company proves it is only performing six of the activities and so the price it is paying meets the arm's length standard. The Korea tax authorities counter this by asking: if the Korean subsidiary is only doing six things in Korea, who is performing the other four? The U.S. parent? Does it have a permanent establishment in Korea? Should it be filing a Korean tax return?

3.6   Double Taxation Relief - Tax Credits

As already noted, one of the major goals of a tax treaty is to encourage trade and investment between two countries by preventing double taxation, that is, two countries are taxing the same income.

Now some countries have enacted provisions in their internal tax laws to prevent double taxation. Some countries do not tax at all the profits of its taxpayers from foreign countries. Others do tax it but allow its taxpayers to (1) deduct any foreign taxes incurred in computing taxable income or (2) take a credit for foreign taxes incurred.

However, not all countries have unilateral double taxation relief, so it is built into an article in tax treaties. A typical article in the tax treaty would be as follows:

1.   *In accordance with the provisions and subject to the limitations of the law of the United States (as it may be amended from time to time without changing the general principle hereof), the United States shall allow to a resident or citizen of the United States as a credit against the United States tax on income*

   a) *the income tax paid or accrued to .... by or on behalf of such citizen or resident; and*

   b) *in the case of a United States company owning at least 10 % of the voting stock of a company that is a resident of ... and from which the United States company receives dividends, the income tax paid or accrued to .... by or on behalf of the payer with respect to the profits out of which the dividends are paid.*

For the purposes of this paragraph, the taxes referred to in paragraphs 1(b) and 2 of Article 2 (Taxes Covered) shall be considered income taxes.

3.7   Exchange of Information

In order to assist each other in making sure global businesses do not evade paying taxes to either country (in circumstances where trade or investment is being done involving one or both of the countries) an exchange of information is built into a tax treaty.

In its simplest form, if a Belgian investor buys shares in a U.S. corporation, that corporation will send a tax form to the Belgium tax authorities alerting them to the fact that a Belgian person has generated income. Similar exchange of information takes place if the Belgian person received interest, royalties, rentals, and similar passive income from U.S. sources.

It may be assumed that non-automatic exchanges of information also take place between the two tax treaty signatories. Such might be the case involving income generated from illegal businesses such as drug trafficking.

It should not be assumed that wholesale exchanges of information take place, however. One time an Asian country's tax authorities asked for a copy of the U.S. Tax Return of every U.S. citizen working in their country. After much consideration that request was denied, possibly on the grounds the tax treaty article did not cover such broad based requests.

3.8   Associated Enterprises and the Competent Authority Process

The competent authority article in a tax treaty is an excellent mechanism for dealing with international tax disputes between two countries, leaving the taxpayer in the middle. A typical example is transfer pricing. A Canadian company sells products to its subsidiary in Mexico. If Revenue Canada contends the price is too low (not arm's length) and the Mexican tax authorities contend the Mexican subsidiary is paying too high a price, the taxpayer could have its income adjusted in both countries with each country saying it belongs to them. Then the taxpayer would be paying taxation on the same income in two countries, hence double taxation.

The mutual agreement procedure set-up in a tax treaty has to be approved by both governments. However, once it is approved, it empowers each country to identify specific people who may serve as competent authority to resolve issues of the type spelled out above. While taxpayers once were hesitant about asking a government person to assist in resolving tax disputes with other countries, the experience has been favourable over the years. To look at it another way, what is the company's alternative? Fight with two countries simultaneously with no guarantee of either country budging?

3.9   Use vs. Abuse

In recent years, a limitation of benefits article has been placed in the tax treaties that the U.S. has either negotiated or renegotiated. For instance, the negotiation of the U.S. - Netherlands treaty had for condition that only Dutch taxpayers could benefit from it. As many international tax people know, the extensive tax treaty network that the Netherlands has, has resulted in it becoming the country of choice for international tax planning.

As a result, people from countries with which the United States have not concluded a tax treaty using Dutch entities through which they could conduct activities with the United States, but significantly reducing the U.S. tax they owed.

The Netherlands is only used for illustrative purposes since similar techniques involved other countries with which the United States has concluded tax treaties. The use versus abuse of tax treaties has been debated for ages. Tax treaty 'shopping' has become an art form. International tax computer software has been developed for structuring how income can flow from one entity through others to its final destination. It will be interesting to see how this 'limitation of benefits' movement permeates the international tax world.

4.   THE ROLE OF MODEL TAX TREATIES

The discussion in this chapter has dealt with the more common situation – a tax treaty between two countries. However, tax treaties have become so prevalent in the international tax environment, that model tax treaties have been developed.

A model tax treaty is a prototype that has been developed so that a country seeking to enter negotiations with another country will have a starting point. The U.S. Treasury Department has developed its own model tax treaty so that any country wishing to enter a tax treaty with the United States will know what the starting negotiating point of the United States will be. It does not mean that all the treaties with the United States are the same. Indeed, given the fact that some tax treaties with the United States went into effect many years ago, there are numerous variations. Nevertheless, as the United States is continuously updating its treaty network, the model treaty indicates the guidelines that will be followed.

The Organisation for Economic Co-operation and Development (OECD) has also created a model tax treaty. The reader should familiarise him/herself with its provisions since not all are similar to the United States Model Tax Treaty. Since the OECD members are the major countries of the world, these differences in model tax treaties often call for extensive negotiations before a bilateral tax treaty is concluded.

STUDY QUESTIONS

1. Why is the concept of residence so important in international tax?
2. Why do tax treaties contain provisions for the exchange of information between countries?
3. What general effect do tax treaties have on withholding tax rates?
4. What is meant by tax sparing?
5. Why would a country or an organisation create a Model Tax Treaty?

Chapter 8

Foreign Tax Credits

ROBERT RICKETTS
Texas Tech University, U.S.A.

Key words: foreign income; foreign losses; tax credits; tax treaties

Abstract: Taxation of the worldwide incomes earned by a country's citizens or residents is an effective method of countering other countries' attempts to lure business activity or investment capital through low tax rates. Regardless of where a country's citizens live or conduct business or investment activities, they will pay at least the level of tax imposed by their home country on their business and investment income. To prevent this policy from resulting in overtaxation of foreign-source income, however, this strategy requires allowance for some form of credit against the domestic income tax for income taxes paid to foreign countries. Thus, most countries that tax the worldwide incomes of their citizens allow a foreign tax credit, subject to necessary limitations and restrictions to prevent abuse. This chapter discusses the basic principles of the foreign tax credit and the necessary limitations and restrictions.

1.   "SOURCE" VS. "RESIDENTIAL" PRINCIPLES OF TAXATION

As local economies become more and more interdependent, inextricably linked to one another through global trade, it becomes increasingly difficult to determine the appropriate tax base against which to apply local taxes. Countries choosing to tax income rather than, or more typically in addition to, other characteristics of taxpaying capacity (e.g., consumption, wealth, etc.) face particularly difficult questions. Whose incomes should they tax, and how heavily should (or can) they tax them? These are not unrelated questions.

The problem, of course, is competition. If one country can lure economic activity away from its competitors, it can maintain existing tax revenues with lower rates. Put another way, it can maintain a high level of social welfare while simultaneously reducing the per capita burden of taxation on its citizens and residents. Other countries can compete by reducing their own tax rates, or by expanding the tax base over which they claim jurisdiction in order to reduce the tax advantage of the low-tax countries. Thus, competitive concerns play a larger role in driving tax policy, as economic activities become more global.

One of the most fundamental issues in designing a tax system is choosing the tax base against which taxes are to be levied. There are many elements to this decision – will the country tax its citizens' income, consumption, or wealth or will it derive some other principle upon which to base its tax system? Additionally, it must decide whether to tax all its citizens equally regardless of income level or family circumstances, whether it will impose equal or unequal taxes on capital vs. labour, whether it will tax citizens and residents alike, and a myriad of other issues. As international competition intensifies, it must also assess the extent to which it can make these decisions independently. That is, as capital and, more recently, highly skilled labour, become more mobile, it also becomes easier for them to escape the jurisdiction of local taxing authorities.

Consequently, one of the most significant choices a country must make is the breadth of its tax base internationally. Essentially, countries choose between two principles – the *source* principle or the *residence* principle. Under the source principle, a country limits its taxing jurisdiction to economic activity taking place within its own borders. It does not attempt to tax activities taking place (sourced) in other countries. Most countries follow this principle with regard to the economic activity of non-citizens, but apply the residence principle to tax their own citizens. Under the residence principle, a country claims taxing jurisdiction over its own citizens (and, in some cases, residents) wherever they conduct business.

Example: Albert Piscani is a citizen and resident of Italy who conducts business in several countries. For the current year, he earns income in the following amounts from business operations conducted in the following countries:

Italy	€50,000
France	€20,000
Germany	€35,000
United States	€45,000
Worldwide income	€150,000

If each of the above countries followed the residence principle, Albert's entire €150,000 income would be subject to tax in Italy, and no other country would tax him. In contrast, if each of the above countries followed the source principle, he would pay tax in each separate country on the amounts of income earned there: €50,000 in Italy, €20,000 in France, €35,000 in Germany and €45,000 in the United States.

If all countries based their tax systems on the source principle, competition would quickly reduce tax rates across the globe, as countries reduced tax rates to bid for economic activity. Taxes on capital in particular would likely fall since it is relatively more mobile than labour. However, taxes on certain types of labour might also decline as countries attempted to attract, say, more engineers, or doctors, etc. within their borders. For that reason, most countries tax foreigners under the source principle but apply the residence principle to tax their own citizens and/or residents.

The residence principle assumes that individuals recognise the benefits of residence or citizenship in their home countries and are willing to pay for those benefits. Moreover, by taxing a country's citizens on their worldwide incomes, to the extent that those citizens are willing to retain their citizenship, using the residence principle to guide tax policy reduces the threat of tax competition from a country's global competitors. It will not matter, for example, to a U.S. citizen that another country imposes a reduced rate of tax on her income since she will still pay at least the amount of tax imposed by the U.S.

Example: Sonja is a resident of the United States who conducts business in different countries. Last year, she earned income in the following amounts from the following countries:

United States	$150,000
Canada	50,000
Ireland	250,000
Worldwide income	$450,000

Because the U.S. claims tax jurisdiction over the worldwide incomes of its citizens and residents, it will not matter to Sonja that Irish income tax rates are lower than those in the U.S. She will pay U.S. tax on her entire

$450,000 worldwide income, and thus will receive no tax benefit by moving her business operations outside the U.S.[1]

As noted previously, most countries apply the source principle to the taxation of foreigners and the residence principle to the taxation of citizens (and residents in many cases). Moreover, in an effort to attract capital, many countries do not tax income from mere investment activities (e.g., bank accounts, stock market participation, etc.) conducted by foreigners within their borders. Of course, as illustrated above, if the foreigners' home countries tax their investment incomes as well as their business incomes under the residence principle, it is not clear how effectively other countries can compete for invested capital merely by reducing or eliminating the tax burden on these activities.

2.   THE POTENTIAL FOR MULTIPLE TAXATION OF THE SAME INCOME

If most countries apply the source principle to tax foreigners and the residence principle to tax their own citizens, then the potential exists for multiple taxation of incomes earned outside one's home country. Some mechanism must exist for settling jurisdictional conflicts between the home and host country.

Example: Otto Garber is a German citizen who conducts business throughout Europe. This year, he earned income in both France and Germany in the following amounts:

| Germany | €300,000 |
| France | €200,000 |

If France applies the source principle to claim jurisdiction over the €200,000 earned in France, and Germany applies the residence principle to claim tax jurisdiction over the same income, then Otto faces the prospect of paying taxes in both countries on the same income. Assume, for purposes of discussion, that both France and Germany impose tax rates of 40% on Otto's French income. He would be left with only €40,000 after

---

[1] This example assumes cooperation among the countries involved about reporting income to one another's taxing authorities. If Irish authorities, for example, refuse to share information regarding Sonja's Irish-source income with the U.S., it would be very difficult, if not impossible, for the U.S. to assess taxes on that income.

payment of taxes. If both countries imposed tax at 50%, he would have no French-source income left after payment of taxes.

2.1 The Role of Foreign Tax Credits

Clearly, countries must implement some mechanism to resolve conflicting jurisdictional claims over the right to tax the incomes of their citizens and others who earn income within their borders. Simply forfeiting tax jurisdiction to the source country (i.e., the country in which the income is earned) is one solution, but if every country followed this policy, competition would gradually erode their tax bases as business activity crossed borders into the countries with the lowest tax burdens.[2]

Alternatively, the source country could forfeit tax jurisdiction to the country of residence, but this is difficult to justify on policy grounds. The taxpayer is receiving the benefits associated with the conduct of business in the source country (such as the freedom to conduct business there, legal protection of legitimate business practices, etc.) and must share the associated tax burden. For this reason, the source country always has primary tax jurisdiction over activities conducted within its borders. The question then becomes how does the residence country maintain its right to tax the foreign income of its citizens without unduly burdening them?

Most countries have implemented some form of foreign tax credit to address this problem. The mechanics of the foreign tax credit are relatively straightforward. The country of residence allows its citizens/residents to offset the domestic tax on their foreign income by the foreign tax paid to the source country on that same income. Thus, the person who earned the income essentially pays only one level of tax – the higher of the taxes imposed by the two countries claiming jurisdiction over his/her income.

> **Example:** John is a citizen of Italy who earned income in the United Kingdom. His U.K.-source income was €250,000. Assume an Italian tax rate of 46% and a tax rate of 40% in the United Kingdom. If Italy, as John's residence country, allows a credit against its income tax equal to the amount of U.K. taxes paid on his U.K. income, he will owe a total of €115,000 in income taxes on that income (46% of €250,000). Of this

---

[2] This discussion oversimplifies this concern. In many cases, higher tax burdens will be preferred if they are accompanied by more skilled labour forces, more reliable legal systems, etc. However, given comparable levels of labour efficiency, stable political and legal systems, etc., and mobile labour forces (e.g., as between the states in the U.S. or the member countries in the E.U.), capital would generally be expected to migrate to those countries where the tax burdens are lowest, all else equal (or nearly so).

amount, €100,000 (40% of €250,000) will be paid to the U.K., and the remainder to Italy. While both countries claim tax jurisdiction, Italy recognises the primacy of jurisdiction in the source country. John's Italian income tax will thus be equal to 46% of his €250,000 U.K. income, or €115,000, less a tax credit equal to the €100,000 paid in the U.K. His net Italian income tax (on the U.K. income) will be only €15,000.

Note that the foreign tax credit allows the residence country to counter the effects of tax competition without imposing a double tax on its citizens conducting business in foreign markets. In the example above, John pays the same amount of tax on the income earned in the U.K., as he would have owed had he earned the income in Italy. He receives no tax benefit from moving his business activities to the U.K.

Two additional issues commonly arise in the implementation of a foreign tax credit. First is the question of what taxes to allow as a credit against one's own tax. Most countries allow only the *income* taxes of other countries to be credited against their own income tax. Not all taxes paid in the source country will be creditable against the residence country's income tax. Property taxes, for example, while perhaps necessary to conduct business in a foreign country, are not taxes paid on income earned in that country and generally would not be creditable against income taxes in the citizen's home country.[3] Likewise, royalties paid to the source country for production of minerals there (e.g., petroleum royalties) would not generally be considered income taxes by most countries (because they are based on the quantity of production, rather than the income resulting from sale of production) and would therefore not be creditable against the income tax assessed by the taxpayer's home country.

The second issue that must be addressed is the extent to which the foreign tax credit can be claimed against a country's income tax. For example, assume a Portuguese citizen conducting business in the Netherlands faces an average Dutch tax rate of 40% and an average Portuguese rate of 35%. The Dutch income tax paid by this citizen exceeds the Portuguese tax against which it is presumably to be credited. Allowance of the entire amount paid as a credit in the current year would effectively allow the Dutch income tax on the Portuguese citizen's Netherlands income to offset a portion of the Portuguese income tax on the citizen's income earned *outside* of the Netherlands. This income may consist of income earned domestically in

---

[3] Property taxes would presumably be owed regardless of the amount of income earned in the source country – indeed, they would be due whether or not any income was actually earned in that country. In this sense, then, they are taxes paid *from* rather than *on* the income earned in the source country. Assessing income taxes against this income in the residence country would not then be double taxation of that income.

Portugal or it may consist of foreign-source income earned outside of both Portugal and the Netherlands. In either case, it is clear that countries that allow foreign tax credits must place some restrictions on their availability.

Example: Gwen is a citizen of country X who has income in Countries X and Y as follows:

Country X	€350,000
Country Y	€400,000

Assume that Country X, her residence country, assesses income taxes at a flat rate of 40% on her worldwide income, and that Country Y assesses taxes at a flat rate of 50% on the income earned within its borders. Thus, she pays €200,000 income tax in Country Y, and faces a pre-credit tax liability of €300,000 (40% of her €750,000 worldwide income). Note that this tax consists of €160,000 on her Country Y income and €140,000 on her Country X income. If Country X, her residence country, allows her to claim a credit for the full €200,000 in Y income taxes paid, this credit will offset not only the €160,000 Country X income tax on her "foreign" income, but also €40,000 in Country X taxes on the income she earned in Country X (domestic income to Country X). Country X would essentially be paying a portion of its tax revenues to Country Y.

2.2   Foreign Tax Credit Limitations

A number of different types of foreign tax credit (FTC) limitations are used (or have been used) around the world. The primary purpose of the FTC limitation is to limit the foreign tax credit to the amount of income tax imposed by the residence country. However, a number of issues must be considered in designing the limitation to be used in a particular country. For example, how is the credit to be imposed geographically? Will it be computed on a country-by-country basis or can citizens combine all their foreign income taxes and compare them to the domestic income tax on all foreign income? Should the credit limitation be computed separately for different types of income (e.g., investment income vs. business income)? Can the citizen carry excess credits forward or backward to different tax years?

The simplest approach is to apply an *overall limitation* under which the foreign tax credit cannot exceed the domestic income tax on a citizen/resident's foreign income. Under this approach, the taxpayer's foreign tax credit is equal to the lesser of the amount of foreign income taxes actually paid or the amount of domestic income tax otherwise payable on his or her foreign-source income. This approach insures that no foreign tax credit will be allowed against the domestic income tax on the taxpayer's *domestic-source* income.

Example: Gertrude is a German citizen with income from both German and Belgian sources. Her income from each country is as follows:

Germany	€500,000
Belgium	€300,000

Assume that Germany taxes her worldwide income, and that the German tax system allows for a foreign tax credit. Assume further that the German income tax on Gertrude's *worldwide* income is €272,000, and that she paid Belgian income taxes of €120,000 on her Belgian income. The German income tax on Gertrude's Belgian income is only €102,000 [(€300,000 Belgian-source income/€800,000 worldwide income) x €272,000 German income tax liability]. Thus, to allow a credit equal to the full €120,000 in Belgian income tax paid by Gertrude would allow Gertrude to offset some of the German tax liability on her *German-source* income by taxes paid in Belgium on her Belgian-source income. This approach would effectively represent a German subsidy to the Belgian tax authorities. In this case, Germany's tax system should limit Gertrude's foreign tax credit to the €102,000 of German tax paid on the income earned in Belgium.

At a minimum, countries using a tax credit mechanism to offset double taxation of foreign-source income must limit the overall foreign tax credit to the domestic tax liability imposed on a citizen's foreign-source income. Some countries may wish to go further, however, and compute the foreign tax credit on a *country-by-country* basis.

Example: Articules, Inc. is a corporation domiciled in Greece with income from the following countries:

Greece	€350,000
Germany	€150,000
Ireland	€300,000
Worldwide income	€800,000

Assume that the Greek income tax on Articules' worldwide income is €280,000 before application of the foreign tax credit. Assume further that Articules paid German income taxes of €63,000, and Irish income taxes of €81,000. If Greece limits the foreign tax credit to the amount of Greek income taxes paid on Articules' foreign-source income, the limitation will be €157,500 [(€450 foreign-source income/€800 worldwide income) x €280 Greek income tax]. If, however, it applies the foreign tax credit limitation on a country-by-country basis, the credit limitation will be as follows:

German limitation (€150/€800 x €280)   € 52,500
Irish limitation (€300/€800 x €280)   €105,000

Note that the foreign tax credit cannot logically exceed the amount of foreign taxes actually paid. Thus, Articules would be able to claim the following foreign tax credits against its Greek income tax under a country-by-country limitation scheme:

	Actual Taxes Paid	Maximum Limit	Allowable Credit
German Limitation	€63,000	€52,500	€52,500
Irish Limitation	€81,000	€105,000	€81,000
Total Credit Allowed			€133,500

Thus, €10,500 of the German income tax paid by Articules will not be creditable against the company's current-year Greek income tax liability.

In the above example, Articules' overall credit limitation of €157,500 exceeds the aggregate credit it would be allowed if the credit is computed on a per-country basis. In effect, the excess credit position the company has in Ireland is not offset by the deficit credit position it is in Germany. Allowing these two positions to offset one another is called *cross-crediting* (i.e., allowing the company to use its credits from one country to offset its taxes paid to another country other than the home country). The decision to allow cross-crediting reduces the complexity of a country's tax system, albeit it at the cost of reducing its own revenues.[4]

Another option is to compute separate credit limitations for different types of income. As noted previously, for example, it is common for countries to tax interest, dividend and other investment income earned by foreigners at lower rates than active business income. Such tax subsidies on investment income are intended to entice capital from foreign sources. If the foreign tax

---

[4]   The complexities arise not only from the additional credit limitations, but also from additional regulations that will be necessary to determine the appropriate allocation of income and deductions between foreign countries. How does the home office, for example, allocate administrative overhead between operations conducted in two or more foreign countries?

credit limitation does not reflect this subsidy, the home country may unwittingly provide incentives for its citizens to make investments in other locales.

Example: Barbara is a U.S. citizen who has business and investment activities around the world. In the current year, she had worldwide business income of $1,000,000, consisting of business and investment income earned from the following sources:

	United States	Europe
Business income	$500,000	$300,000
Investment income	$200,000	
Totals	$700,000	$300,000

Assume that she pays $150,000 (50%) in foreign income taxes on her European business income and owes $350,000 (35%), before credits, in U.S. income tax on her worldwide income. Under the overall limitation on the foreign tax credit, Barbara's credit limitation will be $105,000 [(300/1,000) x 350,000]. Her U.S. income tax liability, after the foreign tax credit, will be $245,000, and her total, worldwide tax liability will be $395,000 ($245,000 U.S. plus $150,000 in European taxes).

Now, assume Barbara learns that if she moved her investment activities to Country X, the Country X tax rate on the resulting income would be only 10%. She moves her investment activities to Country X, increasing her foreign income taxes by $20,000 (10% of investment income) to $170,000. If the U.S. applies only an overall limitation on the foreign tax credit, Barbara's allowable foreign tax credit against her U.S. income tax will be $175,000 (500/1,000 x 350,000). Her U.S. income tax liability will now be $175,000 and her total worldwide tax liability will be $350,000, or $45,000 less than above. Not only will the U.S. have forfeited $70,000 in tax revenues, it will have enabled Barbara to save $45,000 in taxes merely by moving her investments outside its borders. Moreover, the capital Barbara has moved to Country X will no longer be available to supply the U.S. economic system.

For this reason, it is common for countries to impose separate limitations on the foreign tax credit by class of income. A variety of income classes can be imagined, but at a minimum, investment income should be separated into its own class, as should active trade or business income. Other categories will be appropriate depending on the structure of a country's income tax system.[5] In the above example, computation of separate foreign tax credit limitations by income class would allow the U.S. to neutralise Country X's competitive effort to attract Barbara's investment activities. Even if she moved her investments to that country, the income generated would effectively be taxed at the highest of the rates imposed by Country X or Barbara's home country (the U.S. in this example).

Example: Recall from the facts above that Barbara has $500,000 of trade or business income sourced in the U.S., $300,000 trade or business income sourced in Europe and $200,000 investment income sourced in Country X. She pays $150,000 European income taxes on her European trade or business income, $20,000 in taxes to Country X on her investment income, and faces a pre-credit U.S. income tax liability of $350,000 on her worldwide income (because she is a citizen of the U.S.). Applying separate foreign tax credit limitations for each type of income, Barbara would compute her U.S. foreign tax credit as follows:

Trade or business income:	
US pre-credit tax (800,000/1,000,000) x $350,000	$280,000
Credit limitation (300,000/800,000) x $280,000	$105,000
'Foreign' taxes actually paid	$150,000
Allowable credit on trade or business income	$105,000
Investment income:	
US pre-credit tax (200,00/1,000,000) x $350,000	$70,000
Credit limitation (200,000/200,000) x $70,000	$70,000
'Foreign' taxes actually paid	$20,000
Allowable credit on investment income	$20,000
Total FTC allowed	$125,000
Pre-credit US income tax	$350,000
US income tax liability	$225,000
Foreign income taxes paid	$170,000
Total worldwide income tax liability	**$395,000**

Thus, shifting her investment activities from the U.S. to Country X does not reduce Barbara's total income tax liability, despite the fact that Country X taxes her investment income relatively lightly.

---

[5] For example, the U.S. separates income into *nine* separate "baskets" for purposes of computing the foreign tax credit limitation.

3.   CARRYOVERS AND CARRYBACKS

Should a country allow its citizens and domestic companies to carry unused credits to other tax years, thereby offsetting income taxes paid or payable to their residence countries in years other than when the foreign taxes were actually paid? Carryovers and carrybacks may be necessary to measure fairly the actual tax burden on income when the residence country and the source country require different accounting methods to measure the same income. If the foreign country taxes the income in a different year than does the home country, then allowing the taxpayer to carry his/her "excess" foreign tax credit backward or forward may be necessary to properly match the domestic and foreign taxes paid or payable on the same income.

Example: Matchless Construction is a construction company specialising in the construction of large commercial buildings. Its residence country is Country X. Two years ago, it accepted a contract to construct a large facility in Country Y. The contract calls for Matchless to receive a total payment of €14,000,000 for construction. It estimates that its costs will total €10,000,000. Construction began in August, last year, and was completed in September of the current year. Assume that under the tax laws of Country Y, Matchless is allowed to report its entire €4,000,000 profit in the current year, when construction is completed. At that time, it paid €1,600,000 (40%) to the taxing authority of Country Y.

Unlike Country Y, Matchless' home country, Country X, requires that it report its income as it completes major stages of construction (rather than reporting the entire income upon completion of the project). Because it finished half of the construction project last year, Matchless reported taxable income in Country X of €2,000,000 and paid €900,000 (45%) in Country X income taxes last year. It reported the remaining €2,000,000 profit on the project, and paid an additional €900,000 in Country X income taxes, this year.

Because Matchless paid no income taxes last year in Country Y, it could claim no foreign tax credit against its Country X income tax. This year, because it paid only €900,000 income tax in Country X, the most it can claim as a foreign tax credit is €900,000. A carryback provision would allow Matchless to carry the "excess" €700,000 income tax paid this year to Country Y back and apply it against the Country X income taxes paid last year on its construction income sourced in Country Y. If it is allowed to carry this excess credit back, the total tax burden it will face on its

Country Y construction income is €1,800,000, or 45% (€1,800,000 paid to Country X over the two year period, plus €1,600,000 paid to Country Y, less the €1,600,000 foreign tax credit allowed in Country X). If it is not allowed to carry these excess taxes back, the total tax burden on its income from the construction project will be €2,500,000, or 62.5% (€1,800,000 paid to Country X over the two-year period, plus €1,600,000 paid to Country Y, less the €900,000 foreign tax credit allowed in Country X).

Allowing taxpayers to carry excess foreign taxes paid in one year backward or forward to other tax years to be offset against domestic taxes owed on foreign income is an efficient way to address differences in timing in the recognition of income and/or deductions,[6] but it also has drawbacks. For example, when countries change their tax laws, carryback or carryforward provisions in their foreign tax credit rules may allow taxpayers to receive unintended benefits.

Example: Zing Industries is a resident of Country W. It conducts operations in Country W and in the neighbouring country of Z. For the last two years, Zing has earned the following amounts of income in each country:

	W	Z	Total
Last year	€1,800,000	€1,200,000	€3,000,000
This year	€2,500,000	€2,500,000	€5,000,000

For both years, Country Z assessed income taxes against Zing's taxable income at a flat rate of 40%. Country W, on the other hand, implemented a new tax law this year. Last year, it taxed Zing's worldwide income at a flat rate of 35%. This year, anticipating additional revenue needs, it increased its tax rate to 50%. It allows excess foreign taxes paid by Zing to be carried forward 5 years.

Last year, Zing paid income taxes of €480,000 to Country Z (40% of its income from that country). Its worldwide income was subject to taxation in Country W, generating a pre-FTC tax liability of €1,050,000. Of this

---

[6] Timing distortions in the recognition of income arise from a variety of differences between the tax rules in different countries. One of the most common differences is depreciation expense. If one country allows taxpayers to depreciate business equipment over 3 years, while another requires depreciation over 7 years, companies or taxpayers who are residents of one country but doing business in the other may report the same total amount of income to both countries over a 7-year period, yet still have substantial differences in the amounts reported in any one year.

amount, €420,000 was attributable to income earned in Country Z [(1,200/3,000) x €1,050,000]. Thus, its allowable foreign tax credit was €420,000, and the remaining €60,000 is available for carryover to the current year. In the current year, Zing paid €1,000,000 income taxes in Country Z (again, 40% of its income sourced in Z), and owed €2,500,000 in income taxes on its worldwide income to Country W. Of this amount, €1,250,000 was attributable to its foreign-source income (i.e., its income from Country Z). With the carryforward from last year, its allowable foreign tax credit will be €1,060,000 in the current year, and it will pay only €1,440,000 in income taxes to Country W this year.

Note that in this example, the taxes carried forward are *not* attributable to differences in timing in the recognition of income in the two countries. Rather, this carryforward arose because in the prior year, Country Z imposed a higher tax burden than did Country W. When Country W subsequently increased its own tax rate, a portion of the additional revenues it sought to generate was offset by excess taxes imposed by its neighbour, Country Z, in the prior year. This result goes beyond allowing taxpayers to offset the effects of timing differences in the recognition of income in different countries. Indeed, the effect here is to allow the taxpayer to offset partially the effect of the change in tax policy in its home country. Countries concerned about this type of unintended result must carefully weigh the benefits from restricting carryback and carryover provisions against the potential inequities and added complexity that result from such restrictions.

4.   FOREIGN LOSSES AND THE POTENTIAL FOR DOUBLE BENEFITS

A similar policy concern arises when a citizen of one country incurs tax losses in a foreign country in one or more years, followed by profits in subsequent years. If the home country allows the early year foreign losses to offset the taxpayer's domestic income, it must adjust the foreign tax credit limitation in subsequent years when the taxpayer's foreign operations become profitable in order to prevent the taxpayer from reaping double tax benefits from its foreign operations.

Example: Carrerras Mfg. Inc., a corporation based in Country G, reported the following amounts of foreign and domestic income/(loss) over a three-year period:

	Country G	Country H	Country M
Year 1	€650,000	(€400,000)	€200,000
Year 2	€750,000	(€500,000)	€225,000
Year 3	€1,000,000	€25,000	€275,000

Carrerras' worldwide income in Year 1 is €450,000. Assume it paid €90,000 income taxes in Country M, and no income tax in Country H. Its home country (G) imposes a flat 40% income tax rate on its worldwide income. Thus, its pre-credit home-country income tax is €180,000. It is allowed no foreign tax credit because it has no *net* foreign-source income for the year (its net foreign-source income is negative €200,000).

In Year 2, the results are similar. Carrerras reports worldwide income of €475,000, after deducting the net foreign loss of (€275,000). It pays domestic income taxes of €190,000 (40%) and foreign income taxes in Country M of €101,250 (45%), but cannot claim a foreign tax credit because it still has no net foreign-source income. Note that none of Carrerras' Country M income is taxed in Country G. This income, along with €275,000 of Country G income (in Year 2) is offset by the Country H loss.

In Year 3, Carrerras' net foreign-source income is €300,000. Assume that it pays no income tax in Country H (due to carryover of its prior year losses) and €123,750 income taxes in Country M. Its pre-credit tax liability in its home country (G) is €520,000 (40% of its worldwide income of €1,300,000).

Applying the basic foreign tax credit limitation in Year 3, without considering Carrerras' deductions for foreign losses in Years 1 and 2, the company would be allowed a foreign tax credit against its Country G income tax of €116,000: (€300,000 foreign-source income/€1,300,000 worldwide income) x €520,000

Compare the above result with the one that would be reached if the limitation were computed over the full 3-year period. Over the full three-year period, Carrerras had net foreign-source income of (€225,000), and net worldwide income of €2,175,000. If the foreign tax credit limitation were computed over the entire period, it would not be entitled to claim a foreign tax credit, because it had no net foreign-source taxable income. In other words, none of its Country G income tax was attributable to foreign-source income, and therefore none of the Country G tax should be offset by foreign taxes paid.

A variety of approaches can be designed to address the above problem. One approach, as illustrated in the example, would be to apply the foreign tax credit limitation over a multi-year, as opposed to a single-year, window. Of course, this approach will only be effective if all the taxpayer's losses occur within the period covered by the window. Moreover, application of the credit limitation over a multiple year window becomes unwieldy as the number of years that must be included in the calculation is increased.

An alternative is to require that foreign-source income earned in years following a foreign-source loss be reclassified as domestic-source income to the extent of the loss(es) previously deducted. This approach, known as "recapturing" the previously deducted losses, is simpler to implement than the extended window approach described above. This simplicity is especially evident when the home country changes its tax rules during the period shortly after the foreign-source losses.

Example: Bjorn is a citizen of Country J with business activities in that country, Country L and Country R. For the previous two years, Bjorn has reported the following amounts of income or loss in each country:

	Country J	Country L	Country R
Year 1	€750,000	€250,000	(€350,000)
Year 2	€800,000	€400,000	€200,000

Country J taxes Bjorn's worldwide income, allowing a credit for foreign taxes subject to the overall limitation. It imposes a flat tax rate of 30%. Country L taxes his L-source income at a flat rate of 40%, and Country R imposes a flat rate of 35% on his net R-source income.

In Year 1, Bjorn's pre-FTC tax liability in Country J is €195,000 (30% of his net worldwide income of €650,000). He pays Country L income taxes of €100,000 (40% of his €250,000 L-source income), and he pays no taxes in Country R (due to the net loss reported in that country). He is not allowed a foreign tax credit in Country J because he has no net foreign-source income (and therefore his overall limitation is zero).

In Year 2, Bjorn's pre-FTC tax liability in Country J is €420,000 (30% of his €1,400,000 net worldwide income). His Country L income tax is

€160,000. Assume he again pays no Country R income tax (e.g., because Country R allows a carryforward of his year 1 loss).

Note that in Year 1, Bjorn deducted €100,000 of the Country R loss against his Country J taxable income (the remainder offset his Country L income). Assume Country J requires that Bjorn's Country R income in Year 2 be "recaptured" as domestic (e.g., J-source) income to the extent of the previously claimed loss. Accordingly, he will treat €100,000 of his Country R income in Year 2 as Country J income. His foreign tax credit limitation will therefore be (500/1,400) times €420,000 = €150,000.

5. INDIRECT INVESTMENTS IN FOREIGN COUNTRIES

A final consideration for countries in designing a foreign tax credit system is the proper treatment of indirect investments by their citizens in foreign business operations. When residents or citizens (including corporations) of one country make investments in corporations conducting business in another country, the income earned by the foreign corporation will be subject to two layers of taxation unless the home country allows a foreign tax credit against dividend income received by domestic shareholders.

Of course, no credit can be allowed until the foreign corporation's income is subjected to the domestic country's income tax. Thus, unless the foreign corporation's operations are consolidated with those of its domestic parent, the home country will not tax the foreign corporation's income, and should not allow a foreign tax credit, until that income is repatriated to the home country via payment of dividends to domestic shareholders.

The timing issue is quite simple to resolve conceptually, but it can be very difficult to implement. For example, should the home country allow *all* domestic shareholders a foreign tax credit against the domestic country's income tax on dividends received from foreign corporations? If it does, how does the domestic shareholder identify the amount of foreign tax paid on the income distributed to him as a dividend? How can a shareholder who owns less than one percent of the outstanding shares of a foreign corporation, for example, obtain the necessary information regarding the foreign income taxes paid on the income distributed as a dividend? Perhaps out of concern for this difficulty, many countries allow the foreign tax credit only for dividends from foreign corporations in which a domestic shareholder or shareholders own a substantial amount of stock (e.g., more than 10%).

If a country chooses to allow the foreign tax credit to offset its domestic income tax on foreign dividend income, then it must implement provisions to ensure that the foreign income tax and/or the dividend income are measured correctly. Because the dividend received by the domestic shareholder is paid from earnings of the corporation remaining after payment of its foreign income tax liabilities, it is difficult to match up the foreign taxes paid with the income distributed to shareholders. Either the tax attributable to the dividend must be reduced or the income reported by the shareholders must be increased.

Example: Cordon, Inc. is a corporation based in Country Y, but controlled by shareholders in Country X. During its first year of operations, it reported taxable income in Country Y of €800,000 and paid income taxes to Country Y of €320,000. Cordon paid dividends to its Country X shareholders of €100,000. At least two approaches can be taken in matching the Country Y income taxes paid against the dividend income received by Country X shareholders. The company can measure the taxes attributable to the dividend by reference to the amount of the dividend over the corporation's *pre-tax* income – 100,000/800,000 times the €320,000 income tax paid, or €40,000. Note that following this approach will prevent shareholders from claiming credits for the full taxes paid. Because there is only €480,000 of income left to the corporation after payment of its tax liability, it cannot distribute €800,000 in dividends to its shareholders, who therefore cannot claim a credit for the entire amount of foreign taxes paid.

The second approach is to increase the amount of dividend income recognised by the shareholders by the amount of foreign taxes deemed paid on the income from which the dividend was paid. Following this approach, Cordon would measure the taxes attributable to the dividend by reference to the amount of the dividend over the amount of income remaining to be distributed after payment of taxes – 100,000/480,000 times the €320,000 income taxes paid, or €66,667. Under this approach, the shareholders' dividend income is "grossed up" by the taxes deemed paid, to €166,667. The shareholders then report dividend income of €166,667 in Country X, and claim a foreign tax credit of up €66,667 against the Country X tax assessed on that income.

Note that although both approaches in the above example allow a foreign tax credit of up to 40% (Country Y's tax rate) of the dividend income recognised by the Country X shareholders, they can result in different *combined* tax burdens on the foreign corporation's income. The difference arises because the two approaches use different amounts of the foreign tax paid by the corporation as credits against the home country income tax. The second approach captures the most tax revenue for the home country, and thus is likely to be more popular with taxing authorities.

Aside from the timing and magnitude issues, the taxing authority must also consider the problem of classification. That is, if a country has chosen to apply the foreign tax credit limitation separately to different classes of income, then it must consider whether to extend this requirement to foreign corporations making dividend payments to domestic shareholders. Otherwise, taxpayers with both business and investment activities conducted in a foreign country could avoid these "basket" limitations merely by incorporating their foreign activities.

Example: Karen is a U.S. citizen who conducts business both in the U.S. and Country E. She conducts her Country E operations through a wholly-owned foreign corporation. This year, she had U.S. income and her foreign corporation had Country E income as follows:

	U.S.	Country E
Business income	$ 200,000	$ 100,000
Investment income	$ -0-	$ 100,000

Assume the U.S. taxes Karen's worldwide business and investment income at a flat 35% rate. Country E taxes the business income earned by her corporation within its borders at a flat rate of 40%. It does not tax the corporation's investment income.

The corporation paid $40,000 income tax to Country E and distributed $80,000 to Karen (half of its remaining income). Karen must gross up the dividend by half the foreign taxes paid, to $100,000. Thus, her pre-credit U.S. tax is $105,000 (35% times her worldwide income of $300,000). If Karen had received the Country E income directly, rather than through the corporation, she would receive no foreign tax credit on the investment income (because no foreign tax was paid on that income). The U.S. must decide whether she can avoid this separate limitation by conducting her foreign investment activities through a corporation.

To apply the foreign tax credit limitation separately to the different types of income earned by a foreign corporation and distributed to domestic shareholders, the shareholders need to be able to classify *both* their dividend *and* the associated taxes into the separate baskets required for domestic tax purposes. This, of course, requires that the shareholder be able to obtain this information from the foreign corporation. Reflecting the difficulty imposed by this requirement, it is not unusual for countries to require that foreign-source dividends be divided into separate income baskets only if domestic shareholders own a substantial amount of the outstanding stock of the foreign corporation.

6. SUMMARY AND CONCLUDING REMARKS

Taxation of foreign income earned by a country's citizens or residents is an effective method of countering tax competition and maintaining a country's tax base. It is also an effective method of countering other countries' attempts to lure investment capital through low tax rates on investment returns. Regardless of whether a citizen invests or conducts business at home or in a foreign country, he or she will pay at least the level of tax imposed by his or her home country.

To prevent this policy from resulting in overtaxation of foreign-source income, most countries that tax their citizens' worldwide incomes allow for some form of credit against their own tax for income taxes paid to foreign countries on that foreign income. While this approach is very effective at alleviating the burden of double taxation, countries using it must impose limits to insure that only the domestic tax imposed on foreign income is offset by the foreign tax credit. Many countries choose to go one step further, and limit the foreign tax credit on different types of income to the lesser of the amount of foreign taxes paid or the domestic tax imposed on each category of income. Additional limitations should be considered when a taxpayer incurs a foreign loss in one year, followed by net foreign income in a subsequent year so that the foreign tax credit allowed over a period of years does not exceed the domestic income tax imposed on net foreign-source income over the same time period.

Implementation of these limitations and restrictions introduces a substantial amount of complexity into the tax system, especially when the credit is extended to income earned indirectly through foreign corporations. In such cases, the foreign corporation must keep sufficient records, and share a sufficient amount of information, to enable shareholders in the home country to compute the necessary limitations. This complexity is a necessary cost for countries that choose to tax the worldwide incomes of their citizens and residents.

STUDY QUESTIONS

1. Explain the differences between the source and residence principles as a foundation for design of an income tax system.
2. Why might a country apply the source and residence principles differently to its own citizens versus citizens of other countries?
3. How does the use of the residence principle to guide a country's income tax system hinder the ability of other countries to lure investment capital from that country through the use of low tax rates?
4. What types of jurisdictional issues are likely to arise when a country chooses to base its income tax system on the residence principle?
5. How might the jurisdictional issues raised in question 4 be resolved?
6. Isabella is a citizen of country X. She conducts business in both country X and neighbouring country Y. Country X, her home country, assesses income taxes on her worldwide income, but allows a foreign tax credit for income taxes paid to foreign countries on income earned outside country X. Country X imposes a flat rate of 35% on its citizens' worldwide incomes, while country Y imposes a flat tax rate of 25% on incomes earned by non-citizens within its borders. What will be the effective tax rate on Isabella's Y-source income? Explain.
7. Explain how an overall limitation on the foreign tax credit, limiting the credit to domestic taxes owed on a citizen/resident's foreign-source income, protects the home country's tax base.
8. Compare the overall limitation on the foreign tax credit with a system in which separate limitations are imposed on each different country within which a citizen/resident conducts business. Which form of limitation will result in the least amount of revenue loss for the home country? Which form imposes the least amount of administrative burden on taxpayers?
9. How does a system imposing separate credit limitations on different types of income compare to one imposing separate limitations on income derived from different countries? What are the benefits (for the home country) associated with each type of limitation system? What are the costs?
10. Why might a country impose separate credit limitations on investment income and other types of income?
11. What is the purpose of the foreign tax credit? Under what conditions would allowing "excess" credits to be carried forward or backward enhance the effectiveness of the credit in achieving its primary objective(s)? When might carryover or carryback provisions not be consistent with the policy objectives of the foreign tax credit?

12. What policy concerns arise in a country that taxes its citizens' worldwide incomes when a domestic taxpayer incurs foreign-source losses? How are these concerns addressed by "recapture" provisions that reclassify subsequent foreign-source income as domestic-source income?
13. Who is the ultimate taxpayer on income earned by a corporation doing business in a foreign country? How does this complicate the domestic country's tax system, assuming the domestic country bases its tax system on the residence principle?
14. How should the foreign tax credit mechanism be applied when a domestic taxpayer invests in a corporation conducting foreign business operations?

Chapter 9

International Transfer Pricing

JAMIE ELLIOTT and CLIVE EMMANUEL
Deloitte & Touche (London) and University of Glasgow, U.K.

Key words: transfer pricing; advance pricing agreements; corporate tax; multinational
enterprises

Abstract: International transfer pricing (ITP) refers to the prices at which a company
undertakes cross-border transactions with associated enterprises. These
transactions can include tangible goods, intangible property, services and
financing transactions. This chapter explains the importance of ITP in the global
economy, the factors underlying ITP, and recent fiscal developments. In
particular, the chapter considers the approaches adopted by selected tax
authorities when addressing ITP and summarises the prescribed transfer pricing
methods for determining whether multinational enterprises are adhering to the
"arm's length principle

1.   INTRODUCTION

The importance of international transfer pricing (ITP) has increased
alongside the globalisation of business and the increasing importance of
international trade and global marketing. During the 1990s and early 2000s,
the OECD and numerous different countries have published a series of
transfer pricing guidelines, rules, and regulations[1]. These developments have

---

[1]   An example of countries that have introduced Transfer Pricing rules very recently include
countries in all part of the world such as India, Peru and Portugal. India set out a detailed
statutory Transfer Pricing framework to compute income from international transactions
between associated enterprises as part of its Finance Bill 2001. Peru introduced its first
Transfer Pricing enforcement regime that was effective from 1st January 2001. Unlike many
other countries, it has introduced one Transfer Pricing rule for widely traded goods and a
different one for infrequently traded goods. Legislation was approved in Portugal on

raised the profile of ITP and increased the pressures placed on multinational enterprises (MNEs) to ensure that their intra-group transactions reflect arm's length prices[23].

The last 40 years have also witnessed intensive empirical and theoretical research focusing on both domestic and international transfer pricing (see Leitch and Barrett, 1992; McAulay and Tomkins, 1992; Emmanuel and Mehafdi, 1994; Mehafdi and Emmanuel, 1997; and Eden 1998 for extensive literature reviews). The literature emerging over this period also confirms that ITP is complex, multi-disciplinary and remains a puzzle. This body of work has provided us with a limited understanding of ITP within MNEs - it has merely highlighted the gap between theory and practice (Mehafdi and Emmanuel, 1997). There have also been suggestions that many of these previous studies lack the focus required to understand the role of Transfer pricing policies in MNEs and the organisational context into which these policies fit.

2. FACTORS UNDERLYING INTERNATIONAL TRANSFER PRICING

2.1 Transfer Pricing Defined

Transfer pricing refers to the pricing policies and practices that are established when physical goods, intangible property, and services are charged between business units within a group. The prices which are established for cross-border transfers should satisfy the 'arm's length principle'. Essentially, this principle requires that intra-group transfer prices should be equivalent to those that are / would have been charged between independent persons dealing at arm's length in otherwise similar circumstances.

December 29th 2000, establishing a Transfer Pricing compliance programme that applies for tax years starting on or after January 1 2002.

[2] The basis of the arm's length principle is that the result of an intra-group transaction should be similar to the result of a transaction, which would have taken place between unrelated parties in similar circumstances.

[3] A Deloitte & Touche LLP review of various countries' Transfer Pricing enforcement policies and regulating schemes has found that the number of tax authorities aggressively auditing transfer prices has grown from 2 to 12 since 1994 (Tax Management (2000)).

2.1.1   Domestic Enterprises

Domestic enterprises have long decentralised or divisionalised by product specialism or geographical area in order to obtain benefits. At divisional level, the benefits include better market information, quicker decisions, easier identification of strong and weak areas of business, greater local management motivation and, at the centre, top management is released to concentrate on strategy. However, there are certain risks attached to divisionalisation such as loss of economies of scale from the duplication of resources and the potential loss of goal congruence where top management and divisional management follow different goals. The possibility of such dysfunctional behaviour has long been recognised and it is taken into account when setting transfer prices for goods transferred between business units. The setting of transfer prices needs to consider and possibly reconcile a range of factors including autonomy, credible performance evaluation, and goal congruence.

2.1.2   Multinational Enterprises (MNEs)

Once transactions cross national borders transfer pricing takes on a set of added dimensions. Where the group is a MNE that includes subsidiaries and branches that undertake activities in different tax jurisdictions, the transfer prices for these cross-border intra-group transactions cease to be solely an internal concern. There is an external aspect because the accounts of the business units invariably form the basis for determining and assessing liability to tax in each tax jurisdiction (Ogley, 1993). The corporate goal for a multinational is often *perceived* to extend beyond the internal objectives of control and motivation to the maximisation of global after tax profits by using transfer prices to shift income to countries where the corporate tax is lower. If there are corporate tax rate differentials between the parent's country and the subsidiary's country then this might influence the transfer prices on flows between the parent and subsidiary[4].

Take as an example a parent manufacturing in a low tax country with a 10% corporate tax rate[5] and selling in a high tax country with a 40% corporate tax rate, and incurring the following costs and revenue (in £,000):

---

[4]   Aliber (1985) is one of many authors to have suggested that firms can manage transfer prices within an international context to arbitrage national differences in tax rates, interest rates, tariffs, and exchange controls.

[5]   For the purposes of this exercise, we have disregarded any legislation that might apply to tax havens, and concentrate on tax differentials only.

Sales	[in high tax country]	20,000
Cost of sales [in a low tax country]		12,000
Gross profit		8,000
Operating expenses[in a low tax country]		2,000
	[in a high tax country]	4,000
Profit	[in high tax country]	2,000
Tax	[in high tax country] (@40%)	800

If the transfer price is at cost (£12m + £2m) then the tax payable is £0.8m in the high tax country and zero in the low tax country. However, tax would be minimised (ignoring the potential for tax losses) by setting the transfer price at £16m which means that the profit of £2m [Transfer price £16m - Cost of sales £12m - Operating expenses £2m] is shifted to the low tax country where it would suffer tax at 10% i.e. £200,000, the high tax country's tax liability is zero. The group after tax profit would be increased by £600,000.

In practice, there are many other reasons why a decision might be made to set high transfer prices on flows from the parent. A whole list of exogenous market imperfections might influence transfer prices. For example, considerations include ad valorem tariffs, competition, local loans based on the financial structure of the subsidiary, export subsidies or tax credits on the value of exports, inflation rates, restrictions on the value of products that can be imported, profit repatriation regulations, exchange controls, intervention in currency markets, multiple exchange rates, price controls, investment barriers and political instability (Natke, 1985; Arpan, 1988). This demonstrates that any decisions concerning transfer pricing are subject to competing pressures both internal and external to the MNE (Emmanuel, 1999).

2.2   Setting Transfer Prices

One of the problems of setting transfer prices is that there are numerous bases for defining a price and often the setting of transfer prices is not transparent.Transfer pricing may rely on a MNE's internal accounting system being based on cost-oriented transfer prices (internal costs) or being based on market prices (external prices). The question then arises as to which of these is to be preferred and how to reconcile the tax authorities' requirements with the internal requirements of the MNE.

In part, the globalisation of business and the increasing importance of international trade and global marketing have raised the profile of ITP. OECD

(1995), recognising that the role of MNEs in world trade has increased dramatically over the last 20 years, commented on the tax implication:

> 'The growth of MNEs presents increasingly complex taxation issues for both tax administrations and the MNEs themselves since separate country rules for the taxation of MNEs cannot be viewed in isolation but must be addressed in a broad international context. These issues arise primarily from the practical difficulty, for both MNEs and tax administrations, of determining the income and expenses of a company or a permanent establishment that is part of an MNE group that should be taken into account within a jurisdiction, particularly where the MNE groups' operations are highly integrated' (paras 1,2 Preface).

2.2.1 Influences on an ITP Policy

As introduced earlier, one of the main difficulties associated with formulating an ITP policy is that it is driven by many different factors and serves numerous (often competing) objectives. Previous empirical studies and literature have identified numerous factors that influence an organization's choice of transfer pricing method.

Choi and Mueller (1992, p. 518) recognised the difficulties associated with ITP, because it:

a) is conducted on a relatively larger scale internationally than it is domestically (intercompany transactions reportedly account for approximately 50% of the business conducted by MNEs);

b) is affected by a larger number of variables than are found in a strictly domestic setting;

c) varies from company to company, industry to industry, and country to country;

d) affects social, economic and political relationships in multinational business entities and, indeed, in entire countries.

2.2.2 What Role Should an ITP Policy Fulfil Within a MNE?

There have been numerous attempts by commentators to identify the role of an ITP policy. For instance, Abdallah (1989) set out nine objectives for establishing an ITP policy:

- reduction of income taxes;
- reduction of tariffs;
- minimisation of foreign exchange risks;
- avoidance of a conflict with host countries' governments;

- management of cash flows;
- competitiveness;
- performance evaluation;
- motivation;
- goal congruence.

Abdallah (1989) also attempted to identify five criteria that must be satisfied to achieve an efficient ITP mechanism:

1. The international transfer pricing policy should provide an adequate profit measurement to evaluate the performance of foreign subsidiaries and their managers in terms of their controllable divisional contributions to global profits;
2. It should provide adequate information to top management to be used as guidelines in managerial decision making;
3. It should increase the overall profit rate of the MNE; in other words, the MNE's overall performance must be improved by the use of the international transfer pricing system;
4. It should motivate foreign subsidiary managers to increase their efficiency and maximise their divisional profits in harmony with the objectives of top management.
5. It should minimise the international transaction costs for a MNE by minimising border and income tax liabilities, foreign exchange risks, currency manipulation losses, and conflict with the foreign government's policies' (pp. 10-11).

Eccles (1985) adopted a different approach and argued that the two principal determinants of the transfer pricing policy are strategy[6] (determining what a company does) and the administrative process (determining how a company implements its strategy). There are five elements to the administrative process - how transfer prices are set; who sets them; what information is used; when transfer prices are set; how conflict is resolved. Once established, the transfer pricing policy then affects economic decisions (affecting corporate performance) and performance measurement, evaluation, and reward (affecting perceptions of fairness by individuals within the organisation).

---

[6]   Eccles gave many examples of how changes in strategy lead to changes in Transfer Pricing. Strategic changes include changes in product characteristics, market characteristics, technology, competitors' strategies, the balance of internal and external sales, and management of the profit centres.

3. SIGNIFICANCE OF INTERNATIONAL TRANSFER PRICING

3.1 Survey Evidence

The importance of ITP to MNEs is evident in a series of surveys carried out by Ernst & Young. Ernst and Young (1995) interviewed a sample of over 200 MNEs from the Global 1000[7]. 82% of the complete sample (and 92% of UK MNEs in the sample) considered transfer pricing to be the main international tax issue. The study was repeated in a survey (Ernst & Young, 1997) of 393 parent companies in the Global 1000. One of the findings was that 'MNCs throughout the world regard transfer pricing as the most important international tax issue their organisations will face over the next two years' (p. 762). See also Elliott (1998, 1999).

3.2 Statistics

Foreign direct investment (FDI) in the world economy represents a very important part of public policy decision making. UNCTAD (1997a) shows that as at the mid 1990s there were about 44,500 MNEs worldwide with over 275,000 foreign affiliates. UNCTAD (1997b) also stated that the value of goods and services of foreign affiliates are now greater than exports and appear to be the principal means for delivering goods and services to foreign markets. The value of foreign affiliates' worldwide assets was $8.4 trillion in 1994.

Murray *et al* (1995) studied the global sourcing strategies of U.S. subsidiaries of foreign companies. On average, 33% of the total value of all components was procured internally, where most of this was procured domestically from the U.S. (57%). Japanese firms and European firms were significantly different in their internal sourcing strategies. Japanese firms sourced higher levels of internal sourcing from their parent's country (62%) compared to European firms (25%). Murray *et al's* results are consistent with Kotabe (1992) who suggested that European firms would rely more on U.S. production facilities whilst Japanese firms would rely more on exporting to the U.S.

Laster and McCauley (1994) questioned whether the tax revenues paid from foreign-owned firms in the U.S. are fair. Using Bureau of Economic data on the

---

[7] The sample represented 11% of the Global 1000 and a range of businesses (for instance 34% of the MNEs' primary businesses are financial services) with headquarters in Australia, Canada, France, Germany, Japan, Netherlands, UK and US.

operations of foreign-owned affiliates in the U.S. and on U.S. businesses acquired or established by foreign investors, Laster and McCauley (1994) used regression analysis to test several hypotheses. Their results confirmed their hypotheses that very low levels of profits are due to two main factors. First, foreign firms pay very high prices in acquisitions and servicing the debt is very expensive. Second, although there was no evidence to suggest that affiliates manipulated transfer prices when exporting, the regression results showed that those affiliates, which imported the most from their parents, reported lowest profits. They reported that:

> 'The scant profit of foreign firms operating in the United States has emerged as one of the biggest puzzles in international finance. That 4.7 million workers using $1.8 trillion in assets to generate sales of $1.2 trillion could fail to turn a profit strikes many as unbelievable. Could foreign companies have paid $316 billion in the past decade for firms earning $10.7 billion in the year before acquisition only to lose money overall on their holdings in 1992 - a year in which U.S.-owned firms earned record profits?' (p. 44).

However, there have been other empirical studies that do not support the suggestion that the manipulation of transfer prices is widespread. For instance, a study by Grubert (1993) found that 50% of the difference in pre-tax rate of returns between foreign controlled corporations and U.S. controlled corporations were due to start-up costs, historic cost accounting, and exchange rate differentials. Further, the study was inconclusive with respect to transfer pricing because *'a range of other factors may play an important role.... but are difficult to evaluate'* (p. 95).

3.3   Developments in Transfer Pricing Guidelines and Regulations

Over the last 10 years, the OECD has updated its guidelines and many countries have modified existing rules or introduced new rules and regulations to deal with ITP. OECD (1995) stated that *'OECD Member countries are encouraged to follow these Guidelines in their domestic transfer pricing practices, and taxpayers are encouraged to follow these Guidelines in evaluating for tax purposes whether their transfer pricing complies with the arm's length principle'* (para 16). Table 1 provides a summary review of recent developments in selected countries.

3.4 Political Pressures

In the early 1990s, the U.S. fiscal authorities were concerned with capital import neutrality due to one widely held perception that foreign MNEs investing in the U.S. were not paying their fair share of U.S. tax. The House Ways and Means Committee held hearings to investigate the possibility that foreign corporations were benefiting from tax underpayments. According to Jake Pickle, foreign companies were under-paying up to 30 billion dollars of taxes a year through transfer pricing abuses [8]. In his Opening Statement before the Committee on Ways and Means (July 10 1990) he stated that:

> 'The specific purpose of today's hearing is to set the record straight on whether the foreign-controlled U.S. companies the Subcommittee (on Oversight) reviewed have paid the amount of taxes our Federal tax laws require...are they paying the proper amount of taxes?' He explained that '...some of the companies investigated have been operating in the U.S. for years and have never sent a check to Uncle Sam for 'one thin dime' in corporate income taxes....many foreign multinational corporations are setting the transfer prices for their U.S. subsidiaries too high.'

Similarly, U.S. Senator Byron Dorgan complained about perceived abuses due to income shifting in a letter to Congressional colleagues on 19 January 1993:

> 'Foreign-based multinationals have found a new tax haven. It's not the Cayman Islands or the Netherland Antilles. It's the United States. The IRS has conceded to Congress that over seventy percent of the foreign-controlled corporations in the U.S. are paying no U.S. income taxes'.

3.5 Press Coverage

The increased focus on transfer pricing rules has led to inevitable disputes between foreign companies operating in the U.S. and the IRS concerning which country is entitled to tax the profits of a MNE. Similarly, other tax authorities are becoming more aggressive in their approach to transfer pricing. Typical headlines in recent years have included '*Nissan pays Y17bn in U.S. penalty taxes*' (Financial Times 11 November 1993), '*Glaxo loses tax battle on transfer pricing*' (Daily Telegraph 10 November 1995), and '*Multinationals fear transfer pricing squeeze*' (Financial Post 3 September 1997).

---

[8] However, a study by the IRS put the figure at a maximum of 3 billion dollars a year (Economist 25 July 1992).

Usually the disputes between countries will be decided on the basis of competent authority provisions, which are discussed confidentially. Sometimes information about tax adjustments is well publicised. For instance, the National Tax Agency in Japan has imposed heavy tax increases on Roche, Ciba-Geigy (both Swiss pharmaceuticals) and Hoechst (German drugs company). The tax charges are based on the accusation that these companies are minimising Japanese profits by charging excessive royalty payments to the Japanese subsidiaries [9].

Tax Management (2001) reported that the Australian Tax Office (ATO) had completed 33 *transfer pricing* audits during the year ending June 30 2001, generating A\$276 million of tax and penalty adjustments. The 33 *transfer pricing* audits are an increase from the prior year when 27 *transfer pricing* audits were completed and the year before that when 17 *transfer pricing* audits were completed.

4.   RECENT FISCAL DEVELOPMENTS

4.1   The Current Position

Since the mid 1980s, the U.S. has been the prime instigator of the introduction of more onerous and punitive *transfer pricing* rules and regulations, culminating in the s482 Final Regulations which were released on 1st July 1994[10] (US, 1994). At the same time the OECD revised its own draft guidelines, issued the final OECD report in July 1995 (OECD, 1995) and released subsequent updates (OECD, 1997, 1998 and 1999). Since then, the OECD and the U.S. have been refining their guidelines and regulations respectively, and many fiscal authorities around the world have responded by introducing their own transfer pricing rules and regulations.

In order to determine what constitutes an appropriate transfer price for tax purposes, tax authorities need to be able to verify that the transfer prices have been computed in a reasonable manner so that there is a 'fair' level of profits in each country in which a MNE is operating. The arm's length principle is viewed by the majority of parties involved in transfer pricing as the most appropriate method and the principle is enshrined in Article 9 of the 1979 (revised and updated on 1st September 1992) OECD Model Taxation Convention on Income

---

[9]   Up until April 1994, the Japanese authorities had applied penalty taxes for Transfer Pricing on 50 occasions since 1986 - and on just five occasions had this penalty been reduced due to inter-governmental negotiations. (Michiyo Nakamoto, Financial Times 14 April 1994).

[10]   They were published in the Federal Register on 8 July 1994.

and on Capital[11]. The 1979 OECD Model is the accepted blueprint for subsequent double tax treaties (DTT) between different countries. The arm's length principle is a simple concept in theory but has proved difficult to arrive at in practice with a comfortable level of assurance.

4.2 International Transfer Pricing : The Approach of Selected Tax Authorities

Deloitte Touche Tohmatsu (2001) summarises the current transfer pricing position for selected countries as of 1st June 2001 in 'Strategy Matrix for Global transfer pricing: Comparison of Methods, Documentation, Penalties, and Other Issues'. Table 1 reproduces selected extracts for the OECD, Australia, Japan, UK, and the U.S.[12].

4.3 Acceptable Transfer Pricing Methods

Table 1[13] illustrates acceptable transfer pricing methods and the priority of these methods in the selected countries. The OECD has set out details of a range of acceptable transaction-based methods and profit-based methods. Atkinson and Tyrrall (1999) provide an excellent description about how these different methods can be applied in practice; how to successfully manage a transfer pricing policy within a MNE[14]; and how the Inland Revenue conducts transfer pricing investigations.

4.3.1 Transaction-based Methods

Transaction-based methods 'compare the prices charged in controlled transactions undertaken between those enterprises with prices charged in

---

[11] Article 9 states that: 'Where conditions are made or imposed between the two enterprises in their commercial or financial relations which differ from those which would be made between independent enterprises, then any profits which would, but for those conditions have accrued to one of the enterprises, but, by reason of those conditions, have not so accrued, may be included in the profits of that enterprise and taxed accordingly.'

[12] This extract is meant for general information only and should not be relied on without further proper advice.

[13] See end of chapter for Table

[14] 'A sound management framework, based on clear and well-communicated policy on risk, ownership, simplicity, and resources, provides a secure environment for defensible Transfer Pricing mechanisms. This framework should be supported by procedures which ensure that the Transfer Pricing policies are in place and reviewed at regular intervals, including occasions when there is any significant business reorganisation' (p. 150).

comparable transactions undertaken between independent enterprises' (para. 2.5). OECD (1995) identified three transaction-based methods:

4.3.1.1   Comparable Uncontrolled Price (CUP)

The Comparable Uncontrolled Price (CUP) method is the most direct determination of an arm's length price. This method refers to the sales price between unrelated buyers and sellers for a comparable transaction. Ideally the circumstances should be identical but some latitude is allowed to compare with a non-identical CUP (e.g. differences in the terms or timing of the transaction) and make an appropriate adjustment. One of the main problems associated with this method is that it is often very difficult for companies to access data on transactions between 'unrelated buyers and sellers'.

4.3.1.2   Resale Price

The Resale Price method determines the arm's length price by taking the actual price at which goods are sold by a reseller and deducting a normal profit margin, which would be obtained from transactions with unrelated parties. Any difference between the related transaction and the unrelated transaction should be reflected by an adjustment to the normal profit margin.

4.3.1.3   Cost Plus

The Cost Plus Method takes the cost of production and adds the appropriate gross profit margin. Again, this mark-up should be determined by reference to the mark-up earned by a manufacturer's sales to unrelated parties for the same/similar transactions.

4.3.2   Profit-based Methods

Profit-based methods should be applied in '*a manner that approximates arm's length pricing which requires that the profits arising from particular controlled transactions be compared to the profits arising from comparable transactions between independent enterprises*' (para. 3.3)

4.3.2.1   Transactional Net Margin Method (TNMM)

The Transactional Net Margin Method (TNMM)[15] examines the net profit margin relative to an appropriate base (e.g. costs, sales, assets) for controlled transactions and compares this with the net margins earned by the taxpayer in

---

[15] Alternatively, the U.S. regs provide for the use of the Comparable Profits Method (CPM) which compares the overall profitability of controlled and uncontrolled companies rather than the profitability of transactions.

uncontrolled transactions or with the net margins earned in comparable transactions by independent enterprises. This method requires a functional analysis – an analysis of functions performed (taking into account assets used and risks assumed) of all parties that are considered.

4.3.2.2 Profit Split Method

The Profit Split Method splits the total profit earned between the two related parties using an equitable formula (e.g. in proportion to capital employed). This method should compare the split with profit splits between unrelated parties, but as this information is rarely available, an equitable means of division should be found.

4.3.3 Use of Transaction-based and Profit-based Methods

GAO (1995) provided some details about the relative use of these methods. For those transfer pricing issues completed in the fiscal years 1990 to 1992, the U.S. IRS international examiners found that CUP had been used in 25% of the cases, cost plus in 14%, resale price in 12% and other methodologies in 48% (note rounding). As at July 7 1994, 75 methods used in Advance Pricing Agreements (APAs) could be disaggregated to CUP being used in 8% of the cases, cost plus in 7%, resale price in 23%, profit measures in 19%, formulary apportionment[16] in 17% and miscellaneous other allocation methods in 27% (note rounding).

Deloitte Touche Tohmatsu (1998) commented on the 1995/96 Schedule 25A[17] statistics published by the Australian Tax Office (ATO). According to the information, 67% of the 7,787 MNEs lodging a Schedule 25A were able to select and apply one of the recognised transactional based methodologies (for instance 2,220 used CUP and 1,300 used cost plus). However, instead of accepting that MNEs are applying the recommended methods, the ATO has questioned whether this high rate of compliance with accepted methodologies is actually plausible: '*the ATO's experience and efforts to date would suggest that the lack of available comparable data in Australia would not enable companies to apply these methodologies*' (p. 1).

---

[16] Global formulary apportionment allocates a MNE's consolidated profits amongst the business units in different countries on the basis of a single or multi-factor formula (e.g. using sales/assets/staff).

[17] The Schedule 25A form is an additional (mandatory) tax return form that requires the identification and quantification of related party dealings.

4.4   Advance Pricing Agreements (APAs)

In response to the increased rigidity of transfer pricing rules and the increase in both the incidence and amount involved in penalty provisions, there is added emphasis on certainty and getting transfer pricing policies right. One solution gaining recognition is the introduction of Advance Pricing Agreements (APAs)[18]. APAs can be agreed with tax authorities in one (unilateral), two (bilateral) or more (multilateral) countries.

The Inland Revenue has described APAs as a *'mechanism whereby the setting of transfer prices in respect of specified controlled transactions may be agreed with tax administrations in advance of the transactions being undertaken and reported. The mechanism offers certainty for the taxpayer that transfer pricing covered by the arrangement will not be challenged during the period of the arrangement, subject to the terms of the arrangement being observed'* (Inland Revenue (1997), para. 6.38).

At the MNEs initiative, a transfer pricing method or approach may be agreed with the fiscal authorities to cover a fixed number of years (say three to five years) for an agreed coverage of transactions. Therefore, an advance agreement will be reached about how the taxpayer group will be taxed on their international transactions between the countries involved. In order to reach agreement, the MNE must provide a similar amount of information (or potentially even more) to that information that might be required under an audit defense. The required information might typically include:

- A functional analysis of the trade or transaction;
- an industry analysis to distinguish or compare the product or service with the sector;
- a financial analysis of the transaction;
- identification of comparable transactions of goods and services;
- provision of documents to demonstrate the MNEs arm's length policy for pricing.

The advantages of APAs include the provision of certainty to the taxpayer when filing their tax return; the provision of certainty to the taxpayer regarding the elimination of double taxation; and assisting the taxpayer in reaching the right commercial decision, rather than deciding on the arrangement perceived as least likely to attract audit attention. However, they should only be used in complex arrangements that are unlikely to change over time.

---

[18] For example, there is a long-standing APA agreed between the US and Australia for Apple Computers.

Table 2 reviews the status of APAs in the OECD, Australia, Japan, UK and the U.S.

	OECD	AUSTRALIA	JAPAN	UK	US
APA Available	Chapt. IV. F (unilateral and bilateral)	TR 95/23 (unilateral and bilateral)	Circular 8-1, Oct 25/1999	Inland Revenue Statement of Practice 3/99 IV. F	Rev Proc 96-53 (unilateral and bilateral)
APA Term of Agreement	As long as methodology and critical assumptions apply.	Generally 3-5 years forward	Generally 3 years forward, rollback available	Generally 3-5 years forward; either taxpayer or IR may seek rollback	Generally up to 3-5 years forward; either taxpayer or IRS may seek rollback for longer period as appropriate

Table 2: APA Considerations in Selected Countries (Extract from Deloitte Touche Tohmatsu (2001)

According to a recent ATO Media Release (Nat 01/73; 24th August 2001), Australia signed the world's first APA in 1991 and to date has completed around sixty arrangements, either on a unilateral, bilateral or multilateral basis.

The Internal Revenue Service's second annual report on advance pricing agreements (Announcement 2001-32), revealed that the APA Program received 91 APA requests in 2000, executed 63 APAs in 2000, and has executed a total of 294 APAs since 1991. Wrappe and Chung (2001) reviewed the IRS's report and identified that of the APAs negotiated in 2000, 32% related to the transfer of tangible property, 28% related to the transfer of intangible property or cost sharing, 27% related to services, and 13% related to financial products. Those APAs that focused on intra-group services included marketing and/or distribution services (26%), and headquarters and administrative services (21%). Finally, of the 63 APA requests filed during 2000, the majority (62%) was between a non-U.S. parent and an U.S. subsidiary.

In 1999, new legislation introduced in the UK allowed for APAs to be agreed between taxpayers and the Inland Revenue. As stated in Inland Revenue (1999), *'APAs can assist taxpayers by providing certainty in situations where their cross-border activities raise particularly complex or difficult* transfer pricing *issues.'* Before the new legislation, APAs were only available in the UK under the mutual agreement procedure of Double Tax Agreements or unilaterally as a result of a transfer pricing audit.

5.   CONCLUSION

Within MNEs, transfer pricing can serve many roles ranging from securing competitive advantage for a newly established subsidiary to managing foreign exchange currency fluctuations. The benefits to be reaped from efficient management and selection of transfer prices are not trivial. However, many of these potential opportunities are difficult to achieve because they conflict. Not least in significance, performance measurement of subsidiaries and their management teams can be distorted with a possible adverse affect on motivation, behaviour, and rewards.

However, the influence of taxation on international transfer pricing becomes more and more pervasive as an ever increasing number of fiscal authorities introduce transfer pricing rules for the first time; or refine the existing rules to place a greater responsibility on taxpayers to demonstrate arm's length pricing; or implement penalty provisions in the instances in which taxpayers are unable to demonstrate arm's length pricing. The increased interest in transfer pricing also increases the potential for double taxation of the same income in the event that a tax authority makes a transfer pricing adjustment. However, it is possible to avoid double taxation by seeking a corresponding adjustment under the mutual agreement procedure of a double tax treaty or potentially by using the EU Arbitration Convention.

For instance, the UK transfer pricing legislation, which had been in place for nearly 50 years, was 'modernised' in 1998. In brief, for accounting periods ending on or after 1 July 1999, transfer pricing falls within the corporate tax self-assessment system. This means that taxpayers are required to ensure that their computation of taxable profits reflects arm's length prices; taxpayers are required to justify the transfer pricing policy; taxpayers are required to maintain sufficient and appropriate contemporaneous documentation[19]; and

---

[19] The October 1998 issue of the Inland Revenue's Tax Bulletin (issue 37) provides some guidance on the documentation that needs to be maintained in the UK.

penalties might apply to certain tax adjustments based on non-arm's length pricing[20].

Finally, many of the cross-border transactions themselves are becoming more complex as many industries undergo mergers and realignment (e.g. pharmaceuticals); as there is convergence in technology standards (e.g. telecommunications); and as technology allows more cross-border trade (e.g. electronic commerce). In addition, tax authorities are also focusing increased interest on how to deal with transfer pricing when branches/permanent establishments as well as subsidiaries are involved (OECD, 2001). The need for a consistent approach to the taxation of permanent establishments is particularly important for the banking industry and the operation of global trading.

STUDY QUESTIONS

1. We have identified a number of different objectives that might affect a MNE's transfer pricing policy. It has been argued that many of these objectives do not seem to be internally consistent but contradictory. Consider the extent to which the range of objectives can be satisfied in practice

2. Tax Management transfer pricing reported in 'UNITED KINGDOM: Revenue Exchanging Information With Customs in Audits, Official Says' (Volume 9 Number 7 Wednesday, January 10, 2001) that 'The U.K. Inland Revenue is taking steps to streamline the audit process for multinational companies, including exchanging information with U.K. Customs and Excise in transfer pricing audits'. Similarly, Joint consideration for customs and transfer pricing purposes is a growing trend in the United States, Canada, and Latin America. Discuss the implications of this level of co-operation.

3. Review a copy of the most recent Schedule 25A form on the ATO's web site (http://www.ato.gov.au/). Consider the range of information that must be disclosed and how this will be used in practice by the ATO.

4. Identify causes of global market imperfections, giving real-life examples where possible. By concentrating on one real-life example, explain the potential impact on MNE transfer pricing policy.

---

[20] The December 1998 issue of the Inland Revenue's Tax Bulletin (issue 38) provides some guidance on penalties in the UK. The bulletin states that 'The Revenue recognises that the issue of penalties onTransfer Pricing adjustments will be a sensitive one, especially in the early years of the new regime. As a result, and to ensure that a consistent approach is taken across the department, International Division, working in conjunction with Compliance Division will monitor all potential penalty cases'.

5. Describe the potential implications of a MNE taking full advantage of the market imperfections you have identified.

6. USCORP Inc owns a Japanese subsidiary, USCORP (JP), that manufactures products in Japan and sells them to its sister company in the UK, JPCORP (UK), for sale to third party customers in the UK market. The following data is assumed:

   - USCORP (JP) incurs manufacturing costs (cost of goods sold) of $1bn and operating expenses of $100m. The rate of corporation tax in Japan is assumed to be 50%.
   - USCORP (UK) buys all of USCORP (JP)'s production and sells the products to end customers for $2.5bn. USCORP (UK)'s operating expenses are $100m. The rate of corporation tax in the UK is assumed to be 30% and there is an ad valorem import duty of 10%.

   a) Calculate the post-tax profit of USCORP (UK), USCORP (JP), and their combined post-tax profit when the products are transferred at a 'low' transfer price (cost+40%) compared to a 'high' transfer price (cost+80%).

   b) Performance Evaluation - USCORP (UK) and USCORP (JP) are both assumed to have an investment base of $1bn and for residual income purposes, a cost of capital of 10%. Calculate the Return on investment (ROI) and residual income for both USCORP (UK) and USCORP (JP) using the post-tax profits for the 'low' and 'high' transfer prices. Discuss the implications of these results.

   c) Foreign exchange considerations - assume that all the financial data is expressed in Yen and although the current exchange rate is assumed to be Y270-£1 a revaluation of yen is expected. Convert USCORP (UK)'s results to £ sterling and then reconvert to Yen based on an expected 37% revaluation to Y170-£1. Now recalculate the post-tax profit of USCORP (UK), USCORP (JP), and their combined post-tax profit when the products are transferred at a 'low' transfer price (cost+40%) compared to a 'high' transfer price (cost+80%).

   d) transfer pricing – How can USCORP support the arm's length nature of using either a cost+40% or cost+80% transfer price?

7. Describe the relationship between double taxation and arm's length pricing. What methods of arm's length pricing are available and when might each method be used?

FURTHER READING

Some useful web sites include:
http://www.arthurandersen.com/
http://www.deloitte.com
http://www.ey.com/
http://www.kpmg.com/
http://www.pwcglobal.com/

http://www.ato.gov.au/
http://www.inlandrevenue.gov.uk
http://www.irs.ustreas.gov/

There are also two regular transfer pricing journals:
– *International Transfer Pricing Journal* (IBFD Publications)
– *Transfer Pricing Report* (Tax Management Inc, Washington DC)

REFERENCES

Abdallah, W.M. (1989), *International Transfer Pricing Policies: Decision-Making Guidelines for Multinational Companies*, New York: Quorum Books.

Aliber, R.Z. (1985), ' Transfer Pricing A Taxonomy of Impacts on Economic Welfare', in Rugman, A.M. and Eden, L. (Eds), *Multinationals and Transfer Pricing*, London: Croon Helm, pp. 82-97.

Arpan, J.S. (1988), 'International Transfer Pricing' in Nobes, C. and Parker, R. (Eds), *Issues in Multinational Accounting*, Oxford: Philip Allan, pp. 161-177.

Atkinson, M. and Tyrrall, D.E. (1999), *International Transfer Pricing – A Practical Guide for Finance Directors*, Financial Times Management.

Choi, F.D.S. and Mueller, G.G. (1992), *International Accounting*, 2nd edition, Englewood Cliffs, N.J.: Prentice Hall International,.

Deloitte Touche Tohmatsu (1998), *International Transfer Pricing*, Deloitte Touche Tohmatsu, January-April.

Deloitte Touche Tohmatsu (1999), *Strategy Matrix for Global Transfer Pricing: Comparison of Methods, Documentation, Penalties, and Other Issues*, Deloitte Touche Tohmatsu, 1 January.

Eccles, R.G. (1985), *The Transfer Pricing Problem: A Theory for Practice*, Lexington, MA: Lexington Books.

Eden, L. (1998), *Taxing Multinationals –Transfer Pricing and Corporate Income Taxation in North America*, University of Toronto Press Incorporated.

Elliott, J. (1998), *International Transfer Pricing – A Survey of UK and Non-UK Groups*, CIMA Publishing.

Elliott, J. (1999), 'Survey of Multinationals' Responses to New Legislation in the United Kingdom', *Journal of Global Transfer Pricing*, Vol. 1(2), pp. 25-31.

Elliott, J. and Emmanuel, C.R. (1998), 'International Transfer Pricing: Searching for Patterns', *European Management Journal*, Vol. 16(2), pp. 216-222.

Elliott, J. and Emmanuel, C.R. (2000), *International Transfer Pricing – A Study of Cross-border Transactions*, CIMA Publishing.

Emmanuel, C.R. (1999), 'Income Shifting and International Transfer Pricing; a three country example', *Abacus*, Vol. 35(3), pp. 252-267.

Emmanuel, C.R. and Mehafdi, M. (1994),Transfer Pricing, London: The Chartered Institute of Management Accountants and Academic Press.

Ernst & Young (1995), *Transfer Pricing: Risk Reduction and Advance Pricing Agreements*, Ernst & Young.

Ernst & Young (1997a), 'Ernst & Young Transfer Pricing 1997 Global Survey.' *Tax Notes International*, 8 September, pp. 761-777.

General Accounting Office (1995), *International Taxation - Transfer Pricing and Information on Non-payment of Tax*, GAO/GGD-95 101, Washington D.C.: General Accounting Office.

Grubert, H. (1993), 'Taxes and Foreign Controlled Companies in the United States', in U.S. Dept of Commerce (Ed), *Foreign Direct Investment in the United States: An Update*, June, pp. 90-98.

Inland Revenue (1999), *Advance Pricing Agreements (APAs)*, Inland Revenue Press Release 87/99, 31 March.

Internal Revenue Service (1994), Final Regulations Relating to Intercompany Transfer Pricing under Section 482 (TD 8552), Washington D.C.: Department of the Treasury.

Kotabe, M. (1992), *Global Sourcing Strategy: R&D, Manufacturing, and Marketing Interfaces*, New York: Quorum.

Laster, D.S and McCauley, R.N. (1994), 'Making Sense of the Profits of Foreign Firms in the United States', *Federal Reserve Bank of New York Quarterly Review*, Summer-Fall, pp. 44-75.

Leitch, R.A and Barrett, K.S. (1992), 'Multinational Transfer Pricing: Objectives and Constraints', *Journal of Accounting Literature*, Vol. 11, pp. 47-92.

Mehafdi, M. and Emmanuel, C.R. (1997), 'Convergence, Divergence in Transfer Pricing Research: A Forty Year Survey', Department of Accounting and Finance, University of Glasgow, Working Paper 97/9.

Murray, J.Y., Wildt, A.R. and Kotabe, M. (1995), 'Global Sourcing Strategies of U.S. Subsidiaries of Foreign Multinationals', *Management International Review*, Vol. 35, pp. 307-324.

Natke, P.A. (1985), 'A Comparison of Import Pricing by Foreign and Domestic Firms in Brazil', in Rugman, A.M. and Eden, L. (Eds), *Multinationals and Transfer Pricing*, London: Croon Helm, pp. 212-222.

OECD (1994), *Transfer Pricing Guidelines for Multinational Enterprises and Tax Administrations*, Discussion Draft of Part I: Principles and Methods, Committee on Fiscal Affairs, Paris: OECD.

OECD (1995), *Transfer Pricing Guidelines for Multinational Enterprises and Tax Administrations*, Committee on Fiscal Affairs, Paris: OECD.

OECD (1997), *Transfer Pricing Guidelines for Multinational Enterprises and Tax Administrations*, 1997 Update, Committee on Fiscal Affairs, Paris: OECD.

OECD (1998), *Transfer Pricing Guidelines for Multinational Enterprises and Tax Administrations*, 1998 Update, Committee on Fiscal Affairs, Paris.

OECD (1999), *Transfer Pricing Guidelines for Multinational Enterprises and Tax Administrations*, 1999 Update, Committee on Fiscal Affairs, Paris: OECD.

OECD (2001), *Discussion Draft on the Attribution of Profits to Permanent Establishments*, Committee on Fiscal Affairs, Paris: OECD.

Ogley, A. (1993), *Principles of International Tax - A Multinational Perspective*, London: Interfisc Publishing.

Tax Management (2000), 'Around the World', *Tax Management Transfer Pricing Report*, Vol. 9(3), pp. 84-85.

Tax Management (2001), *Tax Management Transfer Pricing Report*, Vol. 10(9).

UNCTAD (1997a), *World Investment Report - Transnational Corporations, Market Structure and Competition Policy*, New York and Geneva: United Nations.

UNCTAD (1997b), *World Investment Report - Transnational Corporations, Market Structure and Competition Policy: Overview*, New York and Geneva: United Nations.

Wrappe, S.C. and Chung, K. (2001), 'The Second Annual APA Report: Reading the Tea Leaves', *Tax Management Transfer Pricing*, Vol.10(2), May 16.

	OECD	AUSTRALIA	UK	US
Tax Authority	Not applicable	Australian Tax Office	Inland Revenue	Internal Revenue Service
Regulations, Rulings, Guidelines	Transfer pricing Guidelines for Multinational Enterprises and Tax Administrations[1]	Final Rulings (TR 92/11, TR 94/14, TR 95/23, TR 97/20, TR 98/11, TR 98/16, TR 1999/1,TR1999/8,TR2000/16) Draft Rulings (TR 2000/D15)[2]	Section 770 and Sch 28AA, Taxes Act of 1988[3] Inland Revenue Tax Bulletins 25, 38, 43 & 46	Reg s1.482[4] Reg s1.6662-6[5]
Documentation Requirement	Pricing decisions should be documented in accordance with prudent business practices. Reasonable for tax authorities to expect taxpayers to prepare and maintain such material. No contemporaneous obligation.	Document pricing decisions in accordance with prudent business practices. Certain documents required. ATO ruling TR 98/11 recommends contemporaneous documentation to reduce risk of audit.	Taxpayers should keep records needed to deliver a correct & complete return. In practice, burden shifts to taxpayer to demonstrate reasonable transfer pricing. Certain documents are required to be prepared and retained.	Must include certain principal documents, as well as supporting documents. Contemporaneous documentation required.

[1] OECD: Various chapters published at July 1995, March 1996, and October 1997.
[2] Australia: All draft and final rulings have retroactive effect to 1982.
[3] UK: This is new legislation that applies to all accounting periods starting after July 1, 1998.
[4] US: Effective for tax years beginning after October 6, 1994.
[5] US: Effective February 9, 1996.

Tax Return Disclosures	Should be limited to information sufficient to allow tax administration to determine which taxpayers need further examination.	Schedule 25A requires disclosure of types of transactions, dollar amounts, countries involved, documentation maintained and methodologies used.	No separate disclosure required (ie on signing tax return taxpayer will be implicitly confirming compliance with arm's length standard).	Forms 5471 and 5472 require disclosure of detailed information on controlled transactions with foreign entities.
Acceptable Methods	CUP, Resale Price, Cost Plus, Profit Split (eg. Contribution Analysis or Residual Analysis), TNMM	CUP, Resale Price, Cost Plus, Profit Split (eg. Contribution Analysis or Residual Analysis), TNMM	CUP, Resale Price, Cost Plus, Profit Split (eg. Residual Analysis), TNMM	CUP, Resale Price, Cost Plus, Comparable Profit Split, Residual Profit Split, CPM
Priority of Methods	Reasonable Method. Transaction-based preferred over profit-based.	Most appropriate method. Transaction-based preferred over profit-based.	Most reasonable method or methods. Transaction-based preferred over profit-based.	Best method

Table 1: Transfer pricing Issues in Selected Countries (Extract from Deloitte Touche Tohmatsu (2001))

Chapter 10

International Tax Aspects of Income Derived from the Supply of Intellectual Property: Royalties vs. Business Profits

KEVIN HOLMES
International Bureau of Fiscal Documentation, The Netherlands

Key words: intellectual property; technology transfer; royalties; tax treaties

Abstract: This chapter describes the international tax aspects of transfers of technology. In this context, the chapter examines royalties and business profits, in terms of the OECD Model Tax Convention. The chapter first describes the principal forms of intellectual property rights and the typical means by which they are transferred. Extensions of the OECD Model definition of royalties adopted by the United Nations Model Tax Convention and some bilateral tax treaties are analysed. The distinction between the taxation of know-how and technical services is examined.

1.   INTRODUCTION

From the time of the discovery of the wheel, technology, even in its simplest form, has been shared. Throughout the ages, all societies have experienced the benefits of technological developments from rudimentary know-how to the techniques mastered in the mechanical, electrical and electronic revolutions. The knowledge behind inventions and other works achieved in these phases of economic and social development in one place has been copied to enhance the well being of users of the know-how in another place.

Historically, the transfers of knowledge have not been confined within national boundaries. International transfers of intellectual property were sufficiently widespread by the end of the nineteenth century to bring about international conventions to protect property rights in know-how from cross-border plagiarism. International transfers of technology (as well as transfers of other intellectual property) accelerated during the twentieth century.

The world experienced a technological revolution in the latter part of the twentieth century, which has continued beyond 2000. Generally more liberal economic policies, which have been adopted since the 1980s by developed and developing economies, and countries in transition from one political order to another, have facilitated the globalisation of trade and investment. These policies, together with the enormous advances in digital telecommunications, have enabled businesses to transfer more freely technology across national borders. Governments have generally embraced this development because of the obvious contribution that the application of the latest technological developments makes to a country's national welfare. As Lainoff and Vaish put it: '[a] great share of both private sector expenditures and government development incentives and other similar programs are designed to speed progress in numerous scientific and industrial fields, for ultimate exploitation in domestic markets and for export.'[1]

However, there is another side to the sharing of knowledge. The development of a new literary or artistic work, or computer program, invention, design or plant variety is a time consuming and costly undertaking. The author, composer, performer, computer programmer, investor, designer or plant breeder desires legal ownership rights in her output in order that she can control its commercialisation to recoup the investment costs and earn a profit from her investment of money, time, knowledge and effort. If the developer were not afforded such legal property rights, she could easily lose control of the commercialisation of her output to 'free riders', and would be quickly dissuaded from further innovative investment. Therefore, through their domestic laws, most developed countries foster the incentive for innovation by protecting the ownership interests in intellectual property of people or other entities that create new literary or artistic works, computer programs or designs, or invent new products or breed new plants.

This chapter begins by describing the nature of intellectual property rights and the international conventions that surround them. It then examines, in an international context, the three major means by which intellectual property (and technology, in particular) is transferred between, or applied for the benefit of, contracting parties, *viz.*:

1. The transfer of rights to use the intellectual property;
2. The absolute sale of the property; and

---

[1]   Lainoff, S. R. and Vaish, R .C., 'General Report', (1997) 82a *Cahiers de Droit Fiscal International - The Taxation of Income Derived from the Supply of Technology*, International Fiscal Association New Delhi Congress, Kluwer, The Hague, 23.

3. The performance of technical services.

The consideration for such transfers is normally payments of royalties or fees. The chapter analyses the manner in which cross-border payments of these royalties and fees are taxed, principally in the context of the relevant articles of the *OECD Model Tax Convention on Income and on Capital*[2] (the OECD Model) and common variations of it, but also citing some specific double tax agreements (DTAs). This approach is adopted, and justified, because (a) the purpose of this chapter is to address general principles and common problems in relation to the subject; (b) it is not practicable here to address all of the relevant articles of all treaties; and (c) to a large extent, most countries adopt broadly the words of the OECD Model or the main variations of it in the articles with which we are concerned.[3]

2.   WHAT IS INTELLECTUAL PROPERTY?

Intellectual property encompasses such things as technological knowledge, products, processes, and ideas. It is intangible property in which property rights vest. Like tangible real and personal property, intellectual property rights can be transferred from one party to another by way of outright sale and purchase or by means of the owner granting another entity the right to use the property. Depending on its nature, property rights inherent in intellectual property commonly take on the form of a:

1. Copyright;
2. Patent;
3. Trade mark;
4. Registered design;
5. Plant variety right; or
6. Geographical indication.

Under the statutes of many countries, an owner's interest in these rights is protected at a national level, often by registration of ownership with the

---

[2]   OECD Committee on Fiscal Affairs, (2000) *Model Tax Convention on Income and on Capital - Condensed Version*, OECD, Paris, April.

[3]   In practice, however, the reader must always remember that the OECD Model is just that - a model - and that the wording of the relevant articles in actual DTAs, while it may be based on the OECD Model, may well differ from it. Further, each DTA is different, so the reader must always make reference to the relevant articles of the particular DTA that applies to the transaction in question and not superimpose the wording of the OECD Model or another DTA onto those circumstances.

relevant governmental agency.[4] Furthermore, some international intellectual property cooperation treaties offer protection in nominated contracting states if an ownership interest is registered in one of the contracting states. For example, the Patent Co-operation Treaty[5] is a multilateral treaty, which facilitates protection for inventions in any or all of the contracting states such that, by filing a single application in one of the contracting states, an inventor simultaneously files in all designated contracting states.

2.1   Copyright

A copyright is an author's right in an original artistic, literary, scientific, dramatic or musical work, sound recording, film, broadcast, cable program, or published edition. Computer programs generally fall within the category of literary or scientific work[6]. Usually registration with a government authority is not required to prevent one entity from copying the work of another.

Although there is no such thing as an 'international copyright', which offers worldwide protection, there are a number of international copyright conventions, which are designed to ensure that copyright interests held in one country are protected also in other countries that are party to the convention. These conventions are not new. The first was the Berne Convention 1886.[7] Other international conventions that address copyright include the Rome Convention for the Protection of Performers, Producers of Phonograms and Broadcasting Organisations 1961, the World Intellectual Property Organisation Convention 1967 (the WIPO Convention),[8] the World Intellectual Property Organisation Performance and Phonograms Treaty 1996, the Universal Copyright Convention,[9] the Geneva Convention for the Protection of Producers of Phonograms Against Unauthorized Duplication of Their Phonograms 1971, the World Intellectual Property Organization Copyright Treaty 1996, the TRIPS Agreement 1994,[10] and the European

---

[4]   For example, in the United Kingdom, the Patent Office; in the United States, the United States Patent and Trade Mark Office; and in Australia, IP Australia.

[5]   Patent Co-operation Treaty 1970 (Washington; revised 1979 and 1984).

[6]   Intellectual property rights generally subsist in a computer program *per se*, rather than in the software medium in which it is embodied.

[7]   The Berne Copyright Convention 1886 (revised 1908 and 1928).

[8]   The Convention Establishing the World Intellectual Property Organisation 1967 (Stockholm; amended 1979).

[9]   Universal Copyright Convention 1952 (Geneva; revised 1971, Paris).

[10]   The World Trade Organisation Agreement on Trade Related Aspects of Intellectual Property 1994, Annex 1C of the Marrakesh Agreement Establishing the World Trade Organisation (Morocco, 1994).

Council Directive on the legal protection of computer programs.[11]

Countries that are party to the Berne Convention 1886[12] and the TRIPS Agreement[13] do not impose formalities; in these cases, the countries' domestic laws, in effect, simply render it an offence to plagiarise artistic or literary work, or films, broadcasts or programs. However, in some countries, which are party only to the Universal Copyright Convention 1952,[14] it is necessary to comply with certain formal procedures in order to claim copyright protection. These include a requirement that foreign authors, who wish to obtain copyright protection in a contracting state that imposes formal copyright protection conditions on its own nationals (e.g. by registration and/or the payment of fees), place the renowned © symbol, together with the name of the copyright proprietor and the year of first publication on the work.[15]

2.2   Patent

A patent is a monopoly right granted, generally upon registration, in such things as a new product or new manufacturing process, an improvement to an existing manufacturing process, a method relating to the testing or control of a manufacturing process; a new chemical compound or composition; biotechnological matter; electrical devices and circuits; and computer technology, all of which have industrial application. Typically, the granting of a patent gives the patentee the exclusive right to make, use or transfer the invention for a given number of years, specified in a country's domestic law, after the expiry date of which anyone may use the invention.

The Patent Co-operation Treaty[16] is a fundamental international convention that pertains to cross-border application of patent rights. Other international conventions that address patent rights include the Paris Convention for the Protection of Industrial Property 1883,[17] the TRIPS Agreement,[18] the WIPO Convention,[19] the Budapest Treaty of the

---

[11] The Council of European Communities, *Council Directive on the legal protection of computer programs* (91/250/EEC), 14 May 1991.

[12] *Op. cit.*, footnote 7.

[13] *Op. cit.*, footnote 10.

[14] *Op. cit.*, footnote 9.

[15] *Ibid*, Article III (1).

[16] *Op. cit.*, footnote 5.

[17] Revised 1900 (Brussels), 1911 (Washington), 1925 (The Hague), 1934 (London), 1958 (Lisbon), and 1967 (Stockholm); and amended 1979.

[18] *Op. cit.*, footnote 10.

[19] *Op. cit.*, footnote 8.

International Recognition of the Deposit of Micro-organisms for the Purposes of Patent Procedure 1997,[20] the Patent Law Treaty 1997, and the Strasbourg Agreement Concerning the International Patent Classification 1971.

2.3   Trade Mark

A trade mark is a means of identification, such as a sign or combination of signs, which can be represented graphically to enable a business to make its goods and services readily distinguishable from similar goods or services supplied by other traders. The sign may include a device or artistic design, logo, brand, heading, label, ticket, name, signature, word, letter, numeral, picture, symbol, graphic, colour, sound or smell, or any combination of these features.

Typically, trademarks are registered in a country if they meet certain statutory standards imposed by the country. For example, in the United States in *Wal-Mart Stores Inc. v. Samara Brothers Inc.*,[21] the Supreme Court held that product configurations could never be inherently distinctive. They are eligible for trademark protection only after acquiring a secondary meaning. 'Secondary meaning' is created in a trademark when the public has learned to identify the name of the product with its source, e.g. *Coca-Cola* ®

Registration of a trademark gives the owner the exclusive right to use the trade mark for a specified range of goods or services and for a period of time, which may be unlimited. Often the owner retains his ownership rights in a trademark in a particular country if he pays renewal fees to the office that administers intellectual property rights in the country.

International conventions that are concerned with trademarks include the Paris Convention 1883,[22] the WIPO Convention,[23] the TRIPS Agreement,[24] the Madrid Agreement Concerning the International Registration of Marks 1891,[25] the Nice Agreement Concerning the International Classification of Goods and Services for the Purpose of Registration of Marks 1977,[26] the Trademark Law Treaty 1994, the Vienna Agreement Establishing an

---

[20] Modified 1980.

[21] (2000) US 120 SC 1339, 54 USPO 2d 1065.

[22] *Op. cit.*, footnote 17.

[23] *Op. cit.*, footnote 8.

[24] *Op. cit.*, footnote 10.

[25] Revised 1900 (Brussels), 1911 (Washington), 1925 (The Hague), 1934 (London), 1957 (Nice), and 1967 (Stockholm).

[26] Amended 1979.

International Classification of Figurative Elements of Marks 1973,[27] and the European Council Resolution on the Community Trade Mark 1993.[28]

2.4 Design

To protect an entity's interest in a novel design, the design is normally registered with a governmental intellectual property office. A registered design protects the owner's interest in the external appearance of an article of manufacture (rather than in the article itself). The design is usually required to be repeatedly produced by an industrial process, rather than produced only once or twice.

Registered design protection does not extend to the materials from which the product is made, how the product is made, or its purpose. Similarly, patterns or shapes on their own cannot be registered as a design. They must be applied to a particular article. When the design of an article is due solely to the function of the article, and when it has no aesthetic value, the design also cannot be registered. Furthermore, designs normally cannot be registered for works of sculpture, wall plaques, medals, clothing, maps or printed matter of a literary or artistic character (for example, book jackets, stamps and advertisements); however, designs of a cast, model or mould to produce an article are usually registerable. What are protected as a registered design are the owner's rights in the shape of the object and any decorative ornamentation that appears on it. The protection is generally for a fixed statutory period, which may be renewable.

A design that is an original artistic work will, in most countries, have an inherent copyright interest. To enforce copyright protection, a designer must prove her ownership of the artistic design and that any infringement has been copied from her design. Unless specifically excluded from registration under a particular country's domestic law (such as those designs described in the previous paragraph), formal registration of a design would normally ease the burden of proof because the registration is evidence of ownership rights in the design and (particularly by notification on a product or packaging) an indication to the world at large of that ownership.

International conventions that relate to designs include the Paris Convention 1883,[29] the WIPO Convention,[30] the TRIPS Agreement,[31] the

---

[27] Amended 1985.

[28] The Council of the European Union, Council Regulation (EC) No. 40/94 of 20 December 1993 on the Community trade mark.

[29] *Op. cit.*, footnote 17.

[30] *Op. cit.*, footnote 8.

[31] *Op. cit.*, footnote 10.

Hague Agreement Concerning the International Deposit of Industrial Designs 1925,[32] the Locarno Agreement Establishing an International Classification for Industrial Designs 1968,[33] and the Treaty on Intellectual Property in Respect of Integrated Circuits 1989.

To distinguish patents, trademarks and registered designs, we can say, in general terms, that a patent protects the inventive aspects of a new product, a trade mark identifies the provider of specified goods or services, and a registered design protects the appearance of a physical object. Thus, patents, trademarks and registered designs give legal recognition to ownership rights in new inventions, brand names and visual designs, respectively.

2.5   Plant Variety Right

A plant variety right is a right granted, generally by a governmental authority, in a new, distinct, homogeneous, and stable, cultivated plant variety. Once granted, the breeder of a new plant variety obtains the exclusive right to produce for sale, and to sell, reproductive material or plants of the variety, and to propagate the variety for commercial production, usually for a fixed period.

The most significant international agreement that relates to plant variety rights is the UPOV[34] International Convention for the Protection of New Varieties of Plants 1961.[35]

2.6   Geographical Indication

In some countries, rights in geographical indications may be registered, which allows the origins of goods to be associated with particular geographical areas; for example, the use of the word *Champagne* on the renowned sparking wine product to indicate the region of France from which the product originates.

2.7   Summary

All of the above rights are valuable property rights, which can be transferred by way of sale and purchase, assignment, licence or lease. The

---

[32] Extended by the London Act (1934), Additional Act, Monaco (1961), the Complementary Act, Stockholm (1967; amended 1979), and the Geneva Act (1999).

[33] Amended 1979.

[34] The International Union for the Protection of New Varieties of Plants.

[35] Amended 1972 and 1978 (Geneva).

legal protections described above, which are afforded to owners of interests in intellectual property (including technological property rights), give an incentive to creators, inventors, developers and breeders to invest in new works, inventions, designs and plants. The innovations clearly contribute to a country's economic and social well being in that they are used nationally. Furthermore, the innovations contribute to the economic and social well being of other countries when the innovations are exported. Conversely, the legal protection in countries where it is offered to ownership interests in intellectual property also enables technology to be imported, which gives citizens of those countries the opportunity to access works, inventions, designs and plants that may not otherwise be released there. Thus, both the exporting and the importing countries can each enhance their national welfare as a consequence of international trade in technology and other intellectual property.

The number of international conventions that apply to intellectual property is indicative of the multinational use of intellectual property and international transposition of technology. These conventions regulate internationally rights in intellectual property in countries that are party to the conventions. It is hardly surprising then that questions of international tax would arise from payments for cross-border use of technology and other intellectual property; in particular, which of the importing country or the exporting country has the right to tax those payments. Resolution of the international tax issues turns on the nature of the particular intellectual property that is supplied.

3. FORMS OF SUPPLY OF TECHNOLOGY

The character of payments received in transactions that involve the transfer of technology depends on the nature of the rights that the transferee acquires under a particular arrangement regarding the use and exploitation of the technology. Once the nature of those rights is determined, the payment can be classified, in general terms, as either a royalty (to which Article 12 of the OECD Model applies) or business profits (to which Article 7 applies).

The interrelationship between Article 12 and Article 7 is important because Article 7 is subordinate to Article 12.[36] This means that countries that wish to tax payments for transfers of technology have a priority right to tax them as royalties (at source, where the OECD Model definition has been

---

[36] Article 7(7) provides that '[w]here profits include items of income which are dealt with separately in other Articles of [the OECD Model], then the provisions of those Articles shall not be affected by the provisions of this Article.'

modified),[37] rather than as business profits, the tax on which is restricted by the requirement of a presence of a permanent establishment (PE) in the country. In other words, a modified Article 12 is an easier route to taxation by a source country than Article 7. Furthermore, if the non-resident exporter is taxable in its country of residence on its worldwide income, it would normally obtain a domestic tax credit for foreign tax paid. In these circumstances, some (if not all) of the tax burden imposed by the source state is transferred to the residence state.

3.1   Royalties

3.1.1   Residence vs. Source Taxation

Article 12(1) of the OECD Model restricts the imposition of tax on royalties to the jurisdiction in which the recipient (being the beneficial owner of the royalties)[38] is resident. However, this general rule is over-ridden by Article 12(3) if the recipient carries on business in the source state through a PE situated there. In that case, the royalties must be effectively connected with the PE.[39]   In essence, Article 12 of the OECD Model provides for exclusive taxation of royalties in the country of residence of the beneficial owner of the royalty income. The OECD Model does not allow for taxation of royalties in the country of source except where the beneficial owner of the royalties carries on business in the source state under the specified conditions that relate to a PE.

At least from the perspective of developing countries, which are technology-importing countries, Article 12 of the OECD Model is inadequate. Unless the supplier of technology has a PE in the developing country, that state obtains no tax revenue from the royalty payments that are made in consideration for the technology. That lost revenue opportunity is exacerbated if technology exporters use untaxed royalty payments to siphon otherwise taxable profits (typically of a subsidiary company) out of the developing

---

[37] See under *Royalties* below.

[38] As to the meaning of 'beneficial ownership', see du Toit, Charl, (1999) *Beneficial Ownership of Royalties in Bilateral Tax Treaties*, IBFD Publications, Amsterdam.

[39] The same principle applies in Article 12 of the United States Model Convention (see 'United States Model Income Tax Convention of 20 September 1996', (2000) *Tax Treaties Database*, International Bureau of Fiscal Documentation, Amsterdam). With respect to the OECD Model, Italy reserves the right to impose taxes under its domestic law on royalties and profits from the alienation of rights or property that gives rise to royalties if the recipient has a PE in Italy, notwithstanding that the rights or property in respect of which the royalties are paid are not effectively connected with the PE (*op. cit.*, footnote 2, 163).

country, leaving it with no direct tax base at all in respect of the use of the imported technology.

This deficiency has been overcome in the United Nations Model Convention (UN Model),[40] which provides that '... royalties may also be taxed in the Contracting State in which they arise...' subject to a maximum, mutually agreed percentage of the gross amount of the royalties.[41]

The following OECD countries (most of which are *not* generally regarded as developing countries) reserve the right to depart from Article 12(1) of the OECD Model and tax royalties at source, largely in accordance with the UN Model: Australia, Canada, the Czech Republic, Greece, Italy, Japan, Korea, Mexico, New Zealand, Poland, Portugal, Spain, and Turkey.[42] Non-OECD member countries (most of which have developing or transitional economies) that reserve the right to tax royalties at source are: Argentina, Belarus, Brazil, China, Estonia, Israel, Latvia, Lithuania, Malaysia, the Philippines, Romania, Russia, Slovakia, South Africa, Thailand, Ukraine, and Vietnam.[43]

3.1.2   What are 'Royalties'?

Article 12(2) of the OECD Model defines 'royalties' to mean:

'payments of any kind received as consideration for the use of, or the right to use, any copyright of literary, artistic or scientific work including cinematograph films, any patent, trade mark, design or model, plan, secret formula or process, or for information concerning industrial, commercial or scientific experience.'[44]

---

[40] United Nations, 'Convention Between (State A) and (State B) for Avoidance of Double Taxation with respect to Taxes on Income (and on Capital) 1980', (2001) *Tax Treaties Database*, International Bureau of Fiscal Documentation, Amsterdam.

[41] *Ibid*, Article 12(2). Although the rate varies between different bilateral DTAs, it is frequently 10 per cent.

[42] *Op. cit.*, footnote 2, 161-162.

[43] *Op. cit.*, footnote 2, 297. Because the influence and application of the OECD Model extends beyond member countries of the OECD, the OECD Committee on Fiscal Affairs invites some non-member countries to contribute their views on the negotiation, application and interpretation of DTAs. Consequently, those countries also identify areas where they have reservations about the text of the OECD Model or the associated Commentary (see footnote 53).

[44] *Op. cit.*, footnote 2, 33. As well as cinematograph films, the UN Model also captures 'films or tapes used for radio or television broadcasting' (*op. cit.*, footnote 40). By contrast, the US Model *excludes* all of the above films or tapes but *includes* 'other like right[s] or property' as those listed in the OECD Model definition; 'information concerning industrial, commercial, or scientific experience'; and 'gains derived from the alienation of any such right or property [as those listed in the OECD Model definition, as modified above by the

Some OECD countries also extend the definition of royalties in Article 12(2) to include payments for transmissions by satellite, cable, optic fibre, or similar technology[45]. Brazil, Estonia, Latvia, Lithuania, and Romania (all being non-OECD member countries) reserve the right to similarly expand the OECD Model definition of royalties.

3.2   Full Alienation of Rights

Where a sum is paid in consideration for the alienation in full of rights attached to intellectual property, the consideration would normally not be a royalty because the definition of 'royalties' in Article 12(2) requires that the payment be made 'for the use of, or the right to use,' the property. Where rights are alienated in full, the payment is not for the use of (or the right to use) those rights. The payment is for the rights themselves.[46]

3.3   Partial Alienation of Rights

There can be a partial alienation of ownership rights in intellectual property when the (pre-existing) owner transfers the exclusive right of use in the property for a specified period or for a defined geographical region. In either of these circumstances, the consideration received for that partial

---

US Model] which are contingent on the productivity, use, or disposition thereof' (*op. cit.*, footnote 39). Remember, however, that the modifications to the OECD Model in the US Model are for the purposes resident state taxation - *not* source state taxation. A definition of 'royalties', which expands that in the OECD Model, is set out in the European Council's Proposed Directive on Interest and Royalties, which is designed to exempt interest and royalties from income and withholding taxes in a source member state where the interest or royalties are paid by a company to certain associated companies or a PE in another member state: ' 'royalties' means payments of any kind received as a consideration for the use of, or the right to use, any copyright of literary, artistic, scientific work or software, including cinematograph films, any patent, trademark, design or model, plan, secret formula or process, or for the use of or the right to use industrial, commercial or scientific equipment, or for information concerning industrial, commercial or scientific experience. Variable or fixed payments as consideration for the working of, or the right to work, mineral deposits, sources and other natural resources shall be excluded, as well as payments for the use of, or the right to use, software when ownership is transferred': European Commission, 'Interest and Royalty Directive', (1998) 41 *Official Journal of the European Communities*, C123, 23 April, Art. 2, Sec. 1(b).

[45] See, for example, the Australia-New Zealand DTA.

[46] Following the US Model, not surprisingly the United States reserves the right to treat as a royalty a gain derived from the alienation of property referred to in Article 12(2) of the OECD Model if the gain is contingent upon the productivity, use or disposition of the property (*op. cit.*, footnote 2, 163).

alienation will again normally fall outside the definition of royalties because the payment is for the (albeit limited) rights themselves, rather than for the use of (or the right to use) those rights. The sum paid in consideration would therefore generally be treated as business income of the alienator (which falls within Article 7) or a capital gain (which falls within Article 13).

3.4 Industrial, Commercial, or Scientific Equipment

Many OECD countries reserve the right to include within the definition of 'royalties' in some of their bilateral DTAs payments for the use of, or the right to use, industrial, commercial, or scientific equipment. This provision has been adopted from the 1977 version of the OECD Model (and the earlier 1963 Draft OECD Model).[47]

Payments for the use of, or the right to use intangible property are *not* payments 'for the use of, or the right to use, industrial, commercial or scientific equipment' because intangible property is not 'equipment'. That some intangible property, such as computer software or other digital products, may be transmitted via a tangible medium (e.g. a diskette or a CD) does not make the acquisition of the content of the medium solely an acquisition of the tangible medium itself.

For those bilateral tax treaties that include within the term 'royalties' payments for the use of, or the right to use, industrial, commercial or scientific equipment, according to the OECD Technical Advisory Group (OECD TAG) on Treaty Characterisation of Electronic Commerce Payments,[48] 'the word 'equipment'... applies to property that is intended to be an accessory in an industrial, commercial or scientific process and could not therefore apply to property, such as a music or video CD, that is used in and for itself.'[49] In addition, products such as computer games, music, or videos,

---

[47] For example, Australia, Canada, the Czech Republic, Hungary, Greece, Italy, Mexico, New Zealand, Poland, Portugal, Spain and Turkey (*op. cit.*, footnote 2, 162). Many non-OECD member countries do the same; for example, Argentina, Belarus, Brazil, China, Estonia, Latvia, Lithuania, the Philippines, Romania, Russia, Slovakia, Thailand, and Vietnam (*ibid*, 297-298). This part of the definition of 'royalties' was removed from later versions of the OECD Model to ensure that payments for the *leasing* of industrial, commercial, or scientific equipment, including the leasing of containers, were taxed as business profits under Article 7, rather than as royalties under Article 12.

[48] OECD Technical Advisory Group on Treaty Characterisation of Electronic Commerce Payments, (2000) *Tax Treaty Characterisation Issues Arising from E-Commerce: Report to Working Party No. 1 of the OECD Committee on Fiscal Affairs*, OECD, Paris, February.

[49] *Ibid*, 12.

which are used by a private consumer, fall outside the 'industrial, commercial or scientific' description of the equipment.[50]

3.5   Know-how

'Know-how' has been defined by the *Association des Bureaux pour la Protection de la Propriété Industrielle* as:

> 'all the undivulged technical information, whether capable of being patented or not, that is necessary for the industrial reproduction of a product or process, directly and under the same conditions; inasmuch as it is derived from experience, know-how represents what a manufacturer cannot know from mere examination of the product and mere knowledge of the progress of technique.'[51]

Therefore, know-how must be more than mere general knowledge.[52] The OECD Commentaries on the Articles of the Model Tax Convention[53] (the OECD Commentary) explains the concept further:

> '[i]n the know-how contract, one of the parties agrees to impart to the other, so that he can use them for his own account, his special knowledge and experience which remain unrevealed to the public. It is recognised that the grantor is not required to play any part himself in the application of the formulas granted to the licensee and that he does not guarantee the result thereof.'[54]

An Australian Tax Office ruling aptly describes some important elements of know-how.[55] Amongst other features, the ruling records that, for know-how, a 'product' (being knowledge, information, a technique, a formula, skills, a process, a plan or the like) *has already been created* or developed; it is *already in existence* and *subsequently transferred*. Furthermore, the product

---

[50] *Idem.*

[51] *Op. cit.*, footnote 2, 155.

[52] In fact, the European Commission regulation on the application of the Treaty establishing the European Community to certain categories of technology transfer requires that know-how is secret: see 'Commission Regulation (EC) No. 240/96 of 31 January 1996 on the application of Article 85(3) of the Treaty to certain categories of technical transfer agreement', (1996) *Official Journal of the European Communities*, L31/2, 9 February, Art. 10(1).

[53] *Op. cit.*, footnote 2, 45-277.

[54] *Op. cit.*, footnote 51.

[55] Australian Tax Office, (1991) *Income Tax: Definition of Royalties, Taxation Ruling IT2660*, 28 November, http://www.law.ato.gov.au/pbrdocs/it2660.doc.

is supplied *for use by the buyer* but remains with the provider who retains the right to also use it himself or to transfer it to another person.[56]

The recognition of know-how turns on the so-called 'imparting principle'.[57] To take van der Bruggen's illustration:

> 'Imparting' is passing on knowledge as a teacher does to a student. The purpose of the exchange for the receiver is to learn how to do something, so that he knows how to do it himself the next time. Applied to know-how, it means paying for information on certain industrial, commercial or scientific experience, with the purpose of using that information and experience to perform that industrial, commercial or scientific process. In those cases, there is ... a right to use information concerning industrial, commercial or scientific experience, payments for which are subject to Article 12 (royalty)...

In most cases, it will be useful to ask the question: 'What can the receiver do with the information he obtained through the exchange?' If the answer is that, predominantly, he can now master an industrial reproduction of a product or process under the same conditions as the grantor, which would have been difficult or impossible without the grantor's experience on the subject, there was an imparting of knowledge.[58]

The same analysis and conclusion can be extended to agricultural products and processes such that, for instance, if, after an exchange the recipient knows how to propagate and produce a plant variety, which she could not do before the exchange, then knowledge has been imparted, the payment for which is a royalty.

These interpretations of the meaning of 'know-how' make it clear that payments made for know-how constitute royalties since know-how falls within 'information concerning industrial, commercial or scientific experience' in Article 12(2) of the OECD Model.

---

[56] *Ibid*, para. 28.
[57] See, for example, Vogel, K., *et. al.*, (1997) *Klaus Vogel on Double Tax Conventions*, Kluwer Law International, 3 ed., London, 709-710, and van der Bruggen, E., 'Source Taxation of Consideration for Technical Services and Know-how with Particular Reference to the Treaty Policy of China, Indonesia and Thailand', (2001) 7(3) *Asia-Pacific Tax Bulletin*, March, 42, 50.
[58] *Ibid*, 50-51.

3.6   Technical Services

3.6.1   Technical Services vs. Know-how

Payments for know-how must be distinguished from payments for technical services, which fall outside the definition of royalties. The OECD Model treats cross-border payments for technical services as business profits to which Article 7 applies.[59] The OECD Commentary again gives us some guidance to distinguish between the provision of know-how and the provision of services:

> '[The know-how] type of contract ... differs from contracts for the provision of services, in which one of the parties undertakes to use the customary skills of his calling to execute work himself for the other party. Thus, payments obtained as consideration for after-sales service, for services rendered by a seller to the purchaser under a guarantee, for pure technical assistance, or for an opinion given by an engineer, an advocate or an accountant, do not constitute royalties .... Such payments generally fall under Article 7.'[60]

The Australian Tax Office ruling also assists in drawing the distinction. In contrast to know-how, the performance of services is an activity that *will result in* the creation or development of a product, which may or may not be know-how. A contractor applies his existing knowledge, skill, and expertise. There is not a supply of know-how, but use by the contractor of his knowledge *for his own purposes*. The product created as a result of the performance of services *belongs to the buyer* for her to use without having to obtain any rights to do so.[61]

---

[59] Portugal and Spain reserve the right to tax at source as royalties income that arises from technical assistance in connection with the use of, or the right to use, rights or information of the ilk set out in Article 12(2) of the OECD Model definition of royalties. In addition, many non-OECD member countries are not prepared to leave technical service fees to be taxed as business profits under Article 7. Argentina, the Philippines, and Thailand reserve the right to tax technical service fees as royalties (*op. cit.*, footnote 2, 297); Brazil reserves the same right for technical service fees *and* technical assistance (*ibid.*); and Malaysia, Russia, and Vietnam reserve the right to deal with technical service fees in a similar way to royalties, but under a separate article (*ibid.*). In fact, India has been the most successful of the developing countries to adopt the latter approach, which is now embodied in most of its DTAs. This approach is also often adopted by African countries; see, for example, DTAs entered into by Gambia, Ghana, Kenya, and Uganda.

[60] *Op. cit.*, footnote 2, 155.

[61] *Op. cit.*, footnote 55, para. 29.

The level and nature of expenditure incurred by the seller is indicative of the nature of the supply. In general, we would expect that the supply of know-how would require little more to be done than copying existing material and, therefore, relatively little expense. The supply of services would generally require a greater amount of expenditure, including such items as salaries and wages paid to the supplier's employees, payments to subcontractors, payments for purchases of materials, and management and overhead expenditure.[62] If A contracts B to create some property (e.g. a report about the efficiency and effectiveness of A's accounting system), which A will own immediately from the time that it is created, no pre-existing property is acquired by A from B. If, on the other hand, A acquires from B property that was not specifically made for A (e.g. an investment report containing confidential, proprietary information), which is supplied to a range of B's customers, the supply is one of data *content* in which A obtains a right of use. Here, there is not a service, but a sale of intangible property rights. The distinctive feature of know-how is that it is a pre-existing asset; it is not brought into existence in pursuance of the contract in question.[63]

In addition, in contrast to know-how, the supply of technical services does not involve the principle of imparting knowledge: '[t]he performer of the service will use his skills to solve the problem himself for the other party. The purpose of the exchange for the receiver is not to learn, but to have the performer of the service execute the work or mission concerned. ... Technological service is, rather than merely imparting knowledge, getting involved with the particular situation of the receiver'.[64] The plumber who fixes our water pipes uses her knowledge and skills to provide us with technical services to complete the job. She does not provide know-how so that we can do the job ourselves next time. If the job needs to be repeated in the future, we call her back to do it again. When a malfunction reoccurs, we are not (nor were we ever intended to be) any the wiser about water pipe repair techniques. Payment received by the plumber for her services is therefore business income and not a royalty for the imparting of know-how. So it is also in an international context. The tax advisor, who is resident in Country A and travels to Country B to give advice to a resident of Country B, uses his knowledge and skills to solve the prevailing problem faced by the resident of Country B. The advisor does not impart his knowledge so that the resident of Country B can solve his next tax problem himself. The payment received by the advisor for his services is therefore business income taxable only in

---

[62] *Ibid*, paras. 31-32.
[63] *Ibid.*, para. 33.
[64] Per van der Bruggen, *op. cit.*, footnote 57, 51.

Country A in terms of Article 7 of the OECD Model.[65] The payment is not a royalty in consideration for imparted knowledge, which would otherwise be subject to (withholding) tax under a modified Article 12.

There are also other distinguishing features between the supply of know-how and the supply of technical services:

1. As the OECD Commentary notes, the quality of services may be guaranteed,[66] but there would not normally be a guarantee associated with the result of the imparting of knowledge;
2. The information in a transfer of know-how, and the grantor and the recipient, are often in the same business sector, and the know-how will be used to generate business income;
3. Know-how remains the property of the grantor S the recipient obtains the right to use the know-how, but cannot do anything else with it, as the owner can; cf. the output of services, which is owned by the recipient; and
4. Payments for know-how can be periodic and based on usage, whereas payments for services are generally singular and made once the service is performed.

3.6.2   Extensions to the OECD Model

It can readily be seen that Article 7 generally confines the tax on technical service fees to the state in which the supplier of the services is resident because the activity of providing technical services would not amount to a PE.[67] The provider of the services would not normally have a fixed place of business in the source state.[68]

Because of the constraints imposed by the OECD Model on source states imposing tax on technical service fees, some countries (particularly, developing countries) veer from the OECD Model and incorporate technical services into the definition of royalties in bilateral DTAs. This most commonly occurs in conjunction with a version of Article 12 that follows the UN Model, which permits the source state to impose withholding tax on

---

[65] Assuming that the adviser does not have a PE in Country B through which he renders his advice.

[66] *Op. cit.*, footnote 60.

[67] The reader will recall that Article 7(1) permits a source state to tax a non-resident's business profits only to the extent that they are attributable to a PE in that state. Article 5(1) defines a PE to be a 'fixed place of business through which the business of an enterprise is wholly or partly carried on.'

[68] Even if the provider of the services were to have a fixed place of business in the source state, through which it provided its services, there would still be no PE if the services were of a preparatory or auxiliary character (see Article 5(4)(e)), which will often be the case for such a service as after-sales service.

royalties and therefore, by virtue of the expanded definition of royalties, technical service fees.

Other countries have introduced a separate article in their bilateral DTAs, which specifically addresses technical service fees. Again, such an article invariably allows the source state to levy withholding tax on the fees.[69]

Although there is no general definition of the term 'technical service fees', it (or variations of it) has been defined in particular bilateral DTAs. For example, the Gambia-United Kingdom DTA defines 'fees for technical services' as 'payments of any kind to any person, other than an employee of the person making the payments, in consideration for any services of a technical or consultancy nature.'[70]

The Kenya-Norway DTA has a broader definition, which encompasses management and professional services. It defines 'management or professional fees' as 'payments ... in consideration for any services of a managerial, technical, professional or consultancy nature.'[71]

Technical services are regarded by the OECD TAG as services that require special skills or knowledge related to a particular technical discipline, such as techniques in the applied sciences (e.g. engineering consultancy), rather than in the humanities.[72] To be treated as a technical service, the special skills and knowledge must be used in producing the service. That such skills are used to *develop* a service, e.g. data warehousing services, does not render the provision of the service a technical service. The service provided to a customer is not the technical development of the data, nor its arrangement and associated software, but the supply of access to the data warehouse. Similarly, the delivery of a service through a technological medium does not in itself render the service a technical service. For example, simply because a distance learning program is delivered on-line does not make the education service a technical service.

The OECD TAG describes managerial services as 'services rendered in performing management functions.'[73] These functions relate to the way that a business is run, in contrast to operational functions performed by line staff.

Consultancy services are regarded by the OECD TAG as services that provide 'advice by someone, such as a professional, who has special qualifications allowing him to do so.'[74] These services may overlap with technical and managerial services.

---

[69] See footnote 59 for examples of countries that adopt these approaches.
[70] Gambia-United Kingdom DTA, Article 14(3).
[71] Kenya-Norway DTA, Article 14(3).
[72] *Op. cit.*, footnote 48, 14.
[73] *Ibid,* 15.
[74] *Ibid,* 16.

These definitions are important because, to the extent that an activity falls outside them, payments for that activity will not, in the absence of a PE, be subject to income tax or, more typically, withholding tax in the country from which the payments are derived, i.e. the source state.

The India-United Kingdom DTA defines 'fees for included services', being services that are associated with rights that give rise to royalty payments, in much broader terms. Subject to some specific exclusions, 'fees for included services' are:

> 'payments of any kind to any person in consideration for the rendering of any technical or consultancy services (including provision of services of technical or other personnel) which:
>
> (a) are ancillary and subsidiary to the application or enjoyment of the right, property or information for which a payment ... is received [in connection with the use of, or the right to use, a copyright, patent, trade mark, design or model, plan, secret formula or process, or information concerning industrial, commercial or scientific experience]; or
>
> (b) are ancillary and subsidiary to the enjoyment of the property for which a payment ... is received [in connection with the use of, or the right to use, industrial, commercial or scientific equipment]; or
>
> (c) make available technical knowledge, experience, skill, know-how or processes, or consist of the development and transfer of a technical plan or technical design.'[75]

The UN Model also expands the definition of a PE in the OECD Model, if there is no fixed base in the source country, to capture certain services based on the duration of their performance. Specifically, the UN Model states that a PE includes:

> '[t]he furnishing of services, including consultancy services, by an enterprise through employees or other personnel engaged by the enterprise for such purpose, but only where activities of that nature continue (for the same or a connected project) with the [source] country for a period or periods aggregating more than six months in any 12-month period.'[76]

---

[75] India-United Kingdom DTA, Article 13(4). The India-United States of America DTA contains a similar, but slightly narrower, definition. It excludes paragraph (b) of the India-United Kingdom DTA definition.

[76] UN Model, Article 5(3)(b). Note that if technical service fees fall within both of the categories of a royalty and business profits because this definition of a PE applies, Article 12 over-rides Article 7 so that the source state can tax the fees (by way of a withholding tax at source) as a royalty: see Article 7(6).

However, time limit and project connection constraints in the proviso to this 'furnishing of services' component of the PE definition would seem to have rendered this extension of the definition inadequate for many countries, which have instead, or in addition, broadened Article 12 of the OECD Model in their bilateral DTAs. Alternatively, as we have seen, some developing countries have inserted a separate article with a wide scope, to catch technical, managerial and consultancy services, which can be taxed at source by the source state.

A separate article that embraces technical, managerial and consultancy fees is undoubtedly the most effective way for a source country to impose tax on service fees under a bilateral DTA because it bypasses the need to conform with any other requirements of an Article 12 royalty definition and it circumvents the constraints of the proviso to the 'furnishing of services' extension to the PE definition, proffered by the UN Model. It is therefore unsurprising that some developing countries have taken the separate article route.

3.7 Mixed Know-how and Technical Service Contracts

Mixed contracts are contracts in which more than one item is supplied under the terms of the contract. A mixed contract could provide for the supply of know-how and technical services in consideration for a single payment; for example, a franchising agreement typically stipulates that the franchisor shall impart not only his knowledge and experience to the franchisee, but also technical assistance. With these sorts of arrangements, one global amount is paid in consideration for the different elements. That sum must be broken down into the two (or more) parts, which are allocable to each element. The apportionment must be based on information specified in the contract itself or on some other reasonable basis. The part of the consideration that is attributable to know-how is then treated as a royalty under Article 12 and the part that relates to technical services is treated as business income under Article 7. Where Article 12 has been modified in a specific DTA to allow for taxation at source, withholding tax may be imposed on the royalty component by the source state.

If, however, one element constitutes 'by far the principal purpose of the contract'[77] and the other element is 'only of an ancillary and largely unimportant character',[78] the whole amount paid should, according to the OECD Commentary, be treated as relating only to the primary element.

---

[77] *Op. cit.,* footnote 2, 155.
[78] *Idem.*

4.   SUMMARY

This chapter has described the main forms of intellectual property in which ownership rights are legally protected both nationally and internationally: copyright, patents, trademarks, designs, plant varieties, and geographical indications. These intangible rights, or the benefits of them, are transferred from the owner to other parties by three principal means:

1. The transfer of the *rights to use* the property;
2. The *outright sale or alienation* of the property; and
3. The performance of *services*.

In transactions that involve the transfer or use of technology, we must determine first whether the vendor supplies intellectual property or a service in order to ascertain the character of the payments given in consideration and, therefore, the correct tax classification.

The provision of a *right to use* intellectual property gives rise to a royalty payment, the international tax treatment of which is indicated by Article 12 of the OECD Model. Payments for the supply of know-how, which involves the imparting of knowledge from one party to another, constitute payments for 'information concerning industrial, commercial or scientific experience' and are consequently royalties, to which Article 12 applies.

Because Article 12 of the OECD Model restricts the taxation rights applicable to cross-border royalty income to the country of residence of the technology exporter, many capital importing countries (particularly developing countries) adopt the royalty article in the UN Model (or a variation of it) in their bilateral DTAs. That article permits the source state to impose tax, including a withholding tax at the time of payment of the royalties. The non-resident technology exporter would normally obtain a credit for tax paid overseas if its worldwide income were taxable in its home state, thus shifting at least part of the source state tax burden onto the home state.

A full or partial alienation of rights in intellectual property generally does not give rise to royalties because the intellectual property rights themselves are transferred. This is a transfer of something more than the granting of the mere right to use the intellectual property. Consideration paid for the alienation of the property rights is business profits, which are dealt with under Article 7 of the OECD Model or a capital gain covered by Article 13. Unless the transaction arises through a PE (as defined in Article 5) that the vendor has in the source state, the source state cannot normally tax the consideration.

Technical services are concerned with the creation of something by a contractor. They do not involve the subsequent transfer of a right to use a pre-existing product. Consequently, payments for services constitute business profits under Article 7 of the OECD Model. However, many developing countries, in particular, extend the OECD Model definition of 'royalties' to catch technical service fees and other service fees. Some bilateral DTAs include instead a broad based separate article to capture fees for technical, managerial, and consultancy services. The UN Model definition of a PE also includes 'furnishing of services' if consultancy services in connection with a project in a source country last for more than six months in a 12-month period. These extensions beyond the OECD Model are designed to strengthen the ability of, especially, underdeveloped countries to derive tax revenue from the activities of foreign technology exporters in their country.

The categorisation and consequential international tax treatment of technology related transactions are summarised in the illustration below:

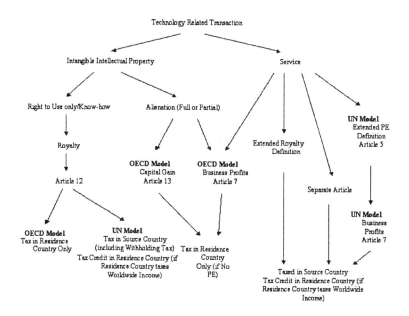

Figure 1. Summary of Technology Related Transactions

Mixed or bundled contracts are common when transfers of technology occur. Here more than one element is given in consideration for the payment of a single sum. Such contracts require a breakdown of the consideration paid into the elements that relate to the provision of rights to use intellectual property and those that relate to the provision of goods or services. In general terms, the former is royalties and the latter are business profits. The OECD Commentary indicates that where one element is by far the principal element such that the other is ancillary or largely unimportant, the tax treatment of the principal element should apply to the whole of the consideration paid.

STUDY QUESTIONS

1. Ten Canadian technicians provide technical assistance for seven months in a car manufacturing plant in China. Where is the payment to the Canadian employer of the technicians taxed? Why?
2. A university library in the United Kingdom pays a subscription to Lexis-Nexis in the United States to enable research students to access a tax legislation and case law database. The students are permitted to search the database, select specific items, and to print out hard copies of the information that they select. How is the subscription taxed?
3. A United Kingdom company sells machinery to an Indian company and sends its technicians to India for two months to set up the machinery, to commence production from it, and to train Indian staff on technological and operational aspects of the machinery. How is payment for this work to be taxed? Would your answer be different if the supplier company was not a resident of the United Kingdom but a resident of the United States?
4. A resident of Country A sells equipment to a resident of Country B. The supplier also transfers the relevant technology to the purchaser, who pays fees for:
   - the proprietary rights in patents;
   - documents and designs in relation to the proprietary rights;
   - documents, designs and training of the purchaser's personnel in relation to the installation and operation of the equipment; and
   - other technical training of the purchaser's personnel.

   How are the fees treated under (a) the OECD Model, (b) the UN Model, and (c) the U.S. Model?
5. The London branch of the ABN-AMRO Bank, a resident of the Netherlands, charges a fee for financial market intelligence reports that it delivers by e-mail each day to subscribers in Germany. The subscribers are prohibited from reproducing the information in any form, except for the purposes of downloading, storing, and reading the reports. The bank also charges these subscribers a fee for banking transactions in sterling, which the subscribers carry out on the internet website of the bank. How is the income received from these two sources treated under the OECD Model and the relevant DTA? (Note: first determine which is the relevant DTA:

United Kingdom-Netherlands, United Kingdom-Germany, or Netherlands-Germany?)

FURTHER READING

Baron, R. (2001), 'Income Characterisation', *Tax Planning International*, Vol. 3(4), April, p. 15.

De Goede, J. J. P. and Holmes, K. J. (Eds.) (2001), *The International Guide to the Taxation of Transfers of Technology*, Amsterdam: International Bureau of Fiscal Documentation.

International Fiscal Association (1997), *The Taxation of Income Derived from the Supply of Technology, Cahiers de Droit Fiscal International*, n.82a, New Delhi Congress, The Hague: Kluwer.

International Fiscal Association (2001), *Taxation of Income Derived from Electronic Commerce, Cahiers de Droit Fiscal International*, n.86a, San Francisco Congress, The Hague: Kluwer.

OECD (2000), *Model Tax Convention on Income and on Capital - Condensed version*, Committee on Fiscal Affairs, Paris: OECD.

OECD (2001), *Tax Treaty Characterisation Issues Arising from E-Commerce: Report to Working Group No. 1 of the OECD Committee on Fiscal Affairs*, Technical Advisory Group on Treaty Characterisation of Electronic Commerce Payments, Paris: OECD.

Sprague, G. D., Whatley, E. T., and Weisman, R. L. (1995), 'An Analysis of the Proper Tax Treatment of International Payments for Computer Software Products', *Asia-Pacific Tax Bulletin*, Vol. 1(6), June, p. 158.

Van der Bruggen, E. (2001), 'Source Taxation of Consideration for Technical Services and Know-how with Particular Reference to the Treaty Policy of China, Indonesia and Thailand', *Asia-Pacific Tax Bulletin*, Vol. 7(3), March, p. 42.

Vogel, K. *et. al.* (1997), *Klaus Vogel on Double Tax Conventions*, 3rd edition, London: Kluwer Law International.

Chapter 11

Taxing Non-Residents: A U.S. Perspective

PEGGY HITE
Indiana University, U.S.A.

Key words: non-residents; resident aliens; U.S. citizens; tax treaties

Abstract: As globalisation increases, so does the need for understanding multijurisdictional taxation. Which countries will try to tax the international traveller's income? Treaties can clarify the tax implications, but too many treaties could become overwhelmingly complex. When treaties do not exist, each host country must establish a set of rules for taxing non-citizens. This chapter describes the basic U.S. income tax laws for taxing resident and non-resident aliens who come to the United States. If international visitors meet the criteria for being a 'resident alien', then the U.S. tax system will tax them on their worldwide income and allow them the same deductions and credits that U.S. citizens enjoy. On the other hand, 'non-resident aliens' are only taxed on their U.S. source income, and they are entitled to fewer deductions and credits. This chapter explains the general concepts along with a few details about how these rules are applied.

1. INTRODUCTION

This chapter examines how non-U.S. citizens are subject to income tax in the United States. Given an increasingly mobile population, international travellers who work or reside in the United States for an extended period may find themselves owing U.S. income taxes. This chapter provides an overview of the major factors that determine one's U.S. tax liability. The primary factor is the determination of whether one is a resident alien or a non-resident alien as the rules of taxation differ by status. Criteria for establishing resident alien status are discussed, followed by special rules for first-year and last-year residency. The effect of tax treaties is discussed next, followed by a discussion about how reported income is affected by the source of income. Income exclusions, exemptions, types of allowable deductions and credits also are discussed. Then, a discussion of how and when the tax is paid is presented, followed by an explanation of departure permits.

2.   RESIDENT ALIEN STATUS

Visiting in the United States could lead to an income tax liability if the visitor has income from sources within the U.S. If visitors are not United States citizens, then they are considered to be aliens, either resident aliens or non-resident aliens. Resident aliens are generally taxed in the same manner as U.S. citizens are taxed—on worldwide income. Furthermore, the same types of deductions and credits are allowed. Non-resident aliens, however, are allowed some but not all of the same deductions and credits. At the same time, non-resident aliens are not taxed on worldwide income. Usually, they are only taxed on income sourced within the United States. In short, understanding who is categorised as a non-resident alien or a resident alien is crucial to understanding the tax requirements.

To be resident aliens, they must meet at least one of two tests. Otherwise, they are non-resident aliens (unless, as discussed later, they can choose to be treated as part-year U.S. residents under the exception for 'first-year choice' that dual-status aliens have). The two tests for resident alien status are the 'green card test' and the 'substantial presence test'.

2.1   Green Card

The green card test indicates that the aliens are lawful permanent residents of the U.S. at any time during the year. That is, according to the U.S. immigration laws, the aliens have been given the privilege to reside in the U.S. as an immigrant. This right continues until the U.S. takes it away by administrative or judicial order. The aliens themselves may relinquish the privilege by either applying for abandonment status or attaching the green card to a letter stating their intent to abandon resident status.

2.2   Substantial Presence

The substantial presence test also leads to treatment as a U.S. resident for tax purposes. The test can be satisfied by being physically present in the U.S. on at least 31 days in the current year and by being present a total of 183 days during the current and preceding two years. However, the 183 days can include only 1/3 of the days present in the preceding year and 1/6 of the days present in the U.S. in the second year before the current year.

Example: If an alien were physically present in the United States on 90 days during each of three years—1999, 2000, and 2001. The total is 270 days in three years, but that is not sufficient. Instead, all of the 90 days in the current year, 2001, are included; 1/3 of the 90 days in 2000 are included, as are 1/6 of the 90 days in 1999. The total for the substantial presence test is 135 (90+30+15), and that does not satisfy the test.

2.3   Exceptions

Being physically present in the United States on any day usually counts as a valid day of presence, however, some exceptions exist. The days may not count if they relate to the following: regular commuters, medical condition, or exempt individuals.

2.3.1   Regular Commute

Having a regular commute in Canada or Mexico is defined as commuting to and from work in the U.S. on more than 75% of the workdays in a working period. A working period can be seasonal or cyclical. Thus, there can be more than one working period in a calendar year, and a working period can begin in one year and end in the next.

Example: Assume Roberto Garcia lives in Mexico. He is employed in Mexico but the firm assigned him to work in its U.S. office four days a week for 20 weeks. He drove back and forth each day when working in the U.S. office, and he worked in his home office in Mexico every fifth day. Four days times 20 weeks is 80 potential days of presence in the U.S. However, during this working period more than 75% of the workdays (80/100) were spent commuting to work in the U.S. Consequently, those days cannot be counted as days of presence in the U.S. for the purpose of passing the substantial presence test.

2.3.2   Days in Transit

Besides regular commuting days, 'days in transit' also cannot be used in the substantial presence test. This refers to time periods of less than 24 hours when the aliens are in the United States because they are en route from one foreign country to another. Of course, if they held a business meeting at the airport when they were en route it would be a valid working day in the U.S. rather than a day in transit.

2.3.3   Crewmembers

Crewmembers of foreign vessels engaged in international transportation cannot count their days temporarily working in the U.S. as days of presence—unless they engage in a different trade or business in the U.S. on those days.

2.3.4   Medical Condition

If aliens could not leave the U.S. when they had intended because of a medical problem that developed while in the U.S., then those days detained for medical reasons do not count as a day of presence for the substantial presence test. However, if the aliens returned to the U.S. for treatment of a medical condition that developed during a prior stay in the U.S., then the days can be included. Similarly, if the aliens were aware that the condition existed before arriving in the U.S., then the extended days can be included in the substantial presence test.

2.3.5   Exempt Individuals

None of the days present in the U.S. count toward the substantial presence test if the aliens are 'exempt' individuals. Although there are a few exceptions, typically, this includes foreign government/international organisation-related individuals and their families (not their employees), teachers or trainees with J or Q visas, students with F, J, M or Q visas (usually for 5 years or less), and professional athletes temporarily competing in charitable sports events. (Days practising are included but days competing are excluded.)

To exclude any days from the substantial presence test (whether for regular commuting, days in transit, a medical condition, as a crew member, or as an exempt individual), aliens must file a form with the Internal Revenue Service (IRS, Form 8843) to timely document the reasons for excluding specific days.

2.4   Closer Connection

Even if the substantial presence test is met, aliens might still be treated as non-resident aliens rather than resident aliens. If during the year, the aliens are present in the U.S. for less than 183 days, they maintain a tax home (main place of business) in a foreign country, and they have a closer connection to any one foreign country that is a tax home than to the U.S., then they can be considered non-resident aliens. (See IRS Publication 519 for resident alien status when there is a 'closer connection' to two foreign countries but not more than two.) Having a closer connection to a foreign country is determined by weighing factors such as the following:

– What country of residence is designated on various documents
– Location of permanent home, family, and personal belongings...
– Location of social, cultural, or religious affiliations
– Location of business tax home
– Jurisdiction for voting and/or holding a driver's license.

2.5   Dual Status

It is also possible to be a dual-status alien, usually in the year of arrival in or the year of departure from the U.S.

Example: If an alien had not been a resident in year 1 (the preceding year) but came to the U.S. from January 6 to January 10 for a business meeting and then lived in the U.S. from the following March 1 through December 31, the alien could be considered a resident alien with a residency starting on either January 6 or March 1, for purposes of the substantial presence test. Generally, it would begin on January 6, but the alien may qualify to exclude up to 10 days (e.g., January 6-10 in this case) if the alien had a closer connection to another country that was his/her tax home during that period. (The alien may prefer to have non-resident status during January and February so that foreign income during that period is not subject to U.S. income tax.) To exclude up to six days, aliens must file a statement with the IRS requesting to exclude those days for the purpose of determining the residency starting date.

If an alien meets the green card test but not the substantial presence test, the residency starting date is the first day in the calendar year in which the alien is present in the U.S. as a lawful permanent resident. If both the green card and the substantial presence tests are met, then the residency starting date is the earlier starting date under the two tests.

A different rule exists if the alien was a U.S. resident in the preceding year. In the above example, the alien would be considered a U.S. resident as of January 1, not January 6 nor March 1 - regardless of whether the green card or substantial presence test is applicable.

2.6   First-year Choice

Other provisions exist - one for the first year of residency choice and another for non-resident spouses. Regarding the first-year choice, if an alien passes the substantial presence test early in the current year, then the alien may elect to be treated as a U.S. resident for part of the preceding year provided the alien was physically present in the U.S. for at least 31 days in that preceding year. In addition, there is a 75% test that requires the alien to be present in the U.S. for at least 75% of the days in the preceding year beginning with the start of the 31-day period and ending with the last day of the year. Up to 5 days of absence during that period can be treated as days present.

> **Example:** Assume Juanita, a citizen of Panama, came to the United States for the first time on November 3 and stayed until December 3 (a total of 31 days) before she returned to Panama. She came back to the U.S. on December 16 and stayed until December 29. During the following year, she qualified as a resident under the substantial presence test. If Juanita makes the first-year choice to be treated as a resident alien for the first year, her residency starting date will be November 3 because she met the 31-day rule and the 75% test. The 75% test was met because her total days in the U.S. were 50 (31 for November 3- December 3; 14 for December 16-December 29; and 5 for the absent days counted as present). Thus, 84.75% of the potential residency period for the first year (total days from November 3-December 31 were 59) was spent in the U.S.

2.7   Non-resident Spouse

The rules tend to be more flexible for married couples. Generally, if the alien is the spouse of a U.S. citizen or resident, then the alien can elect to be treated as a resident for the entire year provided a joint tax return is filed and statements from both spouses are filed documenting they are qualified to make the election. If a married couple does this, then they cannot claim tax treaty benefits as a resident of a foreign country in the same year they choose to be treated as full year U.S. residents. In addition, the couple pays U.S. tax on their worldwide income.

2.8   Last-year Residency

Residency in the U.S. stops at the end of the last year (December 31) in which the alien was a resident, unless the alien qualifies for an earlier termination date. Under the substantial presence test, the residency termination date is the last date the alien is physically present in the U.S. during the last year of qualified residency. Although there are restrictions, if a brief visit or visits occurred later in the year, up to 10 days could be excluded for the purpose of determining the residency termination date.

> **Example:** Assume Desmond Mandela, a citizen of South Africa came to the U.S. from January 1 to June 30 when he returned to South Africa. He came to visit from November 20 to November 28, and since September, he had a closer connection to his tax home in South Africa. For the substantial presence test, Desmond was present in the U.S. for 190 days (181+9). For the residency termination date, the nine days in November can be excluded, making June 30 the residency termination date.

Under the green card test, residency ends on the first day the alien is no longer a lawful permanent resident of the U.S. If the alien meets both tests, the later date of the two tests is the date used as the residency termination date. However, the rule for using a residency termination date that is earlier than December 31 only applies to aliens who at the end of that year had a tax home in a foreign country and had a closer connection to that foreign country.

2.9   Dual-status

When an alien has been both a resident alien and a non-resident alien in the same year, it is a dual-status tax year. To determine the U.S. tax liability, different rules apply for the part of the year spent as a resident and for the part of the year spent as a non-resident. For the part of the year with resident alien status, the alien is taxed on all sources of income. Any income received while a resident alien (not necessarily earned) is taxable. For the part of the year with non-resident alien status, the alien is taxed on income from U.S. sources (unless exempt by the Internal Revenue Code or a tax treaty) and certain foreign source income treated as effectively connected with a trade or business. Dual-status taxpayers cannot claim a standard deduction, but they can itemise their allowable deductions. Any exemption for a spouse or dependents is limited to the taxable income for the part of the year with resident alien status. For the part of the year with non-resident alien status, usually only the personal exemption is allowed.

3.   TAX TREATIES

Each treaty is unique and remains the ultimate authority. For example, the above rules for resident and non-resident alien status do not override tax treaty definitions. Although some treaties require the alien be a national or citizen of the treaty country, most treaties require that the alien be a resident of the treaty country. Consequently, most treaties apply to non-resident aliens in the U.S. The treaty either exempts some income (called treaty income) from U.S. tax or allows it to be taxed at a lower tax treaty rate. Typical tax treaty benefits include exemptions for personal services, for teachers and professors, for employees of foreign governments, for students and trainees, and for capital gains on sales of personal property.

Personal services are sometimes exempt from U.S. tax when the non-resident alien comes to the U.S. for a short stay—usually 183 days or less but some treaties specify a maximum stay of 180 or 90 days. Teachers and professors whose primary purpose is to teach or do research at an accredited institution can sometimes exempt that income for up to 2 or 3 years. Although treaties vary, exemptions for income earned by employees of foreign governments usually apply only to non-resident aliens in the U.S.

If remittances are received from abroad to fund education and training, they are generally exempt from U.S. tax. In addition, most treaties exempt gains from the sale of personal property resulting in a capital gain, but gains from the sale of real property located in the U.S. are usually taxable.

Non-treaty income is taxed at a flat 30% rate if the income is not effectively connected with a trade or business in the U.S. If it is, then the graduated U.S. tax rates are used. In contrast, the treaty income is either exempt or taxed at a lower tax treaty rate. The total tax liability is the sum of the tax on the treaty income and the tax on the non-treaty income, but that tax cannot exceed what the tax would have been without the tax treaty.

Example: Assume Martina is a resident of a foreign country that has a tax treaty with the U.S. For the year, she had $24,000 of income from U.S. sources ($1,000 of dividends that are limited to a 10% tax treaty rate and $23,000 of compensation for services, which is not limited by the treaty). Martina's dividends are not effectively connected with her business, and she does not have any qualifying deductions except for her own personal exemption ($3,000 in 2002). Her tax liability without the treaty is computed as follows:

Income subject to graduated rates (effectively connected with a business)

Compensation $23,000
     Less personal exemption(3,000)
                 $20,000 x .15 = $3,000 Tax

Income subject to 30% rate
     Dividends $ 1,000 x .30 = $ 300 Tax

Tax without a treaty $3,300

The tax with a treaty changes the liability, because the treaty limits the dividends to a 15% tax rate. Hence, the tax liability is only $3,150 ($3,000 + $150 [$1,000 x 0.15]).

4.   SOURCES OF INCOME

The income that must be reported on a U.S. tax return depends on whether the alien is a resident or non-resident. Typically, resident aliens are subject to the same tax rules as U.S. citizens are. In other words, most income will be subject to U.S. income tax whether the income is from sources within or outside the United States. Moreover, the income is subject to the graduated tax rates that apply to U.S. citizens. In contrast, only U.S. source income is usually reported on non-resident aliens' tax returns. The tax rates applied to that income depend on whether the income is effectively connected with a trade or business in the U.S., in which case the U.S. graduated tax rates are used. If the income is not effectively connected with a trade or business in the U.S., then a flat 30% tax rate (or lower treaty rate) is used.

Being effectively connected with a trade or business in the U.S. includes being self-employed or performing personal services as an employee. It also includes being a student or trainee under an F, J, M, or Q visa, being the beneficiary of an estate or trust that is engaged in business in the U.S., or selling real estate located in the U.S. (whether it's a capital gain or not). Even some investment income (if it is an asset used in the current conduct of a U.S. trade or business, or if the conduct of the business was a material factor in producing the investment income) and some foreign income (if a U.S. office significantly contributes to and is an essential economic element in earnings specific types of income) must be treated as effectively connected with a trade or business in the U.S.

Since non-resident aliens pay tax primarily on U.S. source income, rules for determining whether the income source is from within or outside the U.S. must be understood. Some of the most common types of income are presented in Table 1 and discussed below.

4.1   Interest Income

If interest income is derived from bonds, notes, or obligations of U.S. entities (individuals, domestic corporations, state or local governments...), or foreign businesses (partnerships or corporations) engaged in a U.S. trade or business during the year, the interest is U.S. source income. One exception includes payments by resident aliens or domestic corporations whose own income over the preceding 3 years was predominantly (>80%) from sources outside the U.S. because of an active business in a foreign country. Other exceptions exist for savings and loans, banks, credit unions, and commercial banking business operating in foreign countries.

Table 1. Summary of Source Rules for Income of Non-resident Aliens

Item of Income	Factor Determining Source
Salaries, wages, other compensation	Where services performed
Business Income:	
Personal services	Where services performed
Sale of Inventory – purchased	Where sold
Sale of Inventory – produced	Allocation
Interest	Residence of payer
Dividends	Whether a US or foreign corporation
Rents	Location of property
Royalties:	
Natural resources	Location of property
Patents, copyrights	Where property is used
Sale of personal property	Seller's tax home
Pensions	Where services were performed that earned the pension
Scholarships, prizes, awards	Residence of the payer

Source: IRS Publication 519

4.2   Dividend Income

Dividends from a domestic corporation are U.S. source income unless it is a corporation electing to take the Puerto Rico economic activity credit or the

U.S. possession tax credit. Another exception is the dividend from a foreign corporation that had at least 25% of its gross income, in the preceding 3-year period, derived from a trade or business in the U.S. In this case, the dividend is prorated to determine the part that is deemed U.S. source income. The U.S. source part is the dividend times the following fraction:

$$\frac{\text{Foreign corp. gross income derived from a U.S. trade or business for the 3-year period}}{\text{Foreign corp. gross income from all sources for that 3-year period.}}$$

4.3 Personal Services

The source of income for personal services depends on where the services were performed (unless the alien qualifies as an employee of foreign persons, organisations, or offices). If the service is performed both inside and outside the U.S., then the number of days worked in the U.S. relative to the total number of days worked inside and outside for the payment form a fraction. That fraction times the compensation represents the amount of U.S. source income that must be included in gross income.

Example: Assume Pierre Bordeaux, a non-resident alien from Canada, is a professional baseball player from the Toronto Blue Jays. Under his contract, he received $2,000,000 for 290 days of work—either in training, regular season, or playoffs, but 145 of those work days were performed in the U.S. Hence, 50% (145/290) of the $2,000,000 is considered U.S. source income.

4.4 Scholarships and Prizes

For scholarships and grants, the only amount that is potentially taxable is the U.S. source amount that exceeds the cost of tuition and course-related expenses. The source of scholarships, fellowships, grants, prizes, and awards is U.S. income if the residence of the payer is a U.S. entity regardless of who literally disburses the funds. If the payments originate from a foreign entity (even if disbursed through a U.S. agent), then they are considered foreign source payments. Payments from international organisations are usually from foreign sources. Amounts paid because of activities performed or to be performed outside the U.S. are foreign source income, and amounts paid for compensation are determined under the personal service rules (see above).

4.5   Pensions

Pensions attributable to services performed both in and outside the United States must be prorated between the U.S. source and non-U.S. source income. U.S. government employees have U.S. source pension income except for the amount attributable to any tax-exempt pay for services performed outside the United States.

4.6   Rents and Royalties

Rent and royalties derived from property located in the United States is U.S. source income. The source of income for royalties depends on whether the use or right to use the intangible property (e.g., patents, copyrights, goodwill...) is for inside or outside of the United States.

4.7   Real Property

Any real property, such as land and buildings, which is located in the U.S., generates U.S. source income. Thus, rental income, profits and gains or losses from the disposition of that property is U.S. source income.

4.8   Personal Property

Generally, gain or loss from the sale or exchange of personal property is treated as U.S. source income if the alien has a tax home in the U.S. If the alien does not have a tax home but does have a home office in the U.S., then the income is U.S. source income. However, the type of property sold also affects the income source. Income is treated as U.S. source if an income tax of less than 10% is paid to a foreign country for the sale of personal property (other than inventory, depreciable property, or intangibles). The rules vary for inventory, depreciable, intangible, and other types of personal property.

4.9   Inventory

The source of income for inventory depends on whether the inventory was purchased or produced. Sale of inventory that was purchased is sourced where the property is sold. However, when an outside office materially participates in a sale of inventory that will be used or consumed outside the U.S., it is considered to be from sources outside the U.S. More precisely, it is sourced in the country where the title to the property passes to the buyer. If the inventory was produced and sold in the same country, then source follows the place of sale. However, if the inventory was produced in one country and sold in another, the rules require an allocation so that part is U.S. source and part is from outside the U.S. Details on the rules for making the allocation are explained in U.S. Internal Revenue Regulation section 1.863-3.

4.10   Depreciable Property

Determining the source of income for depreciable personal property is a function of whether the gain or sale exceeds the total depreciation adjustments. The part of the gain that does not exceed prior depreciation deduction must be allocated between sources inside and outside of the U.S. based on the ratio of U.S. depreciation adjustments to total depreciation adjustments for the U.S. source part. Although there are some industry exceptions (i.e., transportation, communications...), usually all depreciation deductions are treated as U.S. depreciation adjustments if the property was used predominantly in the U.S.

For the part of the gain that exceeds prior depreciation adjustments, the source of the gain is determined like inventory, generally where the title to the property passes. If depreciable property is sold (after January 10, 1999) for a loss, it is sourced the same as depreciation—U.S. depreciation adjustments proportionate to total depreciation adjustments. However, if the asset was used predominantly in the U.S., then the alien can elect to treat the entire loss as U.S. source income. (See Regulation section 1.865-1T(f)(2)).

4.11   Intangible Property

Income from the sale of intangible property is sourced in the country where the property is used, if the income is contingent on its productivity, use, or disposition. In contrast, if the income is not contingent on its use, then the income is sourced according to the seller's tax home. If the intangible is goodwill and the income is not dependent on its productivity, then the source is the country in which the goodwill was generated.

5.   EXCLUSIONS FROM INCOME

Resident and non-resident aliens can be allowed certain exclusions from income. Resident aliens, for example can exclude foreign earned income and foreign-housing allowances just like U.S. citizens can. The exclusions apply if the resident alien is present in a foreign country or countries for at least 330 full days during a period of 12 consecutive months.

5.1   Interest Income

Non-resident aliens may be allowed to exclude some types of interest income, services for foreign employers, as well as scholarships and grants. For example, interest income that is not connected with a U.S. trade or business can be excluded when it is from deposits with banks, credit unions, savings and loans, obligations targeted to foreign markets, or from a corporation or partnership in which the alien owns more than 10%.

5.2   Services

If the alien worked in the U.S. for a foreign employer for 90 days or less and earned $3,000 or less for those services, then that amount could be exempt from U.S. tax. If the non-resident alien was present in the U.S. as a regular crewmember of a foreign vessel, the earned compensation is exempt from U.S. tax. Students and exchange visitors working for a foreign employer usually exclude the income from U.S. tax. However, if the students and exchange visitors or any other non-resident aliens currently work for a foreign government or a qualified international organisation, the compensation for services is generally excluded when the services performed are similar to those performed by U.S. employees in that foreign country and the foreign country offers a similar exemption to U.S. citizens. In addition, non-resident aliens (but not resident aliens and U.S. citizens) may get to exempt their wages from a foreign government if that government has a tax treaty with the U.S. that has a provision to exempt the income.

5.3   Scholarships

As noted earlier for a resident alien the only amount of a scholarship or grant that is taxable is the amount that exceeds the cost of tuition and course-related expenses. The same is true for a non-resident alien. None of the scholarship or grant, however, is taxable for the non-resident alien if the grant is from sources outside the U.S.

6. EXEMPTION DEDUCTIONS

6.1 Resident Aliens

U.S. citizens can deduct a certain amount each year ($3,000) in 2002 for each taxpayer and dependent—provided each has an assigned identification number. Similarly, resident aliens can claim personal and dependency exemptions. They can even claim an exemption for their spouse who has not come to the United States. Exemptions for dependents must be citizens or residents of the U.S., Canada, or Mexico for some part of the year. In contrast, non-resident aliens can usually claim an exemption only for themselves, not for dependents.

6.2 Non-resident Aliens

In addition to a personal exemption, non-resident aliens may be able to claim an exemption for a spouse and a dependent if any one of three situations exist for the dependent or spouse: resident of Mexico or Canada, or a U.S. national; resident of Japan or South Korea; or a student or business apprentice from India. For U.S. nationals and residents of Mexico or Canada, the spouse must have no gross income and must not be claimed as another's dependent. Dependents must meet the same qualifications as dependents of U.S. citizens (e.g., not too much gross income, receive more than one-half of their support from the non-resident alien, not file a joint return that resulted in a tax liability... See IRS Publication 501).

Tax treaties with Japan and Korea impose additional requirements. The spouse and children must live with the non-resident alien in the U.S. for some portion of the tax year. In addition, the exemption deductions must be prorated based on the ratio of U.S. source income effectively connected with a trade or business relative to the alien's income from all sources.

A tax treaty with India provides a spousal exemption similar to the one for residents of Mexico and Canada (see above). If the spouse has no gross income and is not the tax dependent of another, he/she qualifies for the exemption. Children who meet the U.S. dependency tests can be claimed by these non-resident aliens as long as they were not admitted to the U.S. on F-2, J-2 or M-2 visas.

7.   DEDUCTIONS

7.1   Resident Aliens

Resident aliens are allowed the same deductions as U.S. citizens if they are residents for the entire year. In contrast, non-resident aliens only get to claim deductions that are effectively connected with their U.S. trade or business, such as ordinary and necessary business expenses, and uninsured losses resulting from transactions entered into for a profit.

7.2   Non-resident Aliens

Non-resident aliens may also qualify for individual retirement accounts (IRAs), either traditional or Roth IRAs. The rules are equivalent to those for U.S. citizens and resident aliens. Another possible deduction is the one for non-reimbursed moving expenses if the non-resident alien moves to the United States to take a job (but not to return to a foreign home site). The rules are the same as those used by U.S. citizens and residents. For example, after the move, the taxpayer must work full time for at least 39 weeks out of the next 12 months. If self-employed, the taxpayer must work full time for at least 78 weeks out of 24 months beginning on the date of the move.

Alternatively, non-resident aliens could deduct travel expenses (room, board, and transportation while working in the U.S.) instead of the moving expenses. Moving expenses are allowed when there is a change in your principal place of business while travel expenses are intended for expenses associated with temporary absences from the principal place of business. Other examples of possible deductions include student loan interest expense and penalties for early withdrawal of time savings accounts.

8.   ITEMIZED DEDUCTIONS

8.1   Resident Aliens

Once again, resident aliens are allowed to use the same rules as U.S. citizens in determining their itemised deductions on Schedule A of Form 1040. These deductions allow for the following types of expenses: medical, state and local income taxes, real estate taxes, interest on a home mortgage, charitable contributions, casualty and theft losses, and miscellaneous deductions. Alternatively, a standard deduction can be claimed in lieu of itemising and documenting these specific expenses.

8.2 Non-resident Aliens

The standard deduction is not an option for non-resident aliens (although there is an exception for students and business apprentices from India). Moreover, non-resident aliens can only deduct certain itemised deductions provided they receive income effectively connected with their trade or business in the U.S. Allowable deductions include state and local income taxes, charitable contributions to U.S. organisations, casualty and theft losses, and some miscellaneous deductions. Miscellaneous deductions include items such as tax return preparation fees and job-related expenses. Dues for professional and trade associations and travel expenses for employees on business trips can be deducted in this category. The actual deduction, however, is not the total amount of such expenses. It is only the amount that exceeds 2% of the income reported on the tax return (after certain adjustments). Furthermore, any allowable deductions are denied if they are allocable to U.S. tax exempt income. For example, if a non-resident alien made $10,000 working in the U.S. but $7,000 of it was tax exempt under a tax treaty, then only 30% of any associated expenses would be deductible because 70% ($7,000/10,000) would not be allowed as a deduction associated with U.S. trade or business income.

9. CREDITS

9.1 Resident Aliens

Resident aliens can claim any credits available to U.S. citizens provided they meet the same qualifications for each type of credit. Credits commonly claimed include the child and dependent care credit (for child care expenses when the parents are at work), the child credit (for having dependent children under age 17), credit for the elderly or disabled (for low income elderly taxpayers), education credits (for low and middle income taxpayers who pay college tuition), foreign tax credit (for reducing U.S. tax on income that is also taxed by a foreign country), adoption credit (for expenses associated with adopting a child), and the earned income tax credit (for low income taxpayers).

9.2   Non-resident Aliens

Non-resident aliens can claim some but not all of the credits that resident aliens can claim. Credits can be claimed only if income is received that is effectively connected with a trade or business in the U.S. In that case, the child and dependent care credit, child credit, education credits, foreign tax credit, adoption credit, and earned income credit can be claimed. These types of credits generally reduce the tax liability if taxes are owed. In addition, any taxes that are prepaid (or withheld from the income source) can be claimed subsequently as credits on the tax return. The credits pay the tax if it is owed. If excess amounts have been prepaid or withheld, then the balance will be sent to the taxpayer as a refund.

10.   PAYING THE TAX

Sometimes non-resident aliens are required to file and other times they may choose to file. If too much tax is withheld, they can file for a refund. If they want to claim certain deductions or credits, then a tax return must be filed. Moreover, a tax return must be filed when non-resident aliens have U.S. source income that does not withhold enough tax to satisfy the liability or when they are engaged in a trade or business in the U.S. If they are required to file, they must first apply for a taxpayer identification number (on Form W-7).

10.1   Who Must File

A U.S. tax return must be filed if non-resident aliens work or if they are engaged in a trade or business in the U.S. This is true even if their income is generated from outside the U.S.; they have no income from U.S. sources; or the income is exempt from U.S. tax. Generally, they are considered to be engaged in a trade or business if they perform personal services in the U.S. There is, however, an exception to the personal service rule. The income is not considered to be taxable if they meet all three of the following conditions: 1) compensation for the services is $3,000 or less, 2) the work is performed while temporarily in the U.S. for a total of 90 days or less, and 3) either personal services are performed in an office outside of the U.S. for a business maintained by a U.S. entity or resident; or, personal services are performed for a non U.S. entity or resident that is not engaged in a trade or business in the U.S.

If non-resident aliens have U.S. source income that was not subject to income tax withholding, they must file a return. U.S. source income is subject to U.S. income tax. Examples of such taxable income include 1) wages, fees, tips for services performed in the U.S., 2) most types of interest income and dividend income, 3) profits or losses from the sale of inventory property in the U.S., 4) rents and royalties, and 5) gains or losses from selling real property located in the U.S.

10.2   When to Pay

Non-resident aliens and resident aliens who will owe federal income tax are expected to pay the tax throughout the year either through withholdings or estimated tax payments, just as U.S. citizens must do. If considered employees, taxes are withheld from their wages. Otherwise, most income is subject to a 30% withholding rate. For example, the following types of income could be subject to a flat 30% withholding rate: work as an independent contractor (that is not considered a trade or business), some interest income (but not from most banks or similar institutions), dividend income, rents, royalties, some social security benefits, and annuities from pensions, trusts, etc...). If taxes are not withheld or if they are significantly under withheld, quarterly estimated tax payments must be made. Otherwise, penalties, in addition to the tax due, could be assessed.

11.   DEPARTURE PERMITS

Before leaving the United States, aliens must get a certificate of compliance or clearance. This can be obtained by filing a form with the Internal Revenue Service (Form 1040-C or Form 2063). This is not a final tax return, but any tax paid with the form will be treated as a credit on the final tax return. The form should be filed approximately two weeks before the planned departure date, but it cannot be issued more than 30 days before the departure.

To receive the certificate of compliance several documents are needed: passport and alien registration card (or visa), copies of U.S. income tax returns for the past two years, proof the prior year taxes were paid, proof of claimed deductions, proof of taxes paid for the current year, if self-employed, proof of income and expenses to date, documents proving gains or losses on sales of property, scholarships, and special tax treaty benefits.

Some aliens are exempt and do not have to obtain sailing or departure permits. Generally, no permit is required if the alien (or a family member) has a diplomatic passport, if the alien (or member of the household) is an employee of a foreign government or international organisation whose compensation is tax exempt (provided no income from other U.S. source is received, if the alien (or the family) is a student, industrial trainee, or exchange visitor with the requisite visa (F-1, F-2, H-3, H-4, J-1, J-2, M-1, M-3, or Q visas) with no U.S. source income. Depending on the type of visa, some income is tax exempt such as allowances to cover incidental education expenses, food or lodging, certain interest income, or certain types of employment income authorised by the Immigration and Naturalization Services (INS). In addition, employed aliens who are residents of Canada or Mexico frequently commuting between their country and the United States and whose wages are subject to the U.S. withholding tax are exempt from filing for a departure permit. Lastly, certain military trainees, visitors with B-1, B-2, C-1 or border-crossing identification cards do not have to file for a departure permit if during their temporary stay, they received no taxable income. However, if the IRS has reason to believe that collection of an income tax is jeopardised by departure, then a permit could be required.

12.   CONCLUSION

Visitors to the United States may be subject to U.S. income taxes if they are considered resident aliens or non-resident aliens. A non-U.S. citizen is classified as a resident alien if he/she has a green card or if he/she meets the substantial presence test. Resident aliens are taxed on worldwide income and they receive deductions and credits similar to what U.S. citizens receive. In contrast, non-resident aliens are taxed only on their income from U.S. sources. Consequently, deductions are limited. The tax rates are the graduated U.S. rates for U.S.-sourced trade or business income, and a 30% flat rate on other U.S.- sourced income, unless a tax treaty exempts it or taxes it at a lower rate. In other words, tax treaties can override these general rules. An increasingly global economy may result in more countries establishing and revising tax treaties so that the traveller can be readily informed about the potential consequences of prolonged visits in another country like the U.S.

STUDY QUESTIONS

1. What are the primary differences in the U.S. income taxation of resident aliens and non-resident aliens?
2. How does one qualify for resident alien status?
3. Generally, how lengthy is the substantial presence test?
4. What are some exceptions to the physically present rules?

5. To avoid being taxed as a resident alien even when the substantial presence test has been met, one could claim a 'closer connection' to a different country. What factors are relevant for meeting the 'closer connection' test?
6. How does a tax treaty typically affect the U.S. tax liability of a non-resident alien?
7. How does the source of income affect the tax liability of a non-resident alien?
8. What type of deductions is typically available to non-resident aliens?

REFERENCES

Internal Revenue Service (2000a), *Tax Guide for U.S. Citizens and Resident Aliens Abroad,* Publication 54, Washington, DC: Department of the Treasury.
Internal Revenue Service (2000b), *Tax Information for Visitors to the United States,* Publication 513, Washington, DC: Department of the Treasury.
Internal Revenue Service (2000c), *U.S. Tax Guide for Aliens,* Publication 519, Washington, DC: Department of the Treasury.

Chapter 12

Taxes and Compensation

AMIN MAWANI
York University, Canada

Key words: compensation costs; contracting parties; fringe benefits; non-tax costs and benefits

Abstract: Tax planning can potentially offer a win-win situation for both the employee and the employer since not all forms of compensation are treated in the same manner for tax purposes. This chapter illustrates that compensation planning cannot be done in isolation from tax planning, and tax planning cannot be done in isolation from compensation planning. To appreciate the role of taxes in compensation planning, it is important to consider the tax consequences to both the employee and the employer since taxes can affect both the form and the amount of total compensation paid to employees.

1.   INTRODUCTION

In its broadest sense, compensation can take the form of salary or wages, a variety of fringe benefits, status, non-monetary appreciation, or recognition from superiors and colleagues, and rewards of challenging assignments. To the employee, a compensation package constitutes a source of income, a return on education investment, feedback on performance, and an integral part of job satisfaction. To the employer, compensation costs often constitute the largest component of operating costs, can serve as an important motivational tool, and thereby create a material impact on the success of its business strategy.

Since not all forms of compensation are treated in the same manner for tax purposes, careful tax planning can potentially offer a win-win situation for both the employee and the employer. Thus, compensation planning cannot be done in isolation from tax planning, and tax planning cannot be done in isolation from compensation planning. To appreciate the role of taxes in compensation planning, it is important to consider the tax consequences to both the employee and the employer since taxes can affect both the *form* and the *amount* of total compensation paid to employees. Focusing only on the employer's tax position may make it difficult for the employer to deal with, attract, and retain employees. Employers that consider only their own tax positions may find it difficult to transact or contract with employees in a competitive labour market. For example, insisting on offering compensation in the form that is most attractive to the employer (e.g., 100% deductible immediately) without considering that it may be relatively tax-disfavoured to the employee can potentially make the compensation package relatively unattractive in a competitive labour market, particularly if other employers are offering compensation in forms that are relatively more tax-favoured to employees. Employers pursue the objective of minimising total after-tax compensation costs for a given level of labour services, while employees attempt to maximise total after-tax compensation income for a given level of labour input. When both stakeholders are considered simultaneously, it is not always obvious which stakeholders should have more sway. It is often possible to restructure a compensation transaction in a way that improves the after-tax positions of both contracting parties, usually at the expense of the tax authority. Therefore, while a compensation contract may seem like a contract between two parties (employer and employee), it is usually designed with a third (uninvited) party in mind, namely the tax authority. Figure 1 illustrates the stakeholders involved in compensation planning in a world with taxes.

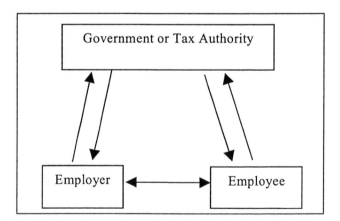

Figure 1. Stakeholders involved in Compensation Planning

Considering *all* parties to a contract – as illustrated in Figure 1 – is often referred to as Multilateral Tax Planning. Compensation schemes serve as an ideal context for multilateral tax planning, since they can be viewed as partnership contracts between the employer, the employee and the (uninvited) government or taxing authority. The objective of multilateral tax planning in this context is to structure the compensation transaction in a way that reduces the government's share, thereby allowing the remaining two partners to competitively share the rest of the pie.

This multilateral approach has been documented by Scholes *et al.* (2002) in the U.S. context, and by Thornton (1993) in the Canadian context. However, the general principles of multilateral tax planning are applicable, and indeed practised in all jurisdictions.

2. TAX TREATMENT OF ALTERNATIVE COMPENSATION FORMS

In a systematic framework that considers both employers and employees, all forms of compensation fall under one or more of the following categories described in Table 1.

Table 1. Alternative Tax Treatments of Compensation Plans

Category	Tax Effects for Employer	Tax Effects for Employee	Example
1	100% immediately deductible	Never taxed	Nontaxable fringe benefits
2	100% immediately deductible	Partial or Deferred tax	Pensions
3	Partial or deferred deduction	Partial or Deferred tax	Employee Stock Options in U.S.
4	Never deductible	Partial or Deferred tax	Employee Stock Options in Canada
5	Partially deductible	Never taxable	Business meals and entertainment
6	Never deductible	Never taxable	Christmas gifts < $100 in Canada
7	100% immediately deductible	100% immediately taxable	Salary, Cash Bonus
8	Never deductible	100% immediately	Shares, Non-performance based compensation > $1

Category	Tax Effects for Employer	Tax Effects for Employee	Example
		taxable	million in the U.S.
9	Partially deductible	100% taxable	Unreasonable or excessive automobile allowances in Canada

Partial taxation includes amounts that may be taxed at a lower capital gains rate. Deferred deduction or taxation can be considered the same as partial deduction or taxation if the cash flows are viewed in present value terms. For example, if the employer's tax rate (t_{er}) is 40% and the opportunity cost of capital is 10% (r), then a deduction to the employer of $D that is deferred for five years can be considered to be equivalent to an immediate partial deduction (P) of 62.5%, as shown in the following derivation:

$$(t_{er} * \$D) / (1+r)^n = t_{er} * P * \$D$$

$$(0.40 * \$D) / (1.10)^5 = 0.40 * P * \$D$$

$$0.25 * \$D = 0.40 * P * \$D$$

$$\text{Therefore } P = 0.25/0.40 = 0.625$$

The mathematical equivalence illustrated above highlights two sources of uncertainty:
- The employer's marginal tax rate (t_{er}) could change over time due to changes in legislation, or tax losses in one or more years over the horizon.
- The employer's opportunity cost of capital may not be constant over time.

In most cases, the above two sources of uncertainty exist jointly. For example, if anticipated legislation or excessive profits are expected to increase marginal tax rates from 40% to 44% by next year, it may be beneficial for the employer to defer deductions and pay taxes sooner unless there exist opportunities to invest $40 today that yield at least $44 in after-tax return in one year. Such opportunities would have to offer at least 10% after-tax yield, or 17.8% in pre-tax yield.

The scope of Table 1 is restricted to categorisation by income taxes only. For example, if an employer is a partnership and an employee is a partner with other family members, then one may argue that both parties would be indifferent to the amount of compensation paid to the partner by the partnership. This is because the partner would be taxed at her personal marginal tax rate on any compensation income received from the partnership, or on her share of the residual profits of the partnership. Reducing the compensation paid out to the partner would increase the partnership's profits by the same amount, and vice versa. Since both are taxed at the same rates, the compensation decision need not be influenced by taxes.

However, effective tax planning encourages us to consider not only all parties, but also all taxes. Non-trivial payroll taxes (approximately 15% in the U.S.) create an incentive to minimise compensation and maximise partnership profits in such a scenario; although combined *income* taxes are not different among alternative compensation amounts.

The nine categories in Table 1 may be considered to be ranked in order of desirability. However, the overall ranking depends non-trivially on the marginal income tax rates of employers and employees, as well as on the non-tax costs and benefits offered by the different categories of compensation. For example, if the employer's marginal tax rate is close to zero due to chronic operating losses, then categories 1, 2 and 7 that offer the employer full immediate deduction may not be as valuable in economic terms, thereby increasing the after-tax cost of compensation offered in those categories and decreasing the desirability of those categories. In such cases, for example, Categories 3 and 4 may be equivalent or even reversed in their rankings. Many employers operate as corporations and most countries tax corporations at rates that are lower than the highest personal marginal tax rates. Personal tax rates exceeding corporate tax rates in most jurisdictions explains why Category 7 offering 100% deductibility and 100% taxable may be worse off than Category 6 offering zero percent deductibility and zero percent taxable.

Another major reason that the categories in Table 1 may not be considered as unambiguously ranked in order of desirability is the *non-tax costs and benefits* that differ across the categories of compensation. For example, compensation in the form of employee stock options may be inferior to non-taxable fringe benefits in their ranking along the tax cost criterion for the employer. However, once the incentive and motivational benefits of compensating in the form of employee stock options are considered, they may end up being more desirable than non-taxable fringe benefits from combined tax and non-tax perspectives. Employers are not in the business of simply minimising taxes, or even simply minimising after-tax costs of compensation. Instead, they are in the business of maximising tax and non-tax benefits, net of tax and non-tax costs. Considering tax and non-tax costs and benefits for all contracting parties (rather than simply the taxpayer) is what differentiates effective tax planning from simple tax minimisation.

The multilateral framework requiring consideration of both the employer and the employee is critical in tax planning for compensation. For example, the denial of deduction at the employer level makes the Canadian tax treatment of employee stock options relatively unfavourable. However,

Sandler (2001) incorrectly ignores this non-deductibility at the employer-level in reaching the conclusion that the tax treatment of [Canadian] employee stock options is generous to a fault. His conclusion that 'employee stock options are taxed more favourably in Canada than in the United States' (page 261) may be reversed if the benefits to the employees in these two countries were compared for a given dollar of after-tax cost to the employer, or if the after-tax [opportunity] costs to the employers in the two countries were compared for a given dollar of after-tax benefit to the employee.

Table 2 offers an alternate way of illustrating the different categories of compensation along the tax dimension. Some jurisdictions may not have any examples of entries in a given cell. Table 2 may be a better way to present the different tax treatments of alternate forms of compensation, since it is silent on any rankings. The two-dimensional nature may make the multilateral perspective clear, in the sense that no contracting party can afford to care just about its own tax position. In considering both stakeholders in this framework, we have to remind ourselves their different objectives: employers wish to minimise the after-tax cost of compensation holding all other non-tax costs and benefits constant, while employees wish to maximise the after-tax value of compensation, holding all other non-tax benefits and costs constant.

Table 2. Alternative Tax Treatments of Compensation Plans

Taxable To Employee		Deductible to Employer		
		Fully deductible	Partially deductible	Never Deductible
	Fully taxable	Category 7 e.g., salary and cash bonus	Category 9 e.g., unreasonable or excessive automobile allowances for mileage in Canada	Category 8 e.g., company shares in Canada
	Partially taxable	Category 2 e.g., company pensions	Category 3 e.g., employee stock options in U.S.	Category 4 e.g., employee stock options in Canada
	Never taxable	Category 1 e.g., non-taxable fringe benefits	Category 5 e.g., business meals and entertainment	Category 6

3.   CONVERTING ACROSS DIFFERENT CATEGORIES OF TAXATION

Tax planning for compensation also involves attempts at changing a particular way of compensating from one category of taxation to another more favourable category of taxation, while making no party worse-off. For example, employee stock options in Canada are not deductible to the employer at the grant date, nor at the exercise date.[1] Suppose an employee receives 10,000 at-the-money stock options with an exercise price of $10 each.[2] If the company stock price increases to $15 before the option expiry date, the employee will exercise her options to acquire shares worth $150,000 for a total exercise price of $100,000, earning a pre-tax income of $50,000. Canadian tax rules further stipulate that as long as the employee stock options were not in the money at the time of granting, the employee is entitled to a deduction from income equal to one-half of the stock appreciation benefit.[3] Hence, if the employee's marginal tax rate (t_{ee}) is 50%, her after-tax income from this source would be $37,500 (= $50,000 - 50% x 50% x $50,000).

The employee's exercise transaction is not tax-advantageous to the employer, since the employer does not receive a corresponding deduction on either the grant or exercise dates. In contrast, a cash payment would be fully deductible to the employer. The cash for this payment to the employee could be financed by selling the employer's shares from the treasury to an investment dealer as a private placement instead of selling it to the employee at a reduced (exercise) price. The amount of cash paid to the employee would have to be greater than $50,000 to keep the employee indifferent on an after-tax basis, since regular cash compensation is 100% taxable, while the stock option benefit is only 50% taxable. A $50,000 cash payment would yield the employee only $25,000 after taxes, whereas a $50,000 stock option benefit would yield the employee $37,500 after taxes.

The minimum cash payment that would make the employee indifferent (to exercising her stock options) would be

$$\$37,500 / (1-t_{ee}) = \$37,500 / (1-0.50) = \$75,000.$$

---

[1] Canadian Income Tax Act: paragraph 7(3)(b).
[2] At-the-money options refer to stock options that have an exercise price equal to the stock price on the date of grant. Employee stock options granted at the money ensure that the recipient employee has no immediate taxable benefit in almost all jurisdictions.
[3] Canadian Income Tax Act: paragraph 110(1)(d).

If the employer's marginal tax rate (t_{er}) were 40%, then the after-tax cost to the employer of paying this tax-deductible cash payment would be

$$\$75,000 \ (1\text{-}t_{er}) = \$75,000 \ (1\text{-}0.40) = \$45,000.$$

This $45,000 amount could be financed by selling 3,000 shares from the treasury to an investment dealer at the current market price of $15 each.

In contrast, allowing the employee to exercise her options would cost the employer 3,333 shares from the treasury computed as follows: sell 10,000 shares from the treasury at a reduced price (of $10 each) to the employee for the exercise transaction, and use the $100,000 exercise price to buyback 6,667 shares from the market (= $100,000 / $15).

Note that if the employer's marginal tax rate went down to 33 1/3%, then its after-tax cost of making the $75,000 cancellation payment would be $75,000 (1 - 0.333) = $50,000. This would require selling 3,333 shares from the treasury (= $50,000 / $15), thereby making the employer no better off than it would be had it allowed the employee to exercise her shares. The employer would be better off disallowing the Category 4 transaction of exercising employee stock options and substituting it with a Category 6 transaction of making a cash payment as long as its corporate marginal tax rate was greater than 33 1/3%.

The basic point of this tax planning scheme is that the option exercise strategy does not offer a benefit to the employee that is sufficient to make up for the loss of deduction to the employer. While the 50% exclusion from income for the employee seems generous, it does not offset the penalty to the employer of completely losing the deduction. Multilateral tax planning suggests that if one party gains a special benefit from one particular method of structuring a deal, then the best approach is often to select that method and find a way to share the benefits with the other party.

Note that to demonstrate that both parties are indeed better off, the exact method by which the benefits will be shared between the parties must be explicit. If this is left implicit, it is possible to derive erroneous conclusions about the benefits of one tax planning strategy versus another. Therefore, considering the tax positions of all parties needs to be done carefully by keeping one party indifferent, and then comparing the costs or benefits to the other party.

One reason why some employers may not pursue this option cancellation strategy and substitute options with a tax-deductible cash payment is that it can reduce their book or financial reporting income, and the corresponding accounting income-based management bonuses. Given the similarity of accounting and tax treatments for many reporting issues, firms often face a conflict between wanting to appear profitable to their capital suppliers, while preferring to appear poor to the government. If a reduction in book income leads suppliers of debt and equity capital to regard the firm less favourably, the firm may have to lower the price on a new equity issue, pay a higher interest rate on its debt, or face restrictions on growth and expansion plans imposed by such capital suppliers. Thus, an important aspect of sound tax planning is due consideration of non-tax costs. Good tax planning is more than tax minimisation.

4.   DEFERRED COMPENSATION

The desirability of a deferred compensation contract will depend on
– the employer's preference for the timing of tax deduction;
– the employee's preference for the timing of tax inclusion;
– the employer's opportunity cost of funds;
– the employee's opportunity cost of funds;
– the employer's non-tax considerations such as incentive and retention benefits;
– and the employee's non-tax considerations such as liquidity needs.

The first two factors require each party to assess their current tax rates versus their future expected tax rates when the deferred compensation becomes due (paid and received). The expected future tax rates are compared with current tax rates, since the implicit benchmark against which deferred compensation is compared is current salary or cash bonus (100% immediately deductible and 100% immediately taxable). A multilateral framework requires that we do not add benefits and costs across time periods, nor across different parties. The only way to determine the mutually superior compensation contract is by holding any one party indifferent between an immediate cash bonus and a deferred cash bonus, and assess the other party's preference between the same two alternatives. It does not matter which party we originally hold to be indifferent, as long as we consider both parties. By considering both parties, we may find that the employer's preference for an immediate tax deduction may be stronger than the employee's preference for a deferred tax inclusion. The multilateral framework analysis would then lead us to compare the employer's benefit from immediate deduction with the employee's benefit from deferred taxation, and recommend that the party with the bigger tax benefit have their way, as long as they share their benefits with the other party, or at least not make them worse off. This exercise could identify the range where both parties could be made better off, usually at the expense of the tax authorities.

The following notation is necessary to evaluate deferred compensation with current cash compensation:
- S is the current cash salary or bonus;
- D is the deferred cash compensation;
- $t_{er,0}$ is the employer's marginal tax rate in time period 0 (or now);
- $t_{ee,0}$ is the employee's marginal tax rate in time period 0 (or now);
- $t_{er,n}$ is the employer's marginal tax rate in time period n;
- $t_{ee,n}$ is the employee's marginal tax rate in time period n;
- $r_{er,n}$ is the employer's annualised after-tax opportunity cost of funds from period 0 to period n;
- $r_{ee,n}$ is the employee's annualised after-tax opportunity cost of funds from period 0 to period n.

4.1   Employer's Perspective:

By not paying \$S in salary now, the employer saves $\$S(1- t_{er,0})$. This could be invested by the employer to yield $\$S(1- t_{er,0})(1+ r_{er,n})^n$ by the end of year n. If the employer pays a deferred compensation of \$D in year n, its after tax cost in year n would be $\$D(1- t_{er,n})$. The employer would be indifferent between paying \$S in current compensation and \$D in deferred compensation if they involve the same outlays. This would be the case if

$$\$S(1- t_{er,0})(1+ r_{er,n})^n = \$D(1- t_{er,n}) \qquad (1)$$

or

$$\$D = \$S(1+ r_{er,n})^n \frac{(1- t_{er,0})}{(1- t_{er,n})} \qquad (2)$$

Note that we are just focusing on the employer's perspective for now, and therefore the employee's tax rate has not yet come into the picture. If the employer's marginal tax rates remain the same over the n years, then the last expression simplifies to:

$$\$D = \$S(1+ r_{er,n})^n \qquad (3)$$

In this case, the employer can afford to give the employee an amount up to the future value of the current salary sacrificed. However, if the employers' tax rate increases, then the last term in expression (2) becomes greater than one (because the denominator is less than the numerator) thereby enabling the employer to offer a higher deferred compensation in exchange for withholding the current salary.

Suppose an employer with an after-tax opportunity cost of capital of 7% wanted to withhold a current salary payment of $1 now and instead offer a deferred compensation of $D four years from now. Table 3 shows the maximum amount of deferred compensation the employer would be willing to offer the employee and still remain indifferent to paying $1 in current salary under different marginal tax rates scenarios.

Table 3. Sensitivity of Deferred Compensation to Employers' Marginal Tax Rates

	$t_{er,0} = 0\%$	$t_{er,0} = 25\%$	$t_{er,0} = 45\%$
$t_{er,n} = 0\%$	$1.31	0.98	$0.72
$t_{er,n} = 25\%$	$1.75	$1.31	$0.96
$t_{er,n} = 45\%$	$2.38	$1.79	$1.31

Table 3 shows that the employer is interested in paying out compensation in the period in which it can get the highest tax deduction for it (and thereby minimising its after-tax compensation cost), and is willing to reward its employees for sacrificing immediate consumption. If employers' marginal tax rates are currently high and expected to decline, then the employer penalises employees who wish to defer their compensation by offering them less in deferred compensation than what the employees could have earned in current compensation.

Employers face zero or low marginal tax rates when they have periods of chronic operating losses that face the likelihood of not being used before the loss carryover period expires. Not-for-profit organisations also face zero marginal tax rates in most cases. The amounts in Table 3 are also sensitive to the returns that the employer could earn on the current compensation that it does not have to pay out immediately. The higher the return, the larger the deferred compensation that the employer would be willing to pay the employee to sacrifice her current compensation.

4.2 Employee's Perspective

The analysis from the employer's perspective above was expressed in terms of how much was the employer willing to reward or penalise the employee for deferring her compensation. The employee will view her decision in a different light, after considering what she could earn on compensation collected immediately. A $1 salary collected now will yield $1(1-t_{ee,0})$ after taxes now, and

$$\$1(1-t_{ee,0})(1+r_{ee,n})^n \tag{4}$$

at the end of n periods. A deferred salary n periods from now will yield $D(1-t_{ee,n})$, where D is expressed in equation (2). Therefore, the after-tax proceeds to the employee from deferred compensation n periods from now is

$$\$D = \$S(1+r_{er,n})^n \frac{(1-t_{er,0})}{(1-t_{er,n})}(1-t_{ee,n}) \tag{5}$$

The employee will prefer to defer her compensation only if (5) > (4). This happens when

$$\frac{(1-t_{ee,0})(1+r_{ee,n})^n}{(1-t_{ee,n})(1+r_{er,n})^n} < \frac{(1-t_{er,0})}{(1-t_{er,n})} \tag{6}$$

Suppose an employee with a marginal tax rate of 50% can earn an after-tax return of 6% on her investment, and wishes to defer her compensation for a period of four years. The employer's current tax rate is 25%, its expected tax rate in year four is also 25%, and it can earn 7% in after-tax return on its investments. Inserting the appropriate values in the left-hand side of expression (6) gives us

$$\frac{(1-t_{ee,0})(1+r_{ee,n})^n}{(1-t_{ee,n})(1+r_{er,n})^n} = \frac{(1-0.5)(1+0.06)^4}{(1-0.5)(1+0.07)^4} = \frac{0.63}{0.65} = 0.97$$

Inserting the appropriate values in the right-hand side of expression (6) gives us

$$\frac{(1-t_{er,0})}{(1-t_{er,n})} = \frac{(1-0.25)}{(1-0.25)} = 1$$

The left-hand side of expression (6) is less than the right-hand side, and therefore the employee would prefer deferred compensation to current compensation. If the employer's tax rate was expected to decline in year four to 15%, then the right-hand side of expression (6) would become

$$\frac{(1-t_{er,0})}{(1-t_{er,n})} = \frac{(1-0.25)}{(1-0.15)} = 0.88$$

Under this scenario, expression (6) would not be satisfied, and therefore the employee would prefer current compensation to deferred compensation.

Expression (6) incorporates the employee's preference of receiving compensation when her tax rate is lower, since that maximises after-tax income. It also incorporates the employer's preference for taking the deduction when its tax rate is high. Finally, it incorporates the after-tax returns that could be earned by both the employee and the employer. Whoever can earn higher after-tax returns should keep the money, and potentially share it with the other party. Similarly, whoever needs the deduction or inclusion the most should likely take it, and share the benefits resulting therefrom with the other party. In summary, expression (6) captures both the employer's preference for the timing of tax deduction and the employee's preference for the timing of tax inclusion.

Employers experiencing operating losses and therefore facing low marginal tax rates may be ideal candidates for deferred compensation. In small owner-managed businesses for example, employers often lend money to the shareholders rather than pay compensation in periods of losses or low tax rate periods. Once the fortunes of the business improve and marginal tax rates increase, the shareholder loans are reversed and compensation paid to the owner-managers. Deferring compensation in periods of operating losses increases taxable income, while paying the deferred compensation in healthier times reduces taxable income. Such smoothing of taxable income is beneficial from a tax perspective, since it allows tax losses to shelter taxable earnings much faster, thereby increasing the present value of the tax shield.

Not-for-profit organisations such as universities and charities may also find deferred compensation to be an attractive and viable scheme in a competitive labour market. The tax-exempt status of such employers can also improve the after-tax rates of return they can earn on their investments.

Note that we have not examined non-tax issues such as the employer's need to offer incentive and retention benefits to the employee, and the employee's need for liquidity. In practice, both parties would simultaneously consider their tax and non-tax benefits and costs in deciding their optimal compensation plan. Finally, the above analysis for evaluating current salary versus deferred compensation is universal in its applicability across jurisdictions.

5.   SALARY VERSUS FRINGE BENEFITS

Fringe benefits have a wide range of tax treatment reflecting the following multiple objectives of any tax system.
1. Raise revenues, or prevent erosion of the cash compensation base;
2. Achieve horizontal and vertical equity;
3. Offer tax incentives for expenditures such as health care insurance and pension.

As in many other cases in taxation, it is difficult to achieve all three objectives simultaneously. Recent tax reforms in many countries have included measures to tax fringe benefits to maintain neutrality across forms of compensation. Tax authorities have been concerned that the growth in fringe benefits may be tax motivated, and therefore are at the expense of growth in cash compensation. Such substitution not only erodes the tax base (violating objective 1), but also potentially redistributes the tax burden across income groups to the extent that high-income taxpayers may have more choices to substitute between cash compensation and fringe benefits (violating objective 2). Taxing fringe benefits can be justified because the recipient has a greater 'ability to pay,' since an expense that would otherwise have been incurred has been avoided.

However, governments without publicly funded health care also wish to offer economic incentives (objective 3) for employers to provide medical benefits – either directly or through insurance plans. Consequently, such fringe benefits are generally not taxable to the employees.

The multiple policy objectives surrounding fringe benefits have produced a wide range of tax treatments such as:
– exclusion of some fringe benefits such as medical care in the U.S., group term life insurance in Canada, merchandise discounts and employee gifts in Japan;
– inclusion of an arbitrary amount in employee's taxable income, generally less than the market value of the benefit – e.g., employer-provided cars in Canada;
– partially or completely deny a deduction to the employer for benefits excluded from the employee's taxable income – e.g., private health care premiums in Sweden, meals and entertainment expenses in Canada; and

– impose a separate fringe benefits tax to the employer (that captures the value of the benefit to the employee) instead of taxing the benefit to the employee – e.g., Fringe Benefits Tax in Australia.

5.1 Choosing the Salary-Benefit Combination

Given the wide range of tax treatments of fringe benefits, an interesting multilateral planning issue is to select a combination of Salary (S) and Benefit (B) that minimises the after-tax cost to the employer and/or maximises the after-tax value to the employee while keeping the other part no worse-off.

Case 1: Fully Taxable and Fully Deductible Benefit
In this case, both parties will only consider the amounts involved in Salary (S) and Benefits (B). If S = B, then both employer and employee will be indifferent. If S > B, then the employee will prefer receiving S and the employer will prefer awarding B. Both the employee and the employer tax rates are irrelevant since both Salary and Benefit are treated the same for tax purposes.

Valuation of the benefit remains an important issue. The employee's subjective value may be less than the fair market value, especially if the employee does not have a choice of accepting or rejecting the benefit offered in certain fixed quantities. Most tax rules generally allow the benefits to be valued at the marginal cost of the employer, and not the higher retail market value. If the cost of the benefit to the employer is different from the value of the benefit to the employee, then employee should be willing to sacrifice or forego salary up to the point where the reduction in salary is less than or equal to the subjective value of the benefit. Similarly, the employer should be willing to offer the benefit as long as the reduction in salary is greater than or equal to the employer's cost of the benefit. In some cases such as an airline seat on a flight with excess capacity, the difference between the employer's marginal cost and the employee's marginal benefit can be substantial, leading to a greater usage of benefits for mutual gain.

Case 2: Non-deductible and Non-taxable Benefits
In selecting a mutually beneficial combination of Salary (S) and Benefits (B), both the employee's and the employer's marginal tax rates will be relevant since S and B are treated differently. The decision on the combination of S versus B depends largely on who has the higher marginal tax rate: employer or employee. If the employer's tax rate is higher than the employee's, then the employer should pay the deductible salary instead of the non-deductible benefit since the value of the tax shield or deduction will be

higher for the employer. For example, if t_{er} = 40%, t_{ee} = 50%, and B = $100, then the employer will have to earn $100 / (1 - 0.40) = $166.67 in pre-tax earnings to pay $100 of non-deductible benefits. In contrast, the employee will have to earn $100 / (1 - 0.50) = $200 in pre-tax income to pay $100 in non-deductible benefits. Therefore, the employer should offer the employee the benefit instead of a $100 salary. In general, the deductible (taxable) salary should be offered (sacrificed) by the party that needs to earn more pre-tax income to acquire the non-deductible benefit. The employer's after-tax cost of paying for the benefit directly would be $100, while paying a grossed-up salary that would allow the employee to acquire the same benefit would cost the employer $200 (1 - 0.40) = $120. If, on the other hand, the employer's tax rate is higher than the employee's tax rate, then the employer should offer the deductible salary (so it can enjoy the higher tax shield), and let the employee acquire the benefit from her own after-tax funds.

Other cases involving partially taxable or partially deductible benefits are analysed in a similar manner. There are also few cases of benefits which are deductible by the employer, but not taxable to the employee, and some which are non-deductible to the employer but taxable to the employee. Again, the analysis is not different from the above two cases.

Two final points to keep in mind. First, the tax rates considered in compensation planning throughout this chapter are *marginal* tax rates. This refers to the incremental tax imposed when taxable income increases by $1. If some government benefits offered through the tax system are lost or clawed back because of earning an extra $1, then their impact should be captured in the marginal tax rate. This rate can be easily and precisely estimated when completing tax returns on various tax software packages by simply adding $1 to income (thereby making) INCOME = $1 in the formula below) and seeing the resulting change in tax liability. More formally, marginal tax rate (MTR) can be computed as follows:

MTR = TAXES / INCOME

In case of a corporate employer, the corporate marginal tax rate depends on the extent of operating loss carryovers and the timing of their expected usage. It is conceivable that a corporation with chronic operating losses may face a marginal tax rate of zero if its losses would otherwise expire.

Second, salary may not adjust dollar-for-dollar when fringe benefits are granted. While the bargaining positions of the two parties may determine how the mutual benefits of compensation planning are shared, it is important to remember that labour markets are often not as competitive or efficient as financial markets. Wages are known to be 'sticky' in part because transition or switching costs in labour markets are much more significant than transaction or switching costs in financial markets. Thus, some people may get more of both salary and benefits.

6. SUMMARY

Tax Planning for compensation requires consideration of the tax positions of both the employer and the employee. Good tax planning requires the planner to know the tax costs and the motivations of both parties so that a win-win situation can be structured. This multilateral analysis need not be limited to tax costs and tax motivations, since good tax planning is more than tax minimisation. An important aspect of sound tax planning is due consideration of non-tax costs such as financial reporting costs. Thus, effective tax planning for compensation strategies should consider all parties, all taxes, and all non-tax costs and benefits.

STUDY QUESTIONS

1. Suggest other business decisions where multilateral tax planning may play a role.
2. Would the (contracting) parties to a multilateral tax plan be willing to disclose all information about their current and expected future tax rates, or their opportunity costs?
3. What are the sources of uncertainty or risk inherent in a multilateral plan involving deferred compensation?
4. Give examples of three non-tax costs and three non-tax benefits that may need to be considered in a multilateral tax plan.
5. Should multilateral tax planning consider taxes other than income-based? E.g., payroll or capital.
6. Since not-for-profit organisations such as universities are not concerned about their tax shield, why don't we observe a greater use of deferred compensation by such institutions?
7. In analysing a multilateral tax plan for a compensation arrangement, Planner A holds the employer indifferent and compares the after-tax benefit to the employee across two alternatives. In contrast, Planner B holds the employee indifferent, and compares the after-tax costs to the employer across the same two alternatives. If done correctly, is it possible for Planners A and B to come up with different rankings across the two alternatives under consideration? Explain.

REFERENCES

Ault, H.J. (1997), *Comparative Income Taxation: A Structural Analysis*, The Hague: Kluwer Law International.

Cordes, J.J., Ebel, R.D. and Gravelle, J.G. (Eds) (1999), *The Encyclopedia of Taxation and Tax Policy*, Washington, D.C: The Urban Institute Press.

Egginton, D., Forker, J. and Grout, P. (1993), 'Executive and Employee Share Options: Taxation, Dilution and Disclosure', *Accounting and Business Research*, Vol. 23(91), pp. 363-72.

Katz, A., and Mankiw, G. (1985), 'How should Fringe Benefits Be Taxed?', *National Tax Journal*, Vol. 48(1), pp. 37-46.

Macnaughton, A. (1992), 'Fringe Benefits and Employee Expenses: Tax Planning and Neutral Tax Policy', *Contemporary Accounting Research*, Vol. 9(1), pp. 113-37.

Macnaughton, A. and Mawani, A. (2002), 'Microeconomic Approaches to Tax Planning' in Lamb, M. and Lymer, A. (Eds), *Taxation: An Interdisciplinary Approach to Research*, Oxford University Press, forthcoming.

Macnaughton, A. and Mawani, A. (1997), 'Tax Minimization versus Good Tax Planning', *CA Magazine*, January / February.

Mawani, A. (2002), 'Cancellation of Executive Stock Options: Tax and Accounting Income Considerations', Working Paper, York University.

Scholes, M.S., Wolfson, M.A., Erickson, M., Maydew, E.L., and Shevlin, T. (2002), *Taxes and Business Strategy: A Planning Approach*, 2nd edition, Upper Saddle River, NJ: Prentice-Hall.

Sandler, D. (2001), 'The Tax Treatment of Employee Stock Options: Generous to a Fault', *Canadian Tax Journal*, Vol. 49(2), pp. 259-319.

Stern, J.J. (1996), *Tax Concepts and Analysis*, Academic Products.

Thornton, D.B. (1993), *Managerial Tax Planning – A Canadian Perspective*, Wiley.

PART THREE

COMPARATIVE ANALYSES

Chapter 13

Taxing Companies and Their Shareholders: Design Issues

LYNNE OATS
University of Warwick, U.K.

Key words: company taxation; corporate tax; dividend imputation; shareholder taxation

Abstract: Given that it is appropriate to treat companies as taxpayers, the potential overlap between taxation of companies and taxation of their shareholders is problematic. To overcome this, a number of different company tax system have emerged, none of which is completely satisfactory from a theoretical point of view. This chapter canvasses the problems that arise and some of the models in use, or proposed, in a variety of jurisdictions.

1.   INTRODUCTION: WHY TAX COMPANIES?

There are a number of different methods of taxing companies. By way of introduction, a study of selected theoretical models for taxing companies and shareholders is presented[1].

Fundamental to any discussion of the imposition of income tax on corporations is whether such a tax is required. There is some debate as to whether separate taxation of corporations, as distinct from their shareholders, is a necessary part of an income tax system. For example, proponents of expenditure tax are of the view that there is no need for a separate tax on companies.[2] However, most countries adopt income tax systems that provide

---

[1] Apart from full integration, which is discussed by way of a benchmark, the other systems of company and shareholder taxation discussed here have been put into practice and are therefore tried and tested. More radical, untested methods, for example Meade's expenditure tax and the IFS's Allowance for Corporate Equity, are beyond the scope of this study.

[2] It is also argued that a comprehensive income tax in the Simons tradition renders a separate company tax obsolete (Cooper, 1980, pp. 25-30). Kay and King (1991, p. 152) also note that

for a tax on both companies and their shareholders. This appears to be largely in recognition of the nature of companies as separate legal entities.

There are a number of possible reasons for continuing to tax companies separately from the ultimate individual shareholders, which hold true regardless of the form of company and shareholder integration mechanism, if any, which is adopted.

The first, and perhaps most important, is ease of revenue collection. It is politically more expedient to collect revenue from entities such as companies than, for example from individual salary and wage earners who are more acutely aware of the burden. Imposing a tax on company profits is therefore convenient for revenue authorities. As Cooper and Gordon (1995, p. 821) note, a separate company tax makes administration easier because there are fewer companies than there are shareholders, and companies are more easily identified.

Secondly, a corporate tax can act as a mechanism for the collecting income tax from foreign resident shareholders of domestic companies. Such shareholders may not otherwise fall within the domestic tax net, and without company tax, the domestic revenue would suffer. In this guise, corporation tax has been described as an additional withholding tax (Cronin, 1985, p. 28). This aspect is particularly important for capital importing countries such as Australia and Canada with substantial foreign ownership of equity capital[3].

Similarly, a corporation tax can provide an indirect means of collecting tax from otherwise tax-exempt entities such as charities and, in some jurisdictions, superannuation, or pension funds that invest in companies.

Finally, in a capital gains tax-free environment, corporation tax can prevent the accumulation of tax-free capital gains through the sale of shares. This arises because to some extend retained profits are reflected in share values and can be realised by shareholders selling the shares. This is not relevant if capital gains are taxed as income. Most capital gains tax systems, however, only tax gains on realisation and to achieve true parity between the treatment of retentions and distributions it would be necessary to tax capital gains on an accruals or unrealised basis. It has also been said that taxes on capital gains are among the more difficult to enforce and collect. (Cooper and Gordon, 1995, p. 819) and therefore not an adequate substitute for an income or profits tax.

---

the argument that companies can afford to shoulder an extra tax burden carried weight in the US debate on the 1986 Tax Reform Act. They reject this proposition, however, as did the Asprey Committee (1975) in Australia.

[3]   In Australia, the Asprey Report (1975) noted that the company tax is the main means of taxing foreign residents deriving Australian income, as did the Draft White Paper Reform of the Australian Tax System (1985) at para. 17.10.

Given the arguments for having a company tax in the first instance, there are then diametrically opposed views of the relationship between companies and shareholders for tax purposes that influence the choice of company tax system adopted. The first view is that it is appropriate to tax companies on profits and shareholders on dividends in light of their distinct legal personalities, which confers separate rights on each. The company, for example, generally has the right to sue and be sued, as well as perpetual existence.[4]

The opposing view is sometimes referred to as the 'conduit' view, under which companies are seen as being mere conduits through which profits flow into the hands of ultimate shareholders. Subscribers to this view state that there is no need for a separate tax on corporations if corporate profits are taxed adequately in the hands of the shareholders.

These two views of the relationship between company and shareholder taxation lead to different conclusions as to the form that company taxation should take. The conduit view leads to the full integration system, whereas the separate view leads to a classical system of company taxation. These two extreme systems and some alternatives are discussed under the next heading.

2.   INTEGRATING COMPANY AND SHAREHOLDER TAXATION

2.1   What are the Alternatives?

The following is a discussion of the various methods by which company and shareholder income tax can be imposed. The discussion is general and not specific to any particular jurisdiction. It does not refer to the design of any one particular system. Between the two extremes of a classical system and a fully integrated system, there lay several alternative compromises, described for the purposes of this discussion as hybrid systems.

The different systems can be shown diagrammatically as per Figure 1, which follows:

---

[4]   As Krever (1985, p. 164) states, it could be that if this is the basis for the separate taxation of companies, a licence fee would be more appropriate. This view is also expressed by Kay and King (1991, p. 152) who point out that there is in fact no reason to assume that the benefits of incorporation are proportional to the profits, indeed the reverse may be true.

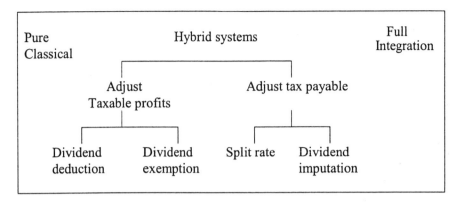

Figure 1. Company Tax Systems

2.2   The Classical System Condemned: The Three Biases

The classical, or separate system, is a manifestation of the separate view of companies and their shareholders. It taxes company profits at two levels: in the hands of the company in the first instance and then again in the hands of the shareholder on subsequent distribution of those profits by way of dividends.[5]. There is still considerable academic debate about the economic effects of a classical system and some uncertainty about the biases it causes (Benge, 1995) and the ensuing discussion must be read with this in mind.

The notion of 'double taxation' is perhaps misleading since the question of incidence of company tax is not fully reconciled. Indeed, there is considerable doubt as to whether the incidence of company tax is actually borne by shareholders.[6] If not, and to the extent to which it is not, there is no actual

---

[5]   It is the system that prevailed in Australia between the start of World War II and the introduction of the dividend imputation system in 1987. A form of the classical system is currently in operation in the US and indeed was the prevailing system of taxing company income world wide until the 1960's. At that time a number of countries began adopting various forms of company tax systems aimed at reducing this 'double taxation' of distributed company profits. See OECD (1973). For example, in 1965 France replaced its classical system with one of imputation; in 1968 Austria replaced its classical system with a split rate system; Norway similarly introduced a split rate system in 1970; in 1972 the UK reverted to an imputation system following a brief time with a classical system; and in the same year Canada introduced a partial imputation system.

[6]   This point was noted by the Carter Commission in Canada. The incidence of a given tax refers to who actually bears the ultimate burden, and in the case of company tax there is doubt as to whether it is the shareholders, the consumers of the company's products in the form of higher prices or the company's labour force in the form of lower wages. In addition,

'double' taxation; perhaps 'overtaxation' would be a more appropriate term. Despite this, the term 'double taxation' will be used as it has wide acceptance in the literature.[7]

Proponents of the classical system justify it on the basis that there is no meaningful interaction between company and individual taxes. The separation of ownership and control, particularly in companies with diverse and widely held shareholding, means that shareholders have no claim on corporate earnings until such time as dividends are declare. Indeed Cnossen (1983, p. 259) describes shareholders as 'little more than subordinate creditors'.

There would certainly seem to be an argument for distinguishing between companies where this is clearly so, and those where shareholders control the company or even use the corporate form as if trading as a sole trader.

A number of problems have been identified as arising from the double taxation of distributed profits. For convenience, these have been divided into three categories as follows:

2.2.1   Bias to Retention

It can be argued that the double taxation of distributed income encourages companies to retain their profits which are then not subject to the 'test of the market place' and may be utilised for less socially productive purposes. Alternative forms of finance such as borrowing, leasing or additional equity issues, come under the external scrutiny of the market through lenders, underwriters, and investments houses (Cooper and Gordon, 1995, pp. 827-8). This phenomenon has been referred to[8] as the nation's savings being directed as 'captive funds' into projects that may be less productive than those to which investors may otherwise direct them given a free choice. This may also place newer firms at a disadvantage compared to established firms (McLure, 1979).[9]

---

there may be a difference between the short run incidence and that in the long run. Such matters go beyond the scope of this paper.

[7]   Indeed Gerardi *et al.* (pp. 307–314) state 'the economic consequences of company tax are one of the most controversial subjects in public finance'.

[8]   *Treasury Taxation Paper No 1* (1974). It has also been referred to as 'survival of the fattest', see the 1973 OECD publication *Company Tax Systems*, Paris.

[9]   According to Benge (1995), under the traditional view, dividend taxes tend to lower dividend payout ratios. In doing this, they may inhibit the signalling and other non-cash benefits of dividends. The Campbell Committee in Australia (1981) was concerned that this would lock capital into existing firms and place impediments in the way of capital flowing to new firms. Holders of the new view also consider that the classical system can penalise new and rapidly expanding companies because the tax system places a higher impost on investment financed by new equity than that financed by retained profits or debt. New and

However, this may be a desired characteristic of the company tax system. Indeed, it was this very bias, favouring established profitable companies, which prompted the UK government in 1965 to adopt a classical system with the stated aim of encouraging companies to 'plough back' their profits.

Of course, the decision to retain profits will not be entirely tax driven, and the distortion effect of this bias may be mitigated by non-tax considerations, which require continued shareholder distributions notwithstanding the tax disadvantages.

2.2.2   Bias to Debt

There is an incentive, under the classical system, for profitable companies to use debt in preference to equity as a source of funds, since dividends are not deductible for income tax purposes, whereas interest generally is. Given that the providers of capital seek the same after tax return, new equity capital is more expensive than new debt. This could lead to excessive gearing exposing companies to the possibility of bankruptcy (Cnossen, 1983). In Australia, the Bureau of Industry Economics (1985) noted that this increased the cost of risk capital for industries such as mining and manufacturing where the non-corporate form is less feasible. As Benge (1995) comments, excessive levels of debt are likely to be costly for a number of reasons including an increased chance of bankruptcy and constraints placed on managers by debt holders to safeguard their interests.

The different treatment of returns on equity and debt also leads to development and abuse of artificial investment forms which can be classified as debt but nevertheless have the desired characteristics of equity (Cooper and Gordon, 1995, p. 825). Indeed, this is one of the more complex areas in tax administration and it is partly to remove the incentive to disguise equity interests as debt that the U.S. Treasury (1992) recommended taxing the income from equity and debt investments at the same, single rate.

2.2.3   Investment Biases

There is potential for distortion of the allocation of resources between the corporate and non-corporate forms of doing business. In its simplest form, if companies are taxed as well as shareholders, effectively on the same profits, investors would not be indifferent to different business entity structures, for

---

rapidly expanding companies need to issue new equity or borrow to meet capital requirements. Further discussion of the differences between the traditional and new views of dividends is beyond the scope of this paper.

example trusts, where there may be only one layer of taxation[10]. This issue is further complicated by the fact that in some industries incorporation may be mandatory[11].

A further source of distortion occurs when the rate of tax applicable to companies is less than the higher marginal personal tax rates applicable to individual taxpayers. In such situations there may be a tax-induced *preference* for the corporate form, particularly where there is no capital gains tax to capture the increase in market value of shares attributable to retained profits. As McLure (1979, p. 24) notes, under-taxation of retained profits at the top end of the income scale (assuming this is higher than the company rate) induces ownership of firms with low dividend payout ratios to be concentrated in the hands of the wealthy.

There are thus indirect effects on the level of national savings and investment, which arise as a result of distortions of payout rates, debt/equity ratios and the forms of organisation through which business may be carried on. (Cnossen, 1983, p. 261) That investors have a choice of conducting business through companies affects tax neutrality[12] in the absence of full integration.

2.3   Full Integration: The Impossible Dream?

If the classical system of company taxation can be viewed as being at one end of the spectrum, then at the other lies the notion of full integration. Full integration stems from the view of companies as merely the vehicle through which shareholders derive profits.

Under a pure system of full integration, no tax is levied on the company[13], but all company profits, whether or not distributed, are attributed to shareholders and brought to tax at the shareholders' appropriate marginal rate of income tax. Company losses are also notionally allocated to shareholders.

---

[10] There is evidence of this in an Australian context when the perceived inequities of company taxation led to many businesses using trusts instead of companies as the vehicle for business operations, refer Draft White Paper (1985) para.17.7. Subsequent amendments were made to tax corporate unit trusts as companies.

[11] For an Australian example see *FCT* v *Bunting* 89 ATC 4358 where a computer systems analyst found it necessary to offer his services to prospective 'employers' via a company.

[12] Tax neutrality in this context refers to tax being non-distortionary, that is, a neutral tax is one which does not impact on economic decisions such as those regarding saving and investment.

[13] Except possibly a withholding tax, which is then credited to shareholders.

Many commentators have acknowledged full integration of company tax and personal income tax[14] as a theoretical ideal. Strong support for a system of integration was enunciated by the 1966 report of the Royal Commission on Taxation in Canada (the 'Carter Commission') where *inter alia* the subject of integration was given significant attention and has often been referred to in subsequent studies[15].

Full integration is sometimes referred to as a 'conduit' system, under which companies are effectively transparent, and are treated, for income tax, in the same manner as partnerships are in most jurisdictions.[16]. As a general rule, profits derived, or losses incurred, by partnerships, are directly attributed to the partners for income taxation purposes thus being immediately exposed to the marginal rate of income tax applicable to the partners.

Krever (1985, pp. 164-5) argues that the economic principles of equity and efficiency *require* integration of company and individual tax rates, in order that the tax ultimately paid reflects each shareholders' ability to pay[17]. Indeed 'ability to pay' is a concept that some commentators consider can only be properly attributable to individuals[18].

Full integration places pressure on companies to distribute in order to provide shareholders with funds to meet their tax liabilities. The 'S Corporation' system in the U.S.[19], under which small companies are effectively treated as partnerships, is the closest approximation of full integration. This failure to embrace full integration is probably explained by perceived administrative difficulties that such a system presents.

Under full integration, tax may or may not be collected from the company in the first instance. If so, it is by way of a withholding tax credited to

---

[14] For example, Cnossen (1983, p. 6) describes it as a perfect solution in an imperfect world.

[15] See for example the Australian Treasury (1974) and the Asprey Committee's Full Report 1975. In an Australian context, the Campbell Inquiry also acknowledged full integration as being a desirable goal in taxation policy formulation.

[16] Partnerships, are not usually legal entities separate from their owners, the partners, and are rarely taxed in their own right. In Australia the partners are directly taxed on the income and deduct their share of losses of the partnership, as is the case in Canada, New Zealand, and the United States of America. In the United Kingdom, there is similar treatment for income tax purposes, notwithstanding that in Scotland partnerships are in fact separate legal entities (*Partnership Act* 1890 s.4(2)).

[17] Of course, if shareholders do not receive a dividend then arguably they have no explicit 'ability to pay' tax on a notional dividend.

[18] According to Cnossen (1983, p. 262) since ability to pay is an equity notion, it can only relate to natural persons.

[19] The 'S' Corporation system in the US allows a partnership election for certain clearly defined companies, having a small number of shareholders, where all shareholders agree. Otherwise, the classical system operates in the US.

shareholders against their individual tax liabilities. It should be refundable in case of excess credit if the progressivity of the personal income tax rate scale is to be maintained. Collection of taxation from the company in the first instance, albeit as a form of withholding tax, provides a degree of administrative certainty and convenience. As previously mentioned, it is also a convenient means of collecting income tax from non-residents and tax exempt entities.

2.3.1 Perceived Advantages of Full Integration

There are a number of perceived advantages of a system of full integration. Firstly, and perhaps most importantly, it achieves tax neutrality as between corporate and non-corporate forms of doing business.[20]

Adoption of a system of full integration also results in greater horizontal and vertical tax equity, as a result of aligning the taxation of company profits with the notion of ability to pay tax.[21]

In addition, it has the advantage of removal of any perceived tax bias in favour of debt financing over equity. This bias is the result of the deductibility for income tax purposes of interest on debt. The non-deductibility of dividends under a classical system leads to a bias towards debt financing. Under full integration, the tax treatment of returns on debt and equity are equivalent.

2.3.2 Perceived Disadvantages of Full Integration

A number of difficulties have been identified which lead ultimately to the abandonment of integration as a workable system in practice.

Timing difficulties arise due to the need for companies to transmit information to shareholders to allow them to complete their own taxation returns.[22] This is aggravated where there is a chain of interposed entities between the originating company and the ultimate individual shareholder.

---

[20] However, not neutrality in the commercial sense, recognising the principle of limited liability.

[21] This presupposes profitability as an acceptable measure of ability or faculty to pay tax - a matter that is itself open to dispute. The principle of horizontal equity in general terms requires that taxpayers with the same ability to pay should pay the same amount of tax. Vertical equity on the other hand, requires that taxpayers with a greater capacity to pay tax should be called upon to pay a greater proportion of tax. It is on this principle that the progressive rate scale, usually applicable under personal income tax, is founded.

[22] This lag between the time profits are derived and taxed gives rise to a cash flow benefit, refer Pope *et al.* (1994, p. 28).

Given that some point in time has to be chosen to identify the relevant beneficial shareholders for the purposes of attributing to them the company's profits or losses for the year[23], there may be an incentive for high marginal rate taxpayers to seek to acquire shares in loss making companies prior to that time in order to obtain the benefit of their attribution. The Carter Commission recommended a variation on full integration to overcome this perceived problem by not allocating losses to shareholders. Another solution is to choose the first day of the fiscal year as being the 'day of record' and allow market forces to determine a sale price for the shares, which will reflect the tax credit likely to accrue before the end of the year. In other words, profits are allocated to the shareholders of record on a given date and the capital market is left to 'parcel out' to others who had been shareholders during the year, their proportion of profits through gains and losses in share values (McLure, 1975, p. 563).

In addition, making shareholders liable for tax on retained profits can lead to cash flow problems by taxing them on income not actually in their hands. Indeed, as Freebairn (1985) suggests that due to the need to fund tax payments, full integration creates a higher demand for dividend payouts.

The introduction of full integration may result in a loss of tax revenue for the government as a direct result of removing one layer of taxation. The Australian Treasury (1974)[24] recognised this as a major consideration, as did the Carter Commission. Even if the loss of company tax is offset by an increase in individual income tax rates, the offset will only be partial as many shareholders are tax exempt bodies, low rate taxpayers or non residents from whom little or no tax can be collected.

Difficulties also arise in an integration system where companies have different classes of shares, resulting in the attribution of profits to the wrong shareholders. For example, a company that wishes to maintain a consistent record of preference share dividends may be forced to pay a dividend to preference shareholders out of previous years' accumulated earnings if there is not enough profit in the current year to fulfil the obligation. Those undistributed profits may have already been attributed to ordinary shareholders for tax purposes in the year in which they were earned (Krever, 1985, p. 171). To overcome the problem it may be necessary to re-open the assessments of the ordinary shareholders to reduce the company profits, on which they were previously taxed, adding to the administrative costs of the system.

---

[23] Since allocation on a day to day basis is clearly not feasible.

[24] This point was also made by the Australian government in its Draft White Paper Reform of the Australian Taxation System, in 1985.

2.4   Classical and Full Integration Compared

The following table compares, under certain assumptions, the impact on taxation revenue under the classical and full integration company tax systems. The full integration system presupposes retention of corporate tax as a prepayment or withholding tax mechanism.

Table 1. A comparison of the effect of the classical and full integration systems under varying marginal personal rates and varying dividend payout ratios [25]

	Item	Classical System						Full Integration	
1	Marginal personal tax rate	20%	20%	20%	40%	40%	40%	20%	40%
2	Percentage of after tax profit retained	0%	50%	100%	0%	50%	100%	N/a	N/a
3	Net company profit bef. Tax & dividends	100	100	100	100	100	100	100	100
4	Company tax @ 30%	30	30	30	30	30	30	30	30
5	Available for distribution (3-4)	70	70	70	70	70	70	70	70
6	Dividend to shareholder	70	35	0	70	35	0	70	70
7	'Gross up' for shareholder	N/a	N/a	N/a	N/a	N/a	N/a	N/a	N/a
8	Assessable personal income (6+7)	70	35	0	70	35	0	100	100
9	Gross personal income tax (1 x 8)	14	7	0	28	14	0	20	40
10	Shareholder credit (from 7)	N/a	N/a	N/a	N/a	N/a	N/a	N/a	N/a
11	Net personal income tax (9 - 10)	14	7	0	28	14	0	(10)	10
12	Total taxes (4+11)	44	37	30	58	44	30	20	40

Note:
1.   Marginal rates of personal income tax of 20% and 40% have been assumed in line with current world-wide trends towards reducing personal income tax rates. Similarly, the company tax rate is assumed a flat rate of 30% in keeping with world-wide trends.
2.   The table ignores any capital gains tax that may capture the increase in market value of the shares as a result of retentions.

---

[25] This table and those following are loosely based on a table produced by McLure (1979, p. 6).

The table illustrates that under a classical system, the degree of 'excess' taxation of dividends increases as the marginal rate of personal income tax increases and the profit retention ratio decreases. Under a system of full integration, however, all company income is taxed at the applicable marginal rate of the individual shareholder irrespective of the payout ratio of the company.

3. COMPROMISES: INTEGRATING DISTRIBUTED PROFITS

Hybrid systems, that is those adopting elements of both the classical and full integration systems, have evolved in light of the administrative difficulties in attributing undistributed profits to shareholders. As is often the case with the manifestation of taxation policy in legislative form, they thus owe their origins to a pragmatic compromise of ideals.

Relief from the classical system of double taxation of company profits can be achieved in a number of ways. In providing relief, adjustment can be made to taxable profits, or to tax payable. In either case, the relevant adjustment can be made at the level of the company or at the level of the shareholder. The four models of integration discussed here are as follows:

	Adjustment to:	
	Taxable profits	Tax payable
At the company level	Dividend deduction	Split rate
At the shareholder level	Dividend exemption	Dividend imputation

3.1   Adjustments to Taxable Profits

3.1.1   At the Company Level: Dividend Deduction

This system reduces company taxable income by dividends paid during the year. Distributed profits are therefore only taxed to shareholders[26]. This addresses the bias to debt, which is a feature of the classical system. However,

---

[26] In Australia, dividend deduction is employed for co-operative companies under section 120 of the *Income Tax Assessment Act* 1936.

it maintains the bias against distributing income in the case of those shareholders whose marginal tax rate is higher than that borne by the company itself. Such shareholders may prefer, capital gains tax considerations aside, the income to be retained by the company notwithstanding its deductibility if distributed.

The effect of a dividend deduction system depends on the proportion of the dividend deduction that is allowed. Subject to company and personal tax relativities, a full deduction imposes a disincentive to retentions in the form of an undistributed profits tax, whilst reduced deductions tend, in effect, to equate to taxes under the classical system (Cnossen, 1983, p. 264).

A dividend deduction system thus corrects the bias in favour of debt financing over equity, since dividends are treated in the same way as interest expense[27]. However, *all* shareholders benefit from the reduction in corporation tax that the deduction provides irrespective of their residency status.

Although it is feasible in theory to deny a deduction for dividends to the extent they are payable to non resident shareholders, difficulties then arise under the various double taxation treaties in place, most of which presuppose a classical system of corporation tax. It is largely for this reason that no major income tax system currently adopts a dividend deduction system.

As Krever (1985, p. 170) notes, without a capital gains tax, a dividend deduction system can achieve indifference between the decision to distribute and retain profits. If there is a capital gains tax, however, there will be a significant bias towards distribution. This is because the capital gains tax will effectively impose another layer of tax on retained profit to the extent that they are reflected in an increase in share value realised on disposal and taxed as a capital gain 'The only way double taxation can be avoided is through the adoption of a cumbersome and complicated credit system in which shareholders' capital gains are reduced by the undistributed income that has been subject to company tax at the time the shareholder realises the capital gain'.[28]

---

[27] Where the withholding tax rates for non-residents in receipt of dividends and interest are different, however, as is often the case under double tax treaties, the bias is not entirely removed for non-resident investors.

[28] The Draft White Paper at para. 17C.5 notes that administrative difficulties could be the reason why apparently no OECD country with capital gains tax and imputation attempts to take into account the effect of capital gains tax on retained income.

Table 2. A comparison of the effect of a dividend deduction system under varying marginal personal rates. (Full deduction)

	Item	Company deduction allowed for dividends at 100%					
1	Marginal personal tax rate (note 1)	20	20%	20%	40%	40%	40%
2	% of profits retained	0	50%	100%	0	50%	100%
3a	Net company profits before tax and dividends	100	100	100	100	100	100
3b	Dividend deduction	100	50	0	100	50	0
3c	Net pre-tax company profits	0	50	100	0	50	100
4	Company tax @ 30%	0	15	30	0	15	30
5	Available for distribution (3c – 4)	100	85	70	100	85	70
6	Dividend to shareholder (note 2)	100	50	0	100	50	0
7	'Gross up' for shareholder	N/a	N/a	N/a	N/a	N/a	N/a
8	Assessable personal income	100	50	0	100	50	0
9	Gross personal income tax (1x 8)	20	10	0	40	20	0
10	Shareholder credit (from 7)	N/a	N/a	N/a	N/a	N/a	N/a
11	Net personal income tax (9 – 10)	20	10	0	40	20	0
12	Total taxes (4 + 11)	20	25	30	40	35	30

Note:
1.	Marginal rates of personal income tax of 20% and 50% have been assumed in line with current world-wide trends towards reducing personal income tax rates. The company tax rate is assumed to be a flat rate of 30%
2.	It is assumed that company tax is funded from retained profits.
3.	The table ignores any capital gains tax that may capture the increase in market value of the shares as a result of retentions.

A full deduction system can be viewed as an undistributed profits tax. It can be seen from Table 2, given full distribution of profits, that a dividend deduction system gives the same tax results as full integration.

3.1.2   At the Shareholder Level: Dividend Exemption

Under a dividend exemption system, dividends are exempt from tax in the hands of the ultimate natural person shareholders; thus, tax is imposed only at the company level. Although one level of tax is eliminated, biases remain, however, in that investment in companies is more or less attractive to individuals based on their respective marginal tax rates relative to the company rate. Thus, the non-neutrality in terms of choice of entity remains where the company rate is proportional and the individual rate is progressive, or if proportional at a different rate to companies.

Where the proportional company rate lies somewhere between the individual progressive rate extremes, the system operates regressively. This means the amount of relief increases as the recipient shareholder's marginal rate increases, with those in the highest tax bracket receiving the benefit of the greatest relief.

Table 3. A comparison of the effect of a dividend exemption system under varying marginal personal rates.

	Item						
1	Marginal personal tax rate	20%	20%	20%	40%	40%	40%
2	% of profits retained	0	50%	100%	0·	50%	100%
3	Net company profits before tax and dividends	100	100	100	100	100	100
4	Company tax @ 30% (note 1)	30	30	30	30	30	30
5	Available for distribution (3 – 4)	70	70	70	70	70	70
6	Dividend to shareholder	70	35	0	70	35	0
7	'Gross up' for shareholder	N/a	N/a	N/a	N/a	N/a	N/a
8	Assessable personal income	0	0	0	0	0	0
9	Gross personal income tax (1x 8)	0	0	0	0	0	0
10	Shareholder credit (from 7)	N/a	N/a	N/a	N/a	N/a	N/a
11	Net personal income tax (9 – 10)	0	0	0	0	0	0
12	Total taxes (4 + 11)	30	30	30	30	30	30

Note:
1.   Marginal rates of personal income tax of 20% and 50% have been assumed in line with current world-wide trends towards reducing personal income tax rates. The company tax rate is assumed to be a flat rate of 30%
2.   The table ignores any capital gains tax that may capture the increase in market value of the shares as a result of retentions.

The total tax revenue under a dividend exemption system remains the same irrespective of the company's dividend payout ratio or the shareholder's marginal rate of tax, that is, in effect for dividend income individual taxpayers are assessed proportionately not progressively on dividend income. This has the merit of simplicity, at the expense of a lack of equity, the result of taxing dividends differently to other forms of income, which are generally subject to progressive tax rates.

3.2   Adjustments to Tax Payable

3.2.1   At the Company Level: Split Rate System

A split rate system taxes the company at different rates for distributed and retained profits respectively. This system is a variation on the classical system, retaining double taxation, albeit at differential rates of tax.

The split rate system discourages retention of profits by imposing a higher rate of tax on retentions, thereby modifying one of the disadvantages of the classical system. Whether or not subsequent distributions from the profits which have been subjected to a higher rate of tax, sometimes referred to as undistributed profits tax, are taxed again in the hands of shareholders depends on the particular type of system adopted.

Criticisms levelled at the classical system are also relevant to the split rate system. The split rate system lacks neutrality as well as both horizontal and vertical equity. It is biased in favour of distributions since the corporate tax burden of the company is a function of its dividend payout ratio. Its effect depends on the differential between the company rate of tax applicable to retained earnings and the shareholder tax rate applicable to distributed earnings, which, of course, will vary across a range of shareholders. If the differential is small, the system is similar to a classical system (Cnossen, 1983, p. 266) as seen in the following table:

Table 4. A comparison of the effect of a split rate system under varying marginal personal rates and company tax rates

	Item	Retentions taxed at 50%, distributions at 30%					
1	Marginal personal tax rate (see note 1)	20%	20%	20%	40%	40%	40%
2	% of profits retained	0	50%	100%	0	50%	100%
3	Net company profits before tax and dividends	100	100	100	100	100	100
4	Company tax @ 30% (see notes 1 & 2)	30	40	50	30	40	50
5	Available for distribution (3 – 4)	70	60	50	70	60	50
6	Dividend to shareholder	70	35	0	70	35	0
7	'Gross up' for shareholder	N/a	N/a	N/a	N/a	N/a	N/a
8	Assessable personal income	70	35	0	70	35	0
9	Gross personal income tax (1 x 8)	14	7	0	28	14	0
10	Shareholder credit (from 7)	N/a	N/a	N/a	N/a	N/a	N/a
11	Net personal income tax (9 – 10)	14	7	0	28	14	0
12	Total taxes (4 + 11)	44	47	50	58	54	50

Note:
1. Marginal rates of personal income tax of 20% and 40% have been assumed in line with current world-wide trends towards reducing personal income tax rates. Similarly, the company tax rate on distributed income is assumed to be a flat rate of 30% in keeping with world-wide trends. The rate of company tax applicable to retained income is assumed to be 50%, i.e. an additional tax of 20% on undistributed profits.
2. It is assumed that the split rate system taxes shareholders on gross dividends received, and that the company tax on retained income is met out of retentions and the company tax on distributed income is met out of distributions.
3. The table ignores any capital gains tax that may capture the increase in market value of the shares as a result of retentions.

Obviously, where the company retains no income, the result for the shareholder is the same as with the classical system. Correspondingly the greater the degree of retention, the higher the level of total taxes, where the rate applicable to the shareholder is less than that of the company. As with the classical system, the total revenue raised is a function of the company's distribution policy, the company tax rate and shareholders' marginal tax rates.

Ceteris paribus, compared to the classical system the split rate system encourages distributions, and thus diminishing the bias in favour of retentions inherent in the classical system. Of course, the decision to retain income within the corporate entity also involves non-tax considerations, for example liquidity considerations or strengthening the company's financial position, to provide funds for the purchase of capital equipment, or to finance other activities or expansion. To this extent, the split rate system may impose constraints on sound corporate management.

3.2.2 At the Shareholder Level: Dividend Imputation

Dividend imputation systems involve levying tax on profits at the corporate level and then notionally allocating or imputing that tax, by way of both assessable income and a compensating tax credit, to the shareholder in receipt of dividends. It is arguably the most complex of the integration mechanisms discussed, but also the most equitable in ensuring that, for distributed profits at least, taxation is imposed at the marginal rate of the individual shareholder.

For example, in very simple terms, assume a company with taxable profits of $1,000 pays company tax at the rate of 30%, i.e. $300 and distributes its entire after tax profits. The natural person shareholder[29] will include in his or her taxable income the cash dividend of $700 and under a system of full imputation, also the company tax paid of $300 as notional assessable income.

---

[29] There are usually different rules for corporate shareholders.

Assuming no other income, the shareholder's taxable income is the same as that of the company, $1,000. A tax credit is then allowed to the shareholder equal to the company tax paid. For a shareholder with a marginal tax rate of 30% or below, this will result in no net tax liability, as the tax on the grossed up dividend is fully covered by the company tax already paid, assuming no refunds of excess credits. For a shareholder with a marginal tax rate of above 30%, the net liability will be $d \times (mtr - t)$ where d is the grossed-up dividend amount (i.e. $1,000 in the example), mtr is the shareholder's marginal tax rate, and t is the company tax rate.

Imputation thus usually operates on a 'gross up and credit' basis[30], that is, the shareholder includes in assessable income, both the cash or credited dividend amount and the company tax attributed to that dividend. Imputation without such a gross up mechanism would provide a result similar to that of dividend exemption, in that the relief would be distributed regressively with respect to income (Cnossen, 1983, pp. 269-70).[31]

Table 5. A comparison of the effect of a dividend imputation system under varying tax credit rates and marginal personal rates.

	Item						
1	Marginal personal tax rate	20%	20%	20%	40%	40%	40%
2	% of profits retained	0	50%	100%	0	50%	100%
3	Net company profits before tax and dividends	100	100	100	100	100	100
4	Company tax @ 30% (note 1)	30	30	30	30	30	30
5	Available for distribution (3 – 4)	70	70	70	70	70	70
6	Dividend to shareholder	70	35	0	70	35	0
7	'Gross up' for shareholder	30	15	0	30	15	0
8	Assessable personal income	100	50	0	100	50	0
9	Gross personal income tax (1x 8)	20	10	0	40	20	0
10	Shareholder credit (from 7)	30	15	0	30	15	0
11	Net personal income tax (9 – 10) (see note 3)	(10)	(5)	0	10	5	0
12	Total taxes (4 + 11)	20	25	30	40	35	30

[30] As does a dividend withholding tax, where in the UK for example, a shareholder in receipt of a foreign portfolio dividend that has been subjected to withholding tax in the country of origin, must include for income tax purposes, not only the cash dividend received, but also the withholding tax. That withholding tax is then allowed as a credit under the foreign tax credit system.

[31] This system operated in Australia from 1923 to 1940.

Note:
1.   Marginal rates of personal income tax of 20% and 50% have been assumed in line with current world-wide trends towards reducing personal income tax rates. The company tax rate is assumed to be a flat rate of 30%
2.   The table ignores any capital gains tax that may capture the increase in market value of the shares as a result of retentions.
3.   This assumes that excess credits are refunded to the shareholder, if not then item 12, column 1 is $30.

Table 5 demonstrates that with full distribution of profits, an imputation system will equate to full integration in that the tax on company profits is at the appropriate individual marginal rate. This effect is diminished; however, to the extent that profits are retained, full integration is only achieved in respect of distributed profits.

There are a number of issues arising in the design of an imputation system. Different approaches to these issues form the basis of differences between imputation systems actually in place in various tax jurisdictions. These issues include whether to allow tax preferred income of companies to pass to the shareholders tax free, the degree of imputation to be allowed and the treatment of imputation credits in the hands of individual shareholders.

3.2.2.1   Pass-through of preferences

In relation to the first issue, three basic methods can be used to impute company tax to shareholders, automatic credit, compensatory tax, and the qualifying dividend approach.

It may be that the government does not require restrictions on the pass through of preferentially taxed corporate profits, in which case a simple automatic credit mechanism can be used. This system allows the shareholder to claim a dividend tax credit of a specified amount, irrespective of whether tax has been paid at the company level. This system has the benefit of simplicity and reduced compliance costs, as no tracking mechanism is required to determine whether the dividend is paid from taxed profits or not.

On the other hand, there are several adjustment mechanisms whereby pass through of tax preferences to shareholders can be prevented if desired. One of the more common forms is the levying of some form of compensatory tax, payable when a dividend distribution is made from untaxed company profits. This ensures that the credit received by the shareholder is matched by actual tax payments by the company.

According to Cnossen (1983, p. 271) 'although the imputation system is meant to promote profit distributions, a compensatory tax negates tax concessions enjoyed by the company and is an inducement to retain exempt profits in the company as a means to minimise the overall tax liability'. In this respect, dividend imputation fails to achieve the objective of overcoming the bias to retention inherent in the classical system.

Another method of ensuring that corporate preferences do not flow through to shareholders is the adoption of an accounting procedure to track whether dividend payments are covered by company tax, and only allowing dividend imputation credit for those dividends. This is sometimes referred to as a qualifying dividend approach.

The difference between the latter two conceptual approaches is merely the stage at which the preference is washed out or negated. With a compensatory tax, it is at the corporate level; with an accounting procedure, it is at the shareholder level.

3.2.2.2   The degree of imputation

In designing a dividend imputation system, the degree of imputation must also be determined, that is, whether it is full or partial. A partial imputation system is one in which only part of the company tax paid is attributed to the shareholder, and it is essentially a compromise between full imputation and the classical system. This is largely a revenue-driven decision, which directly affects the amount of revenue forgone by the government in allowing individual shareholders the benefit of imputation credits.

The smaller the degree of imputation credit, the closer the system moves towards a classical system and all the distortions that entail.

3.2.2.3   Treatment of imputation credits

Decisions must also be taken as to the treatment of imputation credits. Firstly, whether excess credits relating only to dividend income should be able to be offset against tax applicable to other income. Secondly, whether to refund any excess credits to the shareholders. The use of dividend imputation to promote the theory that dividends should be taxed at shareholders' marginal rates in the interests of equity, leads to the notion that refunds should be given. Finally, whether to extend the benefits of imputation to tax exempt shareholders or non-resident shareholders. This is not usually done, as the effect is to subsidise foreign treasuries.

4.   SUMMARY

Various studies (OECD, 1973; Harris, 1996; Avi Yonah, 1990) have shown that systems of corporation tax differ between tax jurisdictions and most entail a compromise on the pure forms of classical and integration systems, exhibiting features of the above systems. Many jurisdictions use a combination of the various systems discussed, adopting one form for individual shareholders, another for intermediate company and another for non-resident shareholders.

The decision as to which method, if any, to adopt for integrating company and shareholder taxation is influenced by a number of factors, including the prevailing view of the benefits of simplicity over equity in tax policy. Simplicity would lead to either a classical system or one of the methods that adjust taxable income either at the company or shareholder level. Equity, on the other hand, leads ideally to full integration, but as a compromise to dividend imputation.

Another issue is the international dimension. As Chua and King (1994) note, providing relief at the shareholder level as opposed to the company level can assist in the bargaining process embodied in the negotiation of double tax treaties.

The company/shareholder tax design, the impact of other relevant taxes such as capital gains tax, or a tax on gains derived from the disposal of shares, will impact on the manner in which company tax systems affect tax neutrality. The bias in favour of retentions in a classical system for example is ameliorated in an environment that taxes accretions in share values resulting from the accumulation of profits by the company.

Each of the alternative systems mitigates one or more of the perceived problems of the classical system of company taxation.

Figure 2. Effect of Company Tax Systems

System	Perceived Problem		
	Bias to retention	Bias to Debt	Investment bias
Pure classical	Present	Debt preferred	Present
Split rate	Mitigated	Mitigated	Mitigated
Dividend deduction	Removed	Removed	Mitigated
Dividend exemption	Removed	Mitigated	Mitigated
Dividend imputation	Reversed*	Mitigated	Mitigated
Pure Integration	None	None	None

* Except where the shareholder's marginal rate of tax is higher than the company's. This assumes that company and individual rates and company rates are the same, and that the company is profitable.

None of the hybrid systems for taxing companies and shareholders achieves the goals of a full integration system, however administrative difficulties render that alternative impracticable, except perhaps in relation to closely held companies.

STUDY QUESTIONS

1. Based on the examples given of the different forms of company tax, what are the differences between them?
2. What are the perceived problems with a 'classical' system of company tax that has led many countries to adopt alternative methods of taxing companies and shareholders?
3. Why has no country tried to adopt a full integration system, despite its theoretical attractions?
4. What design considerations need to be taken into account in introducing a system of dividend imputation?

REFERENCES

Australian Financial Systems Inquiry (1981), Final Report (Campbell Report), Canberra: Australian Government Publishing Service.

Australian Government (1974), *Tax Reform Problems and Aims,* Treasury Taxation Paper No 1, Canberra: Australian Government Publishing Service.

Australian Government (1985), *Draft White Paper: Reform of the Australian Tax System,* Canberra: AGPS.

Avi Yonah, R. (1990), 'The Treatment of Corporate Preference Items under an Integrated Tax System: A Comparative Analysis', *Tax Lawyer* Vol. 44(1), p. 195.

Benge, M. (1995), *Company Tax Integration: Did We get it Right?* Tax Summit Conference, Canberra.

Benge, M. and Robinson, T. (1986), *How to Integrate Company and Shareholder Taxation: Why Full Imputation is the Best Answer,* Wellington: Victoria University Press for the Institute for Policy Studies.

Brooks N. (1986), 'Taxation of Closely Held Corporations: The Partnership Option and the Lower Rate of Tax', *Australian Tax Forum,* Vol. 3(4), pp. 381-509.

Bureau of Industry Economics (1985), 'Imputation of Company Income Taxation' in *Business Income Taxation Paper 2,* Canberra: AGPS.

Chua, D. and King, J. R. (1995), 'The Mechanics of Integration' in *Tax Policy Handbook,* Washington DC: International Monetary Fund.

Cnossen S. (1983), 'Alternative Forms of Corporation Tax', *Australian Tax Forum,* Vol. 1(3), pp. 253-279.

Cooper, G. and Gordon, R. (1998), 'Taxation of Enterprises and Their Owners', in Thuronyi (Ed), *Tax Law Design and Drafting,* Washington DC: International Monetary Fund.*

Cronin, (1985) 'Economic and Revenue Implications of Tax Reform in the Corporate Sector' in Head, J. (Ed), *Reform of Business Taxation,* Sydney: Australian Tax Research Foundation.

Freebairn, J. (1985), paper presented to the Conference on Reform of Business Taxation, Australian Tax Research Foundation Conference, Series No 4.

Gammie, M. (1996), 'The future of UK Corporation Tax', in Head, J. and Krever (Eds), *Company Tax Systems,* Sydney: Australian Tax Research Foundation.

Gerardi *et al* (1992), 'Corporate Integration Puzzles', *National Tax Journal* Vol. XLIII(3), pp. 307–314.

Harris, P. (1996), *Corporate/Shareholder Income Taxation*, Amsterdam: International Bureau of Fiscal Documentation.

Head, J. (1997), 'Company Tax Structure and Company Tax Incidence', *International Tax and Public Finance*, Vol. 4, pp. 61-100.*

Kay, J. and King, M. (1991), *The British Tax System*, Oxford: Oxford University Press.*

Krever, R. (1985), 'Companies, Shareholders and Tax Reform', *Taxation in Australia,* Vol. 10(3), pp. 163-175.

McLure, C. (1975), 'Integration of the Personal and Corporate Income Taxes: The Missing Element in Recent Tax Reform Proposals', *Harvard Law Review,* Vol. 88, pp. 533-582.

McLure, C. (1979), *Must Corporate Income be Taxed Twice?* Washington DC: Brookings Institute.

Oats, L. (1996), 'Taxing Corporations: Systems and Strategies', *Taxation in Australia Red Edition,* Vol. 4(3), pp. 138-145.

OECD (1973), *Company Tax Systems*, Paris: OECD.

Pope J., Fayle, R. and Chen, D. (1994), *The Compliance Costs of Companies Income Tax in Australia*, Research Study No 23, Sydney: Australian Tax Research Foundation.

Royal Commission on Taxation (1966), (Carter Report), Ottawa: Queens Printer.

Taxation Review Committee (1975), Full Report (Asprey Report), Canberra: AGPS.

US Treasury (1992), *Report on the Integration of the Individual and Corporate Tax Systems – Taxing Business Income Once,* Washington DC: Department of the Treasury.

* *Key readings are asterisked*

Chapter 14

Administrative and Compliance Costs of International Taxation

JEFF POPE
Curtin University, Australia

Key words: administrative costs; tax compliance costs; taxation policy

Abstract: Taxation imposes various costs on the private sector including 'hidden costs' arising from the levying and collection process. These 'hidden costs' are known as the compliance costs of taxation. Tax operating costs comprise compliance costs plus the tax authority's administration costs. This chapter focuses on the conceptual, theoretical and methodological issues of administrative and compliance costs from an international perspective. Tax compliance costs are placed in a policy context wherever possible. Their increasing public and political recognition in many countries throughout the world, together with a growing number of research studies, is emphasised.

1.   INTRODUCTION

Taxation transfers resources from the private sector (individuals and businesses) to the Government or public sector, for purposes deemed worthwhile by the Government of the day. As a result, the private sector not only experiences a loss of resources equal to the amount of the tax itself, plus any associated distortionary costs arising from changes in behaviour and decision-making, but also incurs a loss arising from the levying and collection process of the tax. These latter hidden costs upon the private sector are known as 'the compliance costs of taxation'. A country's taxation objectives are important. Objectives such as horizontal and vertical equity, and the use of taxation for other policy objectives, for example, industrial and regional policy, affect the context in which compliance costs need to be considered.

The compliance costs of taxation comprise both economic and non-economic costs. The economic costs, which may be estimated, consist of the monetary and time costs in dealing with the requirements of the tax authorities. For individuals, this includes the cost of time spent by a taxpayer on record-keeping and completing the tax form or in preparing information for a tax agent or accountant; the fees paid to a professional adviser, such as a tax agent; and miscellaneous costs, such as postage, phone calls, taxation guides, and, increasingly, computer software. For business taxation the costs include the monetary costs spent on the professional fees of tax agents, accountants, lawyers and any other advisers; and the time costs of internal staff on maintaining tax information throughout the year; completing the tax returns themselves or in preparing information for professional advisers; dealing with the tax authorities.

Non-economic costs include the psychological costs of stress and anxiety arising from complying with a specific tax or from a tax-related activity, such as a tax authority audit. The existence of such non-economic costs is recognised. Although usually ignored.

The administrative costs of taxation, often referred to as collection costs, are incurred by the tax authority in administering an existing tax code. Administrative costs added to compliance costs comprise the operating costs of taxation. Of particular importance is the relationship of administrative costs and compliance costs. They may be complementary or competitive to each other. In the former case, tax simplification measures may lead to reductions in both administrative and compliance costs. In the latter case, some tasks may be transferred from the tax authority (public sector) to the taxpayer or third party (private sector). Administrative costs would then be relatively lower and compliance costs relatively higher. The reverse situation, namely a transfer of costs from the taxpayer to the tax authority, although probably less likely, could also occur.

Taxation gives rise to three major effects, namely a sacrifice of taxpayer income as determined by the amount of tax paid, the distortionary effects upon the production and/or consumption decisions of taxpayers, and the operating costs of the tax system. The major components of the (economic) compliance costs of personal taxation are mainly tax agent fees, and the time spent in maintaining information, completing the tax return and tax planning. For business taxation, the main forms of compliance costs may usefully be divided into internal and external costs. Internal costs comprise the own time costs of the self-employed and monetary costs, particularly staff costs. External costs, measured in monetary terms, comprise largely accounting and legal fees.

Another important consideration is the tax deductibility of professional fees incurred in tax compliance work, not only by business, as a legitimate expense, but by personal income taxpayers as well. For example, Australia, with its well-established self-assessment system, has a very high use of professional advisers for personal income tax, with 72% of individual taxpayers currently using a tax agent to prepare their returns. Tax agent fees are tax deductible for all taxpayers.

2.   THE TOPIC'S DEVELOPMENT

The pre-eminent work of Sandford *et al.* (1989) comprehensively discusses the historical development of the topic of the compliance costs of taxation in terms of specific studies that attempt to estimate these costs. Sandford *et al.* (1989, pp. 24-25) recognise the very early contribution by (Adam) Smith (1776) to the taxation literature with his four canons of good tax practice: equity, certainty, convenience, and economy. They stress that two of these four maxims are concerned wholly with compliance costs, with a third including both compliance and administrative costs. The psychological costs of tax compliance also received an eloquent treatment by Smith. Unfortunately, word constraints preclude a discussion of the lessons learnt from earlier studies.

Overall, over the past 60 years until the early 1990s, there have been over 50 known studies on the compliance costs of taxation, including in the UK, USA, Canada, New Zealand, the Netherlands and Australia. Moreover, interest in the topic is growing, both in terms of the number of researchers investigating compliance costs for the first time in various countries and continuing investigations, whether in the form of new surveys, updating previous surveys or simulation studies, by established authors in their respective countries. Further, interest is starting to spread out of the traditional stronghold of Anglo-Saxon and European countries, with research studies having been undertaken in Singapore, Malaysia and Hong Kong, and interest in the topic in such diverse countries as Japan, India and Croatia.

3.   RESEARCH METHODS

3.1   Data Collection Methods

Sandford *et al.* (1989, p. 52) have identified seven major methods of estimating the compliance costs of taxation:
1. Highly structured questionnaires and/or interview schedules.
2. Semi-structured or unstructured interviews.

3. Time and motion studies.
4. Participant observation/action research.
5. Other types of case study, e.g. studies of the comprehensibility of tax forms.
6. Archive research, using records held by government departments, tax advisers, etc.
7. Simulation or modelling exercises.

The researcher also has to decide on the means of contacting respondents where a survey method is used. Information may be collected by mail, telephone or face-to-face, or a combination of these techniques.

The advantages and disadvantages of the various methods are fully considered by Sandford *et al.* (1989, pp. 52-54) and this discussion is not repeated here. Suffice it to say that direct contact with taxpayers through time study and face-to-face interviews is generally considered to produce more reliable data as any ambiguities or queries between the researcher and any respondent can be reconciled immediately 'on-the-spot'. On the other hand, such interviews are time consuming and expensive to administer and, realistically, only a very small sample of the taxpaying population may be made. For example, the Wallschutzky and Gibson (1993) study of Australian small business compliance difficulties/issues had only 12 participants.

Historically, the most commonly used and widely accepted technique is that of the postal questionnaire survey, as it enables a relatively large number of taxpayers to be surveyed at a reasonable cost. Any unreliable responses may be easily eliminated. These may arise from deliberate exaggeration (due perhaps to an antipathy towards the tax authority), misinterpretation of the question or respondents interpreting the question differently. There is, however, an increasing emphasis in the international literature towards smaller surveys with much better quality data.

Sandford (1995, pp. 375-413) has made an excellent critique of the various methodologies based on the experience of leading international studies (up to 1994); readers are highly recommended to this text.

3.2   Questionnaire Design and Data Analysis

Questionnaire design for business tax surveys typically elicit information on the characteristics of the business, the time spent on tax affairs by directors, partners or proprietors, accounting/bookkeeping and other staff, fees paid to professional advisers; and any miscellaneous costs incurred. The nature and associated additional costs of any difficulties, and suggestions for improving the taxes, may also be investigated.

The method of data analysis used to obtain the survey results is usually a statistical package such as Statistical Analysis System (SAS) or the Statistical Package for the Social Sciences (SPSS). These 'raw' figures are then grossed-up in order to derive the compliance cost estimates.

3.3 Grossing-up Procedure

This section explains, in straightforward terms, the method of grossing-up to arrive at the compliance cost estimates.

The means of analysis is first decided upon. The measure should reflect the size of the business, although selecting the preferred measure of size may be constrained by the way in which the taxpaying population has been categorised by the tax authority. Usually annual tax remittance is used, as this is the way in which tax authority data is categorised. Other measures include using annual turnover and the number of employees.

The mean compliance costs for each category are derived from survey data. These are multiplied by the taxpaying population in that category in order to give an estimated aggregate compliance costs figure for the taxpaying population by category. The summation of all categories then gives the total overall estimated compliance costs. Table 1 below illustrates the method of grossing-up.

Table 1. Conversion of Survey Mean Compliance Costs into (Aggregate or Overall) Weighted Compliance Costs

	No. of respondents	Mean compliance costs (survey)	Taxpaying population	Weighted compliance costs
		$	Million	$ million
Column No.	1	2	3	2 x 3
Low remittance category	200	100	4	400
High remittance category	300	500	1	500
Overall	500	340*	5	900

* Mean is [(200 x 100) + (300 x 500)] divided by 500 = $340
Mean survey compliance costs: $340
Mean weighted compliance costs: $180 ($900 million divided by 5 million)

The (overall unweighted) mean compliance costs figure derived from the survey is too high, because the survey is biased towards higher remittance category taxpayers. Re-weighting takes the mean compliance costs figure for each income group and multiplies it by the taxpaying population in that category. Thus the weighted overall mean is significantly lower ($180) than the unweighted survey mean ($340). This reflects the fact that 80% of taxpayers are in the lower remittance category and have lower average compliance costs rather than 40% (incorrectly) implied by the unweighted survey responses.

It is important that a clear distinction is made between the two sets of compliance cost data expressed as a percentage of tax, with the first relating to survey tax remittance data and the second to overall tax authority revenue data.

4.   MAJOR MEASUREMENT AND POLICY ISSUES

This section briefly considers the major measurement and policy issues in the tax compliance cost field. Whilst a balanced view is given, it should be recognised that some of these issues e.g. valuing personal income taxpayers' time, remain controversial in some quarters.

4.1   Measurement Issues

4.1.1   The Valuation of Personal Taxpayers' Time

This remains a particularly 'thorny' problem in the literature, and an area where scholars in the field have taken different approaches.

The essential issue is when a personal income taxpayer undertakes tax compliance work, what is he or she sacrificing, and how should this be valued in monetary terms? At one extreme, he or she may be sacrificing an opportunity to earn money (work-substitution), in which case, the economist values the taxpayer's time spent on compliance work at his or her hourly wage rate. This of course may be considerably above the average wage rate in the country. At the other extreme, it could be argued that a taxpayer may be sacrificing leisure activities, for example watching television, and that this has a very low economic value. In other words, the value of a taxpayer's time should be disregarded in any compliance cost estimate (in spite of it probably representing a disutility to the taxpayer). A middle ground, yet to be developed in the compliance cost literature but well established in the field of transport economics (Sandford *et al.*, 1989, pp. 37-38), would be to value a personal taxpayer's time spent on tax work at some percentage value of the average wage rate. Sandford *et al.* (1989, p. 38) argue that tax work should be given a higher value than that used in transport studies (of perhaps around 25% of the average wage rate) 'both because doing tax work is not compatible with other pleasurable activities and because of the disutility associated with it'.

The views of North American scholars follow traditional mainstream economic literature. Slemrod (Slemrod and Sorum, 1984; Blumenthal and Slemrod, 1992) uses the after-tax wage rate as the appropriate measure of the social cost of tax compliance work, on the grounds that it substitutes mostly for leisure.

There are four main approaches that have been used by researchers:
- individual reported values, possibly subject to some maximum rate;
- the sum that taxpayers would pay to be rid of all compliance costs (a hypothetical concept which most respondents find very difficult to handle);
- the before-tax wage rate;
- the after-tax wage rate.

This issue is fully discussed in Pope (1995, pp. 114-118) and Evans *et al.* (1997, pp. 9-12).

4.1.2   The Treatment of Overhead Costs in the Compliance Costs of Business Taxes

The literature has long recognised the difficulty of allocating the overhead costs, such as office accommodation, lighting, heating, computer equipment, used in tax compliance work for business taxes where there is a 'joint use' with normal business activities. Sandford *et al.* (1989, p14) highlight the contribution of Yocum (1961) to this discussion. Sandford *et al.* (1989, p. 16) take the view that the percentage of overhead costs allocable to tax compliance work increases as the size of the business and the complexity of tax work increases. The largest businesses may have an exclusive tax department whereby all the overhead costs of that department may be allocated to tax compliance work. A secondary problem is that of the allocation of overhead costs between different taxes (Sandford *et al.*, 1989, p. 8). The convention adopted in most compliance cost surveys is to leave the allocation of overhead costs implicitly to the respondent, with the deletion of any outlying estimates, for example, for UK employers' PAYE, Sandford *et al.* (1989, p. 268, question 27).

4.1.3   The Measurement of Compliance Costs as a Percentage of Tax Revenue

The usual convention in compliance cost studies is to measure costs in absolute monetary terms and as a percentage of tax revenue for the specific tax under investigation. However, one major study (Arthur D. Little, 1988) measured compliance costs only in terms of time, expressing the aggregate estimate in billions of hours. This avoids the difficulties associated with expressing monetary compliance costs as a percentage of tax revenue, as well as other methodological problems, such as the valuation of time for personal income taxpayers and deriving agent fees by type of tax for business tax compliance work.

Sandford and Hasseldine (1992, p. 2) emphasise that percentage cost figures should be used with caution. Whilst cost as a percentage of revenue is a useful 'input' to 'output' measure, it is only valid for the year to which it relates. This is because revenue may alter significantly due to a policy change that alters the characteristics of the tax. The most likely change may be in the tax rate(s).

In spite of this caveat, researchers in the field continue to compare compliance cost estimates for the same type of tax over time in one country or between countries by using the percentage figure. The explanation is one of convenience: using absolute figures would require adjusting these to common year prices and, for international studies, using an exchange rate conversion. Nonetheless, compliance cost analysis should, and usually does, encompass a range of measures other than absolute dollars and costs as a percentage of revenue, such as average time spent per taxpayer, percentage use and average cost of tax agents, as well as average costs per taxpayer, together with commentary on significant changes to the tax system.

An alternative or additional measure to the percentage of tax revenue measure is that of expressing compliance costs as a percentage of Gross Domestic Product (GDP) e.g. by Sandford *et al.* (1989, p. 191) and Evans *et al.* (1997). Measuring costs as a percentage of GDP, strictly speaking, should be restricted to business taxation because compliance costs include the foregone alternative or opportunity costs of taxpayers' time, using an hourly monetary value of time to convert hours to dollars. But non-working time, however valued by taxpayers, is unrecorded in GDP statistics.

4.2 Policy Issues

4.2.1 The Relationship of Administrative and Compliance Costs

Administrative plus compliance costs comprise the operating costs of the tax system. But what is the relationship between the two? Whilst both may be complementary (for example, tax simplification measures may reduce both these collection and private sector costs), it has long been recognised in the compliance cost literature that there is usually a trade-off between the administrative costs of the tax authority and the compliance costs borne by the private sector (Haig, 1935, as cited by Sandford *et al.*, 1989, p. 27). A tax with high administrative costs is likely to have low compliance costs and vice versa. The explanation is straight-forward: given that the characteristics of a particular tax system, particularly its level of complexity, determine a quantum of operating costs, a significant proportion of these costs are theoretically 'transferable' between the tax authority and taxpayers. For example, computation of tax liability could be undertaken by tax authority officials (the administrative or authority-administered system) or by taxpayers themselves under a self-assessment system. In the former situation administrative costs would be higher and compliance costs lower, and in the latter the opposite would hold.

Such a relationship between administrative and compliance costs is borne out by the limited empirical evidence available. The UK income tax and social security payment system, which is authority-administered, has relatively higher administrative costs (estimated at 1.5% of tax revenue in 1986/87) and relatively lower compliance costs, at 3.4% of revenue, compared with those of Canada, at 1.0% and 6.1% respectively in 1986, which has a self-assessment system (Sandford *et al.*, 1989, p. 110). In other words, administrative costs account for 31% of tax operating costs in the UK, over double the figure of 14% for Canada.

Other countries that have a personal income tax self-assessment system (with varying characteristics) are the USA and Australia. The estimated compliance costs of both these countries are relatively high, at 5-7% of federal and state income tax revenue in the USA in 1982 and 7.9% in Australia in 1986/87, with administrative costs of 0.48% and 1.1% respectively (Pope, 1993, p. 60). Administrative costs therefore account for only six to nine per cent of operating costs in the USA and 12% in Australia. Thus three countries with a self-assessment system have administrative costs which are around one-seventh or less of operating costs, and well below those of the UK with its (then) authority-administered system.

4.2.2   The Relationship of Tax Complexity, Evasion and Compliance Costs

Slemrod (e.g. 1992, 1988) has taken a leading role in relating the topic of the compliance costs of taxation to such conceptual issues as their relationship to tax complexity and evasion. He argues that compliance costs undoubtedly measure the complexity of the tax system, or any particular tax under investigation, at any point in time. However, care should be taken when comparing compliance cost estimates over time, particularly in any interpretation of whether tax laws have become simpler or more complex. The effect of tax reform upon levels of tax evasion and ensuing changes in the level of compliance costs should be assessed. The effect upon planning costs, the use and cost of tax agents and accountants, and attitudes to compliance generally should also be investigated. These cautionary comments also apply to comparisons between different taxes within any country and between the same type of tax across different countries.

4.2.3   The Existence and Relevance of Cash Flow Benefits

Cash flow benefits arise where a business has the use of tax revenue for a period before it must be paid to the tax authority. Conversely, cash flow costs (or detriments) arise where a business has to pay tax revenue to the tax authority in advance of collecting it (from its own clients or customers). The economist assesses the monetary value of such a cash flow benefit by multiplying the cash flow benefit by the cost of capital (rate of interest) to the business, both expressed on an annual basis. Thus the term the value of cash flow benefits (or costs) has been used in several studies to date (e.g. Sandford *et al.*, 1989), with Pope using the abbreviated term cash flow benefit value (CFBV) or cash flow cost value (CFCV).

The CFBV represents an interest-free loan to the taxpayer (usually a business) from the tax authority and, ultimately, other taxpayers. Conversely, a CFCV represents an interest-free loan from the taxpayer to the tax authority.

It must be strongly emphasised that the total amount of resources within society devoted to tax compliance and (authority) administrative work are completely unaffected by the CFBV and CFCV. The legitimate leads and lags in tax payments cancel each other out, as one taxpayer's benefit is a loss to the tax authority, and eventually other taxpayers, and vice versa. In economic terms, it is a zero sum game within the economy as a whole; there are no resource implications to society overall. Some researchers (e.g. Sandford, Pope, Evans) estimate cash flow benefits, whilst others (e.g. Vaillancourt) choose to ignore them.

4.2.4 The Relationship between Compliance Costs and Taxation Policy Objectives

Compliance costs need to be considered in the broader context of the Government's overall taxation policy objectives rather than from a narrower viewpoint

Although the literature varies in terms of emphasis, a useful summary of the consensus of criteria for a good tax system is given by Musgrave and Musgrave (1989, p. 216). The key points are:

1. Adequate revenue yield.
2. Equitable (actual) distribution of the tax burden (equity principle).
3. Minimum interference with economic decisions (efficiency principle).
4. Assist the use of fiscal policy for stabilisation and growth objectives.
5. Fair, non-arbitrary administration and understandable to the taxpayer.
6. Administration and compliance costs should be as low as *is compatible with the other objectives*. (Italics added).

It is important to note the use of the italicised phrase rather than saying that administration and compliance costs should be as low as possible.

Of course, the various objectives are not necessarily in agreement, and there are usually trade-offs between them. For example, equity may require administrative complexity and may interfere with neutrality and preclude low administrative and compliance costs.

5. MAJOR FINDINGS FROM LEADING INTERNATIONAL STUDIES

It is not the intention to provide a comprehensive summary of estimates from the numerous international studies that have taken place. Readers should refer to the references and further reading given at the end of this paper[1]. Evans *et al.* (1997, pp. 58-76) have presented a valuable analysis of international data for the year 1994-95. For illustrative purposes, tax compliance costs for individuals range from 3.6% of tax revenue and 0.38% of GDP in the UK to 7.9% and 1.05% respectively in Australia (Pope estimates). The figures for the USA are 6.1% and 1.00% respectively. Business tax compliance costs show a wide range depending on the country and type of tax. For example, Fringe Benefits Tax (FBT) is estimated to be 17.1% of tax revenue in Australia (ATAX estimates) compared to 1.9% in

---

[1] It is fortunate for students that many disparate references have been summarised in edited books, particularly Sandford (1995), Evans and Greenbaum (1998) and Evans *et al.* (2001).

New Zealand. Business income tax compliance costs are estimated at between 16% and 23% of tax revenue in Australia compared with around 2% in the UK (1.08-0.86% and 0.08% of GDP respectively). The usual qualifying and cautionary statements apply to such international comparisons.

6.   CURRENT MAJOR POLICY ISSUES AND RESEARCH DIRECTIONS

Pope and Sandford (1999) have identified and updated developments in international tax compliance costs. Their key findings are briefly summarised. Tax compliance cost studies in various countries throughout the world nearly all demonstrate three key findings:

1. Compliance costs are high, whether measured in absolute money terms, as a percentage of tax paid, as a percentage of GDP[2] or by comparison to administrative costs (the costs to the revenue authorities).
2. Compliance costs are very regressive, especially for GST[3]. The level of compliance costs is a major concern to small business, unless exemptions or special arrangements for compliance exist.
3. Research into compliance costs and ensuing publicity 'puts compliance costs on the political agenda'. They have played a significant role in the development by governments of the evaluation of the compliance costs of tax regulations; also they have influenced the introduction of Taxpayers' Charters which, amongst other things, stress the duty of the tax authorities to minimise compliance costs subject to other objectives.

Pope and Sandford (1999, pp. 94-95) have identified five major probable phases in the further development of compliance costs research, First, for countries where major studies have already been undertaken, identification of specific 'hot spots' where compliance costs are particularly high. In-depth studies, probably using interview or focus group methods, would identify small, marginal tax policy changes, which might lead to a significant reduction of the difficulties and ensuing cost levels. Government would be made aware of 'where the shoe pinches'. There may also be more sophisticated international comparisons, although this area remains fraught with difficulties.

---

[2] For example, the compliance costs of the tax system are estimated to be around one per cent of GDP in the UK and two per cent of GDP in Australia (Evans *et al*, 1997, p. 83).

[3] For example, in New Zealand, 1990/91, mean GST compliance costs for the smallest businesses were 2.7% of turnover, compared with 0.005% for the largest businesses (Hasseldine, 1995, Table 6.6), a factor of 540 times greater.

Second, the countries which have undertaken compliance cost studies to date are heavily dominated by those with high GDP per capita, as well as a pre-dominance of English-speaking/Anglo-Saxon countries. The next phase should see further compliance cost studies in the richer countries of the Asia-Pacific region e.g. Hong Kong, Malaysia and also in developing countries e.g. Peru and India (where some studies have already been attempted or are contemplated).

Third, the area of psychological costs has been theoretically recognised in nearly all studies since Adam Smith first gave expression to them in 1776, but then generally consigned to the 'too hard basket'. This difficult area is being tackled by a new study in Australia led by Professor Robin Woellner (Woellner *et al.*, 1998).

Next, compliance cost studies will extend into related fields, which has already begun on a small scale, such as tax (incentive) expenditures (Gunz *et al.*, 1995) and subsidies (Allers, 1994).

Finally, for countries with a federal system of government, such as Canada and Australia, the issue of tax harmonisation and a single collection agency and the effects on compliance costs remain a long-term issue. The work of Plamondon (Public Policy Forum, 1997) may be further developed.

Of course, there are likely to be further tax compliance cost studies in various countries throughout the world. Fruitful areas and likely methodologies are fully discussed in Evans *et al.* (2001). Tax reform often acts as a catalyst for further research, as in Australia, with its massive tax reform program, including the introduction of a GST that commenced 1 July 2000[4].

Pope and Sandford (1999, pp. 95-96) conclude by stressing the increasing Government awareness of the political importance of compliance costs in the richer and leading countries in the world, many of whom are incorporating compliance costs into their tax policy decision-making processes. Further, the importance of compliance costs vis-à-vis deadweight losses is beginning to be recognised within the economics profession as a whole.

7.   CONCLUSION

This chapter has focused on the development of administrative and tax compliance costs, with a particular emphasis on conceptual, theoretical and methodological issues, from an international perspective. Many of these

---

[4]   This author, with colleagues, is undertaking such research, particularly regarding GST start-up costs and small business GST compliance costs.

issues deserve a paper in their own right. Further, tax compliance costs have been placed in a tax policy context wherever possible, rather than being treated as a specialist academic topic. The increasing public and political recognition of tax compliance costs in many countries throughout the world, particularly over the last decade or so, should be stressed. Readers are recommended to pursue the various issues identified in this paper through their own further reading. Other issues, such as the use of econometrics, forecasting (particularly in the context of tax reform), specific tax issues e.g. Goods and Services Tax, the particular difficulties of small business, compliance cost impact statements, have been omitted because of the constraint on length. Readers should pursue relevant issues from the reading given.

STUDY QUESTIONS

1. Discuss the reasons for the lack of recognition of tax compliance costs in tax policy making until fairly recently.
2. Identify and critically analyse some of the assumptions and difficult areas involved in estimating tax compliance costs, for example, value of time, allocation of overhead costs.
3. Discuss the advantages and disadvantages of the various methods of estimating tax compliance costs. Why is there a trend towards smaller samples with better quality data?
4. Critically discuss the relationship between the administrative and compliance costs of taxation, and the policy trade-offs involved.
5. Critically review tax compliance cost estimates derived from two or more international studies of your choice. Clearly identify and discuss the difficulties of making international comparisons. (Note: further specialist reading required).

REFERENCES

Allers, M. A. (1994), *Administrative and Compliance Costs of Taxation and Public Transfers in the Netherlands*, Groningen: Wolters-Noordhoff. [A summary appears in Sandford, (Ed.), 1995, pp. 173-195.]*

Ariff. M. and Pope, J. (2002), *Taxation and Compliance Costs in Asia Pacific Economies*, Jitra, Malaysia: Universit Utara Malaysia Press.*

Ariff, M., Loh, A. and Talib, A. (1995), 'Compliance Costs of Corporate Income Taxation in Singapore', *Accounting Research Journal*, Vol. 8(2), pp. 75-87.

Ariff, M., Ismail, Z. and Loh, A. (1997), 'Compliance Costs of Corporate Income Taxation in Singapore', *Journal of Business Finance and Accounting*, Vol. 24(9-10), pp. 1253-1268.

Arthur D. Little Corporation (1988), *Development of Methodology for Estimating the Taxpayer Paperwork Burden*, Final Report to Department of the Treasury, Washington, D.C: Internal Revenue Service.

Bannock, G. and Albach, H. (1987), *The Compliance Costs of VAT for Smaller Firms in Britain and Germany*, London: Graham Bannock and Partners.

Blumenthal, M. and Slemrod, J. (1992), 'The Compliance Cost of the U.S. Individual Income Tax System: A Second Look After Tax Reform', *National Tax Journal*, Vol. XLV(2), pp. 185-202.

Blumenthal, M. and Slemrod, J. (1995a), 'Recent Tax Compliance Research in the United States', in Sandford (Ed.), pp. 142-172.*

Blumenthal, M. and Slemrod, J. (1995b), 'The Compliance Cost of Taxing Foreign-Source Income: Its Magnitude, Determinants, and Policy Implications', *International Tax and Public Finance*, Vol. 2, pp. 37-53.

Bryden, M. H. (1961), *The Cost of Tax Compliance*, Canadian Tax Foundation Paper, No. 25.

Chan, S., Cheung D. and Ariff, M. (1999), 'Compliance Costs of Corporate Taxation in Hong Kong', *International Tax Journal*, Vol. 25(4), pp. 42-68.

Erard, B. (1997), 'The Income Tax Compliance Burden on Canadian Big Business', Working Paper 97/2, Technical Committee on Business Taxation, Ottawa, Canada: Department of Finance.

Evans, C. and Greenbaum, A. (Ed) (1998), *Tax Administration: Facing the Challenges of the Future*, St Leonard's, NSW: Prospect.*

Evans, C. and Walpole, M. (1999), *Compliance Cost Control: A Review of Tax Impact Statements in the OECD*, Sydney: Australian Tax Research Foundation.*

Evans, C., Pope, J. and Hasseldine, J. (Eds) (2001), *Taxation Compliance Costs: A Festschrift for Cedric Sandford*, Prospect, Sydney.*

Evans, C., Ritchie, K., Tran-Nam, B. and Walpole, M. (1996), *Costs of Taxpayer Compliance, Final Report* (prepared for the Revenue Analysis Branch, Australian Taxation Office), University of NSW (ATAX Programme), 1996.

Evans, C., Ritchie, K., Tran-Nam, B. and M. Walpole (1997), *Taxpayer Costs of Compliance*, Australian Taxation Office, Canberra: AGPS. [Referred to as the 1997 ATAX study]*

Gunz, S., Macnaughton, A., and Wensley, K. (1995), 'Measuring the Compliance Cost of Tax Expenditures: The Case of Research and Development Incentives', *Canadian Tax Journal*, Vol. 43(6), pp. 2008-2034.*

Haig, R. M. (1935), 'The Cost to Business Concerns of Compliance with Tax Laws', *Management Review*, pp. 232-333.

Hasseldine, J. (1995), 'Compliance Costs of Business Taxes in New Zealand', in Sandford (Ed.), pp. 126-141 *

International Fiscal Association (1989), *Cahiers de Droit Fiscal International*, Administrative and Compliance Costs of Taxation, Rotterdam: Kluwer.

Lewis, A. (1982), *The Psychology of Taxation*, New York: St. Martin's Press.

Little, Arthur D., Corporation (1988), *Development of Methodology for Estimating Taxpayer Paperwork Burden, Final Report to Department of Treasury*, Washington, D.C: IRS.

Loh, A., Ariff, M., Ismail, Z., Shamsher, M. and Ali, M. (1997), 'Compliance Costs of Corporate Income Taxation in Malaysia, 1995', *Pacific Accounting Review*, Vol. 14(3), pp. 134-176.

Martin, J. W. (1944), 'Costs of Tax Administration, Examples of Compliance Expenses',
      Bulletin of National Tax Association, pp. 194-205.
Musgrave, R.A. and Musgrave, P.B. (1989), *Public Finance in Theory and Practice*,
      Singapore: McGraw-Hill Book Co.
National Audit Office Report (1994), *HM Customs and Excise: Cost to Business of Complying
      with VAT Requirements*, London: HMSO.
Pitt, M. M., and Slemrod, J. R. (1988), 'The Compliance Costs of Itemising Deductions:
      Evidence from Individual Tax Returns', Working Paper No. 2526, Cambridge, Mass.:
      National Bureau of Economic Research.
Plamondon, R. (1991), *GST Compliance Costs for Small Business in Canada*, Department of
      Finance, Government of Canada, (and update by Plamondon and Associates Inc., 1993). *
Plamondon and Associates Inc. (1995), *GST: The Quick Method of Accounting*, A Report for
      Revenue Canada and Customs and Excise, Government of Canada.
Pope, J. (1993), 'The Compliance Costs of Major Commonwealth Taxes in Australia', PhD
      Thesis, Perth: Curtin University.
Pope, J. (1995), 'The Compliance Costs of Major Taxes in Australia', in Sandford, C. (Ed.),
      1995, pp. 101-125.*
Pope, J. (1997), 'Policy Implications of Research on Compliance Costs of Taxation', in Head,
      J. and Krever, R. (Ed.), *Taxation Towards 2000*, Sydney: Australian Tax Research
      Foundation, pp. 617-644.*
Pope, J. (2001), 'Estimating and Alleviating the Goods and Services Tax Compliance Cost
      Burden Upon Small Business', *Revenue Law Journal*, Vol. 11 forthcoming. *
Pope, J. (2002), 'The Compliance Cost Implications of Australian Tax Reform', in Ariff. M.
      and Pope, J. (2002), *Taxation and Compliance Costs in Asia Pacific Economies*, Jitra,
      Malaysia: Universit Utara Malaysia Press.*
Pope, J. and Rametse, N. (2001), 'Small Business and the Goods and Services Tax:
      Compliance Cost Issues and Estimates', *Small Enterprise Research* (The Journal of
      SEAANZ), Vol. 9(2), pp. 42-54.*
Pope, J. and Sandford, C. (1999), 'Tax Compliance Costs', in: Lamb, M. and Lymer, A. (Ed)
      (1999), *Interdisciplinary Research in Taxation: Research Approaches and Bibliographic
      Survey*, London: The Institute of Chartered Accountants in England and Wales, pp. 85-98.*
Public Policy Forum (1997), *Cutting the Costs of Tax Collection Down to Size*, Ottawa.
      [Prepared for Revenue Canada; principal author: Plamondon, R., of Plamondon and Assoc.
      Inc.] *
Regulation Impact Statement for the Introduction of a Goods and Services Tax (RIS, 1998),
      accompanying *A New Tax System (Goods and Services Tax) Bill 1998*, presented to the
      Australian Parliament, December, at www.taxreform.gov.au
Sandford, C. (Ed) (1995), *Tax Compliance Costs Measurement and Policy*, Bath: Fiscal
      Publications.*
Sandford, C. (2000), *Why Tax Systems Differ: A Comparative Study of the Political Economy
      of Taxation*, Bath: Fiscal Publications.
Sandford, C. and Hasseldine, J. (1992), *The Compliance Costs of Business Taxes in New
      Zealand*, Institute of Policy Studies, Wellington: Victoria University of Wellington.
      [Summarised in Hasseldine, 1995, in Sandford, C. (Ed.), 1995, pp. 126-141.] *
Sandford, C. T., Godwin, M. R. and Hardwick, P. J. W. (1989), *Administrative and Compliance
      Costs of Taxation*, Bath: Fiscal Publications.*

Slemrod, J. (1985), 'The Return to Tax Simplification: An Econometric Analysis', Working
  Paper No. 1756, Cambridge, Mass.: National Bureau of Economic Research, [and (1989)
  Public Finance Quarterly, Vol.17(1), pp. 3-27].
Slemrod, J. (1988), 'Complexity, Compliance Costs and Tax Evasion', cited in: Internal
  Revenue Service (1988), Frank M. Malanga Memorial Research Conference Report,
  Washington, D.C., 17-18 November, pp. 61-65.
Slemrod, J. (1990), 'Optimal Taxation and Optimal Tax Systems', *Journal of Economic
  Perspectives*, Vol. 4(1), pp. 157-178.
Slemrod, J. (1992), 'Did the Tax Reform Act of 1986 Simplify Tax Matters?', *Journal of
  Economic Perspectives*, Vol. 6(1), pp. 45-57.
Slemrod, J. and Blumenthal, M. (1996), 'The Income Tax Compliance Cost of Big Business',
  Public Finance Quarterly, Vol. 24(4), pp. 411-438. *
Slemrod, J. and Sorum, N. (1984), 'The Compliance Cost of the U.S. Individual Income Tax
  System', *National Tax Journal*, Vol. 37, pp. 461-474.
Smith, A. (1776), *Inquiry into the Nature and Causes of the Wealth of Nations*, Book 5,
  Chapter 2, Part 2 'Of Taxes', Everyman Edition, pp. 307-309, 1977.
Strumpel, B. (1966), 'The Disguised Tax Burden', *National Tax Journal*, Vol. 19(1), pp. 70-77.
Vaillancourt, F. (1995), 'The Compliance Costs of Individuals in Canada: Personal Income Tax
  and Payroll Taxes', in Sandford, C. (Ed.), 1995, pp. 196-209. *
Wallschutzky, I. and Gibson, B. (1993), *Small Business Cost of Compliance Project*, Report for
  the ATO/Department of Industry, Technology and Regional Development, Canberra.
  [Summarised in Wallschutzky, 1995, in Sandford, C. (Ed.), 1995, pp. 275-298.]
Woellner, R. *et al* (1998), 'Impact of TLIP on Compliance Costs: Progress Report on an
  Empirical Study', Paper presented at the 3rd International Conference on Tax
  Administration, Sydney, April.
Yocum, J. C. (1961), *Retailers' Costs of Sales Tax Collection in Ohio*, Ohio State University
  Bureau of Business Research.

* *Key readings are asterisked*

Chapter 15

Binding Rulings: A Comparative Perspective

ADRIAN SAWYER
University of Canterbury, New Zealand

Key words: Australia and New Zealand, binding rulings, comparative analysis, consultation, tax planning

Abstract: Binding rulings are fundamental in providing business certainty with respect to the taxation treatment of particular transactions. In this chapter the New Zealand rulings regime is reviewed from the perspective of its purposes and essential characteristics, and is then compared to the Australian regime, focusing on the differences in philosophy and substance between the two regimes. The results of an international comparison of rulings systems conclude the analysis, highlighting the differences in approach between countries.

1.   INTRODUCTION

Binding rulings have as one of their major purposes to provide greater certainty (transaction and compliance) to taxpayers and businesses rather than act as some form of legislative power to the tax authorities that issue them. A growing number of countries have introduced or formalised their rulings systems rather than rely on administrative processes operated at the discretion of the tax authority. In this chapter the New Zealand binding rulings regime is analysed in depth commencing on the basis that it is formulated on the Australian legislative regime but with critical differences in operation and scope. The New Zealand regime is reviewed from the perspective of its purposes and essential characteristics, contrasting these with the Australian regime. Much can be learnt through undertaking a comparative analysis of legislative provisions, especially focussing on the similarities and differences. A summary of the findings from an international comparison of twenty seven rulings regimes concludes the discussion in this chapter.

2.   THE NZ BINDING RULING REGIME

2.1   Background to the NZ Regime

New Zealand taxpayers were exposed to a new experience in 1995, the ability to apply for, and utilise, a formalised statutory rulings procedure that binds the Commissioner of Inland Revenue (Commissioner) in his or her assessments of taxpayers relying on applicable binding rulings with respect to specified arrangements. Before this, non-binding (administrative) rulings were available (see Mapp, 1996, for further discussion on the historical development of rulings in New Zealand). An early call for a binding rulings regime emerged in 1986, (Prebble, 1986) although momentum was not evident until 1990 when the Waugh Committee (Tax Simplification Consultative Committee, 1990) recommended that there be a binding rulings regime.

The NZ Government announced in the 1992 Budget that it was its intention to introduce a process of providing binding rulings to deal with the uncertainty created by the possibility of a change in the Commissioner's interpretation of particular legislative provisions. Despite these political overtures, a formal proposal did not emerge until 7 June 1994, when a discussion document (NZ Government, 1994) on the proposed regime was introduced for public examination as part of the Generic Tax Policy Process (Organisational Review Committee, 1994). From the proposals, it was clearly discernible that the Australian regime had provided the greatest influence on NZ Government officials throughout their research of rulings systems in other jurisdictions, including the systems in Canada, Sweden, and the United States.

It was proposed that the Commissioner be able to issue rulings on the interpretation of taxation law that bind the Commissioner on the future application of that law. Submissions were invited from interested parties and were received from fifteen groups and individuals. Support for the concept was overwhelming with the changes recommended being predominantly fine-tuning in nature.

Following consideration of the submissions, draft legislation was introduced to Parliament in December 1994 as part of the Taxation Reform (Binding Rulings and Other Matters) Bill 1994 (NZ). The Finance and Expenditure Select Committee received eight submissions and the draft legislation was returned to Parliament with several recommended changes.

2.2   Purpose of the New Zealand Regime

The introduction of the statutory regime for binding rulings in New Zealand was to give effect to a 1992 Budget announcement of the Government's intention that a binding rulings system on tax matters would be set in place.

2.2.1   The Major Purposes Behind the Regime

Taxpayers frequently desire foreknowledge of the tax consequences of transactions either before the associated arrangements become unconditional, or at least before a tax return is filed and a tax position taken concerning the arrangement. Such a system may enhance efficiency of business operations within a complex tax system, provide greater certainty, and improve the administrative processes of government.

The purpose behind the Australian binding rulings regime (upon which the NZ model is based) has many similarities to the New Zealand system, although an explicit purpose statement is only provided in statutory form in the NZ model. The Honourable Peter Baldwin, Minister Assisting the Treasurer, said with respect to the proposed model for Australia (Taxation in Australia, 1992, p. 49):

> 'The new system of binding and reviewable rulings will promote certainty for taxpayers, and thereby reduce their risks and opportunity costs. It will also be fairer because taxpayers will be able to object to private rulings and have the matter reviewed by an independent tribunal or court.'

The purpose of the NZ regime is encapsulated in the legislation, a feature of the new philosophy behind New Zealand's legislative drafting style in the 1990s. Specifically, section 91A of the Tax Administration Act 1994 (NZ) provides two major and two minor (yet associated) purposes. Binding rulings are intended to provide taxpayers with certainty about the way that the Commissioner will apply taxation laws. In the discussion document that initially outlined the Government's proposals, two categories of certainty were identified: transaction certainty and compliance certainty (NZ Government, 1994). Transaction certainty was described as the form of business certainty that arises when taxpayers know in advance the tax treatment of their proposed transactions. Compliance certainty is the reassurance given to taxpayers that the arrangement will not be subject to a higher tax liability provided the terms of the arrangement are no different to that contemplated by the ruling. The latter form of certainty is particularly important with the new compliance regime that was effective from 1 April 1997.

The second major purpose behind introducing binding rulings was to assist taxpayers in meeting their obligations under the law. An example of the effective implementation of this purpose was evident following enactment of the proposals in the discussion document on taxpayer compliance, standards, and penalties (NZ Government, 1995). Under the proposals, a taxpayer who relied on an applicable binding ruling would have an absolute defence against any penalty for an 'unacceptable interpretation'. However, this proposal was not carried through to the Taxpayer Compliance, Penalties and Disputes Resolution Bill 1995 and the ensuing legislation. Nevertheless, there is a good argument that if a taxpayer relies on a valid and applicable binding ruling then this should be regarded as taking an acceptable interpretation, since this interpretation was 'acceptable' to the Commissioner.

Section 91A also makes reference to the regime recognising the importance of collecting the taxes imposed by Parliament and the need for full and accurate disclosure by taxpayers who seek to obtain binding rulings. Because of the certainty afforded to taxpayers through the availability of binding rulings, strict disclosure requirements are imposed upon taxpayers. Within the proposals, a legislative statement of taxpayer obligations has been provided through sections 15A and 15B of the Tax Administration Act 1994.

2.2.2   Subsidiary Purposes and Benefits

Further subsidiary purposes and benefits of the regime in New Zealand include providing a mechanism to improve the information flows to the Inland Revenue Department (IRD) on current developments in the business sector, especially trends in taxpayer behaviour and 'grey' areas in the law. Second, a reduction in litigation, which, if effective, will cause a reduction in taxpayers' compliance costs and the administrative costs of government (NZ Government, 1994). A reduction in litigation is far from a certainty in the context of the overall regime. For a discussion on compliance and administrative costs and their measurement, see Sandford and Hasseldine (1992).

2.3   Overview of the Key Features of the New Zealand Regime

The Commissioner is able to issue four types of binding rulings in New Zealand: public rulings, private rulings, product rulings, and, from 20 May 1999, status rulings on the application of a change in the law on an existing private ruling or product ruling. In the process of making a private ruling or a product ruling, the Commissioner has the discretion to make conditions and assumptions. Within the legislation, there are a number of exclusions that prevent the Commissioner from issuing a ruling, although these do not include the general anti-avoidance provision. For resource reasons, private rulings were initially limited to specific arrangements entered into after the issue of the ruling by the Commissioner. From 1 April 1996 the regime was extended to enable the Commissioner to provide private rulings on current and completed arrangements. Resource constraints have continued to cause backlogs with the delivery of rulings (see IRD, 1996-2001). The Rulings Group of the IRD's head office issues rulings centrally.

A private ruling is the Commissioner's interpretation of how a taxation law applies to a specific arrangement for specifically identified taxpayer(s), whereas a product ruling is the Commissioner's interpretation of how a taxation law applies to a specific arrangement for a group of taxpayers, all of which need not be specifically identified. A status ruling is the Commissioner's decision concerning whether an amendment or repeal of a taxation law, stated as applying in a specific private or product ruling, has changed the way that the law applies in that ruling. A public ruling is the Commissioner's interpretation of how a taxation law applies to a specified but generally framed arrangement for taxpayers (provided they come within any assumptions or conditions made in the ruling), which from mid 2002 may apply for an indefinite period.

Taxpayers or their agents, who apply for either a private ruling, product ruling, or status ruling, are required to comply with strict application and disclosure requirements and a failure to comply will lead to non-application of the ruling. The arrangement that is to be the subject of the ruling must be seriously contemplated. However, as a matter of practice permission may be given to add some additional information and/or tax laws after the initial application is filed. The level of depth of analysis by the Commissioner with respect to a ruling application may be very extensive, depending upon the nature of the subject matter and tax laws upon which the ruling is sought. There is a statutory right for the applicant to consult with the Commissioner before the issue of a private ruling, product ruling, or status ruling if the content of the proposed ruling differs from that requested by the applicant. A draft ruling is normally required to be provided with the ruling application. A 'team' of three staff members normally deals with an application for a ruling. The first member is a rulings analyst, who has primary responsibility for the ruling and will have the highest level of involvement in the process. The second member is a manager who is responsible for a team of analysts – this person will be involved to the extent of providing direction and guidance to the analysts that report to them. The third member, who will normally have only general oversight or involvement with a particular issue, is a senior manager. This senior manager will be responsible for signing off the ruling before its issue.

The Commissioner will be bound to assess taxpayers in accordance with the position taken in an applicable public ruling, private ruling, product ruling, or status ruling if the taxpayer relies upon the ruling. However, while taxpayers are not bound by a ruling, until 20 May 1999 applicants were required to disclose in their returns that they had applied for a private ruling and whether or not they followed it. They were also obliged, until 20 May 1999, to disclose any material difference between the arrangement described in the private ruling, and the actual arrangement. Applicants cannot appeal an unfavourable ruling, only the consequential assessment in the normal manner.

All rulings will apply to the arrangements entered into for the period for which the ruling is issued, although the period for which the ruling has application may be extended where the original ruling was either a public ruling, or a product ruling until 20 May 1999.

The Commissioner is able to withdraw a ruling or a ruling may cease to have effect, following a change in a taxation law. Withdrawals may not be retrospective in effect and the withdrawal cannot apply before notification of the withdrawal has been provided to the applicant. A withdrawal cannot be effective before the expiry of the period for which the ruling applies if the arrangement has been entered into before the withdrawal. However, tax law changes may cause retrospective cancellation of the application of a ruling.

Status rulings are a new type of ruling that appeared with the enactment of the Taxation (Accrual Rules and Other Remedial Matters) Act 1999 (NZ). The Commissioner may issue a status ruling upon application concerning whether an amendment or repeal of a taxation law, that is stated as applying in the private ruling or product ruling, has changed the way that the law applies in that ruling.

All public rulings, and from 20 May 1999 all product rulings, are published in full in the IRD's Tax Information Bulletins (TIBs), although it there will normally be two months after completion of a product ruling before it is published. Thus while many product rulings are published in full in the TIBs, others are just noted in the *New Zealand Gazette*. Private rulings are not published, but where the content of a private ruling raises an issue of wider significance to taxpayers generally, the Commissioner may decide to issue a public ruling reflecting the approach taken in that private ruling. Status rulings on a product ruling are notified in the *New Zealand Gazette* and generally published within two months of notifying the applicant.

Private rulings, product rulings and status rulings are charged for on a full cost-recovery basis, which for the purposes of the regime until 25 August 1999, implied a non-refundable application fee of $NZ210 (including GST), an hourly rate thereafter of $NZ105 (including GST) and reimbursement of certain fees and disbursements. From 26 August 1999, the fees increased to a non-refundable application fee of $NZ310 (including GST), an hourly rate thereafter of $NZ155 (including GST) and reimbursement of certain fees and disbursements. It is interesting to note that based upon figures in the IRD's Annual Reports to 30 June (1999 – 2001), an estimate of the average cost of a private/product ruling as charged by the Rulings division in 1999 was approximately $NZ4,000, increasing to $NZ6,000 in 2000 and rising still further to $NZ7,000 in 2001.

The Commissioner must provide an estimate of the fees payable in excess of the application fee and must advise the taxpayer of the likely date for issue of the ruling if this is expected to be longer than four weeks after receipt of a complete application. The Commissioner may waive all or part of the fees payable by the applicant. There is provision for the Commissioner to contract out work, such as through using external consultants.

2.4 Consultation and Submissions: Evaluation and Impact

New Zealand's binding rulings model, on its initial introduction, was one of the earliest to experience and benefit from the Generic Tax Policy Process (GTPP), whereby proposed new legislation or amendments are open to public consultation and submissions at both the policy and draft legislation stages (see further Sawyer, 1996). The recent comprehensive remedial review, and for that matter the earlier minor legislative reviews, were open for consultation by way of draft legislation in the form of a Bill and detailed commentary, with submissions heard before the Finance and Expenditure Committee (FEC). Unlike the introduction of the New Zealand model, there was no policy discussion document issued since on this occasion, the model was in place, experiencing only a comprehensive *remedial* review, with one exception. The status ruling 'crept in' though the remedial review process and did not receive the degree of consultation on the underlying policy that public and private rulings received (NZ Government, 1994).

Status rulings were devised in the context of the following general scenario. As a result of the difficulties associated with amendments to legislation, which may or may not render an existing binding ruling inapplicable, the Commissioner must ascertain whether existing rulings remain effective. For example, the Commissioner was required to ascertain whether binding rulings relying upon aspects of the Income Tax Act 1994 (NZ), which have been subsequently amended by the rewriting of the core provisions of the Income Tax Act 1994, remained valid, or whether new rulings must be prepared and issued. A new section 3 Taxation (Core Provisions) Act 1996 (NZ) was added to legislatively facilitate this process. The exercise was initially conducted at the Commissioner's expense rather than by the holders of product rulings and private rulings. Public rulings requiring amendment naturally were altered at the Commissioner's expense. However, legislation will change for reasons other than rewriting the core provisions, and so as to enable continued transaction certainty for taxpayers, the status ruling was devised, a ruling unique to New Zealand.

Government officials made a number of submissions on both the minor and comprehensive remedial reviews of the New Zealand binding rulings model (all of which were accepted by the FEC), along with a few observations and recommendations. Apart from a couple of exceptions, submissions by private sector organisations, requesting amendments to the proposals for change, either yielded no immediate tangible reward or were rejected.

The review process left several areas unresolved in that they were not addressed in the process of discussion and consultation. The absence of an objection facility was not discussed further, neither was whether the issuer of binding rulings should remain the IRD or should become an independent body (for a discussion of this issue in the Australian context, see Bentley, 1997). The issue of whether private rulings should be published in some form was not considered, neither was the issue of the process of withdrawing binding rulings. No progress was made on combining the current processes for issuing determinations and binding rulings.

3.   COMPARING THE AUSTRALIAN AND NEW ZEALAND MODELS - THE EARLY EXPERIENCE

To undertake a complete comparison is beyond the scope of this chapter. Rather, several fundamental aspects that have been taken from the Australian model and adopted in New Zealand are compared. The focus will then turn to differences in the approach and structure between the models, offering reasons for the disparities and their associated implications.

3.1   Scheme of the Australian Regime

The scheme of the Australian legislation, as set out in the Taxation Administration Act 1953 (Aust.), follows a similar approach to the New Zealand legislation with respect to public and private rulings. However, the drafting of the Australian legislation is complex and obscure in parts; there is no statement of the purpose of the regime within Part IVAAA of the Taxation Administration Act 1953. Nevertheless, the purpose behind the Australian regime, which largely mirrors that of the New Zealand regime, is discussed in the case *CTC Resources NL v Federal Commissioner of Taxation* (1994) 27 ATR 403; (1994) ATC 4072, per Gummow J at 407 - 8 and 419 - 20, and Hill J at 427 - 28.

3.2   Similarities Between the Two Regimes

The degree of similarity is sizeable (as noted by Sawyer, 1997), which is not surprising given that the earlier Australian model was the basis for the underlying policy and approach for the New Zealand model. Perhaps the more interesting discussion is that relating to the differences between the models since this can indicate areas where actual or perceived disadvantages of the Australian model are addressed. Alternatively, it may indicate instances where the IRD and the NZ Government have been able to take advantage of the early experience with the Australian model, from the perspectives of users and the Australian Tax Office (ATO).

The most important similarity of the two models was the mutual decision to establish each regime by statute rather than maintain administrative systems, a major cause of dissatisfaction with the previous rulings facility. A statutory basis provides a mechanism for external input into the development phase, vividly illustrated by the consultative process employed in New Zealand. It creates a legitimacy of the process separate from the issuer of rulings, and enables clearer specification of the components, and the rights and obligations of the participants, especially the taxpayer in requiring the Commissioner to assess in accordance with a favourable ruling. However, Harris (1994, p. 36) summarises the Australian model as illustrating '... statutory overkill ... the statutory framework is narrow, uncertain, inflexible and, as usual, too complex.'

Both regimes encompass a broad range of taxation laws upon which the relevant Commissioners may make a ruling, although both systems have restrictions on areas where the Commissioner and Australian Commissioner may make a ruling. Surprisingly, there are fewer restrictions on the areas in which the Australian Commissioner may issue a public ruling when compared to both the issue of all three types of binding ruling in New Zealand and the issue of a private ruling in Australia.

New Zealand's regime draws upon a number of important features of the Australian regime through incorporating both public rulings and private rulings, a predictable situation given that the issue of rulings of a general nature and for specific taxpayers upon request is a dominant feature in most rulings regimes internationally. Australia has recently improved aspects of its public rulings regime through clarification of the publication process and providing guidance to ascertain the distinctive features of a valid binding public ruling; moves which address a few of the earlier criticisms of the Australian regime and place it closer to the environment enjoyed in New Zealand.

Within the private rulings process, New Zealand has incorporated useful characteristics of the Australian regime, including the ability for the Commissioner to request further information, to make assumptions and include these within the ruling, and a series of situations either granting a discretion or placing a restriction on the Commissioner to issue a private ruling. One of the unacceptable restrictions is the discretion granted to the Commissioner to decline to issue a ruling if it would be unreasonable to issue a ruling in the light of the resources available to him or her. Utilising this discretion when a request is received as a means to conceal problems with either resource management within the ATO/IRD or with the allocation of departmental funding from Parliament is unacceptable.

In the course of making submissions to the select committee on the draft New Zealand legislation, the Life Office Association of New Zealand (1995, p. 5) emphasised that '[r]esource constraints are a matter of managing resources'. External consultants can be employed on complex issues or if a short-time frame exists for issuing a ruling. The FEC responded negatively, although it acknowledged that in practice, this discretion would in all likelihood be 'seldom invoked'. The FEC felt that external consultants were not expected to always be available or for that matter, appropriate (FEC, 1995).

With respect to when a ruling will bind the Commissioner, one aspect that has caused concern with tax professionals arises when the underlying arrangement is materially different or there has been a material change from the factual information (and draft ruling in the New Zealand situation) supplied to the Commissioner. In both regimes there is no legislative guidance on the concept of a material difference or material change. Consequently, attention focuses on use of the concept in the common law, where the term 'significant and relevant' has been considered analogous. With written instruments, a significant and relevant change implies alteration of the legal effect of the instrument. To this end, Blaike (1994, p. 133) provides a useful summary of how this test could apply for private rulings, (for New Zealand this approach could be extended to product rulings):

> 'In applying this test in the context of private rulings, a court, if it so chose, would have to identify the legal effect of the arrangement described in the private ruling and compare that effect to the legal effect of the actual transaction into which the rulee entered or proposed to enter. Where the legal effect or substance of the respective transactions, rather than the form, is the same, s.170BB [Taxation Administration Act 1953] would apply ...

Taxpayers will have to take care to include all important details in private ruling applications to ensure that the Commissioner cannot argue that a transaction described in a ruling is 'materially different' from the transaction which the taxpayer has entered into or proposes to enter into.'

In both regimes, the relevant Commissioner is prevented from ruling solely on questions of fact concerning an arrangement where the legal effect of an arrangement under one or more taxation laws is a prerequisite. This restriction has been relaxed in New Zealand for two situations where questions of 'legal' fact are involved with respect to an application for a private ruling; apportionment of income derived partly in New Zealand and partly elsewhere and cross-border arrangements between associated persons (transfer pricing provisions).

3.3 Differences Between the Regimes: Issues of Substance and Philosophy

Major differences highlighted in Sawyer (1997) include the absence of the right for taxpayers to object to unfavourable rulings in New Zealand and the user pays approach (and ensuing private rulings application process), rather than the 'cost-free' service provided in Australia. A further major difference is the mandatory requirement for the Commissioner in New Zealand to consult with taxpayers where the proposed ruling differs from the draft provided by the taxpayer – there is no such requirement in Australia. Furthermore, the obligation to include alternative views and arguments in the application for a binding ruling in New Zealand, the product rulings feature 'unique' to New Zealand, and the contrasting philosophies over 'publishing' private rulings are important differences between the two models. While neither regime includes a feature requiring the publication of private rulings, in Australia databases of private rulings are now to be kept and private rulings will be published in a sanitised form following the developments of the Sherman review of the regime (Sherman, 2000).

Other differences of note include the shorter and more responsive approach and time frame in New Zealand for delivering rulings. However, with resource limitations and shortages of staff, delivery times for rulings in New Zealand have increased dramatically. Another difference is that New Zealand has avoided the uncertainties arising through the vagaries of the withdrawal process in Australia, demonstrating how one country can learn and benefit from the experiences of another.

Sawyer (1997) also identifies other miscellaneous issues of contrast between the two models, including the approach to class rulings (or more correctly, the absence thereof in New Zealand), and the availability of multiple income years (period) for rulings in New Zealand (see IRD, 1996-2001). Other areas of contrast include the content of the public rulings program and allocation of resources to ruling applications, and the location of published rulings in New Zealand in both the *New Zealand Gazette* and in the TIB.

Furthermore, differences arise due to the underlying tax systems of Australia and New Zealand, especially from the administrative side. One example is that rulings are issued centrally in New Zealand while in Australia they are decentralised and issued from different offices of the ATO.

A further major difference is that in Australia there is the right of objection for dissatisfied taxpayers. In New Zealand the decision was made by the Government not to provide a right of appeal to an applicant who receives an unfavourable private ruling or product ruling, the opposite of the position in Australia with respect to private rulings. A New Zealand taxpayer is limited to pursuing their dissatisfaction through the objection (challenge) procedures once the Commissioner has issued an assessment incorporating the arrangement in question. The right to an objection under the Australian regime runs separately to the formal assessment objection process, but should the ATO fail to produce a ruling before the return in which the arrangement in question is assessed, then there cannot be any objection against the ruling, should a ruling ever emerge. An appeal may also be considered from the Commissioner's perspective in 'repealing', or more correctly, withdrawing a ruling.

Explanations for the decision to incorporate an appeal right in Australia include the practical, if not theoretical, requirement that a taxpayer follow a private ruling in Australia once appeal rights have been extinguished; the risk of not following a ruling is the imposition of a 25% penalty on the tax shortfall. With taxpayers 'free' to depart from following a binding ruling in New Zealand, the Government sought to use this feature, amongst others, to reject submissions supporting an appeal facility. The advisers to the select committee incorrectly advance the following argument in support of there being no appeal facility in New Zealand: '[i]n the United States and Canada where the rulings do not bind taxpayers, there is no right of appeal. In Australia, there is a right of appeal, but rulings bind the taxpayer. These two are linked.' (FEC, 1995, p. 41).

The FEC was advised that the New Zealand courts were opposed to the appeal right as this would require them to rule on hypothetical situations; particular concern was expressed in writing by the Chief Justice of New Zealand that an appeal right should not be provided (this statement appears in a letter dated 7 July 1994 by Sir Thomas Eichelbaum, addressed to the Inland Revenue Department and attached to the FEC's Report - FEC, 1995). The advisers to the FEC were of the view that a ruling is the Commissioner's interpretation and not the law itself, and consequently should not be elevated to the status of law. Certainty of the law is the domain of Parliament and the courts, not the Commissioner according to the NZ Government's advisers. While this view is technically correct, it is irrelevant to the issue of objecting to an interpretation of the law as set out in a binding ruling (Slater, 1992).

A preference for early certainty and confidence about the Commissioner's proposed approach to assessing an arrangement (rather than absolute certainty about the law) is advanced by the advisers to the FEC; this is a view with some merit. However, Hill (1995) observes that taxpayers will not perceive this as a preferable form of certainty; furthermore it does not facilitate self-assessment. It may also serve to delay the inevitable dispute and increase the resulting costs when the matter comes within the assessment objection process. One factor in favour of the advisers' view is the statutory consultation facility available to taxpayers if the Commissioner proposes to issue a ruling that differs to that requested, as will permitting withdrawal of the application for a ruling before the ruling is issued. Nevertheless, this approach does not guarantee that the Commissioner will be persuaded to see the taxpayer's view after consultation. Furthermore, the applicant remains liable for the costs incurred as part of any consultation and for the resources utilised until the withdrawal of the application is effective.

While a public ruling may not be appealed, taxpayers and tax professionals in both jurisdictions may offer comment on the earlier draft ruling, which the ATO/IRD will then consider. The cost of obtaining a private ruling in New Zealand may be significant, since the IRD by regulation will charge upon application for a ruling and then for each hour of work in preparing the ruling. In Australia, there is no charging system for public and private rulings, but such a system has been implemented for 'product' rulings. Initially only New Zealand provided for product rulings, although the Australian regime now offers the same feature, albeit as a special form of public ruling. The application process in New Zealand is much more legislative based than Australia, and arguably more onerous on applicants to meet all of the requirements.

In New Zealand, there is prior to the issue of a ruling consultation with the applicant (or with the taxpaying community in general for public rulings), and alternative views on the application of the law (if they exist) are provided in the resulting ruling. Minimal opportunity exists for consultation in Australia, with only significant alternative views included in Australian binding rulings.

A requirement of the New Zealand regime, the disclosure return, was eventually repealed as from 20 May 1999. The disclosure return was required from applicants on an annual basis with their tax return if they had received a private ruling and were required to file a return. Taxpayers in this situation had to take into account the way in which a tax law applies to the arrangement identified in the return, identify the existence of the ruling, state whether the ruling was relied upon, and state if there were any material changes to the arrangement identified in the ruling.

A number of other differences exist between the two regimes, namely that rulings may be issued in Australia on class arrangements and on the tax affairs of another person, but not so in New Zealand (although the product ruling facility may be utilised to overcome some of this potential shortcoming in New Zealand). The period for which rulings are issued is generally longer in New Zealand since Australian binding rulings are issued for only a year at a time, requiring reapplication for further years.

In Australia, the binding rulings and determinations regimes are combined, while in New Zealand they are separate – this is one example of simplification that the Australian regime has over its New Zealand counterpart.

3.4   Evaluating the Two Regimes

Before the components of the two regimes are evaluated in summary, the over-riding factor that will govern whether either regime can achieve its intended purposes of increasing certainty for taxpayers will rest upon the attitudes taken by the ATO and the IRD. Initially the IRD was opposed to a binding rulings regime; it took considerable effort and research to convince the Commissioner and senior staff that the NZ Government's proposal for a binding rulings regime be given statutory effect. It is to a large extent a testament to the research effort and consultative process that several features were added to the New Zealand system in response to difficulties or opportunities experienced in the regimes in Australia, Canada, Sweden, and the United States.

Smith (1995, p. 30) summarises the potential wildcard implications of the IRD's attitude in the following terms (applicable to both private rulings and product rulings, and to a lesser extent public rulings):

'The success of the regime is solely dependent on the IRD's attitude. If it considers that all applicants seek rulings because they have doubt in their minds and issue unfavourable rulings, no one will apply. Any 'if-in-doubt-say-no' approach by the IRD will defeat the potential benefits of the regime.'

Differing views prevail over the ATO's attitude to the rulings system. Lowcay (1995) contends that the ATO attitude is that it has a fundamental responsibility to provide advice to taxpayers via rulings. Hill (1995) argues the opposite; in the event the ATO would be required to issue rulings, then it should be able to charge for their issue.

In evaluating the two regimes, an important proviso is the differing underlying statutory schemes in place; the Australian tax system is close to pure self-assessment, the New Zealand regime has moved in this direction but in a relatively haphazard manner. Both systems are unduly complex and undergoing efforts directed at simplification. Limits on flexibility abound in each countries' tax system, but the New Zealand model offers a more cost effective and efficient process, evidenced in the quality and relative timeliness of rulings, due largely to the charging process and ruling application requirements.

The Australian model offers features with several advantages over its New Zealand counterpart; the appeal process is notable as a mechanism to address disputes over rulings at an early stage. A fortiori, the misinterpretation and the lack of foresight by the NZ Government is evidenced through its reasoning in determining to withhold this facility from the New Zealand regime. Tentatively the slightly wider scope for issuing rulings and the less onerous application requirements would place the Australian regime ahead of New Zealand's.

However, New Zealand's regime takes further steps forward in its more comprehensible procedures for the withdrawal of rulings and the assistance given by the detailed application requirements, which in turn facilitate the timeliness of the issue of private and product rulings, subject to the ongoing problem of insufficient resources and staff. For supporters of removing cross-subsidisation and promoting user pays, the charging process is a positive feature. The provision of product rulings provides a guideline for the ATO to resolve its concerns over privacy. Comparing the current quality of rulings nudges the New Zealand system still further ahead, but it is still relatively early days. The IRD's consultative approach to date is to be applauded when contrasted to the previously unprofessional silence and frequently negative attitude displayed by the ATO. It remains to be seen whether the IRD can maintain this standard and permeate a positive attitude both to rulings requests and in the content of the rulings it issues.

The approach and attitude to the concept of a binding ruling taken by the IRD to date is preferable to the ATO's position during the four years the regime had been in operation, according to Sawyer (2000). Expectations remain high from both sides, with each still experiencing the learning curve effects that accompany relatively new legislation. If the IRD fails to deliver within the spirit and intent of the regime, or reverts to a negative attitude with respect to favourable rulings, the regime will become an expensive 'white elephant', unable to deliver certainty in a positive manner as far as taxpayers are concerned. Both the New Zealand regime and the IRD's associated targets and role are ambitious. Time will be the arbiter of success or otherwise; an open consultative approach is vital to enable continued refinement of the regime.

4.   INTERNATIONAL COMPARISON OF BINDING PRIVATE RULINGS

Binding private rulings have become an increasingly important component of many tax systems and have played an essential role in fostering confidence and trust in the relationship between taxpayer and tax authority. However, binding private rulings are a supplement to, and not a substitute for, clearly drafted legislation. Tax legislation should have a clear purpose, reflecting precisely the circumstances to which it applies. Tax legislation that most countries promulgate is far from clear or precise, hence the need for some form of rulings facility, be it administrative or legislative. While in these circumstances a binding private rulings procedure is often seen as crucial to an effective tax system, even if all legislation were clear and concise such a procedure may still be desirable, even if only to increase taxpayer certainty.

As is the case for virtually all taxation law issues, the design of a binding private rulings system inevitably involves a balance of costs and benefits. On the one hand, comprehensive rulings systems provide security for taxpayers and facilitate individual business decisions based on economic considerations without the risk of unforeseen tax consequences. However, on the other hand, in the context of a mass decision making system, the diversion of resources to the operation of a comprehensive ruling system has the *potential* to bring enforcement mechanisms to a grinding halt, especially if a complex and lengthy appeal mechanism is in place.

Nevertheless, while the increased use of binding private rulings has the potential ultimately to reduce administrative costs, particularly in the areas of auditing and investigation, a complete trade-off will not follow. Hence, the decision in most jurisdictions is to allow binding private rulings in some areas so long as the rulings do not create a precedent. Limiting the scope of the rulings system reduces the need for multiple levels of administrative review and the costs associated with them. Furthermore, generally since binding private rulings are frequently not officially published (although this situation appears to be changing after reviewing the following analysis) and not cited by courts, the potential damage is limited (or confined) if an erroneous interpretation is made in a binding private ruling.

Reliance on binding private rulings varies significantly among the countries surveyed by Sawyer (2001), ranging from limited use in some (a number of jurisdictions were excluded as their use of the binding ruling facility was far too limited to provide useful or interesting comparison) through to perhaps, at the other extreme or end of the spectrum, legislation that virtually requires taxpayers to seek rulings if they wish to avoid penalties and the like. Given the multitude of factors that explain why some rulings systems are limited and others comprehensive, and why advisors' use of rulings varies significantly from jurisdiction to jurisdiction, it is clear that an assessment of the quality and applicability of the incumbent regimes in New Zealand and Australia, and for that matter any recommendations for policy changes and new direction(s), will benefit from comparing the approaches of other countries or jurisdictions.

Group One:
Australia, Canada, Sweden, United Kingdom, and United States - the five major regimes, form the first tier for analysis.

Group Two:
Belgium, Denmark, Finland, France, Hong Kong, India, (Republic of South) Korea, Mexico, the Netherlands and South Africa. These ten countries formed the second tier for analysis.

Group Three:
Germany, Hungary, Iceland, Ireland, Israel, Italy, Pakistan, the Philippines, Portugal, Spain and Switzerland. Interesting features of the regimes in these eleven countries formed the third tier for analysis.

While not explicitly stated in Sawyer (2001), the New Zealand regime formed the status quo upon which to compare the regimes from the twenty-six other countries.

It should be noted that the focus of this analysis, like Sawyer (2001), is on private rulings, not public rulings or any other form of binding ruling (such as New Zealand and Australia's product rulings, and New Zealand's status ruling). Hence, this places a limitation on the scope of analysis, although it can be stated that the vast majority of the twenty-six countries (plus New Zealand) have a public rulings system that accompanies the private rulings system.

4.1   Key Points From Twenty-Six Nations Reviewed

Most regimes that were reviewed by Sawyer (2001) had a formal binding ruling regime in place as compared to a non-binding (or administrative) regime. Most countries stipulated a variety of tax laws that were excluded from being ruled upon, with great variation in the breadth of areas that can be ruled upon. Where information was available, time limits were placed on dealing with applications for rulings for both the revenue authority and the applicant. Almost all revenue authorities had the ability to decline requests (including declining for insufficient resources to handle the request).

In some instances, there are limits as to how long outstanding issues may be debated between the revenue authority and applicant, with some facility or opportunities provided for responses from applicants. Related to this matter is the question of how definitive the arrangement (or transaction) must be that is to be ruled upon, along with the issues that may be ruled upon (the transaction), and the types of documentation that are to be supplied (and whether changes in the arrangement post application are allowed). Considerable variation exists on all of the above between the regimes reviewed by Sawyer (2001). Variation also exists as to whether tax laws can be added (and if so, by whom – the revenue authority and/or the applicant) after the application is filed. In some instances, revenue authorities are permitted to cease work on applications, especially where the applicant has failed to provide all the required information or not responded to queries.

A variety of approaches exist for the preparation and issue of rulings, as between a small central group, widespread decentralisation, or by operational divisions. In almost all instances, it is the revenue authority that is responsible for making and issuing rulings; a notable exception is Sweden with its separate rulings authority.

A minority of regimes utilise some form of charging system for rulings, with most that employ such a regime having fixed or variable rates depending on the complexity of the application, but not to the extent of full cost recovery in the traditional accounting sense of the concept. It appears that most regimes do not provide for contracting out of work (such as to private sector professional firms) and do not draw upon external resources.

The level of depth of consideration of issues and documentation required of applicants by the revenue authority is extensive in almost all of the regimes reviewed, especially in the countries of Group One (as well as New Zealand). Many regimes will only permit prospective arrangements to be ruled upon, with a minority allowing for both prospective and retrospective (post-transaction) arrangements to be ruled upon. It appears that few regimes adopt any form or have any processes in place for determining prioritisation or fast tracking of ruling requests – requests are usually processed in the order of receipt and passed to a particular rulings staff member (although in a few instances the degree of complexity, which frequently affects the time for delivery of the ruling, may be a determining factor in the allocation process).

Many of the regimes have requirements for a business case test to accompany the application, requiring in part that the applicant seriously contemplate the transaction. To this end a test of 'seriously contemplated' may be employed, but it is difficult to establish just what that test entails (see Sawyer, 2001). In New Zealand this means that the applicant must be at least seriously contemplating becoming a party to an actual or proposed arrangement (TIB, 1995). If more than one option is being considered, then the feasibility study into the options must be a substantial exercise in terms of time, effort and expenditure involved, with a separate application for each option to be considered (TIB, 1996). Some contentious issues cannot be ruled upon, which is reflected often through the exclusion of certain statutory provisions (such as the general anti-avoidance provision, if one exists in the tax laws of a particular jurisdiction). It should be noted that some regimes explicitly allow rulings to cover general and/or specific anti-avoidance provisions.

Many regimes require documentation and other information to accompany ruling applications, such as draft documentation describing the arrangement, and in most instances a draft ruling is required or at least encouraged to be provided with the application. Provision of a draft ruling can speed up the process and assist with focussing the application on the core legislative provisions to be ruled upon.

A minority of countries permit or require the publication of private rulings, and where publication occurs, they will be in a sanitised form, removing the identifying characteristics of the applicant(s). A frequent reason for refusing to publish such rulings is the issue of privacy, as against reducing opportunities for certain applicants advisors to have 'inside knowledge' of the revenue authority's interpretation of certain provisions in relation to certain types of arrangement.

The overwhelming majority of countries do not have a formal appeal process in place for objection to unfavourable rulings outside of the normal objection process for tax assessments. If such an appeal process exists, the appeal is normally through a specialist court or body that hears ruling disputes

(Australia is one exception to this where the normal court process is employed). In most instances taxpayers are not bound by an issued ruling, but there is the risk of penalties being imposed if they do not follow a ruling (see further Sawyer, 2002).

5.   CONCLUSIONS AND OBSERVATIONS

As noted earlier, the overriding factor that governs whether either model can achieve its intended purpose of increasing certainty for taxpayers rests upon the attitudes taken by the ATO and the IRD. While the IRD was initially opposed to a binding rulings regime, both the IRD and NZ Government are now supportive of the process, with the main concern being the under-resourcing of the IRD's Adjudication and Rulings Group. Unlike the introduction of the New Zealand model, the subsequent amendments have largely been remedial and in response to developments since 1995. Furthermore, the reforms strongly suggest that there has been minimal tangible effort applied to considering developments in other jurisdictions, especially that of Australia. Part of the reason for the absence of such a wide-ranging review was the benefits gained from reviewing a number of overseas binding rulings regimes (such as Australia, Canada, and Sweden) prior to introducing the proposed regime for New Zealand in 1994-95.

While differing views appeared to prevail over the ATO's attitude to the rulings system, as indicated by Sawyer (1997), the ATO's decision to introduce product rulings in response to requests from the business community is to be applauded. Unfortunately this initiative is confined within the straightjacket of the public rulings legislative framework and the associated problems this situation has caused, including the criminal legal action being taken over the former First Assistant Commissioner of Taxation, Nick Petroulias (see e.g. Laurence, 2000).

In evaluating the two models since the study of Sawyer (1997), the New Zealand tax system has moved even closer to a formalised self-assessment environment, becoming much closer to the Australian tax system in this regard. Both systems remain unduly complex, undergoing protracted efforts directed at simplification (see James *et al.*, 1998). Limits on flexibility abound in each country's tax system, but the New Zealand rulings model still offers a more cost effective and efficient process, evidenced in the past at least by the high quality and relative timeliness of rulings, due largely to the New Zealand model's charging process.

Nevertheless, the Australian model continues to offer features with several advantages over its New Zealand counterpart; the appeal process is notable as a mechanism to address disputes over rulings at an early stage (theoretically at least), albeit with mixed success. A fortiori, the misinterpretation and the lack of foresight by the NZ Government remains entrenched through a reluctance to revisit its reasoning in determining to withhold this facility from the New Zealand model from the outset. While New Zealand's model now offers slightly wider scope for issuing rulings than Australia, the application requirements are about on par between the two models.

New Zealand's model retains its advantage with its comprehensible and less complex procedures for the withdrawal of rulings, and the assistance given by the detailed application requirements that in turn can improve the timeliness of the issue of private rulings, product rulings, and now status rulings. For supporters of removing cross-subsidisation and promoting user pays, the charging process is a positive feature of the New Zealand model, although there is minimal scope for recognising *ability to pay*. Partial (and possibly full) waiver of fees is the only facility provided to recognise ability to pay, although there is no publicly available data on the extent to which the discretion to allow waivers has been applied by the CIR.

It was noted in Sawyer (1997) that the provision of product rulings provided a guideline for the ATO to resolve its concerns over privacy and consider endorsement of a similar feature for the Australian model. Rather than seek legislative backing, the ATO decided to interpret section 14ZAAF Taxation Administration Act 1953 (Aust.) as enabling it to issue a public ruling to a class of persons and call it a *product ruling*; a mere shadow of the equivalent New Zealand feature. There appears to be little evidence to separate the current standard or quality of rulings between the two systems. The IRD's consultative approach to date should still be applauded when contrasted with the previous unprofessional silence and frequently negative attitude that had been displayed by the ATO. The ATO's initiative on product rulings is evidence of an improvement in their attitude towards binding rulings, although in New Zealand frustration is growing that the IRD is failing to deliver many rulings within its stated timeframe.

As noted by Sawyer (2000), expectations remain high from both sides concerning the models, with each still experiencing to a degree the learning curve effects that accompany new (amending) legislation and significant judicial interpretation. In Australia, the private rulings process and the appeal facility in particular have been placed under close judicial scrutiny. In New Zealand's case, the model has come under scrutiny as a result of the recent comprehensive remedial review and introduction of a fourth class of ruling, the status ruling. The status ruling concept is a feature that Australia should seriously consider in relation to the Tax Law Improvement Project (TLIP); the recent amendment to sections 14ZAAM and 14ZAXA Taxation

Administration Act 1953 (Aust.) do no more than expand upon the Australian equivalent to new section 91G Tax Administration Act 1994 (NZ). In respect of the recent amendments in New Zealand, time will once again be the arbiter of success or otherwise. An open consultative approach is vital to enable continued refinement of the model, although private sector organisations have not been highly successful in having their submissions recommending changes to draft legislation accepted.

Australian legislators and the ATO would benefit from examining the Australian binding rulings model as part of a comprehensive review, if they have not already so determined. The recent New Zealand experience in this area would be educative and could, in some respects, form the basis for benchmarking a revised Australian model. However, the New Zealand binding rulings model should not be viewed as the ideal approach, especially concerning the absence of an appeal facility for binding rulings.

From the analysis undertaken by Sawyer (2001) it could be argued that if there were no costs incurred as part of the trade-off with a comprehensive rulings model, then an expanded ruling system drawing upon the favourable aspects of the Australian and New Zealand systems (the former providing a comprehensive, free, ruling system with a full range of appeal options in the case of an adverse ruling) might be a model for consideration for any country seeking to implement a new regime or overhaul its existing regime. Key considerations in any trade-off include the risks to the revenue, the level of resourcing required, and the need to maintain consistency in dealing with all applications for rulings. However, models in other countries also offer interesting features that could be considered in the New Zealand and Australian context.

Indeed, a full binding private ruling system could go even further, providing for publication of sanitised private rulings to create a public check on revenue authorities' decision making and to ensure greater dissemination of administrative practice (even where a binding private ruling does not have the value of precedent). Nevertheless, the practical constraints in the real world of providing interpretations by way of binding rulings may preclude moving to a model with these and other desirable features in anything more than a gradual process.

What must be considered seriously with any binding rulings regime are the costs and benefits of an expanded ruling system beyond, for instance, that which is already in place in New Zealand's system. The focus will no doubt include areas where costs can be reduced and benefits enhanced. Already, the practical constraints in other jurisdictions have impinged on the theoretical model, as the delays in the appeals process illustrate. Whether these concerns can be resolved and a more effectual balance can be struck between tax authorities' resource commitments and ultimate resource savings remains to be seen, and should be key in any decision to alter the current regime model in any country. Thus the level of resources that Governments provide to their rulings bodies has a significant impact upon the practical application of the extent of the regime, and perhaps more fundamentally whether it can carry out its purpose(s) and core features.

STUDY QUESTIONS

1. Are binding rulings regimes that have the backing of legislation more desirable from the perspective of taxpayers and businesses than an administrative scheme designed by a revenue authority? Discuss, providing reasons to support your choice.
2. What should be the benefits and purposes behind having a binding rulings regime?
3. In comparing the Australian and New Zealand binding ruling regimes, which is preferable? Discuss, providing reasons to support your choice.
4. Should a binding rulings regime have an objection or challenge facility solely for rulings, or should this be left to the normal objection/challenge process for the underlying assessment? Discuss, providing reasons to support your choice.
5. Should private rulings be published, and if so, in what format?
6. What are the advantages and disadvantages of status rulings, and should other countries incorporate such rulings into their binding ruling regimes?
7. What role should consultation play between the revenue authority, and taxpayers and their advisors in relation to the preparation and issue of rulings, and also in relation to the design of the binding rulings regime itself?
8. Have the reforms to the Australian and New Zealand binding rulings regimes tackled the most important issues? Discuss, providing reasons in support of your views.
9. From an international perspective, why do countries operate different types of binding ruling or administrative rulings systems? What are the potential implications for taxpayers and businesses with international operations/income as a result of this situation?

REFERENCES

Bentley, D. (1997), 'A Proposal for Reform of the Australian Rulings System', *Australian Tax Review,* Vol. 26, p. 57. *

Birch, B. (1998), *Legislating for self-assessment of tax liability: A Government discussion document,* Wellington: Government Printer.

Blaike, A. (1994), 'Binding Private Tax Rulings: Appearances Can Be Deceiving', *Journal of Banking and Finance Law and Practice,* Vol. 5, p. 130.

Bradford, M. (1998), *Taxation (Accrual Rules and Other Remedial Matters) Bill 1998, Commentary on the Bill,* Wellington.

Chan, W. (1997) 'Binding Rulings', *Fiscal Studies,* Vol. 18, p. 189. *

Finance and Expenditure Committee (1995), *First Report on Submissions on the Taxation Reform (Binding Rulings and Other Matters) Bill,* Wellington. *

Finance and Expenditure Committee (1999), *Taxation (Accrual Rules and Other Remedial Matters) Bill, Officials' Report to the Finance and Expenditure Committee on Submissions on the Bill,* Wellington (available at the IRD's tax policy division's website <http://www.taxpolicy.ird.govt.nz/publications/index>).*

Harris, P. A. (1994), 'Private Tax Rulings: An Advanced System', *Australian Tax Review,* Vol. 23, p. 22.

Hill, P. (1995), 'The Binding Rulings Regime in Action—Comparison with Australia and their Proper Perspective', *Current Taxation,* Vol. 39, p. 75.

Inland Revenue Department (1996), *Annual Report for the year to 30 June 1996,* Wellington, pp. 39-40.

Inland Revenue Department (1997), *Annual Report for the year to 30 June 1997,* Wellington, pp. 31-33.

Inland Revenue Department (1998), *Annual Report for the year to 30 June 1998,* Wellington, pp. 37-39.

Inland Revenue Department (1999), *Annual Report for the year to 30 June 1999,* Wellington, pp. 45-49.

Inland Revenue Department (2000), *Annual Report for the year to 30 June 2000,* Wellington, pp. 69-75.

Inland Revenue Department (2001), *Annual Report for the year to 30 June 2001,* Wellington, pp. 70-74 (available at the IRD's website < http://www.ird.govt.nz/aboutir/reports/annual-01.pdf>).*

Inland Revenue Department (Adjudication and Rulings) (1995), *IR115G, Binding Rulings: A guide to rulings that are binding on Inland Revenue,* Wellington, May.

Inland Revenue Department (Adjudication and Rulings) (1999), *IR 715: A Guide to Binding Rulings* Wellington, October (available at the IRD's website <http://www.ird.govt.nz/library/publications/geninfo/ir715.pdf>).*

James, S., Sawyer, A. and Wallschutzky, I. (1998), 'The Complexities of Tax Simplification: Progress in Australia, New Zealand and the United Kingdom', *Australian Tax Forum,* Vol. 14, p. 183.

Laurence, M. (2000), 'Investigation: The fall of the Tax Office's golden boy', *Business Review Weekly,* Vol. 22(12), available at <http://www.brw.com.au> under 'March 31, business people'.

Life Office Association of New Zealand (1995), *Submission to the Finance and Expenditure Select Committee on the Taxation Reform (Binding Rulings and Other Matters) Bill,* Wellington.

Lowcay, Q. (1995), 'The Binding Rulings Regime: An Introduction to a Useful Planning Tool and a Brief Comparison with the Australian Model', *Current Taxation*, Vol. 39, p. 61.

Mapp, W. (1996), 'Binding Rulings', *New Zealand Journal of Taxation Law and Policy*, Vol. 2, p. 139. *

New Zealand Government (1994), *Binding Rulings on Taxation: a discussion document on the proposed regime,* Wellington: Government Printer. *

New Zealand Government (1995), *Taxpayer compliance, standards and penalties 2: detailed proposals and draft legislation,* April, Wellington: Government Printer.

Organisational Review Committee (1994), *Organisational Review of the Inland Revenue Department,* April, Wellington: Government Printer.

Prebble, J. (1986), *Advance Rulings on Tax Liability,* Institute of Policy Studies, Wellington: Victoria University of Wellington. *

Sandford, C. and Hasseldine, J. (1992), *The Compliance Costs of Business Taxes in New Zealand*, Wellington: Institute of Policy Studies.

Sawyer, A. J. (1996), 'Broadening the Scope of Consultation and Strategic Focus in Tax Policy Formulation: Some Recent Developments', *New Zealand Journal of Taxation Law and Policy,* Vol. 2, p. 17.

Sawyer, A. J. (1997), 'Binding Tax Rulings: The New Zealand Experience', *Australian Tax Review,* Vol. 26, p. 11. *

Sawyer, A. J. (1999), 'Guide to Binding Rulings: Second Edition' in *Butterworths Taxation Service Commentary,* Wellington: Butterworths of New Zealand Ltd, (CD ROM).

Sawyer, A. J. (2000), 'What are the Lessons for Australia from New Zealand's First Comprehensive Remedial Review of its Binding Rulings Regime?' *Australian Tax Review,* Vol. 29(3), p. 133. *

Sawyer, A. J. (2001), *An International Comparison of Binding Rulings Regimes: A Report for the Adjudication and Rulings Division of the Inland Revenue Department,* November.

Sawyer, A. J. (2002), 'A Selected International Comparison of Revenue Rulings Systems and their Features – What is there in Common?' *Proceedings of the Fifth International Conference on Tax Administration,* Sydney NSW, April 4-5.

Sherman, T. (2000), *Report of an Internal Review of the Systems and Procedures relating to Private Binding Rulings and Advance Opinions in the Australian Taxation Office,* Canberra (available at the ATO's website <http://www.ato.gov.au/content.asp? doc=/content/Corporate/sp200007_attachB.htm>).

Slater, A. H. (1992), 'What's the Matter with Future Tax Rulings?' *The CCH Journal of Australian Taxation*, June/July 7.

Smith, N. (1995), 'Binding Rulings: A Step Forward?' *Chartered Accountants Journal of New Zealand,* Vol. 74, p. 29.

Tax Information Bulletin (1995), 'Questions we've been asked', 7:6 December, p. 28.

Tax Information Bulletin (1996), 'Questions we've been asked', 7:12 April, p. 32.

Tax Simplification Consultative Committee (1990), *Final Report,* Wellington: Government Printer.

Taxation in Australia (1992), 'Second Reading Speech, 26 May 1992, of the *Taxation Laws Amendment (Self-Assessment) Bill* 1992', *Taxation in Australia,* Vol. 27, p. 48.

* Key readings are asterisked

Index

Adam Smith 3, 17, 21, 25, 28, 287
Administrative costs 276, 283
Advance pricing agreements 173,
    174, 180
American revolution 28, 34
Avoidance (of taxes) 1, 15, 16, 17,
    64, 78, 84, 85, 87, 89, 90, 118

Banking regulation 1
Bases of taxation 4
Binding rulings 293, 294, 316, 317
Branch 120, 289
Business planning 1
Business transactions 2, 10

Capital 4, 9, 13, 14, 55, 56, 60,
    169, 185, 193, 208
    export neutrality 14
    import neutrality 14
Capital gains 13
Carroll, Mitchell B. 48, 53
Citizenship 6, 120, 139
Civil war 31, 36, 37
Classical system 254, 261
Common market 47

Company taxation
    integration 251, 253, 257, 258,
        259, 260, 261, 262, 265, 270,
        272, 273
    split rate system 266
Comparative analysis 273
Compliance costs 285, 286
Constantinople 44
Controlled foreign companies 83,
    89, 90, 91
Copyright 185, 186, 187

Data collection 277
Deferral system 90
Depression 39, 46
Design 61, 189, 251, 273, 278
Developing countries 5, 16, 57,
    58, 192, 193, 198, 201, 203,
    204, 205, 287
Direct expenditure 3
Dividend imputation 254, 263,
    268, 272
Dividends 217, 218
Domicile 6, 66
Double taxation 8, 10, 11, 14
    relief 127, 132

E-commerce 62, 81
Economic forecasting 111

Equity 4, 251, 272
European Union 81, 99, 104, 119,
    121, 189
  code of conduct 99, 100, 103
Evasion (of taxes) 25, 69
Exchange of information 77, 133
Exemption system 89, 90, 265,
    266
Expenditure 4, 294, 299, 316

Finance 50, 81, 82, 84, 159, 180,
    181, 274, 289, 290, 291, 294,
    299, 316
Financial Action Task Force 87,
    104
Fiscal policy 3, 285
Fixed place of business 10, 131,
    200
Foreign direct investment 165
Foreign sales corporations 89
Foreign tax credit ii, 137, 141, 143
French revolution 35
Fringe benefits 245, 248, 286

G-7 countries 87, 95, 102
Gladstone 36
Globalisation 82, 104, 116

Harmful tax practices 61, 74, 75,
    76, 77, 78, 83, 87, 94, 95, 96,
    97, 98, 99, 102, 119
Heriot 26

IBFD 2, 18, 59, 81, 82, 179, 192
Income
  foreign source 12, 96, 215, 219
Income tax 9, 21, 22, 31, 35, 36,
    37, 38, 39, 49, 64, 73, 75, 76,
    78, 79, 84, 113, 129, 132, 137,
    139, 141, 142, 143, 144, 145,
    146, 147, 148, 149, 151, 152,
    153, 154, 155, 156, 157, 163,
    164, 167, 200, 202, 209, 210,
    213, 217, 220, 224, 225, 227,
    228, 229, 234, 235, 251, 252,
    253, 256, 258, 259, 260, 262,
    264, 265, 266, 267, 269, 277,
    280, 282, 283, 286

Incorporation 6, 67, 253, 257
Industrial revolution 45
Intangible asset 13, 17
Intellectual property 183, 185,
    186, 187, 190
Interest 194, 218, 222
International tax 15, 83, 88, 134
  system 15
International trade 44
  transactions 1
Internet 61, 62, 63, 64, 66, 67, 68,
    69, 70, 71, 72, 73, 74, 75, 76,
    78, 79, 80, 107, 108, 114, 115,
    119, 207
Investment appraisal 2

Know-how 89, 196, 197, 198, 200,
    203, 208

League of Nations 8, 48, 51, 52,
    53, 54, 55, 57, 59, 60
Licence fee 253
Local economy 5
Low-tax 84, 90, 138

Mesopotamia 23, 41, 44
Model tax treaty 9, 125, 129, 131,
    134, 135
Money laundering 86, 87
Multinational 46, 48, 51, 58, 59,
    60, 85, 104, 161, 179, 181

Napoleonic wars 26, 35
National neutrality 14

OECD
  guidelines 56, 59, 60, 104, 181
  Model Tax Treaty 9, 10, 129
Offshore financial centre 94

Parent company 13, 54, 89
Patent 185, 186, 187
Pax Romana 44
Permanent establishment 10, 11,
    14, 17, 49, 53, 61, 65, 68, 81,
    88, 125, 127, 131, 163, 177,
    192

Phoenicia 44
Pitt, William 35
Place of management
    effective 7
Portfolio investment 85

Residence 6, 66, 67, 130, 214
    dual 7
    non-resident 210, 214, 218,
        222, 223, 224, 225, 226, 227
    taxing residents 7
Resident aliens 210, 221, 224,
    225, 228
Return on investment 178
Right to tax 6, 7, 9, 10, 11, 49, 52,
    53, 141, 191, 192, 193, 198
Roll-up 13
Royalties ii, 71, 183, 192, 193,
    194, 197, 218, 220
Russian Revolution 46

Social security 3, 108
Source
    principle 7, 115, 138, 139, 140
STEP analysis 107, 108, 109, 112
Subsidiary 296
Subsidies 3, 146, 162, 287

Tax
    authority 14, 15, 72, 76, 177,
        232, 275, 276, 278, 279, 280,
        283, 284, 293, 308
    avoidance 15
    avoision 15
    break 16
    collection 4, 23, 24, 25, 63
    competition 86, 118
    complexity 284
    cross border 73, 82, 180
    deduction 239, 241, 243
    equity 86, 88, 259
    estate 21, 24, 25, 26, 27, 29, 30,
        31, 32, 33, 224
    gift 21, 22, 25, 32, 33, 129
    harmonisation 119
    haven 16, 84
    incentives 86, 244

    minimisation 15, 96, 235, 239,
        247
    neutrality 257
    planning 231, 237
    stamp tax 28, 29
    system 76, 114, 115
    year 8, 143, 148, 149, 160, 215,
        223
Tax treaties 128, 223
    treaty shopping 15, 89
Tax-what-you-can system 78, 80
Trade mark 186, 188, 189
Transfer pricing ii, iii, 72, 82, 91,
    131, 159, 160, 164, 165, 166,
    169, 172, 179, 180, 181
    cost plus method 92

United Nations 9, 52, 54, 55, 56,
    57, 60, 181, 183, 193
US Revenue Act 49

Value added tax 7, 73, 79, 81, 289,
    290

Withholding tax 10, 14, 49, 53, 70,
    78, 88, 126, 127, 131, 135, 194,
    201, 202, 203, 204, 228, 252,
    258, 259, 261, 263, 269
World Trade Organisation 89, 118,
    187
World War I 27, 30, 31, 32, 33,
    34, 38, 39, 45, 46, 47, 49, 53,
    254
World War II 39, 46, 47, 49, 53,
    254

Zollverein 50, 51